TRULY OUR SISTER

Truly Our Sister

A THEOLOGY OF MARY
IN THE COMMUNION OF SAINTS

Elizabeth A. Johnson

continuum

NEW YORK • LONDON

2009

The Continuum International Publishing Group Inc
80 Maiden Lane, New York, NY 10038

The Continuum International Publishing Group Ltd
The Tower Building, 11 York Road, London SE1 7NX

Grateful acknowledgment is made to Rosemary Broughton for permission to reprint the poem "Liturgy" by Irene Zimmermann, SSSF, from *Womensprings*, compiled by Julia Ahlers, Rosemary Broughton, and Carol Koch, and published by St. Mary's Press; also to *Theological Studies* for permission to use "Mary and the Female Face of God" (*Theological Studies* 50 [1989]: 500–526) as the basis for chapter 4.

Library of Congress Cataloging-in-Publication Data

Johnson, Elizabeth A., 1941-
    Truly our sister : a theology of Mary in the communion of saints /
Elizabeth A. Johnson.
        p. cm.
    Includes bibliographical references (p.   ).
    ISBN 0-8264-1473-7
    ISBN 0-8264-1827-9 (paperback ; alk. paper)
    1. Mary, Blessed Virgin, Saint—Theology. 2. Catholic
Church—Doctrines. I. Title.
BT613.J65 2003
232.91—dc21

                                                2003005640

Dedicated to
all the women of the world
who struggle for the flourishing
of their own human dignity

Mary is "truly our sister, who as a poor and humble woman fully shared our lot."

—Pope Paul VI

"For poor women Mary is not a heavenly creature but shares their lives as a comrade and sister in struggle."
—María Pilar Aquino, Mexico

Mary is our "sister: a woman in solidarity with other women and the oppressed."
—Chung Hyun Kyung, Korea

"It is the Mary of the Gospels, on whose lips is placed the Magnificat, who is seen as a colleague by women around the world who are rediscovering that they have a mission in society and church. . . . [Her] face is no longer only that of Our Lady, glorious Queen of Heaven, but also and primarily an elder sister and traveling companion."
Ivone Gebara and María Clara Bingemer, Brazil

"Perhaps for our time her best title is not 'mother,' but 'sister in faith,' not one who directs or defines our way, but one who reminds us of the resources we carry with us as we go."
Patricia Noone, United States

Contents

PART 5
MARY IN THE COMMUNION OF SAINTS

Acknowledgments

I t is a distinct pleasure to acknowledge the many persons and institutions which have contributed to this work. My leading thanks go to Fordham University, whose generous and enlightened sabbatical policy provided the time for research and writing. The university's library staff, led by James McCabe, gave unending, superb service. My graduate researchers, Antoinette Gutzler, Kathryn Lilla Cox, Patricia Houlihan, and Gloria Schaab, assisted me generously and with joy; they have my heartfelt thanks. Gloria Schaab in particular deserves credit for casting a sharp editorial eye over the final text and notes, and doing yeowoman's service on the index.

For over twenty years I have taught graduate courses on this subject in universities and schools of theology. John Ford, chair of the Theology Department at Catholic University of America, deserves credit for my beginnings, insisting that I design and teach such a course despite my initial reluctance. The questions and insights of younger Catholics and of students from Protestant and Anglican traditions, and in a special way from women, have immeasurably enriched and challenged my own thinking, as any teacher knows. I am honestly and happily in my students' debt. As a member of the Lutheran/Catholic dialogue in the United States, I participated in an eight-year round on Mary and the saints, delving deeply into official Catholic and Reformation sources and wrestling with ecumenical aspects. This was challenging, enriching work, and I learned much from my colleagues in dialogue.

Warmest thanks go to my colleagues Mary Catherine Hilkert, Nancy Dallavalle, Ellen Umansky, Mary V. Maher, and John Perry, who read and critiqued chapters of this text in progress. In a special way Anthony L. Rubsys, biblical scholar, teacher, and friend, accompanied me with criticism and encouragement through the scripture passages that form the heart of this book. Our conversations shortly before the book was finished and, unknowingly, shortly before his life was finished, led to a wholesale revamping of the flow of the book's argument. I honor this unpayable debt. Other friends provided me with substantive material on the subject: Constance Fitzgerald, Thomas Shelley, Aristotle Papanikolaou, Connie Loos, and Jack Healy. Through e-mails and other communiqués, Terrence Tilley, Catherine Patten, Margaret Galiardi, Robert Sadowski, John Cabrido, Miguel Lambino, Ginny Gerace, and Kathryn Lilla Cox sent invaluable questions, suggestions, and their own wisdom.

In its early stages this work received a hearing as the keynote lecture at Villanova University's 26th Theology Institute. Midway through, some of its ideas were presented at the Los Angeles Religious Education Congress. When it was at a more advanced stage, the John Courtney Murray lecture, sponsored by the journal *America,* provided another airing with a discerning audience. I thank the organizers of these events for the opportunity to engage a wider public, with resulting benefits to my own thinking. With elegance, wit, and grace, my editor Frank Oveis supported this work. His personal encouragement, laced with humor, lit up long days of writing; his professional interest ensured publication in a more than timely manner. He is a marvelous ally, and my gratitude knows no bounds. My religious community, the Sisters of St. Joseph, Brentwood, has never ceased supporting my work, including this book; I am deeply, continually grateful. Finally, I thank all the women from different parts of the world who have shared with me their stories, struggles, and insights about faith over the years, both orally and in writing. Our ongoing dialogue sparked this book. It is to them that this work is dedicated.

Introduction

This book proposes that one fruitful approach to the theology of Mary, historically the mother of Jesus, called in faith the *Theotokos* or God-bearer, is to envision her as a concrete woman of our history who walked with the Spirit. Keeping faith through the days of her own life, she is now counted among the great "cloud of witnesses" that surrounds the church on earth with encouragement. This proposal entails picturing her historical world and pondering the theological glimpses of her life in scripture, so as to remember her today as our sister, herself a friend of God and prophet in the communion of saints. In a previous book, *Friends of God and Prophets: A Feminist Theological Reading of the Communion of Saints* (New York: Continuum, 1998), I have already explored the history and theology of the great doctrinal symbol of the communion of saints, that intergenerational community of the living and the dead stretching across time and space and comprised of all who are made holy by the Spirit of God. Here I explore the intellectual, practical, and spiritual understandings that result when we place Miriam of Nazareth in that blessed company. Since *Friends of God and Prophets* forms the theological framework of this book, the two are companion volumes. At the same time, since major ideas are reprised here, this work can be read on its own.

While it draws on the history of marian doctrine and devotion and seeks precedent there for my proposal, this is not a work of doctrinal theology in the traditional sense. It does not aim to present the full teaching of the church about Mary, which is amply available elsewhere. Following the practice of Vatican II, it does not "have it in mind to give a complete doctrine on Mary, nor does it wish to decide those questions which have not yet been fully illuminated by the work of theologians" (*Lumen Gentium* §54). Its purpose is to explore a new avenue of approach to Mary, one grounded in scripture, liturgy, and ancient Christian preaching, and able to evoke appreciation of the presence of God's Spirit in the community of faith today. Toward that end, convinced that history is the arena of encounter with God, I do not begin, as does so much contemporary mariology, by thinking about Mary as a religious symbol. Rather, I seek to understand her meaning as a particular person with her own life to compose. She has been symbolized to such an extravagant degree divorced from her own history—symbol of the maternal face of God, of the eternal feminine, of the disciple, of the idealized church—that approaching her as an actual human being surprises us with the discovery that she too struggled, that her own life's journey, in Vatican II's poetic phrase, was a pilgrimage of faith, including sojourning in faith's dark night. Remembering her in the great cloud of witnesses that surrounds the community of disciples, we draw strength from "the lessons of encouragement" flowing from her life.

In seeking thus to interpret the meaning of Mary within the logos of faith for our day, this work goes forward as part of the broader wave of women doing theology, a new phenomenon.

Around the world, large numbers of women are slipping the bonds of male control and seeking instead a partnership that honors the equal human dignity befitting themselves as human persons. This liberating movement, which is more than ever a sign of our times, reverberates in theology as in other disciplines, where it brings new voices to the table. When it comes to the subject of Mary, women's judgment is decidedly ambiguous. On the one hand, the marian tradition has functioned negatively to promote an idealized notion of the obedient female self, a construal that legitimates women's subordinate place in the church. On the other hand, the living remembrance of this woman can function positively to inspire the struggle for God's compassionate and liberating justice. Sorting out this blessing and bane, mariology done by women in the last decades has served up groundbreaking critique as well as creative new interpretations. Particularly rich insights have poured forth from women in situations of dire suffering caused by injustice. In different cultural situations of poverty, racial and ethnic prejudice, and violence, they consistently find connections to the biblical story of Miriam of Nazareth as herself also a poor woman, "someone like us." They form alliance with her as a companion in the struggle for voice and fullness of life. Vastly indebted to this scholarship and engaging it, this book joins the effort to articulate a theology of Mary that will promote the flourishing of women and thereby all the relationships and communities of which they are a part.

The context in which I write, a postindustrial culture often characterized as postmodern, provides an interesting opening for the reception of
this approach to a theology of Mary. For a variety of reasons, this culture
has little time for faith symbols configured to medieval or premodern sensibilities. One visible sign of this is the diminishment of traditional devotion to Mary in the years since the Second Vatican Council in the Catholic
Church in the United States. Neither Mary nor indeed the rest of the company of saints has found much of a suitable place in the contemporary pattern of faith. This holds true especially for the generations born and raised
after the council. In fact, the issue of Mary can even be deemed irrelevant
to the burning religious questions of the day, chief among which is the
search for God in a world of suffering and secularity. My social location in
precisely this context precludes interpreting Mary through appeal to a tradition of veneration of ancestors, such as is done in African theology, or to
vibrant traditions of popular religion intrinsic to faith in Latin America
and in Hispanic communities in the United States, or to local customs of
immigrant ethnic groups. These sources of marian reflection not only
deserve respect; they also have much to teach, as scholars among them
show. But such are not the experiences of many who live their lives and
express their faith in the postindustrial mainstream. This book seeks to
make sense of Mary so as to sound the challenge of discipleship in precisely
this setting, drawing people into deeper friendship with the heart of divine
mystery and turning them toward the praxis of justice and compassion for
the world, both human beings and the earth. It is my thesis that women's
work on Mary as a friend of God and prophet can do precisely that.
Thereby part of the living Christian tradition being lost in postmodern
culture can find an avenue to perdure into the future.

Truly our sister: this proposal is worked out in five steps. My point of
departure is the global chorus of women's voices today, which, heard in all
fullness, offers both critical and creative theological interpretations of the
marian tradition (part 1). Counterposed to this, the next section analyzes
two types of androcentric marian theology that form the chief alternative
to women's liberating approach and judges them paths to be avoided (part
2). Thus fortified and warned, part 3 explores in a preliminary way the
proposal of this book and the precedents for it in ancient and recent theology and church teaching. Now begins the heart of the book, remembering Mary in a theologically and practically fruitful way. Part 4 pictures the
world she inhabited, including political, economic, religious, and cultural

conditions that impinged on her life. This forms the context for part 5, which engages in a close reading of thirteen scripture passages in which Mary appears. These stories encode the theological memory of the early church, which wrote her into the faith event of salvation coming from God in Jesus through the power of the Spirit. Each story is like a tile of colored stone. Assembled together they form a mosaic of this Spirit-filled woman, who, in company with other significant gospel persons, partnered the redemptive work of God. Stepping back and viewing the mosaic as a whole, the last chapter situates Mary in the whole cloud of witnesses who accompany the church on its following of Jesus, ending with her own revolutionary prayer, the Magnificat.

Theology today is nothing if not multicultural and pluralistic. I stress at the outset that this proposal is but one of several fruitful approaches in current theology of Mary. Its purpose is to seek understanding of an aspect of the Christian faith confession for our era. As Karl Rahner famously noted, however, not all who are alive at the same time are contemporaries. My own respect runs deep for the elders of the community whose lifelong relationship with Mary, formed in the context of preconciliar mariology, has been a source of strength and for whom the approach of this book may be jarring. I also appreciate views of Mary arising from different ethnic cultures. Coming from a perspective that is American, Catholic, and feminist, in dialogue with women's work on Mary around the world, my criticism is reserved for patriarchal mariologies that function to subordinate women. Otherwise, different approaches are possible and, to the degree that they offer intelligible and liberating directions, definitely desirable.

We have arrived at a new moment in the history of interpretation. Concentrating on Mary as a concrete, graced individual in the company of all God's friends and prophets, this book develops a marian theology rooted in scripture read through women's eyes with feminist hermeneutical methods. It seeks a glimpse of the raw, mostly unknown historical reality of Miriam of Nazareth, a Jewish woman in a relatively poor, politically oppressed, first-century peasant society. It tries to understand the presence, call, challenge, and creativity of the Spirit of God in her life, as in the lives of all who believe and love down through the centuries. It connects her unique vocation, which included but was not limited to mothering the Messiah, to the stories of the women and men disciples of Jesus then and now, finding challenge and encouragement for disciples today. In a word, this proposal invites Mary to come down from the pedestal where she has been honored for centuries and rejoin us in the community of grace and struggle in history. Far from dishonoring her, this connection esteems her and the whole company of the saints in one liberating way appropriate to our time and place.

Doing research for this book, I requested Jeanette Rodriguez's book *Our Lady of Guadalupe* from my university's library on a sister campus. When it arrived, the student on duty notified me by phone, mentioning, according to custom, the book's title. Here is what I heard on my voice mail: "Dr. Johnson, Our Lady of Guadalupe has come in and is waiting for you at the front desk." One of my colleagues, with whom I shared this humorous message, paused and then responded quietly, "May she be there for you." A striking thought, and one with which I end this introduction. Remembering Mary as a friend of God and prophet in the communion of saints, a woman who is truly sister to our strivings, allows the power of her life to play in the religious consciousness of the church, encouraging ever-deeper relationship with the living God in whom our spirits rejoice, and allying us with God's redemptive designs for the hungry, the lowly, and all those who suffer, including in an unforgettable way women with their children in situations of poverty, prejudice, and violence.

PART 1

Women's Voices in a New Key

1

Fragments in the Rubble

A RICH TAPESTRY

The first-century Jewish woman named Miriam of Nazareth, mother of Jesus, also proclaimed in faith to be *Theotokos,* the God-bearer, is the most celebrated female religious figure in the Christian tradition. What would be a theologically sound, ecumenically fruitful, spiritually empowering, ethically challenging, and socially liberating interpretation of Mary for the twenty-first century? What is her significance in the light of Christian faith in the gracious mystery of God? What difference does remembering her, along with all the friends of God and prophets, make in the life of church and society? How in particular can her image be construed so as to be a source of blessing rather than blight for women's lives in both religious and political terms?

The figure of Mary referred to by these questions is extraordinarily complex. Whether studied from the point of view of theology, spirituality, or culture, this Galilean woman has been interpreted and explained, imagined and rejected, loved and honored in ways so diverse as to be impossible to codify.[1] The diversity begins in scripture, where each of the four Gospels portrays her in a different way according to the theological perspectives of the evangelists. This biblical difference is so real that in ecumenical circles it serves to explain the variety of approaches in different church bodies. Protestants traditionally follow Mark's rather negative assessment of Jesus' mother; Catholics take from Luke a positive, personalistic view of her as full of grace and favor from God, a woman who cooperated with the divine adventure of bringing the Redeemer into human flesh; while Orthodox approach Mary in the iconic, symbolic manner of John.[2]

3

From the fifth century on, creative artists have used their imaginations to depict Mary in paintings, sculptures, and icons, musical compositions from classical motets to simple hymns, poetry, dancing, dramatic arts, and contemporary films that reflect cultures as different as Byzantine, European baroque, and Latin American. Soaring cathedrals, parish churches, and simple chapels in cities and in the bush have been dedicated to God in her name. Annual liturgical feast days along with a wealth of sermons, devotional practices, and private prayers including the rosary have brought her memory into the midst of the church community in divergent times and places. Meditations and litanies of her praises, belief in her appearances and miracles, pilgrimages, legends, folk customs, and street festivals make her figure accessible to ordinary folk, even to those with less than strong attachment to the institutional church.

When this devotion passes into scholarly theology and church doctrine, it remains true that, as Els Maeckelberghe phrases it, "Mary" is a collective noun.[3] From Ephraem to Augustine, Hildegard to Julian of Norwich, Aquinas to Luther, Rahner to Ruether, generations of thinkers in eastern and western churches and on northern and southern continents have offered different explanations of the meaning of her life for the community of faith. They have used categories coherent with the diverse theologies of their day, whether scholasticism, the Reformation's *sola gratia,* transcendental Thomism, or liberation and feminist insights. Exercises of papal power in the nineteenth and twentieth centuries added another dimension when they defined as doctrine that God freely bestowed gifts on Mary at her coming into the world (the Immaculate Conception) and departing it (the Assumption), while virtually every pope in the modern era has also exhorted the faithful to cultivate proper devotion to her in varied ways.

In recent decades ecumenical dialogue among Protestants, Catholics, and Orthodox Christians has sought a common root in the Bible and creeds for understanding Mary's significance, each making a case for the coherence with scripture of its traditionally distinct patterns of thought and prayer.[4] Dialogue between Christians and members of other world religions further widens the scope of diversity in marian matters. The *Qur'an* of Islam gives Mary, named Mariyam, a relatively important position as mother of the prophet Jesus whom she conceived by the Spirit. She herself is one of God's chosen ones in the line of the great prophets. It is not uncommon for Muslims to venerate the mother of Jesus, a factor highlighted in the Second Vatican Council's groundbreaking call for mutual understanding: "They also honor His virgin mother; at times they call on her, too, with devotion."[5] Speaking of the great religions of Asia, scholars point out pictorial and devotional parallels that developed as people with a long tradition of venerating *Kannon* or *Kwan Yin*, the Buddhist female image of compassion in Japan, or *Guanyin*, the popular Chinese deity who gives herself for the salvation of others, or *śakti*, the divine female principle of power in Hinduism, interpret the meaning of Mary in their own context.[6]

The picture becomes even more complex in the light of recent scholarship that highlights how this adaptable marian image functions to promote particular social-political agendas. In Constantinople the Virgin *Theotokos* protected the scepter of orthodox emperors and flew on the banners of their armies, guiding the civic religion and military might of the Byzantine empire especially in times of invasion.[7] The nineteenth-century Roman Catholic marian revival cannot be separated from the church's sense that it was in a state of siege against the modern world. Barbara Corrado Pope's analysis of this period's image of Mary crushing the head of the snake demonstrates that "while the outstretched arms of the Immaculate Conception promised mercy to the faithful, the iconography of this most widely distributed of Marian images also projected a militant and defiant message that through Mary the church would defeat its enemies."[8] Robert Orsi's beautiful study of *The Madonna of 115th Street* clarifies how the struggle of newly arrived Italian immigrants for spiritual and economic survival in New York City was aided and abetted by their Madonna brought from the old country.[9] Militant cold-war opposition to the Soviet Union among Catholics in the United States drew strength from devotion to Our Lady of Fatima, as does continuing opposition to modern trends in society.[10] César Chávez's struggle for just wages and living conditions for migrant workers in the California vineyards invoked the supportive protection of Our Lady of Guadalupe.[11] From right-wing imperial power to the struggle of the poor for justice, the figure of Mary has been pressed into service for goals that are far from neutral.

There is no one thread that would knit this exuberant tradition into a unified whole. The apt title of George Tavard's work gets it exactly right: *The Thousand Faces of the Virgin Mary*.[12] While an historical woman obviously dwells at the root of this whole phenomenon, there has been a plasticity to her image that has allowed the Christian imagination to create widely different marian symbols and theologies in relation to spiritual and social needs.

A living tradition calls forth new interpretations in keeping with changing historical contexts. Now artists and theologians need to do for our age what former eras did for theirs. How does this generation, living in a multicultural church at the beginning of a new millennium, interpret and honor Miriam of Nazareth within a faith context, and with what social and political effects? Obviously, more than one answer is possible. The historical diversity regarding Mary is mirrored geographically today around the world as local churches on different continents express her significance in accord with their own cultures. So too do local communities within pluralistic nations such as the United States, where, for example, Hispanic practices of popular religion honor *María* in warm, colorful, identity-building ways, while among most Anglos even major marian feasts meet with restrained celebration.

HEARING WOMEN'S VOICES

Amid this pluralism a genuinely new development is occurring around the world, namely, the rise of women's voices. It is a sign of the times that women, marginalized for millennia in male-dominated cultures, are becoming increasingly conscious of their human worth and, in the prophetic words of Pope John XXIII, "will not tolerate being treated as inanimate objects or mere instruments, but claim, both in domestic and in public life, the rights and duties that befit a human person."[13] As part of this emerging awareness, women for the first time in history are publicly and corporately interpreting the figure of Mary from the perspective of their own struggle to be independent, strong, lively, and holy, that is, from their option for full human dignity. They are raising criticisms of the ways traditional idealizations of her privileges and perfections have been used to short-circuit women's own quest for wholeness. They are also making creative moves toward reclaiming this woman as an ally of women's flourishing. Now the tapestry of marian tradition becomes ever richer as twenty-first century women weave their insights into the great cloth.

The heritage women have received and set out from is nothing if not ambiguous. On the one hand, for centuries Mary was the only female figure allowed in or near the sanctuary. This kept the image of a woman in full view, an important and frequently powerful woman, which not only counterbalanced a heavily patriarchal view of God but also made cultural room for promoting respect for the dignity of women. In unintended ways the role of Mary worked subversively to denote female power and possibility. The history of spirituality reveals that women found in prayer and companionship with her a source of inspiration, comfort, and strength, precisely as a woman and particularly in times of trial.

On the other hand, official views of Mary have been shaped by men in a patriarchal context and have functioned powerfully to define and control female lives. Women were not consulted, nor were they permitted to bring their knowledge of their own lives before God into this official portrait. Almost inevitably the marian symbol became that of an idealized woman, created as an act of men's definition of women, whose voices were officially silenced. Strong emphasis on Mary's obedience, virginity, and primary importance as a mother shaped a religious symbol that satisfied the needs of a monastic or ecclesiastical male psyche more adequately than it served women's spiritual search or social capabilities. Throughout the centuries this did not exhaust interpretation, for those outside the circles of power had their own depictions. One can sense the hidden, repressed power of the female breaking through in popular piety, as Rosemary Radford Ruether has pointed out:

> there is the Mary of the monks, who venerate her primarily as a virgin and shape her doctrines in an antisexual mold. But there is the Mary of the people who is still the earth mother and who is venerated for her power over the secret of natural fecundity. It is she who helps the woman through her birth-pangs, who assures the farmer of his new crops, new rains, new lambs. She is the maternal image of the divine who understands ordinary people in their wretchedness.[14]

However, the official marian symbol perdured as the fruit of a history of socially powerful men's interpretation of the ideal woman. On balance, this ideal has functioned effectively to keep women in their preassigned place subordinate to patriarchal authority.

The wind of female empowerment blowing throughout the land disturbs this traditional arrangement. Bringing about a sea change in women's own self-definition, it casts up new understandings of women's nature, capabilities, role, status, and relationship to men and male-created structures. As women today take charge of their lives, their explorations of what it takes to be a liberated, whole human being in relation to others lead to far-reaching critical rejection as well as creative reimagining of various aspects of the marian tradition. Something new is occurring in the encounter between women and the figure of Miriam of Nazareth.

CRITICAL JUDGMENTS

Not surprisingly, many express negative assessments, even if reluctantly.

• In South Africa an elderly woman, Margaret Cuthbert, confided an incident that happened in her women's prayer group. They met weekly to recite the rosary and the Litany of Loreto, a traditional compendium of Mary's praises. One day, after much discussion and with some distress, they decided to omit forever two of the litany's encomiums, "Mother inviolate, Mother undefiled." Their reasoning went this way: if Mary is an undefiled mother because she conceived without having sex, then we are defiled because we have had sex. However, our experience of our own bodies, of making love with our husbands, and of bearing children has not sullied us but has been, despite the suffering, a source of joy and blessing from God. These praises of Mary insult us; they do not make sense; so we dropped them.[15] The cognitive dissonance between women's present experience of God and the traditional marian symbol sets up a conflict in which the latter, inevitably, loses.

• During a basic Christian community prayer meeting in Oaxaca, southern Mexico, Sabina Lopez de Hernandez reflected with the group on her strong reaction to a recent sermon. The gospel reading had depicted Mary at the foot of the cross. The priest said that she stood there in accord with God's will, freely offering up her son for the salvation of the world. As a mother, Sabina found this abhorrent. A mother, even a woman of faith, wants her child to live, not to be killed. Did the others not think so? They did. This preacher did not understand a mother's heart. The prayerful discussion turned toward the idea that the God of life passionately abhors people killing or hurting each other. The violence of the cross is not what is salvific in and of itself. The long-standing idea that Mary willingly joined in a divine plan for the suffering of her son was rejected.[16]

• British writer Marina Warner crafted a massive study brilliantly entitled *Alone of All Her Sex*, analyzing the harm done to women by idealizing Mary, who alone among women is honored as unsullied and privileged. At the end of her research she found herself in Notre Dame cathedral in Paris, weeping, torn between her heart, which was still moved by love of Mary, and her new-found insight that "in the very celebration of the perfect human woman, both humanity and women were subtly denigrated."[17] Her study of the exalted marian myth and cult, its images, prayers, and practical effects, concludes:

> The Virgin Mary has inspired some of the loftiest architecture, some of the most moving poetry, some of the most beautiful paintings in the world; she has filled men and women with deep joy and fervent trust; she has been an image of the ideal that has entranced and stirred men and women to the noblest emotions of love and pity and awe. But the reality her myth describes is over; the moral code she affirms has been exhausted.[18]

The legend might live on in its lyricism, she suspects, but it will have lost its power to heal and to harm, for women now see right through the myth and reject it.

• That this is not the experience of just a few isolated individuals is indicated by a story told by Professor Mary Hines at a school of theology in Washington, D.C. At the beginning of a semester she discovered that all the students registered for her course on theology of Mary were young men; all the students in her course on feminist theology were women. When asked to explain their choices, the men said it was because they knew next to nothing about the church's teaching on Mary but as ordained ministers would be expected to. The women, on the other hand, avoided that course because of their negative feelings about what they already knew. "Some responded with a sense of betrayal and disillusionment, some with a sense of undefined unease, . . . some said there was just too much baggage for them to summon up interest in studying Mary."[19]

• Reflecting on the experience of women in the Philippines, Hilda Buhay, O.S.B., focuses on how during the Spanish colonial period the ideal Filipino woman was the *María Clara,* a young female whose purity, docility, and winsome feminine qualities resembled Mary. That period may have passed, "but our society still puts a premium on submission, blind obedience and passivity in Filipino women. Mary, then, when imitated, becomes an extremely useful means of domesticating women and other oppressed people."[20]

• A young Christian woman in India, Astrid Lobo, expresses the frustration of many of her peers who find Mary too high, too holy, and too innocent to be of much use for their own spiritual growth.

As a human being constantly struggling through difficult choices I could find no comfort in this docile Mary who said "Yes" so easily to God. As a young woman faced with the challenge of taking up my rightful role in society, I just could not understand this Mary tucked away inside her four walls. She was the "virgin most pure" with whom I could never share the excitement of my flowering sexuality. What could this sinless woman understand of my weakness and failure?"[21]

• Reflecting on the prevailing idea of Mary in the Orthodox church, Elisabeth Behr-Sigel laments the exclusion of women from the development of marian theology. "Rather has this been largely the preserve of men who, unwittingly perhaps, left the imprint of their dreams upon it. Hence the vision of an ideal woman, which could go hand in hand with the way in which actual women might be despised or devalued in societies where patriarchal norms prevailed."[22] If one should think that idealization of Mary might redound to the benefit of other women, just observe the practical consequences: "In actual fact, idealised women are kept from functions in the Church which imply authority and involve the making of decisions."[23]

• Addressing problems of identity and self-esteem in Hispanic women in the United States, psychologists Rosa Maria Gil and Carmen Inoa Vazquez teach their clients to recognize the socially learned set of behaviors called *marianismo*, the flip side of men's *machismo*. Taking as the model of perfection the Virgin Mary herself, *marianismo* cultivates the notion of feminine spiritual superiority and teaches women to live a life of self-sacrifice in order to please men. Its "Ten Commandments" include: do not forget a woman's place; do not be single, self-supporting, or independent-minded; do not forget that sex is for making babies, not for pleasure; do not be unhappy with your man or criticize him for infidelity or verbal and physical abuse; do not challenge things which make you unhappy. In the old country, the reward for this total surrender of self was a certain measure of protection and power in the family. But in today's North America, this ideal becomes a yoke that binds capable Latinas into self-defeating behavior and unhappiness. These psychologists issue a stirring call: "open your heart, your mind, your soul, and your spirit to the winds of change as you travel beyond *marianismo* through acculturation to self-esteem, and become your own woman at last."[24]

• Speaking for a generation of women, American novelist Mary Gordon famously observed how in her Catholic high school, "Mary was a stick to beat smart girls with. Her example was held up constantly: an example of silence, of subordination, of the pleasure of taking the back seat." Describing the move made by countless others, she continues: "For women like me, it was necessary to reject the image of Mary in order to hold onto the fragile hope of intellectual achievement, independence of identity, sexual fulfillment."[25]

It would be difficult to underestimate the depth of repugnance, both existential and intellectual, felt by women who become conscious of the negative ways in which the marian symbol has worked upon them. Interpreted largely by the imagination of men, Mary has been depicted as one kind of woman rather than another and has been held up by male preachers and church leaders as the ideal for women's virtue and social roles. The symbol of Mary functions. Much traditional theology makes her a means to keep women in their subordinate place, for, as Rosemary Haughton argues, "with all her glory she is always obedient, she is not 'ordained,' she is the busy but submissive, patient and suffering auxiliary who can intercede but not decide."[26]

Now engaged in a historic struggle for equality in political and familial structures and for freedom from male dominance with its all too often physically violent manifestations, women have found this traditionally gendered marian model decidedly unhelpful. Women of color who resist the racial prejudice that ravages their communities, economically poor women who struggle daily to raise their children on mean streets, women of different sexual orientations who seek respect for their embodied life, heterosexual women who find their sexual pleasure to be a source of gladness and grace: these and many others now judge this religious symbol to be deficient. Notice that the charge is not that Mary is irrelevant, a criticism now heard from the cultural quarter. It is rather that the figure of Mary is harmful, functioning as it does to support the patriarchal oppression of women. The marian tradition is accused of distorting women's reality, of promoting a restrictive ideal of human fulfillment, of constricting women's social roles, of blocking their access to God's blessing in the fullness of their lives. It has presided over the evil of sexism rather than challenged it.

Paul Tillich's often used analysis of how a symbol works sheds useful light on these critical women's voices.[27] Any symbol arises from a dimension of the human spirit not under immediate rational control. It is born and grows from the depths of the psyche and takes root in particular historical circumstances insofar as it feeds the human hunger for transcendent meaning. Just as a symbol cannot be created by a conventional decision, neither can it be replaced at will. It goes on living in dynamic interchange with the spirit of a group even in the face of attempts to crush it. But once a symbol no longer opens up the "power of being" the human spirit is thirsting for, then it will die in relation to a group. No official command can keep it functioning in a living way if it contradicts what the community yearns for. The critical voices above make clear that the traditional marian symbol has died out among hosts of women by just such a deeply intuitive process.

CREATIVE INSIGHTS

At the same time, rigorous criticism does not exhaust contemporary women's response to the marian tradition. The struggle for fullness of life together creates a context for discovering new sources of empowerment from her image. Mary Jo Weaver's query, "What would it mean to read the symbol of Mary differently?"[28] now resonates across cultural boundaries and sets an agenda for the future. Stubbornly unwilling to abandon this woman to her imprisonment behind patriarchal bars, women are risking new, liberating interpretations of her meaning in the light of their lives before God. Growing in their ability to appreciate themselves and each other precisely as women, they are reclaiming her as a woman into the sisterhood of struggle. These voices resonate with fresh, even if tentative, appreciation.

• Moved to explore the symbol of Mary once again by giving birth for the first time, Mary Gordon, who had rejected this figure for the sake of her own maturity, begins to see new possibilities. We must begin, she advises, by understanding that the history of human thought about women has been a history of error, leading to degradation, oppression, and "the idealization whose other side is tyranny." The image of Mary has been a prime example of this distortion. If women wish to take our place in the Christian tradition rather than leave it, the only option is "forgiving vigilance." From that stance, we can sift through the nonsense and antiwoman hostility of the marian tradition, to find some images, shards, and fragments, glittering in the rubble. One must find isolated words, isolated images; one must travel the road of metaphor, of icon, to come back to that figure who, throughout a corrupt history, has moved the hearts of men and women, has triumphed over hatred of women and fear of her, and abides, shining, worthy of our love, compelling it.[29]

• In Latin America, women in situations of poverty and violence pioneer the insight that María was like them, a poor woman of the people. As Pilar Aquino makes clear, "poor women identify with her because they share the same hope and the same language as women."[30] A villager who lived her trust in God in the midst of hard daily labor, she knows their struggle and their pain. A widow who survived the violent public execution of her son, she is a companion on women's shared Calvary. As one lilting hymn sings, "she is our *compañera*." And it is to *this* woman that God has done great things. Honoring her puts one in solidarity with God's own option for the poor, and with the poorest of the poor, colonialized women in violent situations, most of all.[31]

• In search of Mary as a credible woman who could serve her own maturing spirituality, Euro-American literature teacher Sally Cunneen movingly recalls her grief at the death of her oldest son. Being able to relate to the woman of Nazareth who knew the same loss was a source of consoling strength. "I no longer saw Pietàs, in which the mother holds the body of her son across her knees, as simply pious images; they became representations of a completely human woman who shared the pain of all mothers—all parents—who have lost their children."[32] Such alliance between women's experience and what can be seriously imagined as Miriam of Nazareth's own life history begins to renew appreciation.

• Speaking not as a white woman or as a black man but as one who combines oppressed gender and race in one person, African American Diana Hayes presses the similarity between the life Mary lived as a Jew under Roman oppression with the poor and marginalized existence of black women in our racist society and church. Like the Galilean woman, black women keep on keepin' on despite prejudice and hard days, giving birth to the future with their very lives. What commends Mary is not her passivity, of the type classically inculcated into slave women, but the way she models strong, righteous, behavior in alliance with God's liberating justice for her people. Paying a high compliment drawn from the black community, Hayes describes her as "womanish."[33]

• Women in Hispanic communities in the United States analyze how the figures of Mary in various traditions—Mexico's Our Lady of Guadalupe, Cuba's Our Lady of Charity—function to encourage a strong sense of self in women whom society otherwise devalues. Jeanette Rodriguez discovered that the bond Mexican-American women have forged with Our Lady of Guadalupe influences their lives for the better, providing them with a spiritual form of resistance to their marginalization in society and church. Reflecting the merciful, maternal face of God to women whose humanity is systematically denigrated, this icon offers them an experience of being accepted, embraced, and loved by someone of the highest value. Thereby their sense of being worthwhile and valuable persons grows: "certainly she is a source of empowerment."[34] This stream of reflection continues despite the ambiguity pointed out by other scholars, insofar as devotion to Mary has not liberated Hispanic women from sexual or economic oppression.[35]

• Living in strongly patriarchal cultures pervaded with religious diversity, Asian women rediscover not the bejeweled Mary crowned Queen of Heaven but the poor, courageous Mary, herself a west Asian woman. Meeting in Manila, a group of church women from across the continent write, "We saw Mary, the mother of Jesus, no longer as a passive, ethereal being, detached from the suffering of millions in Asia. We now see her in a new light, as a strong woman who can identify and be with today's grieving mothers, wives, daughters in the bitter fight for freedom."[36] Rather than adhere to a marian cult that vitiates her person and minimizes her partnership, these women assume the responsibility to reclaim and redefine Mary with regard to the liberation of all people, especially women. As in Latin America they hear Mary's song, the Magnificat, which tellingly has found no place in traditional marian theology, as a rallying cry for the poor and oppressed to overcome injustice. A striking sign of the reversal announced in that song is the virginal conception. This strong woman of Israel conceives her child without a man. God and a woman together bring forth the Christ. Thus the end of the patriarchal order is announced, and the revolutionary vision of a new creation where women claim their human dignity comes into view.[37]

• From Appalachia comes a Christmas card with a line drawing of the creche and a text that reads in part: Imagine yourself young, inexperienced, pregnant, and poor. You are forced to leave home. On your journey you give birth, but because you have no money you do not receive adequate care or comfort. Right up to the time of delivery you have experienced unjust accusation about your pregnancy, near abandonment by your young husband, and the cruelties of discrimination from society. Now a refugee, you give birth in an unkempt place, a lean-to where animals move about freely. Your name is Ana of Brazil, Debbie of West Virginia, Michelle of Brooklyn, Mary of Nazareth . . . .[38]

• The quest widens as women of the Reformation tradition, whose religious horizon holds no strong female image, begin to attend to this lack from their own religious perspectives. "I fear we are so concerned not to fall into the trap of making her co-Redemptor that we are wary of acknowledging her at all," writes Pauline Warner, a Methodist; "I am saying that we should be wary of our wariness."[39] Commenting on the Church of Sweden's decision to dedicate the fourth Sunday of Advent to Mary, Mother of the Lord, Dr. Margit Sahlin credited a growing feminism which stresses the importance of women and the need to counter a masculine tradition in the church; "it seems important to have a woman painted before your eyes as an object of identification."[40] Once while I was teaching the theology of Mary in a graduate course populated largely by men, a young Lutheran woman studying for the ordained ministry shot her hand into the air and shouted, "I *like* this woman!" In the lecture she was sensing something beneficial in the story of a female like herself, someone who walked by faith, a companion she was determined to bring to light for others in her future preaching. German theologian Dorothee Soelle makes the case to Protestant and Catholic women alike: let us not be too hasty to abandon Mary to our patriarchal opponents. The millions of women before us who have loved Mary were not simply blind or duped. They, too, sensed her subversive power and offered resistance from which we can learn. Uniting the militancy of the Magnificat with the charity of a lover of God, "she becomes an image of hope for those who have been cheated of their lives."[41]

THEOLOGICAL SIGNIFICANCE

The quest for "fragments, glittering in the rubble" now goes on in women's prayer and poetry, art and midrash, conversation and religious reflection.

Laying their own religious desires side by side with the official symbol of
Mary, women struggle intensely for a liberating rather than restricting
interpretation. They read her stories in the Bible from their own location
outside the corridors of ecclesiastical power, discovering meanings that
would never be apparent to a patriarchal mind. Rather than letting her
stand alone, they link her to the other women around Jesus. They catch
glimpses of her as a companion, sister, and friend with her own human
experiences that connect her to women across the centuries. Their uneasi-
ness, rejections, and creative new insights are crafting theologies of Mary
that ally her with women around the world as they contest for the recognition and exercise of their full human dignity and that of their girl children. The sound of these voices cannot be hushed, however urgently one
insists on traditional understandings.[42]

In a perceptive analysis Mary Catherine Hilkert presents the argument
why women's voices resound with legitimate power in the Christian community.[43] Though banned from ordination and thereby officially marginalized, they nevertheless speak with authority. The source of this authority
is the Spirit of God, ultimately the only source of authority for the church.
Women are gifted with this Spirit in three ways: through their vocation as
baptized persons, which makes them into prophets, priests, and leaders as
part of the body of Christ; through their actual experience of living the
Christian life every day, which gives them a growing wisdom in discerning
the truth in love; and through their negative experiences of suffering,
which engenders knowledge of what should not be. With courage born of
mutual support, women speak as persons of faith with the authority of
their experience of questing for the living God. Partners with the Spirit,
they ultimately appeal to the authority of the future in accord with the
reign of God when the fullness of life, *shalom,* is poured out on everyone,
the lowest and least most of all.

In a theological sense, this new phenomenon is a sign that the Christian
tradition is indeed a living one, empowered by the Spirit of God, who
forever vivifies and recreates the world. As John XXIII realized, signs of the
times arise because this God continues to speak and act in and through
human history. History in this view ceases to be the place where the church
simply applies binding principles derived from eternal truths known from
philosophical reasoning. Rather, it becomes the place of ongoing interpretation of revelation. The church therefore needs to look to the world to
discover God's designs for the present time. Like the two other signs of the

times that Blessed John XXIII pointed to, namely, the demand of the poor for economic justice and the right of colonialized nations to self-governance, the rise of women's claims to human dignity and their concomitant power to speak are rooted in God's design for the world.[44]

In a farsighted essay Karl Rahner noted that the image of Mary in the church has always been closely tied to the image of women at any given time. Since the culturally conditioned image of women in our day is undergoing radical change, this raises serious questions about the image of Mary that have not yet been adequately recognized. Consequently, he suggested, perhaps it is time for men to stop writing books about Mary and let women have a go at it, since there is much wisdom in that quarter that has not yet come to light: "Mariology today and in the future still has a great deal to do if it wants to have an image of Mary that will really be true for the religious existence of woman as such. It is an image that can perhaps be produced authentically today only by women, by women theologians."[45] There is more consequence to this suggestion than he could have imagined.

2

℮

Women's Theological Work

THE ICE CRACKS

On every continent, women scholars with their ear to the ground of women's religious experiences are bringing this harvest of insights about Mary into the formal language of theology. Their writings in mariology form but a small part of the much broader endeavor of doing theology "with women's eyes," work made possible by the new sociological phenomenon of women's advancing into the academy and gaining there a public voice. As historically practiced, theology, classically defined by Anselm as "faith seeking understanding," has been almost exclusively a field of men's endeavor. Inevitably, the result has been a male-inflected set of understandings. The sheer fact of the omission of women has led to ambiguous results. While carrying forward the good news of salvation in Christ through changing eras and cultures, sometimes with heart-warming success, theology has been marred by deeply embedded attitudes of men's privileged place before God coupled with definitions of women's inferiority that support practices of exclusion.

As part of the social movement on a global scale for the betterment of women's lives, women in increasing numbers have gained access to theological education. When they begin to practice their craft as professionals, their unique position as "insider-outsiders"[1] inevitably gives rise to new theological approaches. Like theologians everywhere, women scholars engage in careful, honest dialogue with scripture and Christian tradition to arrive at wisdom for practice and belief in their own cultural contexts. Given their explicit commitment to do this from the position of those who have been long silenced, they pay specific attention to what traditionally disparages women and to what could contribute to the flourishing of women in all dimensions of their lives. In a critically negative step, their diverse methods confront bias against women and their communities based on gender, race, class, ethnicity, age, sexual orientation—the whole inter-structured edifice of oppressions, based on religious belief, that allow some to lord it over others and even over the earth. The enemy in every instance is not men as such but systems and thought patterns that disparage and abuse the genuine humanity of women in all their differences along with their communities. In a critically positive step, they seek understanding that will promote "the full humanity of women,"[2] who are created in the image of God. It is a mistake to think that this theology is concerned simply with "women's questions." Rather, it reflects on the entire realm of Christian faith, seeking to interpret beliefs, moral values, rituals, symbols, and structures in ways that give life to the heretofore excluded half of the human race. Women of color who suffer the ravages of racial prejudice stemming from slavery's inheritance, women in economically poor circumstances, women whose ethnic communities differ from the majority, women of different sexual orientations, and women caught up in violent situations in their home or society push this project to utter inclusiveness. The genius of this approach is that by promoting the full humanity of the diversity of women it also enhances the Christian gospel's hope for the well-being of the whole human community and the earth, insofar as women exist in and profoundly sustain whole living networks of relationships.

To signal their intent to interpret religious truth with the flourishing of women as a goal, women on every continent employ certain adjectives. They name their work feminist theology, or womanist theology in the case of African American scholars, or *mujerista* theology in the case of Hispanic/Latina scholars in the United States.[3] As is always the case in theology, they utilize theories taken from other disciplines such as philosophy, sociology, and psychology to help interpret matters of faith.[4] Some concepts have proved enduringly useful as analytic tools.

Sexism, prejudice against women precisely because they are female. At the end of the twentieth century the U.N. world conference on women held in Beijing describes this in striking phrases:

> While women have made significant advances in many societies, women's concerns are still given second priority almost everywhere. Women face discrimination and marginalization in subtle as well as in flagrant ways. Women do not share equally in the fruits of production. Women constitute 70 per cent of the world's poor. . . . Women and men still live in an unequal world. Gender disparities and unacceptable inequalities persist in all countries. In

1995 there is no country in the world where men and women enjoy complete equality.[5]

Patriarchy, the rule of the father. Poet Adrienne Rich offers a comprehensive definition: "Patriarchy is the power of the fathers; a familial, social, ideological, political system in which men—by force, direct pressure, or through ritual, tradition, law and language, customs, etiquette, education, and the division of labor—determine what part women shall or shall not play, and in which the female is everywhere subsumed under the male."[6] This is a complex system of subordination and domination that has functioned throughout much of recorded history as the paradigm not only for the family household but also for church, society, and the state. As historian Gerda Lerner insists, patriarchy does not render women totally powerless or totally deprived of rights, resources, and influence. The permutations of patriarchy are many, and it has shifted and adapted throughout history in response to female pressure and demands.[7] Still, its web of regulations never grants women equal rights or equal opportunities for participation and decision making.

Kyriarchy, rule of the lord and master. Broader than patriarchy, this neologism encompasses the whole range of exploitation practiced around the world wherever certain powerful persons assume the right to control individuals or groups who might benefit them. It refers to multistranded, interstructured layers of oppression based on gender, race, class, ethnicity, colonial status, sexual orientation, age, disability, and other markers used to denigrate peoples' human dignity. This analytic concept makes it clear that while all women are marginalized by law and custom in kyriarchal systems, in some instances women themselves may benefit at the expense of other women—think of white women in the South during slavery, or first-world consumers who buy apparel made by women in sweatshops in developing countries. Indeed, "the full oppressive power of kyriarchy is manifested in the lives and struggles of the poorest and most oppressed wo/men who live on the bottom of the kyriarchal pyramid."[8]

Sex refers to the biologically distinct designs of the male and female body that function in reproduction, a physiological constant normally needing surgical intervention to be changed.

Gender is not a given in the same sense. It is the socially constructed expectation of how sexually embodied male and female persons should act, what characteristics each should develop, and what social roles they will be allowed to play. As Gerda Lerner writes, gender is "the cultural definition of behavior as appropriate to the sexes in a given society at a given time."[9] Complete with linguistic and symbolic expressions, gender organizes the relation between the sexes in a given time and place. Because they are historical constructions, gender definitions can and do change from age to age—including in spectacular ways in our own—while sex remains a constant.

Feminism, that much-maligned but still beautifully meaningful term, is the intellectual and practical stance that promotes the well-being of women as genuine human beings, fully gifted while very diverse, and worthy of equal dignity, rights, and power in every sphere of life. In Sandra Schneiders's lucid description, it is a comprehensive body of ideas "which is rooted in women's experience of sexual oppression, engages in a critique of patriarchy as an essentially dysfunctional system, embraces an alternative vision for humanity and the earth, and actively seeks to bring this vision to realization."[10] Multicultural and pluralistic, academic feminism has grown by listening to the challenge of women of color to avoid false universalism, which would define all women by the narrow range of white women's experience. "Those who are willing to engage us," Ada María Isasi-Díaz points out, "must embrace our difference instead of making us a reflection of who they are."[11] Dialogue marks the way ahead.

Inheriting a patriarchal religious tradition, women use these analytic tools to do Christian theology in a way that seeks liberation from all forms of kyriarchal oppression, including an unjust sex-gender system, for the benefit of church and society. There is no uniform approach. Depending on their analysis of the situation and the strategies utilized, women's theological work is variously labeled as liberal, social, cultural, radical, reform, reconstruction, liberation, or postmodern, depending on the feminist theory utilized.[12] Regardless of the particular methods used, the goal is profound. This theology works to heal patriarchy's broken heart, in Rita Nakashima Brock's peaceable metaphor, or to liberate women and men together into a community of the discipleship of equals, in Elisabeth Schüssler Fiorenza's powerful symbol, or to mediate the Spirit's offer of transforming grace to the church in this age, as Anne Carr prophetically proposes.[13] Both critical and hopeful, it is drawn by the power of the Spirit to believe in the biblical promise that what exists in the present is not all there is, that God's deepest hope for humanity is the liberating wholeness of all people and indeed of the whole world itself. This is faith seeking understanding so passionately that it enables an encounter with the living God that challenges a whole calcified pattern of structured sinfulness. Spiritually, it expresses a hunger and thirst for justice that includes women of all kinds, for the benefit of the whole community. In the course of this work, the ice of centuries of women's public silence and invisibility begins to crack.

Different though their "adjectives" may be, women theologians on every continent who have turned their attention to the subject of Mary note that elements oppressive to women pervade the marian tradition. These need to be uncovered and corrected so that "the liberation of Mary," in Sally Cunneen's telling phrase, in union with her sisters, can be accomplished.[14] The wealth of women's theological work on Mary done to date cannot be neatly systematized. Their work has yielded a raft of critical judgments and a wealth of creative interpretations. Taking note of key contributions makes clear just how rich these emerging options are and depicts the colorful spectrum on which the proposal of this book is situated.

CRITICAL JUDGMENTS

In order to move forward, one must identify obstacles that are blocking the way. When women begin to analyze the marian heritage, one basic problem emerges that undergirds all others, namely, this tradition is just saturated with sexist construals of gender. Drawing from the unquestioned assumption that men are by nature active, rational, and capable of exercising authority, while women are naturally receptive, emotional, and oriented to obedience and service, male theologians over the centuries created an image of Mary as the ideal feminine person. They then either contrasted her unique virtue with that of all other women or held her up as the norm whom all other women should seek, impossibly, to emulate. In the process, the marian symbol functioned powerfully to legitimize patriarchal social structures. Without these sexist gender assumptions, which result inevitably in male social dominance and female subordination, the classic construals of marian theology would fall apart.

Parsing this basic critique, we can see that the baleful effect of patriarchal mariology operates in at least three ways. It idealizes this one woman to the detriment of all others. It construes her holiness with virtues conducive to women's subservience. And it draws sociological lessons from her relationship to Christ that point to female subordination. These strategies are clearly interrelated, but each unveils a different aspect of the problem. Together they set parameters for what a liberating theology of Mary at the very least should *not* be, and guide thought onto a more promising path that avoids these dead-ends.

Idealization

Picturing Mary as the most perfect of women, the patriarchal marian tradition functions paradoxically to disparage all other women. One would think it might work in the opposite way, that honoring one would lead to honoring all members of her group. But praise of Mary in theology and cult redounds to her benefit at the expense of other women because of the fundamental assumption that Mary does not *exemplify* the capacity for God of redeemed humanity including women. Rather, she is the great exception. "Alone of all her sex" she stands pure and blessed by God.[15] Her glorious precedence prevents any analogy between herself and other women, all of whom fall short by comparison with her perfection.

Historically, this idea first emerged in the Mary–Eve analogy. Introduced by Justin in the second century and developed by Irenaeus and others with great embellishment, this analogy takes the biblical Adam–Christ contrast and extends it to their female partners. "As in Adam all die, so also in Christ shall all be made alive," Paul writes (1 Cor. 15:22). Similarly, through her disobedience Eve is responsible for the fall of humankind with all its attendant misery. Through her obedience Mary, the new Eve, is responsible for bringing forth the conqueror of that sin, the Savior. As Irenaeus writes, "Just as Eve, while wife of Adam, was still a virgin . . . and became by her disobedience the cause of death for herself and the whole human race, so Mary too, espoused yet a virgin, became by her obedience the cause of salvation of both herself and the whole human race. The knot of Eve's disobedience was loosened by Mary's obedience."[16] Death through Eve, life through Mary became the axiom. A greater contrast could hardly be imagined.

Where do the rest of women fall in this dichotomy of female behavior? Since no other woman is as obedient, pure, or holy as the mother of God, women are ranked with the sinful temptress Eve. As Tertullian so disastrously exclaimed to women:

Do you not realize that you are each an Eve? The curse of God on this sex of yours lives on even in our times. Guilty, you must bear its hardships. You are the gateway of the devil; you desecrated the fatal tree; you were the first to betray the law of God; you softened up with your cajoling words the one against whom the devil could not prevail by force. All too easily you destroyed the image of God, Adam. You are the one who deserved death; because of you the Son of God had to die.[17]

Eve is the cause of sorrow, condemnation, corruption, and death. Identified with Eve, women are sinful, seductive accomplices of Satan. Note that women's sexuality here is deeply connected with sin, which is not at all what the biblical text of the so-called fall in Genesis 3 suggests. By contrast, Mary alone is pure and undefiled. Unfortunately, as Susan Ashbrook Harvey points out, Tertullian's invective became the hallmark of preaching about women.[18] Chrysostom, Jerome, Augustine, and many others projected primary responsibility for the sinful condition of humankind onto Eve and all other women who are like unto her instead of perceiving clearly the solidarity of the whole human race, both men and women, in sin and grace. The pattern is repeated throughout the history of theology. A fascinating study by William Cole documents how even so rigorous a thinker as Thomas Aquinas was less than consistent on this question. To compare Aquinas's texts that describe women as defective and misbegotten males, inferior not just because of sin but originally and by nature, with his texts on the woman Mary, which exalt her above all creatures, even the angels, is to expose a logical gap in his thought that he never resolved.[19] A modern articulation of the same idea comes from the early Schillebeeckx, who wrote, "It is clear that she must be a creature of matchless wonder, this *Immaculata* and *Assumpta*, with whom even the most physically and spiritually beautiful women in the world cannot in any way be compared."[20] Some of this is the language of devotion, but the practical effect on women is deadly.

The Eve–Mary contrast has been used to disparage women much more vehemently than the Adam–Christ distinction was ever used to men's disadvantage. By idealizing Mary, splitting her off from Eve and all other women, the denigration of the many became the shadow side of the glorification of the one. Now male authors could deploy women as a theological code signaling weakness, sexual temptation, and even depravity. And practical consequences could be drawn: Eve spoke and sin entered the world, which is the reason why women must keep silent in the churches.

As Australian Orthodox editor Leonie Liveris laments, "Always women carry with them the past reputation of Eve; always they travel towards the sinless and unobtainable but beloved Mary, the Mother of God."[21] Raising this one woman onto a pedestal became a strategy of patriarchal disparagement and control of all other women.

Those who approach this critique from a contemporary psychological point of view note that the official, exalted view of Mary, insofar as it is created primarily by patriarchal minds and hearts, bears an overload of male projection. Men split off what is uncomfortable in their own nature and identify it disparagingly with the "other" who is different from themselves. Similarly, they sense what could inspire their lives and idealize it in the "other" who draws them on like a good angel. Thus dividing women's human reality into good and harmful elements, they project the good onto Mary in an idealized fashion and the weakness onto the rest of women, who must then be kept subject because of their very nature. Truth be told, this view comes nowhere near the experience actual women have of themselves. Nor, given the opportunity, would women ever theologically define themselves this way. As Rosemary Ruether analyzed early on, this is a classic example of the "madonna–whore" syndrome, which exalts the symbol of the spiritual feminine but denigrates the sexual, maternal, carnal reality of actual women in the concrete.[22] The pattern is powerfully harmful because it allows churchmen to love and revere their ideal of woman in the transcendent woman Mary, but to ignore and dominate concrete women with impunity and with immunity even from the searchings of their own conscience. Further evidence for this judgment is provided by sociological observation. In those countries where devotion to Mary still flourishes strongly, women find great difficulty in claiming significant involvement in public and political life. The same holds true for those churches that have the strongest official attachment to Mary: they are the least likely to be open to full participation of women in ecclesial public life and ministry.

Feminine Modeling

In addition to idealizing Mary, the patriarchal marian tradition also operates to harmful effect by construing the image of Mary with virtues and roles conducive to women's subservience. With no little irony, since Mary has already been classified as beyond the reach of her sinful sisters, she is set up as the supreme model whom all other women should emulate. This second strategy uses strong gender dualism that assumes, contrary to

Christian faith, that Mary models the ideal spiritual path for women while leaving Jesus for the men. It mounts this argument with particular emphasis on Mary as handmaid, as virgin, and as mother. Let me be very clear. To be responsive to the call of God, to live a life of freely chosen virginity, and to be a loving mother are fine and excellent things in and of themselves. But patriarchal interpretation has derailed these options into a wreck of oppressive expectations.

Handmaid. Luke's gospel narrative of the annunciation presents a powerful example of a young girl's positive response to the invitation of God operating within history. But rather than seeing Mary's response as the radical free decision of a young woman to risk her life on a messianic adventure, patriarchal mariology interprets it as an act of feminine submissiveness to the will of God, imaged here in literal fashion as a male authority figure. In preaching, spiritual writing, and theological treatises, Mary stands forth as the feminine epitome of dependence on this male God's initiative, a model of humility understood as lack of a personal ego or will of one's own. She models obedience understood as acquiescence: "I'll do whatever you say." The overwhelming passivity connected with this construal has rendered Mary, in the words of famed mariologist René Laurentin, "a psychological model of a perpetual minor," hidden and enclosed, timid and sweet, taking direction from others with no inner purpose of her own.[23] Such a presentation of Mary, as Sri Lankan theologian Tissa Balasuriya critically observes, does not present her as a strong women "who can respond to a world seeking justice"; nor does it encourage those devoted to Mary to play their part "in the liberation of humanity from the social evils which are part of the cause of our misery."[24] Presented with this ideal, women learn that they find their true path to God by being obedient, submissive, self-sacrificing, silent, and deferential, rather than exercising independent, responsible thought and action, especially in the face of social and political evils. This construal of Mary the obedient handmaid legitimates the idea that women's virtue lies in being receptively obedient to the authority of males, be they divine or human, God, fathers, husbands, or priests. Note how the problem is compounded by the thoroughly masculine character of the deity.

Growth in their own autonomy as human persons ensures that women find this model increasingly intolerable. Kari Børresen speaks for many when she argues that to make Mary a model for women is absurd if the essential connection between femininity and subordination is not broken. Only when the divine is no longer pictured in predominantly male metaphors, and only when human dependence on God is not cast in terms of female subordination to male authority, will the figure of Mary stop being "a patriarchal construct: virgin, wife, and mother, an adjunct to the male."[25]

New depth is brought to this critique by African American women who inherit the legacy of chattel slavery. Clarice Martin, noting that the Greek word *doulos/doulē*, which the annunciation scene translates "servant" or "handmaid," literally means "slave," lists the degradations of slavery, including violence, which enormously complicate its use as a metaphor for relationship to God.[26] The experience of slavery, furthermore, was different for women and men insofar as women had to be bodily available to serve the physical requirements of the males of the household, not only feeding and cleaning them but servicing them sexually. Delores Williams's analysis of the coerced roles of the slave "mammy" in the American South who had to be wet nurse, concubine, and breeder for her master removes any possibility of glorifying the position of handmaid.[27] Shawn Copeland argues that Christian teaching and preaching on the plantation sought to bind slaves to their condition "by inculcating caricatures of the cardinal virtues of patience, long-suffering, forbearance, love": the more compliant the woman, the better.[28] Today these virtues are being reevaluated in light of women's need for their own integrity, a rethinking that engages a hermeneutic of suspicion to subvert the value of submission. No longer is religious promotion of self-surrender and humble obedience bearable if black women are to live in the freedom of the gospel. Jacquelyn Grant's work on the symbol of the servant reveals the ambivalence of this motif even when applied to Jesus: when servanthood instead of discipleship is offered as an ideal to black women, especially if it be shorn of concomitant emphasis on resistance to evil, it is nothing short of sinful.[29]

Virgin. Postbiblical theology of Mary grew in an intellectual and religious environment that was increasingly suspicious of the human body and its sexuality. The early church's move from a Hebraic to a Hellenistic environment entailed using the intellectual tradition of that culture, including a philosophy that posited strong, underlying tension between spirit and matter. This translated into a Christian spirituality that prized as the highest value detachment from the world and its fleshly pleasures. The end of persecution in the fourth century gave additional impetus to the path of asceticism, including abstinence from sex, which was considered a new form of martyrdom. Theologians developed a strong bias against marriage and sexual pleasure, which in their view enmeshed the soul in earthly goods and distracted from the things that are above. They valorized lifelong virginity as the holier way, achieved by special graces and leading to a higher position in heaven. Interpreting Jesus' parable of the sower and the seed, innumerable patristic authors taught that marriage brought forth thirtyfold, widowhood sixtyfold, and virginity the hundredfold harvest that was so desirable. Jerome did famously grant that marriage was good for one thing: it produced virgins, who could then avoid the fate of their pitiable mothers. As for those already married, he offered the consolation that they could become holy if they stopped having sex and practiced virginal chastity within the married state.

In the battle between the spirit and the flesh, waged by men who aspired to God, women were placed on the side of the flesh owing to their role as marriage partners as well as their messy connection with pregnancy and childbirth. You can watch it develop in the literature of the early Christian centuries: an increasingly strong torrent of misogyny against women and their bodies.[30] In this context, the resulting powerful aversion of Christian male thinkers to female sexuality gave them a strong impetus to honor Mary for her virginity. If virginity was the highest ideal for women, then the mother of the Savior epitomized this ideal. The New Testament affirmed that Mary had conceived Jesus by the overshadowing of the Holy Spirit. Her virginity at his conception was now extended to include the idea that she gave birth virginally, with her hymen unbroken, and remained ever afterwards a virgin par excellence. It got to the point where in the fourth century Pope Siricius even said that Jesus would have rejected his mother if she had conceived other children. He would not have chosen to be born of Mary "had he been forced to look upon her as so unrestrained as to let that womb, from which the body of the Lord was fashioned, that hall of the eternal king, be stained by the presence of male seed. Whoever maintains that, maintains the unbelief of the Jews."[31]

A series of vicious debates in the fourth century showed that the intertwining of marian doctrine and ascetical theology was not universally accepted. Arguing that marriage, sex, and children were the gift of God, both Helvidius and Jovinian opposed the ascendent view of Mary's perpetual virginity because its accompanying rhetoric degraded those gifts. It also drove a wedge between all baptized Christians, profoundly devaluing all who were not virgins. Baptism made both married women and virgins equally sanctified in Christ, they argued, and while Mary conceived Jesus virginally, her marriage to Joseph involved sexual relations, as can be seen from the presence of the brothers and sisters of Jesus in the Gospels. While their views were arguably more in accord with church tradition up to that point, their opponents Ambrose and Jerome ultimately won the day. In the end, Mary's virginity was detached from its original Gospel significance and came to stand alone as a physical value in itself. "What was once a testimony to the presence of God in Christ had become an affirmation of absence, an emblem of exclusion and closure; what was once a sign of salvation extended to all, became a symbol of holiness possessed by the few."[32] When this view was wedded to the Mary–Eve dichotomy, the patriarchal imagination not only scapegoated female sexuality as the cause of sin and death. It also created a marian tool with which to disparage all women who engaged in sexual behavior, even if they were legitimately married.

There was one bright light in all of this. Historians of the ascetic movement in early Christian centuries underscore how revolutionary the possibility of virginity was for women. Ancient patriarchal society "conscripted" young women without question into marriage and childbearing as their duty to family and state. Once married, a woman became her husband's property, meant for his pleasure, the service of his life's needs, and the reproduction of his progeny. Virginity offered a new option. It opened up possibilities for women that departed dramatically from the traditional role expectations of patriarchal marriage. Dedicated to Christ, virgins could resist family demands for unwelcome marriage alliances and a life of bearing children for the clan. They could, in effect, choose a more independent lifestyle that included private time, cultivation of the mind, and empowering association with other women in female-run communities.[33] Seen in her social context, the virgin was "intact" not only physically but also socially from patriarchal pressures.[34] An index of the consternation this caused is the degree to which women had to struggle for the right to be virgins or, in social terms, for the right to dispose of their bodies as they pleased by keeping them out of circulation. What is clear is that this choice was not imposed upon women by men. Rather, as Jo Ann McNamara's research demonstrates, "it was a revolt against an earlier set of male definitions, a rejection by some women of the sexual roles they had played for so long. No early Christian Father recommended virginity to women until they had already claimed it as a new role for themselves in Christian society."[35] Indeed, it was only after women chose this way of life in large numbers that male theologians and church leaders began their voluminous outpourings in the effort to regulate their lives.

One strategy in this effort to tame the virgins' freedom involved setting Mary up as the ideal virgin who was not only chaste but silent, submissive, and obedient.[36] If they emulated her, independent groups of women could be controlled by church authorities. Despite some success along these lines, the image of the virgin Mary did subversively signal that women could be valued as persons in themselves without being identified with a man. As Sydney Callahan writes, "All of Mary's powers and privileges, her strengths and virtues, were seen as independent of her status as a wife."[37] Emphasis on Mary's virginity served paradoxically to strengthen women's search for freedom.

On balance, however, the glorification of Mary's virgin status, part of the larger spiritual suspicion of the body, functioned to the detriment of other women's holy exercise of their own sexuality. Theoretically Jesus might still have been the Son of God however conceived, since God's power is unlimited; but concretely Mary could hardly have been found worthy of the honor unless preserved from the contamination of sexual desire and activity, which theologians began to equate with sinfulness or at least a lesser degree of holiness. Consequently, as Susan Roll observes, "the virginity of the mother of God captured the imagination of male theologians and inspired extraordinary poetic images and discourses: Mary as a sealed fountain, an enclosed garden, and so forth, to the point of morbid fascination, embarrassing to read."[38] The fundamental hostility of this theology to women's sexuality has perdured through the centuries. As the feminist critique has laid bare, the results are derogatory to women whose embodied human reality is disparaged in direct proportion to Mary's unearthly, asexual exaltation. Today as women reclaim their own sexuality as part of their blessed human and spiritual wholeness, they emphatically reject this disparagement. In South Africa, Sister Bernard Mncube, ex-prisoner in the struggle against apartheid and campaigner for justice for women, typifies the attitude when she exclaims:

> Women in the Church need to re-affirm their sexuality against the cult of virginity. I am a Roman Catholic nun and proud of it. But why must I be ashamed of my sexuality? . . . Our sexuality has been so mystified today that we fear even to talk about it. I can talk about my hand, face, and every part

of my body, but when it comes to my vagina, I dare not even whisper the word. As if God has created something so evil that we are not even allowed to say a word about it.[39]

She suspects that God, too, who created and loves women, feels marginalized in the church by the antisexual tradition that so disrespects women at the very core of their being.

One promising development stems from the discovery that the archetypal virginity of goddesses in ancient mythology lay not so much in their lack of sexual activity as in their personal independence. "The virginity of a goddess is a symbolic statement of her spiritual purity," writes James Preston from the perspective of cultural anthropology; it is "not to be taken literally or confused with human sexuality."[40] A virgin goddess might engage in sexual activity or she might not, but her virginity was not thereby affected so long as she remained one-in-herself. C. G. Jung's work on archetypes came to the same insight. More than a biological reality, being a virgin indicates a state of mind characterized by fearlessness and independence of purpose. Whether wife or mother, the virgin retains an inner autonomy. "She does what she does . . . because what she does is true," as psychologist Jean Shinoda Bolen describes it.[41] When this becomes the lens for interpreting Mary's virginity, the resulting image can function spiritually and politically to encourage women's integrity and self-direction. Korean theologian Chung Hyun Kyung approvingly describes a virgin Mary who is a self-defining woman, connected to her own inner self and free to serve God. She does not lead a derived life as merely daughter, wife, and mother of men. Rather, she lives from her own center with a power that only gets stronger as she ages. In a similar vein, Marianne Katoppo in Indonesia and Rita Monteiro in India, arguing that virginity refers to the state of being whole in oneself rather than biological abstinence from sex, relate Mary to poor women who struggle to be the subjects of their own actions.[42] European Catharina Halkes suggests that since virginity denotes "an attitude of being open and available to the divine mystery, to the voice and power of the spirit in us," then we can learn from the virgin Mary "to live from our own centre, our own roots, in independence, and not in one-sided and alienating dependence."[43] Thus Mary's virginity functions as a symbol of autonomy, signaling that a woman is not defined by her relationship with a man.

This symbolic interpretation of virginity is not as implausible as it might sound at first to those familiar with traditional church teaching.

Spiritual writers have long held that, in essence, virginity connotes an openness of spirit to God. Considering incidents of rape during military invasion, Augustine held that purity is not lost even when the body has been violated, if the will remains pure. Hence, a woman who is raped has no cause to commit suicide.[44] In holding Mary up as model of the church, Vatican II points not only to her role as mother, which typifies the church bringing forth new children in the body of Christ by preaching and baptism, but also to her role as virgin, which typifies the church following Christ with wholehearted fidelity. "The church herself is a virgin who keeps whole and pure the fidelity she has pledged to her Spouse. Imitating the mother of her Lord and by the power of the Holy Spirit, she preserves with virginal purity an integral faith, a firm hope, and a sincere charity."[45] Since *Lumen Gentium*, the Dogmatic Constitution on the Church, has already defined the church as the whole People of God, its virginity is obviously something other than sexual abstinence. Rather, it signifies a quality of religious commitment.

With these notions of virginity, the church's official position about Mary's perpetual virginity, which teaches that she was a virgin before, during, and after the birth of Christ, takes on a strangely liberating power. Here is a woman whose worth is not dependent on a man; a woman whose yes to God's invitation was at the same time an assent to the totality of herself; a woman who acted with integrity from her own center. Saying that she is perpetually virgin encourages women to relate to the world with freedom all their life long. Poor women have used this approach subversively to emphasize Mary's strength, autonomy, and prophetic spirit, which empowers their own earthly struggle against forces of death. Many Asian women have come to realize that "when a woman defines herself according to her own understanding of who she really is and what she is meant for in this universe (and not according to the rules and norms of patriarchy), she is a virgin. Therefore her virginity persists in spite of sexual experience, child-bearing, and increasing age. Actually her virginity, her ability to be a self-defining woman, grows because of her full range of life experience."[46]

Despite these attempts at reinterpretation, many other women find the whole discussion of Mary's virginity depressing and obnoxious. One New Yorker dismissed the whole issue in inimitable fashion: "Mary's sex life is her own business. She, like all of us, needs some privacy."[47] Feminist analysis has laid bare the fundamental problem. Cast in a dualistic framework profoundly inimical to the body and sexuality, the patriarchal construction of Mary's ideal virginity disparages actual women in their embodied, sexual, beautiful reality.

Mother. Historically, Miriam of Nazareth was indeed the mother of Jesus of Nazareth and can be assumed to have had influence on the kind of compassionate, courageous man he became. However, concentration on Mary's motherhood in the tradition has served to reinforce the teaching that motherhood is the raison d'être of a woman's life, her one divinely approved accomplishment. It thereby shores up the patriarchal social expectation that reproduction with its accompanying domesticity is the primary vocation for women. Equally problematic, Mary's motherhood is construed in absolute separation from eroticism and sexual love, handing women a virtually celibate ideal even in their motherhood. In addition, the kind of mothering portrayed in marian hymns and prayers entails total, lifelong devotion to the needs of her children, which precludes any idea that she might develop as an independent individual. Her perpetual availability suffocates women, in Susan Harvey's strong language, "with threats of innate enslavement to a self-abnegating motherhood."[48] The other side of that relationship is that all too frequently it keeps devotees in a state of perpetual childhood, narcissistically looking to the mother for the satisfaction of needs, a state that is the antithesis of adult responsibility for the world.[49]

Traditional construals of Mary as mother have yet another drawback. They promote a spirituality that imaginatively takes the social experience of the patriarchal household and projects it into heaven. One of the key roles of the mother in a patriarchal family, where she is supposedly the "heart," is to intercede on behalf of her children with the rather more distant father, who is supposedly the "head." Her merciful influence can soften punishment and obtain benefits that would otherwise not be forthcoming. Reinscribing this human institution into heaven makes Mary the merciful mother who intercedes for her wayward children before a basically loving but definitely just, perhaps testy, sometimes even angry God the Father. The whole theology of her maternal mediation derives from this scenario.[50] While we have no adequate idea of heaven, however, we can be quite sure that since it is supposed to be a state of bliss, one thing it decidedly does not resemble is a patriarchal household.

Feminist research makes a distinction between women's experience of being a mother, which involves relationships of giving and nurturing that can be deeply fulfilling, and the patriarchal institution of motherhood, which is invariably restrictive.[51] To be a mother is to give life abundantly out of one's own body and to nurture its well-being with power. Far from pusillanimity, mothering awakens fierce protective instincts as the one who gives life fights like hell to ward off what will harm the young.[52] Retrieving and renaming this rich, life-changing relationship in their own voices, women are freeing up from patriarchal definition an experience that is uniquely female. In this context, Mary's mothering has the potential to promote the "ripeness of maturity" that enhances the dignity of all women who nurture and serve the life of others, whether biologically or in other ways.[53] Indeed, given Christian faith in the identity of the one she bore, her act of mothering rings with subtle power for all believers. As a popular axiom would have it, we are all meant to be mothers of God, for God is always needing to be born. The strength of patriarchal gender definitions, however, makes women's recovery of Mary as mother a continuingly dicey proposition.

For women who now enter into mutual partnership with their husbands in marriage, or who yearn to transform their relationships in this direction, or who run single-parent households, or who combine mothering with a career, or who live with their female partner, or who just root for fullness of life for women, the whole patriarchal paradigm of motherhood is simply ignored or even rejected. Discussing the unreality of Mary's motherhood as construed by the male celibate tradition, Ute Ranke-Heinemann notes that "they have ignored the fact that a woman is also something more than the bearer of a child according to a plan."[54] A woman's personal worth does not depend on having children. Valuable though it is, being a mother is not the only choice of vocation a woman can legitimately make. In fact, persistent emphasis on the importance of having children has but served to undermine the human dignity of women who are childless whether by choice or necessity.[55] Even when she is a mother and happily stamped forever by her childbearing, a woman's identity is not exhausted in this fact. There are more facets to her person as a mature woman.

Sociological Subordination

Besides idealizing Mary and assigning her stereotypical feminine roles, a third strategy uses Mary sociologically to divide women from other women and all women from men. In the first instance, emphasis on the value of Mary's virginity implies that women who live a vowed life of virginity are closer to the ideal, are living a holier life, are more favored by God, than women who actively exercise their sexuality even if this be in the context of the sacrament of marriage. Thus Mary in patriarchal hands is used to drive a wedge between women by assessing them to be of greater or lesser spiritual worth, thereby replicating hierarchy instead of promoting solidarity. Women on both sides of this divide are increasingly rejecting this sexual stratification, along with women who are neither virgins nor mothers. Appreciating the great diversity of women's ways to God, affirming the sexually active female body as blessed, and refusing to consider marriage inferior to religious life, they are finding each other as allies in a community of celebration and resistance rather than rivals in a hierarchy of holiness.

A further insidious use of Mary occurs when her relationship to Jesus Christ as perceived by Christian faith serves as the model for the sociological relationship between concrete historical women and men. Despite heroic efforts to the contrary, this strategy inevitably relegates women to a subordinate position. Jesus Christ is the Savior and Mary is caught up in the mystery of salvation coming from God through Christ in the Spirit. But this sound theological pattern is corrupted by patriarchal construals of gender. God is envisioned as male, and *she* obeys *him*. Jesus' human maleness is brought to the fore and interpreted in naive ontological fashion: he is Messiah and *she* is oriented to *him*. This pattern is then translated into normative social structures that shape the relationship between women and men in the church. Men take initiative, women respond; men are slated for the public sphere, women for the private; men exercise authority, women are supportive of them.

Even without Mary, this is an argument as old as scripture. Christ is the head of the church, his body. In a parallel way the husband is the head of his wife: "as the church is subject to Christ, so let wives also be subject in everything to their husbands" (Eph. 5:24). Granted, the husband is exhorted to love his wife as Christ loves the church. But there is no mutuality of equal partners here. The human analogy is patriarchal marriage, with dominance–submission the fundamental pattern of relationship. In subsequent theology, when Mary, again because of her gender, is construed as a model of the church, the biblical Christ–church metaphor shifts to a Christ–Mary one. In the resulting ideal, the patriarchal authority exercised by men is complemented by women's loving obedience and publicly silent but privately supportive role. Theologian Jean Galôt framed the argument in a blatant way: since Christ operated while Mary, who was totally dependent, cooperated with him, the roles of men and women in the church are clear. Man leads, woman follows. Man preaches the word, woman receives it. Her role is her listening silence by which she renders service to the man who speaks.[56] The point to note is that the argument is being mounted from the marian symbol in relation to Christ, applied sociologically in direct fashion. For women and men who have glimpsed the new vision of a community of the discipleship of equals, who yearn for it with a passion born of their encounter with the Holy One, this construal is a distortion of gospel truth. It exalts Mary the woman precisely for accepting the secondary role assigned her in view of the priority of Christ the man. Any woman who does otherwise is judged to be not living up to the ideal limned by the mother of God. Little wonder that independent women walk away.

To sum up: separated and idealized, given a life story in which she is submissive, desexualized, and fixated on motherhood, and then sent back as a model for women subordinate to men, the traditional image of Mary emerges from critical feminist analysis as a male-designed creation that functions to define and control women. This image shores up patriarchal social structures and inculcates in women the legitimacy of their restricted place. This, of course, is not the whole sum and substance of the marian tradition. But the burden of proof is on those who would deny this analysis, which points to the deep problems that women face when they turn to the work of liberating Mary from patriarchal interpretation.

CREATIVE INTERPRETATIONS

Despite the problems delineated above, "religious images do not belong just to the powerful in the church,"[57] as South African Megan Walker points out. Gleaning wisdom from those disenfranchised, a legion of women scholars now deals with the question of Mary in new ways. Their creative proposals move the conversation to more spacious quarters of the mind. One of the most significant interpretations is that of Rosemary Radford Ruether, who envisions a liberation mariology based on Luke's gospel. The primary text is Mary's song, the Magnificat (Luke 1:46–55). Here, with her declaration that God casts down the mighty from their thrones and lifts up the lowly, Mary proclaims the saving power that enters history to reverse the present order of power and powerlessness. As a woman from among the poorer classes of a colonized people, she herself "represents the oppressed community that is to be lifted up and filled with good things in the messianic revolution."[58] Her story embodies God's preferential option for the poor and challenges economically advantaged people to be converted to their cause. Insofar as Mary represents the church as redeemed humanity, a new paradigm comes into being. Rather than the typology of Christ and the church as dominant male and submissive female, we now have the kenotic Christ self-emptying divine power out into the human situation of suffering and hope, and the church being empowered and lifted up as the transformed community of the poor and those in solidarity with them. Together Christ and church/Mary/we ourselves begin to live the reversal of values characteristic of the coming reign of God. While some have criticized this construal because it continues to use gender as a basic category, its strength lies in turning the Mary–Christ relationship into a liberating rather than repressive symbol.

Mary Jo Weaver puts forth the intriguing suggestion that we should commit an act of symbolic integration that would conflate all the different women named Mary in the New Testament into one composite figure. This would both heal the separation of Mary from other women and function as a powerful icon for feminists.[59] Another suggestion, put forward by Elisabeth Moltmann-Wendel, would be to reinstate and honor the tradition of women's friendship with Jesus rather than Mary's motherhood. Critical of the way mainstream tradition has tamed Mary of Nazareth "from a living, critical, angry, unadapted mother into the symbol of femininity,"[60] this theologian argues that in the Gospels friendship rather than motherhood is the constitutive mark of the eschatological community of the disciples. Though nativity scenes and *pietàs* would not lead one to think so, Jesus' life was shaped not only by relation to his mother but also by adult friendship with his women disciples, chief among whom was Mary Magdalene, first witness of the resurrection, which is the central proclamation of Christian faith. Until the women disciples are given their rightful place, mariology has no future.

Women's theological work on Mary is by now voluminous enough to permit classification into distinct models. In an enlightening essay, British theologian Sarah Coakley connects five different forms of theological mariology to the kinds of feminist theory that they utilize.[61] *Liberal* feminism and its ensuing mariology seek to promote equality, autonomy, and self-determination for women as individuals. In this vein, Rosemary Radford Ruether parses Luke's annunciation scene to mean that in a free act of faith Mary makes her own choices about her body and sexuality without consulting male authority figures. She thereby enters into a real co-creatorship with God, possible only if we understand that faith consists not in obedience to external authorities but in response to God, which is intrinsically united with growth in our own autonomy. *Radical* feminism and its concomitant mariology deconstruct the tradition in an entirely negative way, finding it nothing more than an elaborate set of projections of the "feminine" by and for the benefit of men. Mary Daly is a prime example here, interpreting Mary as a male-controlled shadow of the once-powerful Goddess. Placed on a pedestal, she answers men's psychological need and serves their purpose with no purpose of her own. In her inimitable style Daly dismisses the result: "Dutifully dull and derivative, drained of divinity, she merits the reward of perpetual paralysis in patriarchal paradise."[62] Even here, however, there is some hope, as Daly sees the Goddess enchained in the figure of Mary set free to foretell women's future independence. The Assumption image of "Mary rising," for example, has a prophetic dimension that portends women's reclaiming their true identity; it foretells "women rising." *French postmodern* feminism, eschewing a fixed, definable view not only of "feminine" nature but also of human nature, approaches Mary with a psychoanalytic interest. In this vein Julia Kristeva's reading shifts attention to motherhood, uncovering how language, institutions, and individual consciousness in patriarchal society coalesce to repress and distort this experience unique to women. She substantially deconstructs the virgin-mother image of traditional dogma and calls for a profound new discourse on the dynamics of motherhood that incorporates not only suffering unto death but also erotic pleasure, *jouissance*.[63] *Socialist* feminism and its *liberation* mariology bring women's struggle against patriarchy into the cultural, economic, and political realms. The Magnificat is clearly relevant here, and its use is exemplified by Latin American theologians Ivone Gebara and María Clara Bingemer, who pursue the theme of God's favor to Mary because she is a poor, socially insignificant woman. It is precisely on this basis that God begins with her the messianic work of liberation of the people, which affects not just spiritual matters but all aspects of society. Finally, *romantic* feminism and the mariology aligned with it construct a "feminine other" complementary to the male psyche, updating traditional gender stereotypes with Jungian psychology. In Leonardo Boff's work, for example, the feminine is characterized by "life, depth, mystery, tenderness, interiority, and caring."[64] Its pinnacle can be found in Mary's humility and discretion: "Mary never lived in or for herself. Mary was a woman ever at the service of others."[65] In this woman, Boff argues, the feminine person of the divine Trinity, the Holy Spirit, became embodied, just as the Word of God became incarnate in Jesus. Because of this special relationship between Mary and the Spirit, the "feminine" so described reigns now at the very heart of the Trinity, while Mary shows the world the maternal face of God. Judging this romantic model to be reflective of a perspective spun out from the needs of the male psyche, Coakley calls it weak-kneed and limping compared with the other options now in play, options that even if fragmentary begin to illuminate how women are developing new readings that may truly liberate.

A different take on the current scene is presented by Elisabeth Schüssler Fiorenza, who describes four models of mariology prevalent in the patriarchal tradition, two centered on the human qualities of Mary and two on aspects that relate her to the divine. She cautions that harmful effects of these same approaches tend to surface in feminist reconstructions whenever women do not scrutinize carefully enough how much their thinking still remains within dominant male paradigms. The *historicizing Reformation* approach cuts through the excesses of marian piety by a return to scripture. There, the focus is on Christ, who alone is the Savior worthy of our absolute trust. Mary's story, written around the margins of the story of Jesus, is read historically, and her importance in the scheme of salvation is consequently diminished. The result did not reform patriarchy, as Reformation views on the subordinate position of women in marriage and ministry make clear. Rather, it threatened to turn Protestantism into a purely masculine religion: "The elimination of Mary and the saints from the spiritual cosmos of theology and church had as a consequence—probably unintended—that women no longer appeared in the religious symbolic cosmos nor in the public of theology and church at all."[66] Likewise drawn from scripture, the *ideal-typical ecclesiological* approach was adopted by Vatican II when it confirmed Mary to be an ideal representative or "type" of the church, symbolizing the faith, charity, and union with Christ that should mark the whole community. The difficulty here is that old dualistic sex/gender framework continues to prevail, undermining what could

be this symbol's liberating power. Mary as feminine symbolically represents the church or the new humanity, whose virtue resides in obedience
to God. In the context of male imagery for God and an all-male clergy that
excludes women from ordained leadership, this symbolism has political
ramifications. Some men exercise the authority of God the Father and
Christ, while the remainder of men and all women are exhorted to imitate
Mary, who perfectly represents the qualities of receptivity, humility, obedience, and passivity. Thus the typology reinscribes women's secondary
status.

In contrast to the minimalist tendencies of these two models, two other
approaches to Mary place her at the center of attention and exalt her
above the heavens. But here again the basic dynamic of what Schüssler
Fiorenza calls kyriarchal theology, centered on the dominant male *kyrios*
lording it over others, undermines their benefit for women. The *doctrinal-
mythologizing* approach, which governs Catholic tradition, separates
Mary from all other women and gifts her with privileges far beyond their
ken: virginal conception, mothering of God, immaculate conception,
assumption into heaven. In a feminist sense these doctrines can be seen to
carry a double message, signaling as they do female power in both historical and heavenly realms. However, by making Mary here the exception
rather than the type, these doctrines, as we have seen, subtly disparage
women's sexuality, holiness, and independence. Within the patriarchal
structure of the church they allow one glorified woman to function, which
inhibits the fullness of life for other women. "Only when Mary is no longer
the exception but rather has become the rule for the socioecclesial status of
women can her cult be credible and her image develop transformative
power for solidarity, justice, and liberation."[67] The *cultic-spiritual* approach
of popular religion, finally, appeals not so much to reason and doctrine as
to emotion, the desire for security, and the intimate experience of divine
presence. Through feast days and private altars, candles and flowers,
visions and pilgrimages, Mary is celebrated as our loving mother, Queen
of Heaven, in such a way as to mediate an experience of divine goodness
and redemptive power in female form. The problem here is that official
theology insists that this so-called "feminine face of the divine" must
remain subordinated to an idea of God on analogy with the dominant
male. Even when recourse to intercession of the merciful mother Mary is
encouraged, her symbol remains fixed in a patriarchal cosmos and even
reinforces it by making a softer, more appealing approach to the patriar-

chal God possible. The whole setup remains trapped in the inherited framework of gendered masculinity and femininity, which does not offer a way forward toward the liberation of women. Schüssler Fiorenza concludes that only a genuine transformation of church structures and rhetoric in the direction of a genuine community of the discipleship of equals will provide the context in which mariological discourse can truly be set free for the benefit of women.

A third attempt to organize the wealth of women's work is the doctoral dissertation by the Belgian scholar Els Maeckelberghe, published as *Desperately Seeking Mary*,[68] which lists eleven different approaches on three continents. First she probes the work of Catharina Halkes, which employs various disciplines such as comparative religion, history of religion, psychology of religion, and theology to yield flashes of insight into the historical Mary, the basis for the symbolic Mary who reveals the *Magna Mater*, the great divine mother. In more systematic theological fashion Rosemary Radford Ruether deconstructs and then reconstructs the idea of Mary in relation to women and redeemed humanity freed from patriarchy. Focusing on tradition, Elisabeth Schüssler Fiorenza analyzes the Mary myth to uncover its psychological and ecclesiological functions, querying whether this story ever provided women with a new vision of equality and wholeness. Elizabeth Johnson's earlier work on the symbolic character of theological discourse about Mary, proposing that speech about Mary actually points to the graced existence of all believers, occupies a spot on the chart. So too does the liberation mariology of Ivone Gebara and María Clara Bingemer, who ally Mary with the struggle of poor people, especially women, for justice and peace. There is the shifting work of Mary Daly, who moves from rejecting Mary out of hand as an impossible model for women of flesh and blood to perceiving a hidden, prophetic message in her figure: a remnant of the ancient Goddess, she is also a precursor of a new age of women's divine power. Carol Ochs, Christa Mulack, and others identify Mary with the feminine "side" of the divine, especially because she shares major characteristics of the classical Goddess: mother of God, bride of God, powerful virgin, mourner of the dead, Queen of Heaven, and source of salvation. These authors promote Mary as revelatory of the divine female in order to give women a foothold in the sacred according to their own image. Maria Kassel undergirds this approach with Jungian psychology, seeing Mary's function as embodying the feminine archetype; in the Catholic Church her presence provides a continuous link to the primeval, all-embracing feminine divine principle. Then there are historical studies by Marina Warner, P. Shine Gold, and Barbara Corrado Pope that show how the history of marian thought has been ruled by images that correspond to the society in which they function. Changes in economic, social, and cultural arrangements bring about multiple variations in images of Mary. Accordingly, one main interest of these researchers is to track the effect of these changes on the status of women, for better or worse. Corrado Pope, for example, analyzes how marian visions and pilgrimages in nineteenth-century France promoted conservative nationalistic feelings at the same time that they offered a new measure of religious power to poor and poorly educated women. After critical assessment of all these approaches, Maeckelberghe's own contribution is to offer a method drawn from history and hermeneutics by which traditional symbols may be appropriated. With the lens of symbolic imagination, she demonstrates, the community of women may use sources as disparate as papal pronouncements and popular holy cards to reinterpret Mary in an empowering way.

There is much more creative work than these typologies have codified. Asian theologians Chung Hyun Kyung and Marianne Katoppo limn the contours of Mary as a prophetic woman and fully liberated human being in Korean and Indonesian contexts, respectively. María Pilar Aquino and Ada María Isasi-Díaz explore her image as not only liberated but liberating for Hispanic/Latina women who struggle against gender, ethnic, and class bias.[69] Carol Frances Jegen edits a book of essays, *Mary according to Women*, that presents the fruit of an entire festival built around marian themes, including her significance for the afflicted and those who work for justice and peace.[70] Mary Grey calls for a new discourse of motherhood that would honor the birthing energies in Mary and the rest of women, while Patricia Noone pens a beautiful literary reflection on Mary's relations to herself and others that culminates in claiming her as our sister.[71]

The work of women's theology in this field shows no sign of abating, motivated by a spirituality whose hunger and thirst for justice includes women in all their differences.

Within this chorus of women's voices in a new key, I am going to explore the option to consider Mary as a genuine human being who acted according to the call of the Spirit in the particular circumstances of her own history. This entails viewing her as a first-century Jewish woman living a hard-scrabble life in a land occupied by a foreign empire. Naming the grace of her choices in this context and the long-term influence of her life, I propose that we situate her within the communion of saints and develop a theology of her significance within this community. This will be a pneumatological mariology with emphasis on a dangerous memory that encourages the whole community of disciples to ally themselves with the reign of God, the God for whom Mary believed that "nothing will be impossible" (Luke 1:37).

To pursue this option with clarity, I wish to address two other prevalent interpretations. One, arising in the field of theological anthropology, views Mary as the perfect embodiment of the feminine principle or essence, which makes her the ideal face of "woman." The other, working on the turf of the theology of God, views her as bodying forth the feminine dimension of the divine, which makes her the maternal face of God. At first glance, these construals may seem beneficial to women. Indeed, when placed within restrictive patriarchal settings, they do ameliorate women's invisibility and promote their dignity, at least symbolically. But a stance that unapologetically affirms the full humanity of women sees through the restricted boundaries of such approaches as they operate in the practical order, so that they now appear to be cul-de-sacs. I do not call them dead-ends because in traveling their length we can garner usable insights. They are, however, roads that curve around and arrive back at their starting point, nowhere going forward toward the goal of the understanding and praxis of women's equality. We need to map them clearly.

PART 2

Roads Not Taken

3

℘

Cul-de-Sac:
The Ideal Face of Woman

ONE HUMAN RACE

As a result of rapid social changes, the traditional discipline of theological anthropology is today a field of dispute. At issue is the fundamental question of what it means to be a human being, or what it means to be human together in a small ecological community of life in an enormous universe created and energized by the Spirit of God. Within this broad question lies the particular topic of what it means to be a male or a female person in this one human race. It is hardly possible within the contours of this book to give an account of the diverse views now being argued. But the cul-de-sac in mariology marked out in this chapter uses one precise interpretation that is easy to trace. Based upon an essentialist view of gender, it ascribes to women and men two virtually separate kinds of human nature, each gifted with its own characteristics, a position commonly described as dualistic anthropology or an anthropology of complementarity. Upon this grid it projects Mary as the ideal woman who embodies the best of feminine nature, or what poets and philosophers have called the Eternal Feminine.

For women to attain equal human dignity in a just and inclusive society, this dualistic anthropology needs to be reordered into a multiple-term schema, one that allows women and men of all races and classes to connect in all their differences rather than constantly guaranteeing identity through gender opposition. Toward this end feminist liberation theology proposes an egalitarian anthropology of partnership, a set of ideas whose parameters are still emerging in keeping with new facts of women's advance on the ground.[1] In this view of the human race, sexual difference is vitally important, but it does not become the sole, essential marker of a person's human identity. Rather, sex combines with other anthropological constants such as race, class, family relations, social structures, historical era, and geographical and cultural location to define persons as uniquely themselves. Here Mary can take her place as the distinctive person she is in solidarity with other women and men in all their diversity.

Dualistic Anthropology

Influencing centuries of marian theology, this view of the human race starts out from the obvious biological sex differences between women and men. Thinking in binary terms, it elevates sexual difference to an ontological principle that cleaves the human race into two radically different types of persons—men who have a masculine nature and women who have a feminine nature. Each comes equipped with a distinct set of characteristics. Masculine nature is marked by reason, independence, and the ability to analyze, take initiative, and make judgments, while feminine nature is marked by emotion, receptivity, and the ability to nurture, show compassion, and suffer for love. Gender dualism then extrapolates from the qualities endemic to each nature to assign men and women to different social roles played out in rigidly preassigned spheres. This, it is claimed, is according to the law of God laid down in nature.

This pattern of thought comes with a long historical pedigree. It first appeared in theology when early Christian writers sought to speak intelligibly about faith drawing on their own culture's Hellenistic philosophy. The medieval reappropriation of classical Greek thought gave this earlier dualism a new lease on life. In each instance theology utilized a philosophy that divided all reality into two spheres, spirit and matter. It also ranked these spheres in order of importance with spirit, which signifies the higher realm of light and eternal life, being prized over matter, which embodies the lower realm of darkness, change, and death. Everything that exists belongs to one sphere or the other. Regarding human beings, men are classed with spirit while women are identified with matter, in the latter case especially because of the obvious changes that take place in women's bodies through menstruation, childbearing, and menopause—female flesh being forever the stumbling block to equality, in patriarchal thinking. Consequently, men by nature are nearer to the divine, endowed with a full measure of soul, while women for their own good need to be governed by men who can guide them toward the higher realm. This dualistic vision results in a world where men function as the normative human beings fit to exercise authority in the public realm while women are destined for the private domain of childbearing, homemaking, and care for the vulnerable. Even in this domain the man should ultimately rule because his innate ability to reason and make decisions provides for smooth ordering of the household. As Thomas Aquinas writes, "woman is naturally subject to man, because in man the discretion of reason predominates."[2] Casting women and men as polar opposites and defining women in terms unfit for personal freedom let alone social leadership, gender dualism gives the advantage, by nature and therefore immutably, to men. The only exceptions to this status quo are women who dedicate themselves to virginity. By renouncing the exercise of their female genital sexuality with all it entails, they are in fact taking leave of their feminine nature and "becoming male," thus moving closer to the divine. In Jerome's view: "As long as woman is for birth and children, she is different from man as body is from soul. But when she wishes to serve Christ more than the world, then she will cease to be a woman and will be called man (*vir*)."[3]

Such separatist thinking about the sexes gives rise to a series of equations that frames classical theology like a procrustean bed: men are to women as spirit is to matter, as act is to potency, as mind is to body, as head is to heart, as cool thought is to feeling and passionate sexual arousal, as conscious is to unconscious, as initiating is to receiving, as call is to response, as ruling is to obedience, as public is to private, as light is to darkness, and, theologically, as heaven is to earth, as the Creator is to the world, as Christ the bridegroom is to the church the bride, as the Spirit is to the soul. Each of these pairs entails another in the practical order: as superiority is to inferiority, as control is to subordination. Let it not escape notice that the whole speculative edifice comes about because patriarchal structures have allowed educated men to commandeer the power of naming. They have used this power to label those who differ in distinctly disadvantageous terms. Given the chance, women would not define themselves in these dichotomous designations even while claiming their own female powers and needs.

A famous aphorism of Claude Lévi-Strauss quips that "women are good to think with." In the theoretical world of gender dualism, women do not appear as historical agents in their own right but as rhetorical codes for many other concerns, a phenomenon that we shall trace with Mary. Constructed as man's "Other," their feminine nature functions as a stand-in for abstract theological concepts, cosmological powers, or distressing forces in male consciousness. Whether they are placed on a pedestal as a symbol of virtue or blamed as the originators of sin and death, however, they are treated as symbolic representatives of male experience rather than as persons in their own right. "The feminine figure shuttles between the sublime and the debased, but always as the psychological 'other', and never as the person who herself experiences spiritual anguish, who is fired by messianic dreams, and who craves closeness with the creator."[4] Some feminist analysis suggests that, far from being accidental, opposition between masculine and feminine is essential for the very existence of patriarchal discourse. Carol Newsom argues that in patriarchal thinking it is woman's lack of the phallus and the privilege that men associate with its possession that ground woman's inferiority. Hence, male authority is established on body symbolism. When the self is defined as male in this way, woman *qua* woman enters all-male discourse possessing a strange and foreign quality, either what discomforts and even repels the male or what attracts him and inspires him to redouble his efforts. In either case, opposition between male and female is fundamental to the symbolic order of patriarchy. Without such opposition and its construction of the female as the receptive or mediating principle of male sovereignty, most serious patriarchal thought would evaporate. But its use is not simply symbolic. When carried forward in relation to concrete persons, symbolic statements implicate behavior. All use of the patriarchal feminine in symbolic representation, therefore, is freighted with significance for action toward actual women in the real world.[5]

Egalitarian Anthropology

As early as 1838, during the first wave of feminism in the United States, the Quaker Sarah Grimké penned a startling rebuttal to gender dualism. Actively working for the abolition of slavery, she espied an analogy between the condition of enslaved black people and that of white women like herself, subjugated by male dictates about their "proper nature" and "special role." Founding her argument on Jesus' teaching, she argued that, contrary to what the Massachusetts clergy might say, it revealed a message of freedom and equality. The emphases in the following citation are her own:

> The Lord Jesus defines the duties of his followers in his Sermon on the Mount. He lays down grand principles by which they should be governed,

without any reference to sex or condition. . . . I follow him through all his precepts, and find him giving the same directions to women as to men, never even referring to the distinction now so strenuously insisted upon between masculine and feminine virtues: this is one of the anti-christian "traditions of men" which are taught instead of the "commandments of God." Men and women were CREATED EQUAL: they are both moral and accountable beings, and whatever is *right* for man to do, is *right* for woman.[6]

Drawing on this same resource, Catherine LaCugna echoes and broadens this sentiment in contemporary language: "The life of Jesus Christ is at odds with the sexist theology of complementarity, the racist theology of white superiority, the clerical theology of cultic privilege, the political theology of exploitation and economic injustice, and the patriarchal theology of male dominance and control."[7] British theologian Janet Soskice reports a more visceral response. To the Bishop of London's painstaking elaboration that the "masculine" is associated with giving and the "feminine" with receiving, she replies that this is "a piece of gender construction as intolerable for men as it is dishonest about women, and among the latter is liable to produce some hilarity in those who have become aware of and articulate about their role in securing the well-being of men without any firm expectation that the converse will obtain."[8] The laughter is a sign of dismissal. Women know that equating femininity with dependence inevitably privileges men in terms of social, political, and spiritual power while leaving women themselves to do the daily work that sustains life.

Moving to theory, egalitarian anthropology of partnership takes its cue from the first chapter of the book of Genesis, where God creates humankind in the divine image and likeness, "male and female" (1:26–27).[9] Scholars note that there is no assignment of masculine or feminine qualities here but simply the fullness of being human persons in God's image in one's distinctive sexuality whether male or female. We are one human race, and attention must be paid to what we historically have in common as a species. Most basically, all human persons share in being embodied spirits in the world, who are conceived, at least as of this writing, when egg and sperm unite to produce a growing organism that is ultimately delivered from a woman's body. Through the body all human beings are connected to the earth in an ecological community that includes all other living creatures in mutual interdependence on the life-supporting systems of the planet. To stay alive all humans have common needs for breathable air, drinkable water, nourishment, and sleep. Feminist theory is pouring attention on the vital importance of the body, so neglected in classical anthropology but a starting point of commonality for all humans. All persons, furthermore, starting in the first minutes of life are connected to significant other persons and develop personality in and through these intimate relationships. All interact with political, economic, and social structures, for better or worse. All are shaped by their culture, geography, and the historical time in which they live. And all are destined to die. When a plane crashes into the tower where you work, you burn to death the same way. When you breathe anthrax spores into your lungs, you die from the same bodily breakdown whether male or female, of African, European, or Asian descent, old or young, employed in a skilled or unskilled job. In all our differences, we have more in common than what divides us.

In this matrix, personal identity is forged not only by sex but also by race, class, family dynamics, ethnic heritage, social location, and political, cultural, and ecological environment in interaction with the way each person uniquely appropriates these markers.[10] Diversity of personal characteristics and gifts is not predetermined by sex but ranges across a wide spectrum for women and men of all races and cultures. In fact, the range of differences among women themselves can be just as great if not greater than differences between some women and some men.[11] This is not a unisex anthropology that devalues sexual or heterosexual difference, even as it insists that gay and lesbian persons are fully human persons who contribute to the definition of what it means to be a woman or a man. Egalitarian anthropology recognizes that the sex chromosomes XX or XY with their attendant differences abide in every cell of a woman's or man's body and that biological sex difference is irreplaceable for healthy reproduction of the species.[12] It acknowledges that deep mutual love between a woman and a man, where it is achieved and sustained, ranks as one of the most profound relationships on earth, life-giving in literal and metaphorical ways. Nevertheless, in contrast to dualistic anthropology, it argues that male–female differences, rather than predestining persons to public or domestic social roles, are compatible with social equality.

Here strategies differ. Liberal feminists interested in transforming power arrangements tend to emphasize women's capacity to function in social roles traditionally denied them. Why, they ask, are courage, authority, and rationality mainly properties of the male person rather than of *human* persons, including mature women? By what criterion are the abilities to relate, to respond, and to nurture primarily called female qualities rather than *human* ones, attributable also to mature men? Indeed, the sexist stereotype of the feminine shrinks the vast diversity of women's gifts into a narrow set of characteristics. But nurturing and tenderness simply do not exhaust the capacities of women; nor do bodiliness and instinct define women's nature; nor are intelligence and creative transformative action beyond the scope of women's power; nor can women simply be equated with receptivity and mothering without suffocating their human dignity. Respecting individual differences, such a stance calls for social equality across the board. At the same time cultural feminists, seeking to cherish and enhance female qualities typically demeaned in patriarchal thought, emphasize that while each has a capacity for psychic wholeness, women and men tend to perceive and integrate the relational and rational elements of their lives in different ways. This leads to studies of women's moral development and psychology, women's ways of knowing, women's ways of loving, and women's ways of living bodily that promote the exercise of autonomy with a care for relationships.[13] Rather than the ideal of the solitary, self-contained individual so prevalent in classical and contemporary patriarchal culture, the power to connect should pervade all of society for the good of the whole. In symbol, ritual, and story, women's spirituality movements seek to tap into and let loose their nurturing powers of relationship, such as they are at this point in time, for themselves, other persons, and the whole earth itself.[14] Indeed, as Sara Ruddick argues, maternal thinking itself is a boundless resource for social justice and peace, requiring that the world's business be done so as to nurture rather than destroy what women have labored to bring forth.[15] The obvious danger in this approach lies in the ease with which it may cross over the line into gender essentialism. With its uncompromising esteem for what has been denigrated, however, it stands as a sentinel against the idea that equality means sameness. Both liberal and cultural feminist insights contribute vital pieces to the still-developing egalitarian anthropology of partnership utilized by feminist liberation theology in its quest for a world where women in all their differences can flourish.

The position I espouse protests not difference between the sexes but the patriarchal idea that these differences signify masculine and feminine natures equipped with rigidly preassigned characteristics, which fact then assigns women and men to play predefined, separate social roles. Even if the two sexes are theorized to be equal and related in a complementary way, the assignment of characteristics in traditional dualism does not grant women an equal say in how the world is run, thus keeping them in the status of a minor. In place of this gender dualism, so influential in theology, an egalitarian anthropology envisions a redeemed humanity with relationships between women and men marked by mutual partnership. This signifies a relation of equivalence between persons, a concomitant valuing of each other's gifts however they are distributed, and a common regard marked by trust, respect, and affection in contrast to assertions of superiority. It is a relationship on the analogy of friendship, where a dialectic of reciprocity and independence joins whole persons together for their mutual benefit. In this egalitarian environment, sexual difference between women and men assumes its rightful proportion and does not translate into a strictly genderized division of human characteristics or labor. A companionable community between the sexes on a broad scale then becomes possible without detriment to the intense relationship that develops when a man and a woman form a coupling bond. Rosemary Radford Ruether has beautifully described the journeys of conversion that need to be taken to arrive at this kind of relationship. In a sexist society women need to journey from socialized inferiority and lack of self-worth toward a grounded personhood replete with self-esteem. Men must journey from overweening masculine pride toward a grounded self replete with humility. Then they can join hands in the struggle to create a way of being together in mature mutuality that will humanize the world and salvage the planet.[16]

MARY AND THE PATRIARCHAL FEMININE

Time and again the fundamental pattern of gender dualism has formed a grid for interpreting Mary. Theology has placed her, obviously, on the distaff side of the human divide, envisioning her as the ideal embodiment of feminine essence. Whether her perfection then serves to disparage other women or to inspire them, her obedient, responsive, maternal image is at play in the community as the norm for women in contrast to men. When combined with an understanding of God and Christ as essentially masculine, the result reproduces in theology, spirituality, and church polity nothing less than the patriarchal order of the world, now with divine sanction. The sampling of authors below demonstrates the problematic nature of mariology done in this framework of the patriarchal feminine and illuminates why interpretations of Mary based on dualistic anthropology form a cul-de-sac rather than a way forward.

Leonardo Boff

Doing theology in the Latin American context of enormous popular devotion to Mary, Boff seeks to interpret this woman in the light of what he takes to be a momentous contemporary event that occurs only once every several thousand years. This is the emergence of the "feminine" from humanity's collective unconscious, apparent in our culture's reappraisal of the intuitive, of everything concerning subjectivity. "Recent decades have seen a devastating assault on rationality and its airs. The 'nonrational' has come into its own." Part of this emergence entails women's struggle for recognition as persons who enjoy equality in social relationships. Wishing to promote this equality, Boff defines his task as recasting standard patriarchal mariology into a new mold defined by the broad horizon of the newly emerging feminine. His project thus chooses "the feminine as the basic mariological principle,"[17] an organizing axiom that synthesizes all marian privileges and interprets them as revelatory of the importance of the feminine, even for God.

Given such a project, everything obviously stands or falls on the meaning assigned to the feminine. Boff's discussion is clear about the fact that this idea is not a raw datum of experience but rather a construct drawn from philosophy and the human sciences, especially depth psychology. His all-important description proceeds in this manner. The feminine is the ontological dimension of humanity that "expresses the pole of darkness, mystery, depth, night, death, interiority, earth, feeling, receptivity, generative force, and the vitality of the human." Its antithesis is the masculine, which expresses the opposite pole of "light, sun, time, impulse, surging power, order, exteriority, objectivity, reason." Each expresses itself in traits: the feminine shows itself in "repose, immobility, immanence, a longing for the past, and a certain darkness," while "aggressiveness, transcendence, clarity, the thrust toward transformation, the capacity to impose order and project into the future" belong to the masculine.[18] The feminine is allied with the dark unconscious as opposed to the broad daylight of consciousness; with the nonrational as opposed to the rational; with chaos as opposed to order; with *eros* as opposed to *logos*; with the body as opposed to the mind; with the desire to preserve and protect as opposed to risk and challenge; with silence as opposed to the word.

With this idea of the feminine clearly in view, Boff's mariology then interprets the traditional doctrines of Mary's motherhood of God, virginity, immaculate conception, and assumption into heaven to demonstrate that this woman embodies the best of this ontological principle. In keeping with its social location, this is a self-described maximalist mariology. It situates Mary, humble, silent, and given in service to others, at the apex of the revelation of the very femininity of God to the world. As with all mariology constructed on a dualistic anthropological foundation, Boff encounters a problem with Jesus' function as universal savior, namely, that his humanity connects men to God in a more straightforward way than it does women.

> Jesus the male reveals God's plan for the masculine explicitly. But he also reveals God's plan for the feminine (implicitly), since his reality, as the reality of a human being, contains both the masculine and the feminine.... But Jesus' humanity, being male, contains the masculine and the feminine in the proportion proper to a male. Thus, while the masculine acquires an ultimate, divine meaning in him directly, the feminine does so only implicitly, as the recessive component. But if there has been a full and direct divinization of the masculine—in Jesus—can we not expect the feminine to be ordered to a full and direct divinization as well?[19]

The answer fits with the way the question is set up. Just as the Son of God became incarnate in the male Jesus of Nazareth and thereby divinized the masculine, so too the Holy Spirit, whom scripture portrays as feminine, has the mission of divinizing the feminine, directly and explicitly. The Spirit has done so by entering into historical union with the Blessed Virgin Mary. Thus Mary is cast as the salvific feminine complement to the masculine Jesus—a theologically unacceptable place one arrives at by a commendably stringent application of the logic of dualistic anthropology.

In an intriguing way, the logic of this argument falls apart in Boff's chapter "Mary, Prophetic Woman of Liberation," which sojourns like an alien in this book. Here he attends to the view of Mary newly arising from small local faith communities (*comunidades de base*) in situations of poverty, violence, and oppression, where poor people pray, discuss, and carry out actions that express the political dimension of the faith. Such Christians, committed to the process of liberation, discovered Mary's hymn of praise, the Magnificat, with a special appreciation. Her role of denouncing oppression and critically proclaiming liberation in the name of God's mercy puts her in solidarity with their efforts and inspires their flagging spirits. Boff rightly notes that traditional mariology pays little or no heed to Mary's prophetic song or to her ethical indignation as she prays of God to scatter the proud in the conceit of their hearts and feed the hungry. The masculine–feminine framework provides part of the explanation: "Christian ideology, always in charge here, has had a difficult time deciding between not ascribing any importance to Mary's prophetic words, superficially so male and so strange-sounding on the lips of a woman, and spiritualizing them."[20] Opting for a prophetic, liberating image of Mary, Boff proceeds to abandon all the assumptions he has adopted. Instead of the feminine expressing silence, darkness, repose, immobility, and a longing for the past, this woman assertively and joyfully proclaims God's word about the coming messianic redemption, when the whole unjust order of things will be overturned. In Boff's artful description and despite his intentions, this singer of the song of justice in the name of the God of Israel reveals the feminine stereotype for what it is: a patriarchal construct that has little to do with actual women. Boff's illogic sounds a pleasing note.

Hans Urs von Balthasar

At the other end of the theological spectrum, this mystical, conservative Swiss theologian also interprets Mary with the categories of dualistic anthropology, appealing more to symbol and metaphor than to philosophy or the human sciences. A guiding idea in Balthasar's theology is that the symbol of man and woman as a married couple provides a most effective way to illuminate the plan of God for the world's salvation. The archetypal and final couple is Christ and his church, bridegroom and bride par excellence. Prefiguring them is Yahweh's covenant relationship with Israel, whose people are depicted responding to God in various texts as virgin, sinful and repentant spouse, and daughter Zion. Linking the two couples is Mary, who brought forth the Messiah from one people to be head of the other, his body the church. Her multivalent spiritual relationship to God as virgin, spouse, daughter, and mother sets her up as the type of the church par excellence. She does not just model the theological vocation of church in an extrinsic way, but lives it out in her historical life and in heaven as the symbol for the whole community. Thus Balthasar approaches mariology with a deep christocentric vision and a strong ecclesial interest. On the one hand are God and Christ, implicitly masculine; on the other hand are Israel, Mary, and the church, explicitly feminine. The most profound dimension of salvation is expressed when these two relate on the analogy of reciprocity between man and woman in a patriarchal conjugal relation.

Within this framework Balthasar reflects on scenes from the gospels, construing Mary with typically feminine virtues: she is silent, self-effacing, self-giving, lovingly obedient, and so forth. One example is the wedding feast at Cana. Mary notices the embarrassing lack of wine and brings it to Jesus' attention, revealing her awareness of the needs of the poor and her instinctive feeling that her son could somehow provide help. Marching toward his hour, Jesus tries to put her off. But her response, telling the servants, "Do whatever he tells you" (John 2:5), symbolizes the church at its best. It expresses "her complete disinterestedness and surrender to his will, but also her confident hope; and it is precisely by not making a fuss, by her lack of self-will, that she wins and the hour of the Cross is anticipated." By appealing to Jesus despite his initial brushoff, Balthasar explains, Mary gives evidence of the simplicity and cunning of a mother who knows how to penetrate from the level of justice in God to the more profound level of mercy; "and she is convinced that in this she is behaving correctly in a more profound way than might be dictated by all the abstract justice worked out by men for their state." Balthasar pays tribute according to his own lights with an encomium that is one of the most exquisitely weird statements about Mary I have ever come across: "As a woman she has her heart where it ought to be and not in her brain."[21] The traditional dichotomy between feminine and masculine, equated with heart and head respectively and further equated with mercy and justice, is here on full display. It defies common sense to interpret Mary's taking initiative in this story as lack of self-will, her influence over her son as surrender to his will, and her smart observation of need as love divorced from intelligence. Yet Balthasar is more logical than Boff, and the feminine stereotype that governs this interpretation allows for nothing else.

Gender-inflected complementarity of man and woman also governs Balthasar's symbolic use of Mary. Along with a constellation of other historical figures, including Peter, John, and Paul, she is pressed into service to represent what he calls "dimensions" of the church.[22] The most important dimension is the spiritual one of response to God's gift of grace. Mary symbolizes this dramatically. Her yes to God at the annunciation signals the very beginning of the church. The responsive human consent of this handmaid, one of Israel's *anawim*, symbolizes the mystery of grace at the heart of the church: "the bride is 'prepared' and 'presented' by the bridegroom to himself in such a way that the bride is solely for the bridegroom, is offered to him as a sacrifice, is exclusively at his disposal . . . ."[23] Indeed, it is too little to say that in this act of faith and in the unconditional, self-effacing obedience to her Son that characterized the rest of her life Mary is a model of the church. Rather, her *fiat,* "the maiden-saying of Mary by which she consents to her total dispossession in order to become the receptacle of the Holy Spirit,"[24] is the very *form* of the church, the inmost spiritual reality that should mark every ecclesial person and activity. It is the interior, receptive response to God that makes the church more than just a sociological group. Balthasar argues that this "marian element holds sway in the Church in a hidden manner, just as a woman does in the household."[25] Spreading a protective mantle of warmth, it shows itself in service, humble love, and quiet being there for others. This "marian face of the church" is deeper and closer to the center than any other aspect. It will last for all eternity. Without it, the church would not be fruitful, for the feminine bears fruit in response to the divine (read: masculine) gift of grace.

At the same time, the church needs "objective" means to promote this all-important "subjective" holiness. Thus there is also Peter, charged with leadership, mission, and, in the case of the petrine office itself, unity. The petrine face of the institutional church is expressed through sacraments, preaching, and administration of canon law, which assure members of the church that they are encountering Christ in a stable way. "Institution is the guarantee of the enduring presence of the bridegroom Christ to the bride the Church. This is why it is entrusted to men who, although they belong to the comprehensive femininity of the Church, are taken from her midst and, while remaining in her, embody Christ who approaches the Church to impregnate her."[26] The marian tradition of holy obedience complements this petrine tradition of orderly hierarchical rule.

Mediating between these two dimensions stands the apostle John, whom Balthasar conflates with the Johannine beloved disciple. John symbolizes the archetypal experience of contemplative love. Receiving from the dying Jesus the charge to become son and protector of Mary, on the one hand, and frequently coupled with Peter in the missionary beginning of the Acts of the Apostles, on the other, he "slides thereby into an unemphasized but fully indispensable mediating center (between Peter and Mary, church of office and of men, and church of women) which points out to both dimensions of the mystery of the church their place and their proportion."[27] In addition there is Paul, who expresses the missionary dimension of the church. Not having known Jesus during his public ministry, Paul witnesses to the step forward that must be taken after the resurrection. Faith that comes from hearing rather than one's own seeing is now the founding experience of the church. His archetypal encounter with the risen Christ, and its expression in zealous proclamation guide the later witness of the church, always in submission to Peter. I note here that Mary Magdalene, first witness of the resurrection, missioned to preach by the risen Christ who presumably had a choice whom to send, does not appear in this constellation of figures.

Compared to the usual patriarchal pattern of male over female, Balthasar poses the petrine and marian dimensions in reverse order of importance. The marian dimension relativizes the hierarchy, he argues, pointing it always to its primary purpose, which is to facilitate the encounter between God and human beings in Christ. It cannot be forgotten that Peter denied knowing Jesus at the moment of supreme crisis, while Mary's *fiat* lasted all the way to the foot of the cross. Thus the marian takes precedence over the petrine in what is of ultimate importance: "Before male office makes its entrance in the Church, the Church as woman and helpmate is already on the scene."[28]

Note how this kind of language allows marian symbolism to segue into ecclesial symbolism to the erasure of the existence of actual historical women in the church with their spiritual and political agency. Mary gets equated with an idealized spiritual reality called church, which equates with the abstract "woman," which equates with receptive response to grace. Framing the entire discussion is the all-male hierarchy, governing in the name of the male Bridegroom, which this type of symbolism serves to maintain. In a discerning essay James Heft notes the criticism that Balthasar's idea of the masculine–feminine polarity may be more rooted in German idealism and modern psychoanalytic thought, especially that of C. G. Jung, than in the scriptures.[29] The concept of dimensions of the church, furthermore, is a nonbiblical idea not at all necessary for ecclesiology. In any event, this Swiss theologian's symbolizing of different ecclesial dimensions serves to clarify the unspoken agenda in the standard use of Mary as model of the church. She may take precedence over Peter in spiritual matters and may be said to have no use for apostolic power because she exercises a higher power, but the net effect of this symbolism is to relegate women to nurturing the inner life of the spirit, which of course is of no little importance, but to block them from participation in the public ministry of the church.

John Paul II

Departing from centuries-long tradition, Pope John Paul II teaches in no uncertain terms that women and men are equal as persons before God: "Both man and woman are human beings to an equal degree, both are created in God's image."[30] The power of this theoretical affirmation of spiritual and metaphysical equality, however, is compromised in practice by the pope's commitment to gender dualism. His work consistently draws upon the traditional view that men and women embody human nature in two radically contrasting ways, which means that they must play distinct social roles. The unique essence of "woman" lies in the notion that she is made for the "order of love": "Woman can only find herself by giving love to others."[31] Given her orientation to love, the proper vocation for every woman is motherhood, or the spiritual form of motherhood that is exercised in virginity. Even here, however, the masculine–feminine dichotomy, interpreted as acting versus responding, prevents women from taking initiative in love. As the pope conceives the dynamic, "The bridegroom is the one who loves. The bride is loved. It is she who receives love in order to love in return."[32] This is the case not because of personality or economic conditions or any other social circumstance, but because of nature: "This concerns each and every woman, independently of the cultural context in which she lives and independently of her spiritual, psychological and physical characteristics, as for example age, education, health, work, and whether she is married or single." Consistent with the tradition of this dichotomy, furthermore, the pope warns against women departing from their own rich essence even when they muster "rightful opposition" to sinful domination by men. This "must not under any condition lead to the 'masculinization' of women," he warns. Although never spelling out just what that would mean, his writings make clear that this would entail assertiveness, rational argument, and independent action. "In the name of liberation from male 'domination,' women must not appropriate to themselves male characteristics contrary to their own feminine 'originality.'"[33] Instead, as woman, each one must live according to the "special qualities" proper to the "fact of her femininity."

What makes this papal position an advance from previous official teaching is that he declares the two sides of the masculine–feminine divide to be of equal value in the eyes of God, which must lead to equal respect in human relationships. Especially in marriage, man and woman should relate to each other in a communion patterned on the life of the Trinity, which entails respect for each person's dignity. This equality of essence as persons, however, does not mean that man abandons his leadership position. To illustrate, the pope points to the ordained priesthood: "Since Christ in instituting the eucharist linked it in such an explicit way to the priestly service of the apostles, it is legitimate to conclude that he thereby wished to express the relationship between man and woman, between what is 'feminine' and what is 'masculine.'"[34] It is surely an idiosyncratic interpretation of the gospel narratives, unsupported by biblical scholarship, to posit that Jesus' concern at the Last Supper was to teach the gender difference between man who essentially acts and woman who naturally receives. But to stay on point: equal in dignity but separate in social roles stamps this new version of gender dualism.

When this pattern of thought deals with Mary, it produces the same difficulty we have already encountered in Boff and Balthasar. Mary is intensely exalted, assigned feminine functions, and held up as the model for women, with the result that women continue to be subordinated in fact if not in intention. The main focus for John Paul II's reflection is Mary's role as mother of God, which ineffable truth stands at the center of the mystery of God's plan of salvation. What is most important about this real motherhood, to which she gave her free consent, is that it places her in union with God, uniquely so on a physical level and also, in an archetypal way representative of the whole human race, on a spiritual level through grace. Since all of this happens to her precisely as a woman, she also signifies "the fullness of the perfection of what is characteristic of woman, of what is feminine. Here we find ourselves, in a sense, at the culminating point, the archetype, of the personal dignity of women."[35] Anything true said about woman's dignity and vocation must remain within this marian horizon. Her role in the divine plan of salvation "sheds light on women's vocation in the life of the church and society by defining its difference in relation to man. The model Mary represents clearly shows what is specific to the feminine personality." Indeed, "Mary is the model of the full development of women's vocation."[36] Unpacking this specificity, the pope declares that, like Mary, women have as their true vocation motherhood, whether physical or spiritual. Like Mary, women should emulate a "style" that makes no proud demands but maintains an attitude of humble service. And like Mary, women should develop certain characteristics that will enable them to live their true vocation to the utmost. In the encyclical *Redemptoris mater* (Mother of the Redeemer) the pope lists these virtues as follows:

It can thus be said that women, by looking to Mary, find in her the secret of living their femininity with dignity and of achieving their own true advancement. In the light of Mary, the church sees in the face of women the reflection of a beauty which mirrors the loftiest sentiments of which the human heart is capable: the self-offering totality of love; the strength that is capable of bearing the greatest sorrows; limitless fidelity and tireless devotion to work; the ability to combine penetrating intuition with words of support and encouragement.[37]

Note that whatever may be the praiseworthy value of this list of virtues, the fact that they are "feminine," applied to women but not to men, makes them suspect. They are the habits of the helper, the auxiliary, the handmaid, not that of the resister of oppression—let alone the self-actualizing, creative leader. In situations of abuse where it is essential for women to say NO, such sentiments can even be dangerous to life and limb. Assigning these qualities to women in the private domain may challenge women to develop a spiritual life, but it also serves to block their mature growth as active subjects of their own history and to deny them opportunities for equal partnership in society.

Bringing Mary's archetypal feminine function into ecclesiology, the pope borrows explicitly from Balthasar to note the distinction between the marian and petrine dimensions of the church.[38] The marian dimension, seen most clearly in Mary's *fiat*, symbolizes the church in its identity as the handmaid of the Lord, as the one who believes, as the virgin dedicated to God's service, as the spouse made fruitful by the Spirit, and most of all as mother, bringing forth new children of God in Christ. This marian, maternal dimension functions in a discreet and hidden way. It is the field of spiritual union with Christ, of prayer, of self-giving service, of abiding faith. It is, however, distinct from the petrine dimension. Mary "represents one face of the Church, different from and complementary to the ministerial or hierarchical aspect."[39] Interpreting the scene where Mary prays in the upper room in the midst of the disciples at Pentecost, the pope notes that this was the moment when Peter and the apostles received power from on high to preach the gospel to all nations. He then notes explicitly that "Mary did not directly receive this apostolic mission."[40] Here dualistic anthropology controls interpretation, glaringly so, because the biblical text makes no such distinction but rather states just the opposite: "When the day of Pentecost had come, they were all together in one place. . . . And they were all filled with the Holy Spirit and began to speak in other tongues, as the Spirit gave them utterance" (Acts 2:1, 4).

On balance, John Paul II's genuine desire to promote the dignity of women is subverted by the unrelenting dualism of his thought. It holds women in such idealized regard that they are judged to be too good to get involved in the messiness of the public realm, being relegated to a discreet if influential vocation. Many women respond to this romantic papal feminism as did one of my college students in a paper on the encyclical *The Dignity and Vocation of Women:* "As a young woman of the late twentieth century do I want to be so highly exalted? No, I would rather be equal." One young man in that same class also had a fascinating insight: "Saying that women are more fitted to love means that they are better able to follow Jesus' teaching to love God and your neighbor. Where does that leave me? Second best?" The point being, of course, that by boxing women's and men's abilities into innate differences based on traditional gender stereotypes, dualistic anthropology inevitably compromises the human and spiritual potential of both.

Myriads of Others

Hosts of additional thinkers across the theological spectrum accept and use the masculine–feminine dichotomy for mariology without questioning whether or not it is an adequate tool of interpretation or even whether it is true. In an article aptly titled "Mary: Miriam of Nazareth or the Symbol of the Eternal Feminine?" John van den Hengel names, in addition to Boff and Balthasar, Henri de Lubac, Leo Scheffczyk, Andrew Greeley, Claus Newman, and Teilhard de Chardin, all of whom present Mary as the Christian personification of the eternal feminine.[41] There are myriads of others. In a meditation on the marian dimensions of life, Raimundo Panikkar suggests that the relationship between human beings and God is none other than that between a created femininity and a Creator. Mary the woman, mother, and handmaid of the Lord, incarnates the eternal feminine and thus best represents this feminine—that is, receptive, responsive—aspect of life. "We see in tradition that Mary said practically nothing and did very little," he writes. "It is her 'being,' her existence that causes her to be called, and truly, blessed among women."[42] It must be noted that this view of Mary's passive existence, her non-speaking and non-acting, does not cohere with the testimony of scripture. Nor does the idea that women are blessed because of their silence and inactivity remotely do justice to women's struggle for life and human dignity.

In a similar pattern of thought, John Macquarrie reflects "that it is possible to characterize the feminine in broad strokes—it is a type of mentality responsive rather than initiating, concerned with the whole, with the inward, with the ideal, with what can be intuited rather than deduced," while the masculine style is opposite on every point. Applying this to Mary, he notes how she is the pattern of womanhood because she as feminine responds to the initiating activity of God (read: as masculine) and has great inward depth along with the feminine capacity for patient endurance of pain. But then, pointing to the Magnificat, he finds that there is also "another side" to her personality. The only language on hand, that of gender dichotomy, is barely adequate to his purpose: "Mary then did not conform to any stereotype and she sometimes showed characteristics that we would normally call masculine, yet she is perfectly woman and perfectly feminine."[43] Why is Mary masculine when she utters prophecy against powerful oppressors? Can a woman not speak in a critical vein? Not according to the ideal of the feminine, which Macquarrie interestingly admits is a stereotype. From the perspective of feminist liberation theology, one must note that a woman who proclaims the downfall of the rich and the feeding of the hungry in the name of God is a strong woman, period.

Yet another example exists in Jaroslav Pelikan's sweeping study of Mary in the history of culture. He raises the important question of how "this humble peasant girl from Nazareth," about whom the New Testament has relatively few references, became the subject of such reams of sublime, even theologically extravagant, speculation. With reference to the arts, in particular music, painting, and church architecture, he finds the answer to his query in a line from Goethe's *Faust*: "the Eternal Feminine leads us upward."[44] To demonstrate this, his study observes that Mary has been the subject of more discussion about what a true woman ought to be than any other woman in Western history. He also takes passing account of the problematic nature of that history for women today, citing critics such as Elisabeth Schüssler Fiorenza and her conclusion that, since mariology has its roots and development in a male, clerical, and ascetic culture in which women were silent and invisible, the whole construction is a theology "preached to women by men [which] can serve to deter women from becoming fully independent and whole human persons."[45] However, Pelikan thinks to offer a "historical corrective" to feminist studies like this on a number of points. He criticizes women's scholarship that exposes the invective hurled at women through the fallen figure of Eve by noting that the same patristic and medieval authors heaped praise on a counterpart, Mary, the second Eve. Here he avoids the critical analysis that reveals how both the overwhelmingly negative portrait of women in Eve and the positive portrait of the feminine in Mary are but two sides of the same coin, namely, male projection ignorant of and dominant over the actual lives of real women. By not critically analyzing the patriarchal bias of the history in which the construct of the eternal feminine originates, Pelikan can revel in its aesthetic outcome but ignore its effect on women struggling for human wholeness who are not included in the "us" being led upward. A little hilarity is in order.

In light of this tour of the perennial dualism that afflicts so much interpretation of Mary, it is instructive to revisit Vatican II for a final example. The conciliar treatment of Mary as model of the church, despite its ecumenical advantage, is hobbled by gender-inflected notions of masculine and feminine. The wording of the key text contains the clue: "the Mother of God is a model of the Church in the matter of faith, charity, and perfect union with Christ" (*Lumen Gentium* §63). Beautiful and true though this might be, what is not said is equally significant. Mary is not the model of the church in its institutional aspects, most particularly in its exercise of pastoral leadership. She is not the model of the church in its official role of governing, preaching, and administering the sacraments. She is not the model of the church's ordained priesthood. Priests may look to her as the model of their own faith and charity but not of their ministry, except insofar as they symbolize it as the maternal role of bringing persons to birth in Christ. There were no debates about this during the council. It was simply taken for granted, mentioned in speeches and commentaries, sometimes rounded off by indicating that the complement to the marian model of the church is Peter, model of the church in its formal structures and sacraments. The underlying assumption is the split between men's and women's natures characteristic of dualistic anthropology. The so-called feminine is not fit for the public, official sphere, at least in the church. Put another way, for the patriarchal imagination, women are by nature incapable of exercising the authority of Christ.

LIGHTING OUT FOR THE TERRITORY

The views presented above are not exceptions but are overwhelmingly typical of the way Mary is construed in patriarchal, dualistic theology. Now it becomes clear why women's negative assessments presented in chapters 1 and 2 are so strong and will not go away. It is not a question of this or that image or questionable virtue being assigned to Mary, but of the whole system of gender dualism that frames the interpretation. Within that framework, construals of Mary are inevitably shunted onto a track that runs toward idealization of the feminine as opposite to the masculine. Caught in this binary way of thinking, women's lives are forever restricted. So long as the essential connection between femininity and subordination stays unbroken, so long as theology uses the feminine to mean the receptive principle complementary to masculine initiative, Mary will signify a lesser place in the world for women.

It is not possible to interpret Mary in a liberating way within the confines of this traditional masculine–feminine dichotomy. An old American expression from frontier days reflects what happens when staying in town becomes too uncomfortably hot for unconventional characters: they light out for the territory. Escaping the clutches of stereotyped definitions of the feminine and taking Mary with us, women are doing just that. Our task now is to free theology from hierarchical power relations encoded in dualistic views of women, situating interpretation of Mary instead within an egalitarian anthropology of partnership. The goal is to arrive at a place where we can remember her as a blessing rather than a detriment to women's struggle for full human dignity in all their diversity, and ultimately to allow her life to be part of the church's word about God that advances loving praxis for the good of the world.

Before leaving town, however, it will help to plant seeds for future transformation to lay out the inadequacies in theory and practice of the dualistic anthropology being left behind.

• It originates in patriarchal society and reflects the status of women in that setting. Women were said to lack reason, for example, in a society that blocked them from receiving an education. Of course they were using their powers of reasoning, but not in the way learned men did; the latter could not recognize intelligence born of experience and the wit to survive. Cultural expectations socialize children into specific ways of being male and female. Change these, and new ways of being women and men emerge. This is indeed happening in postindustrial society today—think of women in sports, business or government, law or medicine, ministry or university education.

• In addition to its unexamined roots in traditional societal structures, which are passing away, gender dualism functions to maintain unjust distribution of social power between women and men. By defining the feminine as dependent, devoted, and receptive, and thereby declaring the essential woman incapable of representing any authority beyond herself, it denies women access to the task of shaping the community's cultural institutions, laws, and symbols. Indeed, the feminine ideal projected onto women is vigorously defended because it functions so well to keep men in positions of public power and women in service to them in predetermined, private, politically powerless roles.

• Gender dualism also suppresses the fact that persons actually exist who are homosexual or bisexual or intersexed. This dualistic theory does not do justice to their concrete humanity, basically rendering them invisible. Numerous empirical studies demonstrate that real gay and lesbian persons do not fit the standard stereotypes of masculine and feminine, any more than heterosexual persons do. But since their way of being human more clearly departs from the traditional standard, the former provoke fear and hostility. All too often, gross injustice results.[46]

• Gender dualism is racist and classist. Womanist and *mujerista* theologians note how the patriarchal concept of the feminine reflects the societal privilege of *some* women, those belonging to the race and class of the men in elite positions who thought it up. In American society at this time, it is white, middle-class women who can (if they wish) live out the feminine ideal, for they have not known the struggle for survival engaged in by generations of slaves or marginalized immigrants. In fact the existence of such "non-feminine" women to do the sexual and domestic scut work of society is required if some women are to occupy positions of privilege. Poor women have never had the luxury of staying home in their own domestic realm, even if they wanted to. Sojourner Truth, a nineteenth-century freed slave, tellingly put her finger on this racist and classist underbelly of the notion of the feminine in her famous "Ain't I a Woman?" speech:

> That man over there says that women need to be helped into carriages and lifted over ditches. . . . Nobody ever helps me into carriages or over mud puddles, or give me any best place. And ain't I a woman? Look at me! Look at my arms! I have ploughed and planted and gathered into barns, and no man could head me! And ain't I a woman? I could work as much and eat as much as a man—when I could get it—and bear the lash as well. And ain't I a woman? I have borne thirteen children, and seen them most all sold off to slavery and when I cried out with my mother's grief, none but Jesus heard me! And ain't I a woman?[47]

Indeed, what is a woman? And—the vital subtext here—who gets to decide? Sojourner Truth's poignant and challenging query, born of suffering, disrupts patriarchy's discourse about the ideal feminine, as does the concrete historical reality of millions of other women.

• Finally, gender dualism fosters the development of distorted human psyches. "Men fail to integrate into their own identity those repressed capacities which they project onto women. Women in turn are denied those capacities for autonomous selfhood, decision-making, and critical intelligence monopolized by males."[48] The result is truncated human beings whose relationships, even the most intimate, can only be less than mature. Two role-playing halves trying to make a whole never succeed, for authentic relationship requires two fully human persons in all their differences standing independent from and lovingly responding to one another.

Historically outdated, unjust to women, exclusive of those who do not fit the norm, racist and classist, and productive of psychological immaturity, patriarchal gender dualism is an obstacle on the journey toward a liberating future. Governing all of these failings is the need patriarchal discourse has to think by means of opposition to what is "other." As Newsom observes, "So long as a society's discourse is carried on by males alone, that fact is scarcely noticeable. But as women enter into public discourse as speaking subjects, the habit of patriarchy to think symbolically by means of woman is thrown into confusion. Woman cannot occupy the same symbolic relation to herself that she does to man. With that change the long, slow crisis of the symbolic order is at hand."[49] It is this crisis, now at a full boil, that leads women to reject those construals of Mary that have been created by traditional dualistic thinking. In this new moment of the living tradition, the uprising of women's consciousness is refusing such definitions of female reality. Crafting a view of Mary from the perspective of the poor, Latin American theologians Ivone Gebara and María Clara Bingemer provide a helpful description of the view of the one human race so needed to arrive at the territory ahead. A truly liberating mariology, they reflect, must move from a male-centered to a human-centered anthropology; from a dualistic to a unifying one; from an idealistic to a realistic, historical view of human nature; and from a one-dimensional to a pluridimensional view of humanity that includes but goes beyond sex.[50] The poet Irene Zimmerman expresses best what lies ahead in this territory for marian theology:[51]

All the way to Elizabeth
and in the months afterward,
she wove him, pondering,
"This is my body, my blood."

Beneath the watching eyes
of donkey, ox, and sheep
she rocked him, crooning,
"This is my body, my blood."

In the moonless desert flight
and the Egypt-days of his growing
she nourished him, singing,
"This is my body, my blood."

In the search for her young lost boy
and the foreboding day of his leaving
she let him go, knowing,
"This is my body, my blood."

Under the blood-smeared cross
she rocked his mangled bones,
remembering him, moaning,
"This is my body, my blood."

When darkness, stones, and tomb
bloomed to Easter morning,
she ran to him, shouting,
"This is my body, my blood."

And no one thought to tell her:
"Woman, it is not fitting
for you to say those words.
You don't resemble him."

By now it is clear why considering Mary the ideal face of woman or the feminine face of the church is a cul-de-sac that this book will not take. Our proposal to interpret Mary within the communion of saints will certainly honor the fact that she is a woman, a Jewish woman of a particular time and place, with her own familial and social relationships, her own journey toward God, and what turned out to be her historic vocation to partner God in bringing to birth the Messiah. It will not, however, interpret her in terms of the patriarchal feminine. As women claim the power of naming themselves in their own right, an egalitarian anthropology of partnership is emerging to the fore. This is the fresh context for theologizing about Mary as a woman with her own originality in the community of the saints.

4

❧

Cul-de-Sac:
The Maternal Face of God

MINING A RICH LODE

A second road that this book will not take interprets Mary as the woman who in her merciful, ever-loving care makes present to people the maternal face of God. This is a fascinating idea that goes a long way toward illuminating the dynamics of marian devotion. The exuberance of this tradition indicates that much of its growth is not explainable by the needs of preaching the gospel alone. Despite correct official formulations of doctrine, more is going on here than immediately meets the eye. A surprisingly diverse number of women and men scholars have proposed that, since standard images of God as lord and king along with the trinitarian formula of Father, Son, and Holy Spirit inevitably set up in the human imagination the notion of a male person or persons, the human psyche seeks intuitively to balance this one-sided relationship with other images that mediate the divine in female form. Teilhard de Chardin, for example, gave voice to this view when he defended the veneration of Mary because it served to satisfy an "irresistible Christian need" in the church, namely, the need to correct "a dreadfully masculinized" conception of the Godhead. When the dogma of Mary's Assumption into heaven was defined, he wrote that he was "too conscious of the bio-psychological necessity of the Marian—to counterbalance the masculinity of Yahweh— not to feel the profound need for this gesture."[1] Even though female images of God are present in the Bible and in Jewish and Christian mystical traditions, they have been excluded from the church's official language about God. Thus, the explanation goes, these divine images have migrated to the figure of Mary.

Thanks to this dynamic, Mary has functioned beautifully as an icon of

71

God. For innumerable believers her *persona* has revealed divine love as merciful, close, interested, always ready to hear and respond to human needs, trustworthy, and profoundly attractive, and has done so to a degree not possible when one thinks of God simply as a ruling male person or persons. Consequently, in devotion to her as a close, compassionate mother who will not let one of her children be lost, what is actually being mediated is a most appealing experience of God's saving love. The criterion for discerning where marian symbolism is actually harboring a word about the living God, rather than the woman of Nazareth, is the prayerful movement of the human spirit in adoration. Wherever Mary is described or addressed so as to evoke the ultimacy of God as expressed in scripture, liturgy, and creed, or wherever people direct their trust to her with ultimate devotion, there it can be supposed that, rather than idolatry taking place, the reality of God is being named in female metaphors.

Most scholars who have posited this relation between the figure of Mary and the need for some feminine quality in the divine have been content to let the issue rest there. Feminist theology takes a further step, proposing that thinking of God in exclusively male images is the result of patriarchy and subject to reform, rather than a necessary state of affairs in need of compensation. Holding strongly to the claim that women are created in the image and likeness of God and affirming with equal vigor the incomprehensibility of the living God who can never be captured literally in finite words or symbols, such theology argues that the holy mystery of God can be represented by female symbols in as adequate and inadequate a way as by male symbols.

In view of this conviction, the ordinary habit of Christian language that uses a few male images for the divine to the exclusion of all others appears restrictive and even distorted. Theologically the words tend to be reified so that God is wrongly understood to be masculine in a literal sense, however subliminally. The human heart thus creates an idol. Spiritually and psychologically, all male imagery of the divine also deprives women of seeing themselves as created directly in God's own image and likeness unless they abstract themselves from their own bodies. They are thereby deprived of a source of spiritual power. Socially and politically this language maintains the patriarchal arrangement of church and society, legitimating men's domination over women and nature since they rule in "his" image as king and lord. Indeed, the long omission of female images from standard speech about God has not been accidental. Historically it has been wedded to a view of humanity that holds that men alone embody the fullness of God's image and likeness. Compared to them women are defective in body and spirit, which makes them less than worthy as reference points for the divine. It is good to report that no reputable theologian today holds this position, which has been so harmful that it has even drawn a papal apology.[2] The implications for God-talk have not been as quick to follow, but they are clearly in view. Reclaiming the basic revolutionary teaching that precisely as female they are created with unsurpassable dignity in the image and likeness of God, women today are proposing that female images along with cosmic ones be used, not exclusively, but to enrich the poverty of the traditional vocabulary about the holy mystery of God.

Given this program, the insight that divine images have clustered around the figure of Mary affords a new opportunity. Rather than leave them there, we can invite them to travel back to their source, where they belong. The marian tradition then becomes a rich mother lode that can be "mined" in order to retrieve maternal and other female imagery and language about the living God.[3] Relieved of bearing this burden, the figure of Mary is freed to return to her own history as a woman of faith and to rejoin us in the graced community of struggle in history. Toward that end, our trip around this cul-de-sac explores key instances where female images of God that were going homeless in official doctrine found a place in Mary's image to shelter and thrive.

HISTORICAL SOUNDINGS

Early Christian Centuries

It is commonplace today for scholars to note the similarities between the veneration of Mary in the early Christian centuries and the pervasive veneration of the Great Mother Goddess in the Mediterranean world into which Christianity was moving. Very little is known precisely about how elements of the Hellenistic cults of female deities accrued to the person of Mary, but, as Hugo Rahner notes in the course of his argument for the essential differences between them, such similarities at least in superficially observable matters are simply a matter of historical fact.[4] The church was not fashioned in a vacuum but absorbed many of the assumptions, verbal and visual imagery, and rituals of the surrounding culture into its own theology and liturgy.

In his classic study of this adaptation in the case of Mary, Jean Daniélou stresses the radical distinction between the mystery cults and the Christian veneration of Mary.[5] Insofar as the latter originated in a historically unique revelation of God in Jesus Christ, and furthermore portrays Mary as virginal rather than as the sexually fecund Earth Mother, there is more dissimilarity than similarity between them. Once these essential differences are established, Daniélou argues, one is then free to examine the ways in which Christianity's marian cult adapted elements from the mystery cults and substituted itself—historically in the fourth-century world, and psychologically in the human spirit—for the cults wherein the female deities played an absolutely central role. The officials of the church allowed this assimilation of pagan elements for two reasons: it was an excellent missionary strategy in a world where goddesses were highly honored; and it reflected a sacramental view of reality in which, once "baptized," female images could evoke the God revealed in Christ. Among the people, however, it must be asked whether such purification was actually accomplished, or whether instead in a form of syncretism the cult of Mary simply continued the veneration of the maternal power of the goddess. In either case, Daniélou concludes, the power of the marian cult lies in the fact that it corresponds to the aspirations of the human heart, by which it seems he means the desire for a mother's love.

Starting in the fourth century, devotion was transferred to Mary in innumerable ways. Places in nature where female deities had been honored with pilgrimage and prayer, such as grottoes, springs, promontories, mountains, lakes, and woods, became associated with Mary.[6] Shrines and temples to the goddess were rededicated to Mary the Mother of God, outstanding examples being found in Rome, Athens, Chartres, and Ephesus. Artistic symbols of the goddess accrued to Mary: her dark blue cloak, turreted crown, link with the moon and the stars, and with water and the sea. The iconography of Mary seated with her child facing outward on her lap is patterned on the pose of Isis with Horus, the mother herself an upright royal throne that holds the god-king facing the world. Hymns reminiscent of the self-praises of Isis acclaimed Mary with familiar titles and attributes of female deities, such as Queen of Heaven, all-holy, merciful, wise, the universal mother, giver of fertility and the blessings of life, protector of pregnant women and their children, sailors at sea, and all who call to her in need. The still-venerated statues of the black madonna at Le Puy, Montserrat, Chartres, and elsewhere derive from ancient black stones con-

nected with the fertility power of earth goddesses, black being the benefi-
cent color of subterranean and uterine fecundity. Adapted into the iconography of the classic Gallo-Roman mother goddesses, this symbolism was
then conserved in the sculpted images of the black madonna.[7]

The earliest written trace of this devotion is the prayer *Sub tuum prae-
sidium*, a papyrus fragment of which is variously dated to the late third or
fourth century. Used for centuries as a liturgical antiphon in the churches
of East and West, the prayer casts Mary in the role of divine protector: "We
fly to your patronage (or protection, shelter), O holy Mother of God;
despise not our petitions in our necessities, but deliver us from all dangers,
O glorious and blessed Virgin." Hilda Graef notes that this prayer dares to
use the same verb (*rhyomai*) as does the Lord's Prayer when asking Our
Father in heaven to "deliver us" from evil, suggesting that the mother of
God has access to divine power and will use it for merciful purposes.[8] The
same plea for deliverance from calamity resounds through the *Akathistos
Hymn* developed in the sixth century, a magnificent exuberance of twenty-
four stanzas, each in dazzling poetry hailing Mary worthy of all praise for
having brought forth the Logos.[9]

The mass demonstration that took place during the council held in
Ephesus in 431 gives further evidence of this transfer of devotion. When it
became clear that the bishops would decide in favor of the disputed marian title *Theotokos,* or God-bearer, the populace, which had been demonstrating outside the church, greeted the verdict with an explosion of joy.
They led the bishops to their lodgings with torchlight processions and
shouts of "Praised be *Theotokos!*" This outpouring is reminiscent of an
enthusiastic rally in this same city several centuries before, when Paul's
preaching threatened the livelihood of the silversmiths who crafted like-
nesses of the city's goddess. As reported in Acts, enraged crowds shouted
for hours, "Great is Diana of the Ephesians" (Acts 19:23–24), practically
forcing a riot and causing Paul to leave. Four centuries later the scene
repeats; *Theotokos* had taken Diana's place in the hearts of the people.[10] In
at least one instance, popular assimilation of the goddess cult seemed to
destroy the fundamental structure of Christian faith. The fourth-century
sect of the Collyridians, made up mostly of women, worshiped Mary as
herself divine. Devotees sang, prayed, and offered sweet breads before her
throne as had so many before them to the Great Mother. Against them
Epiphanius, bishop of Salamis, inveighed, "The body of Mary is holy but
she is not God. . . . Let no one adore Mary."[11]

For all the real differences in structure and content between Christian devotion to Mary and the veneration of the goddess, the evidence at hand indicates a strong process of assimilation and adaptation of ideas, texts, and artistic imagery in the case of the emerging marian cult. As Daniélou argues, while remaining independent, Christianity yet used the rich symbols of paganism purified of their ancient content to express its own revelation and thereby to insinuate itself into the hearts of new believers so recently accustomed to the beneficence and maternal power of the goddess. This comparative approach to the origin of marian symbolism yields a clear insight: the marian tradition is one conduit of imagery and language about divine reality flowing from the veneration of the Great Mother in the pre-Christian Mediterranean world. Even when well integrated into a Christian gestalt, the historical origin of this symbolism opens up the possibility of drawing upon Mary to reflect upon the mystery of God in female metaphors.

Medieval Growth

Scholars of the medieval European period, documenting its extensive growth in popular devotion and learned speculation about Mary, note that by the sixteenth century the figure of Mary had taken on attributes and functions borrowed not only from the ancient goddess but from the Christian Trinity itself.[12] While the Protestant Reformers roundly criticized this development and while the Catholic reform sought to correct it, more contemporary interpreters perceive it as a quest for religious experience through the compassionate feminine image, an experience not available through the patriarchal idea of God at the time. On a popular level supported by religious orders and bishops, these centuries saw the multiplication of marian feasts, prayers, hymns, sculptures, paintings, and magnificent cathedrals, expressions of devotion that still stand. The marian theology that arose in this context is complex. Theologically, scholasticism drew on the Hellenistic idea that feminine/maternal qualities were and perforce had to be totally absent from God, for it was intrinsic to the feminine to be passive and receptive; technically, to be potency rather than act. Since God is Pure Act, only the active power of the masculine/paternal could be allowed to enter the notion of "Himself." As the scholarly medieval idea of God consequently became ever more rigorously androcentric with no room for anything feminine, views of Mary became commensurably ever more laudatory. Her privileges and honors grew according to the premise *potuit, decuit, fecit*: God could do great things for his mother, he should do them, therefore he did them. Freed by the logic of this axiom to imagine what they would give their own mothers if they could, the minds of medieval male theologians generously heaped gifts of personal perfection and public influence on the mother of God.

In the process, Mary at first paralleled and then occasionally outshone the Godhead. The creative power of God the Father was mirrored in Mary, who at the incarnation gave the world the Savior, thereby becoming the source of the world's renewal. As Anselm praised, "So God is the Father of all created things, and Mary is the Mother of all recreated things."[13] Psalms were rewritten substituting Mary for God as the acting subject of divine deeds: "Sing to Our Lady a new song, for she hath done wonderful things. In the sight of the nations she hath revealed her mercy; her name is heard even to the ends of the earth" (Psalm 96/97).[14] Standard hymns of divine praise such as the *Te Deum* were refashioned to honor Mary:

> We praise thee, O Mother of God; we confess thee, Mary ever Virgin. . . . Thee all angels and archangels, thrones and principalities serve. Thee all powers and virtues of heaven and all dominations obey. Before thee all the angelic choirs, the cherubim and seraphim, exulting, stand. With unceasing voice every angelic creature proclaims thee: Holy, holy, holy, Mary Virgin Mother of God![15]

In time, Mary was gifted with omniscience and a certain omnipotence over earth, heaven, and hell. Biblical affirmations of God the Father were attributed to her, such as she so loved the world that she gave her only Son (John 3:16).[16] She was addressed as Our Mother who art in heaven, and asked to give us each day our daily bread and deliver us from danger. In moments of critical reflection there was universal insistence that these and similar honors redounded to the glory of God, who "himself" had so honored Mary. In effect, however, this kind of devotion to the Mother of God was actually devotion to God the mother, to the ultimate mystery of the creative and recreative God glimpsed in female form.

While Jesus Christ was acknowledged as gracious Savior, the increasingly juridical penitential system in the church led to the sense that his role as judge superseded his mercy. The latter in turn was attributed abundantly to Mary. She was depicted as restraining Christ's wrath, placing back into its sheath his sword, which was raging against sinful humanity. She was particularly kind to the undeserving, saving all manner of rogues and wrongdoers so long as they called upon her. As the period progressed, she went from being merciful mediatrix with the just judge, to being sharer of common dominion with Christ through the pain she suffered on Calvary, and thence to having power over the mercy of Christ, whom she commanded by her maternal authority. So great was the essential role of Mary's mercy that medieval theologians wrote of her what biblical authors wrote of Christ: in her the fullness of the Godhead dwelt corporeally (Col. 2:9); of her fullness we have all received (John 1:16); and because she had emptied herself, God had highly exalted her, so that at her name every knee should bend (Phil. 2:5–11). Medieval parallels between Mary and Christ in nature, grace, and glory, in virtue and dignity, resulted in the figure of Mary assuming divine prerogatives. As co-redemptrix, she merited salvation; as mediatrix, she obtained grace for sinners; as queen and mother of mercy, she dispensed it herself. All of this power resided in Mary as a maternal woman who represented ultimate graciousness over against divine severity. While theology today criticizes the deficient christology that made this compensation necessary, it is nevertheless clear that the figure of Mary functioned more than adequately as a female image of the saving mystery of God.

In scripture the activity of the Spirit of God is pictured in a multitude of metaphors taken from the natural and human world. One such constellation of images centers on the bird and her wings, long a symbol of female deity in ancient Near Eastern religions. Whether hovering like a nesting mother bird over the egg of primordial chaos in the beginning, or sheltering those in difficulty under the protective shadow of her wings, or bearing the enslaved up on her great wings toward freedom, the Spirit's activity is evoked with allusion to femaleness.[17] Early Syriac Christianity kept this connection between the Spirit of God and female imagery, consistently depicting the Spirit as a brooding or hovering mother bird, mothering Jesus into life at his conception and into mission at his baptism, and bringing believers to birth and mission in the waters of baptism. This doctrine of the motherhood of the Spirit fostered a spirituality of warmth which found expression in characteristic prayers: "As the wings of doves are over their nestlings, and the mouths of their nestlings toward their mouths, so also are the wings of the Spirit over my heart."[18] In time this biblical and patristic imagery migrated away from the Spirit toward the church, called holy mother the church, and by the Middle Ages to Mary, the mother of Jesus, venerated as mother of the faithful as well. The Spirit's outstretched wings "morphed" into the outstretched cloak of the strong medieval

Madonna of the Protective Mantle, and the Spirit's birthing and renewing powers were attributed to her gracious work in salvation. The figure of this woman became the bearer of profoundly important characteristics of the Spirit of God.

As this brief sampling shows, those who were devoted to Mary experienced first and foremost a relationship of trust to a transcendent, powerful mother figure ready to hear human needs and profoundly sympathetic to human weakness. In her symbolism, the maternal, merciful, caring metaphors that the Bible uses to describe God's unbreakable love for the people of the covenant found continuing, concrete expression.

European Theology

As the Roman Catholic tradition developed after the Protestant Reformation, the priority of God and the centrality of Christ in the mystery of salvation were made officially clear. There was still more than enough room, however, to attribute to Mary important functions in the mediation of God's saving love. The pressure to do so built up into a "marian movement" from the nineteenth to mid-twentieth centuries, a period marked by marian apparitions, innumerable treatises on her privileges, and papal definition of two marian dogmas, the Immaculate Conception and the Assumption. In a highly influential work, *Mary, Mother of the Redemption*, written at the peak of the marian movement a decade before Vatican II, Edward Schillebeeckx sought to provide a theoretical foundation for the church's actions. He reasoned that while God's love is both paternal and maternal, the latter quality is not and cannot be fully expressed in the man Jesus because he is a male. Thus God chose Mary to embody the feminine qualities of the divine, namely, all that is tender, mild, simple, generous, gentle, and sweet in divine love. "Mary is the translation and effective expression in maternal terms of God's mercy, grace and redeeming love which manifested itself to us in a visible and tangible form in the person of Christ, our Redeemer."[19] What is so interesting in this treatment of the theme is the choice of active verbs to express a relationship: Mary represents, makes manifest, explicates, translates, effectively expresses something of God that cannot come to light in Jesus Christ. This quality is the feminine, maternal aspect of divine love which needs expression through the figure of a woman. Schillebeeckx's statement is one of the most explicit preconciliar treatments of the Mary–God connection. While he clearly would not treat the subject the same way today, having criticized his own position and wishing, after his monumental work on Jesus, to hew to a more biblical approach;[20] and while his reduction of the feminine to the maternal and of the maternal to mildness and sweetness is highly questionable from a feminist viewpoint, his thesis is still being used by theologians who wish to affirm Mary as the maternal face of God. In an interesting development, some Anglican and Lutheran scholars have favored this idea, finding in Mary a life-giving symbol of divine creativity and saving love that helps to correct Christianity's heavy masculine emphasis with reference to God.[21]

In the ecumenical climate after the Second Vatican Council, theologians such as Yves Congar, René Laurentin, Heribert Mühlen, and Léon J. Cardinal Suenens paid careful attention to the Protestant critique that in the Catholic tradition Mary has substituted in a particular way for the action and experience of God the Holy Spirit.[22] Catholics have said that Mary forms Christ in them, that she is spiritually present to guide and inspire, that she is the link between themselves and Christ, and that the spiritual seeker goes to Jesus through Mary. But are these not precisely the roles of the Spirit of Christ? Furthermore, Mary is called intercessor, mediatrix, helper, advocate, defender, consoler, counselor. But are these not titles that belonged originally to the Paraclete? Catholics have thought and preached that all grace comes from God through Christ by way of Mary. But is this not a dislocation of the Holy Spirit, who is essential to the trinitarian gift of grace in this world? The observation of Protestant student Elsie Gibson is frequently quoted as Catholic thinkers attempt to come to grips with this issue: "When I began the study of Catholic theology, every place I expected to find an exposition of the doctrine of the Holy Spirit, I found Mary. What Protestants universally attribute to the action of the Holy Spirit was attributed to Mary."[23]

Finding this critique basically substantiated, Laurentin has observed that Mary occupied spaces left vacant by an undeveloped pneumatology in medieval Latin theology and even more in post-Tridentine theology. The way forward, he suggests, is to be found by a return to the scriptures. There the Spirit has obvious primacy, while Mary is overshadowed by, filled with, made fruitful by, and enabled to prophesy in the power of the Spirit. Consequently, the privileged sign and witness to the Holy Spirit in the community of the church is the person of Mary, whose role of mediation and intercession occurs only within the primordial role of the Spirit. At the same time, the consistency with which Mary has been conflated with the

Holy Spirit, the person in the Trinity most connected with divine intimacy and presence to human beings, suggests that here again the figure of Mary is expressing important but overlooked aspects of the reality of the living God.

To summarize our explorations to this point: soundings of the marian tradition's historical origin, medieval growth, and modern European interpretation reveal workable connections between the figure of Mary and the creating, redeeming, and sanctifying God in both popular piety and theological reflection, and often there is not a hard and fast distinction between these two. The need to compensate for an overly masculinized idea of God, seen especially in a deficient christology and a woefully undeveloped theology of the Holy Spirit, is never far from the surface. Rounding the bend into our contemporary era, we find the same insight being articulated by theologians in the southern and northern hemispheres of the new world.

South and North American Theology

Interpreters of Latin American Catholicism universally note that massive devotion to Mary is one of the most popular, persistent, and original characteristics of its peoples' piety. Seeking to ground this piety, Brazilian theologian Leonardo Boff proposed a daring hypothesis: just as the Word became flesh in Jesus Christ, so too Mary is the embodiment of the third person of the Holy Trinity. "We maintain the hypothesis," he wrote, "that the Virgin Mary, Mother of God and of all men and women, realizes the feminine absolutely and eschatologically, inasmuch as the Holy Spirit has made her his temple, sanctuary, and tabernacle in so real and genuine a way that she is to be regarded as hypostatically united to the Third Person of the Blessed Trinity."[24] This union is an ontological one so profound that the Spirit can be said to have taken flesh in the Virgin Mary, who in turn personifies the Spirit.

Two major presuppositions underlie Boff's hypothesis. One is the venerable Catholic understanding that human nature as such is created with a capacity for the hypostatic union, so it is not unthinkable for divine nature to be ontologically united with a woman, provided women be understood as fully human. The other is the more controverted idea that the Holy Spirit is the feminine divine person in the Trinity. While in the incarnation Jesus Christ assumed human nature in its totality, Boff argues, still it is the "masculine" that is assumed in direct and immediate fashion, while the feminine is assumed and divinized only indirectly as a secondary component of the male. Conscious of the long-standing subordination of women, he proposes that it is only fitting that the feminine itself should also be assumed and sanctified directly and immediately. This occurs in Mary, immaculately conceived, virgin mother of God, assumed into heaven, and co-redemptrix and co-mediatrix of salvation. In her, the feminine is "hypostatically assumed" by the Spirit, with the result that the created feminine is now eternally associated with the mystery of the being of God and is a vehicle of God's own self-realization. Mary rightly belongs not subordinate to Christ but by his side. Widespread attribution to her of the functions of the Holy Spirit is legitimate.

While obviously reflecting the pattern of prayer of millions of people in the Latin American churches, Boff's hypothesis has come in for severe criticism.[25] The point to note for our purpose is that, unlike theologians who would judge exalted tendencies in the veneration of Mary negatively, Boff sees them as revelatory of a neglected aspect of God. His work underscores the clue we have already been following, namely, that it is especially in maximalist marian development that female images of the divine are coming to expression.

In the United States a rich body of theological work is growing as scholars from Hispanic communities interpret the revelation encoded in popular religious practices.[26] Central to this experience is the figure of Mary, more precisely of different images of Mary, according to various communities' countries of origin. The marian configurations from Cuba, Dominican Republic, Colombia, Mexico, and other countries differ, reflecting as they do the particular histories in which they arose. But they all inspire a spirituality of struggle for life that stretches from their countries of origin to the challenge of struggling for life within a dominant Anglo culture.

Mexican American theologian Virgil Elizondo's detailed interpretation of Our Lady of Guadalupe is particularly illustrative of the connection between marian imagery and the idea of God. He advances the thesis that the origin of devotion to Our Lady of Guadalupe involved resistance by conquered native people not only to the European invaders but also to the all-male God in whose name they conquered. In the process of this resistance, the poor and vanquished people became the recipients of a major disclosure in the development of the Christian understanding of God, namely, that the mystery of God embraces both male and female identities. Consequently this living marian symbol has significance not just for Mexican Americans but for the whole church: it liberates everyone from a restrictive, masculinized view of God.

Analysis of the genesis of this Mexican gestalt of Mary supports this contention. The place of the original sixteenth-century apparition was the site of an ancient temple dedicated to Tonantzin, the Indian virgin mother of the gods. The flowers and music of the vision were part of Tonantzin's temple worship. The dark skin of the woman of the apparition, the language she spoke, the colors she was wearing, and the celestial symbols surrounding her were all reminiscent of the goddess of the defeated people. Yet it was not Tonantzin who was appearing, but the virgin mother of the Christian God. As Elizondo interprets the creative result of this cross-cultural encounter, the figure of Our Lady of Guadalupe combined the Indian female expression of God, which the Spanish had tried to wipe out as diabolical, with the Spanish male expression of God, which the Indians had found incomprehensible, since everything that is perfect in the Nahuatl cosmovision has a male and a female component. Here "the male Father God of militaristic and patriarchal Christianity is united to the female Mother of God (Tonantzin), which allows the original heart and face of Christianity to shine forth: compassion, understanding, tenderness, and healing."[27] Each understanding of God was expanded by the other, yielding a new *mestizo* expression that enriches the very understanding of the selfhood of God.

At the same time, at the very moment when imperial conquerors imbued with religious absolutism on one side were meting out death and defeat to indigenous peoples considered "pagans" on the other, this marian revelatory event signals the birth of a new reality, a new humanity, a new church, in continuity with both traditions and yet transformative of both into something new. "Both had so much to offer to each other, but neither could see it or even think about it. God breaks through—with flower and song! This is no longer an exterminator God but is, rather, the God of pleasure and harmony."[28] In order to appreciate this, one must proceed through the ways of thought of the oppressed people of the new world. Then one discovers that God is on the side of the poor, the raped, the defeated, the exploited, pouring out compassion and challenging consciences.[29] The figure of Guadalupe is a living locus of the experience of the compassionate God in female form.

Shifting focus, Orlando Espín ventures a different, intriguing theological interpretation that keeps Guadalupe's connection with divinity while setting Mary free into history. Using Hispanic theological method, which attends to popular religion as a genuine expression of faith, Espín argues that the profound devotion to Guadalupe should be mistaken for neither heresy nor idolatry, for this figure is not identical with the historical Mary of Nazareth, mother of Jesus. "When I am confronted by the depth of trust and affection that Latinos have for the *Virgen*, and when I see the beautiful, reverential relationship they nurture with her, and also how deeply touched and empowered they are by her, then as a theologian I have to wonder."[30] His wonder leads him to question whether the ecclesiastical insistence that this is a marian apparition does not fly in the face of the *sensus fidelium* of everyday people. It leads him to suggest that instead of an experience of mariology, what we have here is a superbly inculturated experience of the Holy Spirit. Espín is not implying that Mary *is* the Holy Spirit, or that Mary of Nazareth *appeared* in Indian guise and mediated the maternal or feminine face of God. He is implying that the historical Mary has nothing much to do with this phenomenon at all. It is not the Jewish woman Miriam of Nazareth whom Latinos venerate in their devotion to *la Virgen de Guadalupe*. It is rather the Holy Spirit of God, expressed not in the categories of Greek myth or European culture and philosophy but in culturally meaningful marian categories borrowed from the conquerors and transferred in a colonial Mexican context to the indwelling, reconciling Creator Spirit. Theological and ecclesiastical elites at the time of Juan Diego's encounter insisted on a marian interpretation in an understandably defensive move to protect doctrinal purity, since the only female imagery for the divine they knew was associated with the religion they were trying to stamp out. Besides, too much talk of the Holy Spirit could bring you to the attention of the Inquisition! But in the experience of the people then and now, references to the Mary of the gospels is notably absent in connection with devotion to Guadalupe. What is mediated instead is a profoundly engaging experience of God present in their midst with love and compassion. Therefore, is it not the case that "what we have here is not mariology but pneumatology in an unexpected and brilliantly achieved cultural mediation?"[31] The marian practices of Latino Catholicism thus come to signify an orthodox popular pneumatology.

To support his thesis, Espín lists a growing number of thinkers who are making similar suggestions that manifestations of the *Virgen* are not always the same as manifestations of Mary the mother of Jesus but signify the presence of the Spirit.[32] The net effect of this way of positing a deep connection between the strong marian symbolic presence in Hispanic faith experience, prayer, and liturgy and the actual presence of the Spirit of God is to make this phenomenon a *locus theologicus* for pneumatology rather than for theology of Mary. This is an interpretation that simultaneously respects the orthodoxy of the religious experience of millions of people while allowing the proposal to view Mary as a friend of God and prophet in the graced community to go forward.

As Miguel Díaz observes, one would be hard pressed to find a theological consensus among U.S. Hispanic theologians about the referent of the marian symbol. However, it is always and everywhere a symbol of grace, of God's faithful solidarity in the midst of struggle. "Whether understood as the female face of God (Rodriguez, Elizondo), a symbol of the Holy Spirit (Espín), the poetry of the trinitarian God (García), or the *mestizo* face of the divine (Goizueta), it is clear that U.S. Hispanic theologians understand Marian symbols as mediators of the life of grace, especially to and within the experience of the poor and marginalized."[33] In other words, the figure of Mary mediates an encounter with the liberating, compassionate God herself in female form.

In view of its basic tenet that the full human dignity of women makes female imagery of God both legitimate and necessary, feminist theology is at ease with the interpretation that the marian symbol portrays the female face of God. Reflecting on her own childhood in Catholic Bavaria, Elisabeth Schüssler Fiorenza analyzes the local experience of marian devotion in this light.[34] In postwar southern Germany, the God presented for belief had been shaped by a long process of patriarchy and militarization to become ever more remote and judgmental. Enormous devotion was poured out toward Mary, the beloved "other face" of God. She became the figure who bore the life-giving, compassionate love so characteristic of the *Abba* whom Jesus preached. On the intellectual level pastors insisted on the distinction between adoration of God and veneration of Mary; but on the affective, imaginative level, the Catholic child experienced the saving love of God in the figure of this woman. Schüssler Fiorenza's analysis leads her to conclude that the Catholic cult of Mary is one fruitful source of theological discourse that speaks of the divine in female terms, images, and symbols. Following that thread, she suggests, will enable divine compassion, power, and care to be spoken about in female terms directly, in the full light of day.

One critical point where feminist liberation theology takes issue with most other approaches canvassed above is the idea that Mary represents the feminine "dimension," "side," "aspect," or "traits" of the divine. Theologically speaking, God does not have a feminine dimension, or a masculine dimension, or an animal dimension (think of the winged bird, the angry mother bear), or a mineral dimension (the rock). God is simple. Names, images, and symbols do not aim at part of the divine mystery, were that even possible, but intend to evoke the whole. Consequently, female imagery by itself points to God pure and simple and has the capacity to represent God not only as nurturing, although certainly that, but also as powerful, creating-redeeming-saving. This entails, obviously, that women's capacities not be reduced by gender stereotyping to what is sweet and mild or compassionate alone. When this happens, as can be seen in the examples of Congar, Schillebeeckx, and Boff cited above, the predominant image of God remains that of the ruling lord, but now one whose sternness is tempered by the nurturing, maternal traits reflected in Mary. Problematically, the female is not allowed to function as an icon of the divine in all fullness but only supplements what remains an overarching male image. To the contrary, if women are created in the image of God, then God can be imaged in female metaphors in as full and as limited a way as God is imaged in male ones, without talk of feminine dimensions or sides or traits reducing the power of this language.

GIVING BACK: THE MIGRATION BEGINS

This exploration of diverse ways in which the marian symbol bears images of the divine indicates how strongly the Mary–God connection has been welded. Historians of the development of doctrine, Catholic theologians with a classical doctrinal interest, ecumenically minded theologians of the Reformation tradition, liberation, Hispanic, and feminist theologians all affirm in different ways that marian devotion and theology are sources of female language and symbols for God. Certainly not all would agree that this phenomenon is due to the patriarchal tenor of the dominant idea of God, nor that there is pressing need to change the status quo. To my mind, however, it makes no lasting theological sense to use Mary as a coverup for defective notions of God, Christ, or the Spirit. Rather, this female imagery should be allowed to travel back to its source and begin to fertilize the church's imagination and piety in relation to the mystery of God, who is beyond gender but Creator of both women and men in the divine image. Without claiming to be comprehensive, at least five marian elements present themselves as viable candidates for this return: maternity with its nurturing warmth and fierce protection; compassionate love; power that empowers, heals, and liberates; all-pervading presence; and energy that recreates the earth.

The first and most obvious transfer is the symbol of God as mother. The metaphors of birthing and maternal care that the Hebrew scriptures use to describe God's unbreakable love for the covenanted people have been concretized and carried forward in the figure of Mary. Throughout tradition she has been portrayed predominantly as the mother par excellence. Transferring this maternal language back to its source enables us to see that God Herself has a maternal face. All that is creative and generative of life, all that wills the young to live, all that nourishes and nurtures, teaches and corrects, cherishes and sustains, all that is full of solicitude and sympathy originates in Her. Warm, indispensable mother-love flows from God the Mother toward all creatures. As Sallie McFague points out, this symbol points intrinsically to God's option for the poor and fierce desire that those who are threatened be safeguarded, for do not mothers care for the most vulnerable among their brood and want all at their table to be fed?[35] All mothering on earth has its source in Her. She exercises a maternity that does not leave us orphans. As Pope John Paul I declared in a Sunday talk, God is our Father but even more God is our Mother, the one who comes to our aid especially when we are bad or feverish with war.[36] The image has the capacity to release profoundly attractive characteristics of God long suppressed in a patriarchal system. Notice that what is overcome here is a popular concept of heavenly interaction modeled on a patriarchal household in which a distant and judgmental God the Father is inclined to be approachable and more lenient through the intercession of Mary the mother on behalf of wayward children. Praying to and speaking about God our Mother rearranges that whole scenario. Maternity itself is predicated of God equally with paternity, and female images of the creative caring intrinsic to healthy mothering evoke the reality of God.

Another, closely related element that has been cherished in the marian tradition is divine compassion. As Phyllis Trible's biblical studies have shown, the Hebrew word for mercy is linguistically rooted in the term for a woman's womb. Traveling from the wombs of women to the compassion of God, the metaphorical resonance of divine compassion evokes the idea of God's "womb-love" for the ones whom she has carried and shaped from her own flesh.[37] Despite the New Testament's overwhelming witness that the mercy of God is made effectively present in Jesus Christ, and the symbolizing of that fact in such images as Jesus as the mother bird gathering her brood under her wing (Matt. 23:37–39), the medieval split of the kingdoms of justice and mercy resulted in the marian tradition being the primary bearer of this good news. In much preaching and piety Mary has been presented as more approachable than Christ, especially when one is conscious of human weakness. In this vein the classical marian antiphon *Salve Regina* salutes Mary as "mother of mercy, our life, our sweetness and our hope"; to her the poor banished children of Eve send up their sighs and pray: "turn then, most gracious advocate, thine eyes of mercy toward us." In the end Mary is asked to show us Jesus, but the form of the prayer itself casts her in the life-giving role of the merciful one. Returning this language to God to whom it properly belongs enables us to name God's own self as essentially and unfathomably merciful.

In her insightful essay entitled "Mother of Mercy: Reclaiming a Title for God,"Australian theologian Patricia Fox models this reclamation, showing how reimagining mercy flowing from God who is Mother of Mercy gives a new, strong impetus for commitment to living lives of mercy in this broken, needy world.[38] God is the Mother of mercy who has compassionate womb-love for all her children. We need not be afraid to approach. She is brimming over with gentleness, loving-kindness and forgiveness, lavishing love and pity on the whole sinful human brood. Her judgment is true, most devastating to those who refuse the call for conversion to the same kind of mercy toward others: their self-righteousness is to no avail. Yet to the most ordinary as well as to the most blatant of wrongdoers who wish to repent, she is a true Refuge of Sinners (a marian title). In addition to mercifully forgiving sin, God consoles in all troubles and, bending with care over those who suffer, is the true Comforter of the Afflicted (another marian title).[39] It is simply not the case that God is essentially just with a justice that needs to be tempered by Mary's merciful intercession. Rather, compassion is primordially divine, as is suitably disclosed in the divine symbol of the merciful mother.

The marian tradition also carries images of divine power and might. In this instance it is not a power that dominates but a strength that seeks to protect and to save. There is a persistent sense that Mary's power is not restricted by the demands of ecclesiastical law, or bound by the power of Satan, or even by the male God-figures of Father and Son to whom she is supposedly subject. Her sovereignty is unbounded, saving whom she loves if they but turn to her.[40] This is graphically illustrated by the widespread medieval iconography of the Madonna of the Protective Mantle. Under the umbrella formed by her draped, outstretched arms huddle a family, a religious order, a king, even a whole town's populace. There they find protection from evil which threatens, be it plague, war, temptation, or even God's eternal judgment. Understanding all of this as primarily imagery of the divine unlocks the realization that the power of God is neither destructive, aggressive, overbearing, or bound by law. Rather, divine power comes forth as an expression of unbounded love and operates wisely and justly in a form of advocacy for human beings who suffer. Her might is effective in breaking the stranglehold of evil and freeing those whom it has held in bondage, putting down the mighty from their thrones and exalting those of low degree. Like the Gospel homemaker searching for her lost coin, she powerfully seeks and finds what is lost (Luke 15:8–10). This kind of power, carried in the imagery of a female figure of "might and mercy,"[41] most accurately belongs to God's own being.

The immanence or indwelling nearness of God, attributed to the Holy Spirit and so often underplayed in classical theism, is yet another element emphasized in the marian tradition. Indeed, it is a traditional Catholic experience that, as John Paul II tellingly observes, the eternal love of the Father manifested in history through the Son "comes close to each of us through this Mother and thus takes on tokens that are of more easy understanding and access by each person."[42] This closeness of the love of God, this sense of the divine presence surrounding and pervading the creature, is given striking expression in Gerard Manley Hopkins's poem "The Blessed Virgin Compared to the Air We Breathe":

> Wild air, world-mothering air,
> Nestling me everywhere . . .
> Minds me in many ways
> Of her . . .
>   I say that we are wound
> With mercy round and round
> As if with air: the same
> Is Mary, more by name.
> She, wild web, wondrous robe,
> Mantles the guilty globe . . .
> And men are meant to share
> Her life as life does air . . .
>   Be thou then, O thou dear

> Mother, my atmosphere . . .
> World-mothering air, air wild,
> Wound with thee, in thee isled,
> Fold home, fast fold thy child.[43]

The imagery of this stunning poem refers most properly to the Spirit of God. Redirecting it enables us to realize that it is the wild Spirit who is our true atmosphere, surrounding and nestling us. Most truly it is in her that we live and move and have our being (Acts 17:28). God the Spirit is closer to us than we are to ourselves. She holds fast to all who spring from her being, continuously creating them into life. All beings awaken and sleep, develop and decay in the presence of her holy love. In the end, all are finally enfolded into her eternal presence. Rather than Mary being the figure who functions to make a distant patriarchal God close, a more adequate theology of the Spirit makes clear that God already is inexpressibly near. This interiority of God to creation can be effectively evoked in the image of a woman, matrix of all that is gifted with life.

Lastly, the understanding of God as source of recreative energy is one more element that can be drawn from the marian tradition. "May is Mary's month," writes the poet Hopkins, and all that is swelling, bursting, and blooming so beautifully does so under her aegis. Marian symbols entwined with earth and water, vines, flowers, eggs, birds, and young animals evoke her connection with fertility and the motherhood of the earth.[44] The theme of overturning the ancient sin and beginning again, so connected with her historic pregnancy, finds its parallel in the springtime renewal of the earth. As Anselm praised: "plenty flows from you to make all creatures green again."[45] Attributing this imagery directly to God allows us to affirm that it is God's own being that is the source of transforming energy among all creatures. She initiates novelty, instigates change, transforms what is dead into new stretches of life. Fertility is intimately related to her creative divine power. It is she who is ultimately playful, fascinating, pure and wise, luring human beings into the "more." As mover and encourager of what tends toward stasis, God herself is ever young and imaginative, taking joy in creating and recreating all that exists.

Maternity with its nurturing warmth; unbounded compassion; power that protects, heals and liberates; all-embracing immanence; recreative energy—thus is borne out the hypothesis that the marian tradition is a rich source of divine imagery. Not just "feminine dimensions" but analogies for the whole incomprehensible mystery of the divine are available here. In a manner of speaking, Mary has treasured these things in her heart (Luke 2:19), awaiting the day when what has been guarded in her symbolism can find its rightful place in the living God again.

PASTORAL JUDGMENT

This chapter has proceeded under the rubric of the cul-de-sac, tracing an influential path of contemporary interpretation that this book's proposal to understand Mary in the communion of saints will not take. We will not seek to understand Mary as the maternal or feminine face of God because this stops female images from pointing all the way to the loving God who is their true source. Such limitation allows patriarchal construals of the divine to perdure and blocks women from their full identification with the divine image and likeness. At the same time, there is a hugely important lesson to be learned from this whole development, namely, the capacity of the female figure to represent God. The fact that divine mercy and power have indeed been successfully carried in the image of Mary reveals how theomorphic women actually are. Not just Mary's face but the face of every woman is created in the image and likeness of God. Not just Mary's vocation but that of every woman and man is to partner with Holy Wisdom in bringing about the reign of mercy and peaceful justice. Such a strategy does no dishonor to Mary, for beneath the rich evocations of the divine feminine which Catholic devotion has celebrated in her symbol for centuries exists an actual, powerful female model of holiness.[46] Relieved of her historic burden of safeguarding female images of the divine and positively signaling the depth of women's dignity vis-à-vis God, Mary becomes free to rejoin the community of saints.

Fully aware of the logic of this approach, some of my colleagues have nevertheless sounded a salutary warning. If one redirects all this female symbolism back to God in a church that remains institutionally patriarchal, then will it not get lost again? The marian shrines, devotions, titles, sacramentals, and elaborate theologies of maternal mediation are all keeping something womanly alive at a time when it still has no other official place to go. Transferring these symbols to God without reforming the church's language and practice could result in a totally masculine public square, similar to the Protestant churches before women moved into official ministry.

In a pastoral sense I think this criticism is well taken. I recall one Sunday evening in Munich after the devotion of benediction of the Blessed Sacrament had concluded in a great baroque church. Most people left; the lights were all but turned out. In the marian chapel at the back, however, a small knot of people knelt or stood. One man buried his face in his hands; others prayed with an intensity that was palpable. The silence was absolute, the darkness broken only by flickering candles. For a long moment it seemed as if no one even breathed. Here, I thought, an encounter with the living God is taking place. The high altar is abandoned; the clergy have left. In this cavelike setting the loving Mother who gains the heart's absolute trust is found.

On another day in Mexico City, I sensed the same experience happening in the great plaza outside the cathedral wherein the original image of Our Lady of Guadalupe resides. It was December 12th, the feast day of *la Moreñita*. Under a blazing sky, bands of people arrived from different villages. Entering the plaza from all directions, each group announced its arrival with live music; all carried bright red flowers. Processing across the plaza, faces concentrated, lips moving, people dropped to their knees, crossing the cobblestones in this difficult position of humility and need. Amid the sun and the mariachi music, these people, mostly poor, honored their Guadalupe with an ardor that was palpable, a sense that only intensified when they finally gained the presence of the sacred image inside.

Clearly it would not do to take away these places and experiences in the present patriarchal situation of the church and secular condition of the world. Seeking the living God in prayer and letting oneself be found by the Spirit are precious acts, and there are times and places where devotion to Mary mediates this encounter. All the same, many people do not resonate with this pattern of mediation, especially the young in postindustrialized society. And some, especially women, are becoming increasingly comfortable with prayer to God herself mediated in female imagery. Thus I am not making a judgment about pastoral practice, which needs to be done with wisdom and prudence in accord with the needs of local people. But I am making a theological judgment, the practical effect of which will work out over time. For the renewal of the doctrine of God liberated from the restrictions of patriarchy, for empowering women to claim their own dignity made in her image and likeness, and for the transformation of the church into a community of the discipleship of equals, this female imagery needs to disperse beyond Mary back to its source. Let God have her own maternal face. Let Miriam the Galilean woman rejoin the community of disciples.

PART 3

A Way Forward

5

A Modest Proposal

FROM TRANSCENDENT SYMBOL
TO HISTORICAL PERSON

I am proposing that one fruitful way to work out a liberating feminist theology of Mary is to locate her in the communion of saints and there to remember her, dangerously and consolingly, as a woman with her own particular history among her contemporaries and before God. At first glance placing Mary in the company of the saints may seem strange to those accustomed to more traditional Catholic practice, even though the title "Saint Mary" adorns many churches, schools, and other institutions. It may even seem a diminishment of the honor that is her due as the *Theotokos,* or bearer of God. But at root it grants her the greatest honor the Christian tradition acknowledges for a human being, namely, the core dignity of being created in the divine image and likeness and gifted, in community with others, with a graced relationship to the living God.

The idea that this woman should be thought of in historical terms bears closer scrutiny because the history of marian doctrine and devotion gives clear evidence that this has not been standard practice. The fact that Miriam of Nazareth has been depicted in so many diverse ways, from the humble handmaid to the powerful Queen of Heaven, indicates that the human imagination has been at work crafting symbols. This holds true not only for artistic and literary depictions but also for some biblical and doctrinal texts. By contrast, situating this woman in the communion of saints focuses on the fact that she is in truth a very concrete historical human being with her own ultimate destiny in God. A basic issue that arises at the outset, then, is whether and to what extent the figure of Mary is or should be symbolic. Over the years my mind has changed considerably on this issue.

One of the most promising approaches of recent years for both ecumenism and spirituality has been the move to symbolize Mary as the ideal or perfect disciple. Writing in the late 1960s from a Protestant perspective, theologian Wolfhart Pannenberg mounted an intriguing argument in favor of this idea. There is a significant formal difference between christology and mariology, he suggested. This difference lies in the fact that christology is the explication of the meaning of a historical event, namely, the life, death, and resurrection of Jesus the Christ, while mariology, possessing no such historical basis, is the personification in symbolic fashion of the characteristics of the new humankind of faith.[1] In other words, because so very few historically attested events surround the figure of Mary, her *persona* is more open to being shaped by diverse projections regarding the virtues and values of the ideal believer.

This insight triggered biblical scholar Raymond E. Brown's interest to the point that he decided to test it by a quest for the historical Mary. After scrutinizing the four gospels and other biblical data, he returned from his travels rather empty-handed, declaring "I find confirmed more than I had ever expected Pannenberg's contention that the NT does not give us much knowledge of Mary as a historical character."[2] It is precisely this lack of knowledge, he continued, that allows the figure of Mary to lend itself more freely than that of Jesus to a symbolic trajectory through Christian history. Luke and John took the first step in this direction by depicting Mary as the ideal disciple both at the annunciation (Luke) and at the foot of the cross with others (John). In later ages the church continuously translated the virtues of discipleship into descriptions of Mary's character. In the fourth century, when martyrdom had ceased and asceticism was on the rise, Mary became the model of virtuous women who withdrew into the desert to lead the abstinent life of the nun: voice low, eyes shut when undressing, heart always in prayer. In the Middle Ages she became the fair lady of the knights, the symbol of chaste love. The Renaissance saw her become the tender mother caring for her spiritual children. In the early twentieth century she appeared as part of the "holy family," the church's rebuttal to divorce. Influenced by the women's movement in the 1970s, the U.S. Catholic bishops hailed her as model of the liberated woman. Brown's survey led him to conclude: "One cannot historicize all these diverse and even contradictory pictures of Mary; but in having her assume these symbolic roles, the Church has been contemporizing the ideal of Christian discipleship. The Church has been diagnosing a way in which Christians of various times needed to hear the word of God and keep it."[3]

This insight is a valuable tool for critical interpretation as far as it goes. For one thing, it connects Mary deeply with the community of believers rather than letting her stand alone as an exotic character. For another, it places emphasis on her active relationship to God in faith and charity rather than to the gendered roles of handmaid, virgin, and mother that women find so problematic. Intellectually, the symbolic interpretation of ← Mary as the ideal disciple sheds light on all manner of marian statements, images, and practices that through this filter can ultimately point to humanity's graced relationship with God. Reflecting the custom of honoring Mary with special prayers and ceremonies during the fertile month of May in the northern hemisphere, Karl Rahner expressed this in memorable fashion: "It is quite possible to say that when we are involved in our May devotions, we are engaged in a Christian understanding of the human situation. It is God's word concerning us that we are there concerned with, a blessed and holy understanding of our own life."[4] By honoring Mary we are ultimately saying something about ourselves, namely, that God has addressed us with a word of grace and called us to discipleship.

The Second Vatican Council took the idea of Mary as the ideal disciple and cast it into an explicitly ecclesial framework. It teaches that Mary is a model or type of the church, the one who signifies to all the people of God their own call to be fully committed "in the matter of faith, charity, and perfect union with Christ."[5] Indeed, the council writes, while celebrating the annual liturgical cycle focused on the mysteries of Christ, the church also gazes at Mary. There the church "joyfully contemplates, as in a faultless model, that which she herself wholly desires and hopes to be."[6] Carrying this insight forward, the U.S. Catholic bishops teach in a pastoral letter that "the Church saw herself symbolized in the Virgin Mary. The story of Mary, as the Church has come to see her, is at the same time the record of the Church's own self-discovery." This means that "what the Church has said about the effect of redemption in Mary, she has affirmed in other ways and at other times of us all."[7] Theology of Mary is thus closely linked to ecclesiology insofar as she typifies the community redeemed by God's grace. This approach has been enormously fruitful for ecumenical understanding, giving Protestant thinkers a way into the conversation about Mary, the figure and symbol of the church, while safeguarding the Reformation sensibility that Christ alone saves by grace through faith alone.[8] Despite its subliminal androcentrism, as we have seen, it has also borne fruit in feminist theology. Rosemary Radford Ruether reasons, for example, that as "the feminine face of the church," the symbol of Mary serves to criticize ecclesiastical sexism and points to the full participation of women in the church's life and ministry.[9]

Some time ago, enthusiastic about this idea of Mary as a symbol of discipleship in the church, I joined the conversation with an essay about language. I saw a problem in the way Catholic speech about Mary tended to be taken literally in a historicized way, while Protestant speech about Mary, what little there was of it, tended to reduce statements about her to mere meditations, as if she herself had nothing to do with the history of God with the world. Seeking a more satisfactory middle ground between these two, my study sought to illuminate the meaning of talk about Mary, from popular hymns to official doctrines, by using Paul Ricoeur's analysis of the symbol. In brief, the thesis of my argument stated:

> Theological statements about Mary have a symbolic structure, so that while they refer immediately and in an obvious way to this one woman, they reach their intended theological referent when interpreted finally as statements about the church, the community of faithful disciples, of which she is a member and in which she participates.[10]

Unlike a sign, a symbol participates in the reality which it signifies. According to Ricoeur, furthermore, a symbol has a structure of double intentionality which carries the human subject beyond the literal intent of an image or word into the surplus of meaning conveyed by it. For this to happen, one must first make a wager that the symbol will prove of value and so enter into its circle. Dwelling in its first level of meaning, one is carried through the literal reference by its surplus of meaning to what it signifies, which in the case of religious symbols is the infinite mystery of the living God. So too, I aimed to show, does the symbol of Mary serve the life of faith. This symbol itself is created from the church's experience of encounter with a gracious God.

When we dwell with this symbol it gives rise to thought about the life of discipleship lived in response to God's salvific approach in Jesus Christ. My examples drew on language about Mary as mother, virgin, pilgrim of faith, prophet, and disciple, all of which ultimately deliver awareness of the graced life and calling of the people of the *ekklēsia*. "Such speech does so not by sleight of hand," I argued, "but by its very character as symbolic speech whose origin lies in the graced reality of the church finding expression in the image of this key member."[11]

Such a hermeneutic, I suggested, can be especially helpful in giving an intelligible reading of the two much disputed marian dogmas declared in the modern era. The U.S. Catholic bishops recommended this interpretive key when they wrote that the Immaculate Conception and Assumption "are not isolated privileges but mysteries filled with meaning for the whole Church."[12] At the beginning of life, the Immaculate Conception witnesses to the grace of God freely offered without merit to every human being who comes into the world, a grace that is always more powerful than sin. At the end of life, "Mary in her Assumption, as in other aspects of her God-gifted personality, is a figure of the Church as perfected through union with Christ."[13] This point had already been made by Vatican II, which sees in Mary in heaven "a sign of sure hope and solace for the pilgrim people of God,"[14] signaling as she does that the corporate human journey will reach its blessed goal.

Despite the benefits of interpreting Mary as a symbol of discipleship, I have grown increasingly dissatisfied with this position taken as a first, only, or predominant step.[15] One reason lies in the inability of this symbol, given its emphasis on Mary's perfect response to grace, to name and account for sin in the life of the graced individual. When this symbol is placed in an ecclesial context, furthermore, it whitewashes the sinfulness of the church of which there is such ample, scandalous, public evidence. Nor can it account for all the data of tradition. In numerous instances marian images have clearly functioned not as symbols of discipleship but as symbols of either the eternal feminine embodied in the ideal woman or the maternal face of God.

My greatest dissatisfaction arises from the fallout of a symbolic Mary on the flourishing of women in all the concreteness of their actual histories. What happens to a woman when she is made a symbol? How much of her own reality is lost? One amazing loss that has resulted in Mary's case is her historical Jewish identity. This is totally eclipsed in the symbol of Mary as the ideal Christian disciple. Perhaps some would say that this is not too important. But, to engage in a thought experiment, if someone in the future were to lift up the story of my life for inspiration and omit my commitment to the Christian faith or, even more strangely, describe me as a member of a community with highly developed doctrines and structures that evolved only long after my lifetime, I would be uneasy. I would feel that something important had been left out, indeed, that the depiction lacked a certain truthfulness regarding the life I actually led.

And what happens to all other women when one woman is made a symbol of discipleship? I have in mind Mary Magdalene, whose discipleship entailed following Jesus on the roads of Galilee, using her own resources to support his ministry, going up to Jerusalem on his last trip, keeping vigil by the cross while he died, being part of the burial party, leading the other women to the surprisingly empty tomb, encountering the risen Christ in her grief, and preaching the good news to the disbelieving, ridiculing male disciples. Without her courageous initiative and witness and that of the "many other women" (Mark 15:41) with her, there would be no continuity in the story surrounding the end of Jesus' life, no paschal narrative. Holding up a mirror to the struggle over women's ministry in the early church, later apocryphal gospels depict Peter's attempts to suppress her leadership in the community. Losing Magdalene into the false fog of a fallen but repentant woman has had incalculably negative consequences, which is why women greet the recovery of her image as "apostle to the apostles" so intensely. Many others too, outstanding among them Martha of Bethany, Joanna, and the Samaritan woman, along with church leaders such as deacon Phoebe of Cenchreae, apostle Junia of Rome, and missionary Prisca with her husband Aquila also model discipleship in excellent ways. Does not loading the ideal disciple image on one woman lead to the exclusion of all the others—another version of the "alone of all her sex" critique?

Moreover, we have seen what happens to a woman who is made a symbol largely through the male imagination in a patriarchal context. A large portion of men's own experience and needs shapes the symbol to the detriment of actual women's human and religious well-being. Insofar as this symbolizing has gone on in an institution publicly governed solely by men, it also has social-political effects, idealizing one woman as the flip side of marginalizing the rest. Symbolizing is rife with problems. In truth, I know that religious worldviews are inevitably symbolic, reaching beyond the immediate here and now to encounter divine presence in the depths of the concrete world and beyond it. Speech about Mary arising within a religious milieu will therefore always have a symbolic character. But my view now is that to be true to this woman who actually lived a life some two thousand years ago, and to honor her in a liberating way, whatever we say should be tightly moored to her historical reality at every point.

Hence, the proposal to interpret Mary within the company of the saints entails this corollary: *First and foremost Mary is not a model, a type, an archetype, a prototype, an icon, a representative figure, a theological idea, an ideological cipher, a metaphor, a utopian principle, a feminine principle, a feminine essence, the image of the eternal feminine, an ideal disciple, ideal woman, ideal mother, a myth, a persona, a corporate personality, an every-woman, a cultural artifact, a literary device, a motif, an exemplar, a para-digm, a sign, or in any other way a religious symbol.* All of these terms are drawn from contemporary religious writing. To the contrary, as with any human being, as with every woman, *she is first and foremost herself.* I am not saying that the contemporary religious imagination cannot make use of her in a symbolic way. But it is the luminous density of her historical existence as a graced human person that attracts my attention. As Rahner argues, "We, however supremely elevated our spiritual nature may be, still remain concrete historical beings, and for this reason we cannot consider this history as something unimportant for the highest activity of our spirit, the search for God."[16]

Mary is a concrete woman of history who had her own life to figure out, a first-century Jewish woman in a peasant village with a culture very different from twenty-first century, postindustrial society, though similar to peasant culture in those countries where it still exists. About the chronology and psychology of her life we know very little. We need to acknowledge this void in our knowledge, respect it, and inhabit it knowingly. Then we can rightly interpret the Christian discourse of the gospel writers who present glimpses of her life connected with the coming of the Messiah and his community. This location in the gospels offers good reason to think of her as a woman of faith, one whose life was a "pilgrimage of faith," in the poetic words of Vatican II.[17] Even these gospel depictions, of course, have a symbolic character, reflecting the theology of the different evangelists. There is no raw historical data. The construals of later interpreters, including women today who constructively ponder the meaning of her story for life and faith, also enter into the realm of the symbolic, being a type of religious discourse. My point is not that we can dispense with symbolic construals, but that because we are dealing with an actual person, however much unknown, her historical reality should tether down insight at every point.

A PNEUMATOLOGICAL THEOLOGY OF MARY

The proposal to interpret Mary in the communion of saints situates our thinking in the third article of the creed, which testifies to God the Holy

Spirit. "We believe in the Holy Spirit, the holy catholic church, the communion of saints, the forgiveness of sins, the resurrection of the body and life everlasting," the Apostles' Creed affirms. The nonbiblical phrase *communio sanctorum* was a late addition to this creed, but in the west its sweeping, inclusive meaning was ancient. As Nicetas, bishop of Remesiana, explained to his people in the fifth century:

> What is the church but the congregation of all saints? From the beginning of the world patriarchs, prophets, martyrs, and all other righteous people who have lived, or who are now alive, or who shall live in time to come, comprise the church, since they have been sanctified by one faith and manner of life, and sealed by one Spirit, and so made one body, of which Christ is declared to be the head, as the scripture says. . . . So you believe that in this church you will attain to the communion of saints.[18]

Clearly here the communion of saints stands for a relationship among all holy people of all ages, including the whole company of heaven, which is anticipated and partially realized in the community of the church on earth. In addition to this text's recognition of illustrious persons who have died, Jewish and Christian alike, it also includes the future in a fascinating way, for generations as yet unborn also belong to this community. Similarly, the whole company is not settled in the present but moving toward the eschatological fullness yet to come—"you will attain." The whole church through time shares in a communion of hope in the Spirit.

Placing a theology of Mary within the communion of saints in this creedal framework has a double advantage. It profoundly connects her life to that of other women and men whose lives are shaped by response to the Spirit of God. And it allows female imagery of God, traditionally associated with the Spirit, to play a guiding role in interpretation. Already the structure of this proposal prevents major problems of the patriarchal marian image from arising, chief among them the idealized isolation of a patriarchally feminine Mary and the gender system that interprets her relationship to God in masculine/feminine stereotypes. We are seeking to understand her meaning in light of the third article of the creed, which professes belief in the Holy Spirit, Lord and Giver of life, who makes people holy and who in the end raises the dead to life, which article at the same time is never separated from the first article of the creed regarding God who creates the world out of love, nor from the second article regarding Jesus the Wisdom of God, born of Mary, crucified, and risen for the world's salvation. Taken together, all three articles of the creed constitute the framework for this book's theological interpretation of Mary:

• First and last there is God, Creator of heaven and earth, whose care is bent on the well-being of the world, humankind and the natural world together. When the antagonistic forces of evil tear apart the world that God so loves, the divine response is to "be there" in order to heal, redeem, and liberate. The voice from the burning bush reveals as much: "I have seen the misery of my people who are in Egypt; I have heard their cry on account of their taskmasters; I know well what they are suffering; therefore I have come down to deliver them . . ." (Exod. 3:7–8). In the history of suffering and joy on this planet, the bitter question of whether life has any meaning has received a positive and unique answer: God's own faithfulness guarantees the good purpose of life. Identifying especially with the poor, the exploited, those stunned by meaningless agony, the sinner, and the dead, divine concern wants to re-create and save. The flaming bush made clear that God's name is YHWH, "I am who I am," the dynamism of which means "I will be with you." Divine honor lies in the flourishing of what God freely created out of love.

• The nucleus of God's saving history with the world lies in the person, life, and destiny of Jesus, God's only beloved given as a gift to humankind. His message and lifestyle embody divine care for the world, especially those most marginalized and in need; his ministry sounds the call to others to join in solidarity with this way of loving. Jesus advocated for human beings as God's cause and suffered for it, even unto death. The great Amen resounding in his resurrection from the dead affirms God's solidarity with the suffering of the world beyond all expectations. Now it is disclosed that God indeed is love; that sin, suffering, and meaninglessness do not ultimately define the future. New life awaits.

• The continuing presence of God in Christ is accomplished through the power of the Holy Spirit. Effective throughout the world and in the heart of every person, the Spirit in the church awakens discipleship, which allows the history of Jesus the Living One to continue through time. Remembering his life, death, and resurrection, the church is empowered to follow him in passion for God and loving care for the world: "the living community is the only real reliquary of Jesus."[19] Gathered together by the Spirit, this "little flock" has as its mission to witness to the effective presence of Christ, bent over suffering. "By following Jesus, taking our bearings from him and allowing ourselves to be inspired by him, by sharing in his *Abba* experience and his selfless support for 'the least of these,' and thus entrusting our own destiny to God, we allow the history of Jesus, the living one, to continue in history as a piece of living christology, the work of the Spirit among us."[20] In the course of history, suffering multiplies, massive public evil has its day, the death of each individual keeps breaking the threads of human flourishing. Therefore the work of the Spirit does not stop in this known world. The church treasures the word of future resurrection as an eschatological promise. While final salvation reaches far beyond words or imagination, hope is awakened here and now in fragments of healing, liberation, justice, peace, and love. Without the mediation of these human experiences, the word of promise is illusory. With them, hope is carried forward in history to that day beyond time when God will wipe away all tears.

I propose to read Mary's story in light of the mystery of salvation coming graciously from God through Jesus in the power of the Spirit, made present in the community of disciples for the world, and oriented, through fragmentary experiences of salvation in the midst of suffering, to an eschatological future that exceeds all expectations: a world without tears. The paradigm of Mary as Spirit-filled friend of God and prophet within the circle of disciples, this grand company of saints living and dead, situates her within the basic Christian confession without distortion and with new potential to empower the praxis of liberating faith to the benefit of women's flourishing, even now. The primary angle of vision will be pneumatological, seeing Mary as a graced woman. Since she is embraced by and responsive to Spirit-Sophia, she is a sister to all who partner with the Spirit in the struggle for the coming of the reign of God.

ISSUES OF INTERPRETATION

I want to flag two danger zones where this project could run aground. One is the tendency to make Mary into someone like the intended audience of this book, educated, mostly middle-class Christians. The other is the idea that the privileges defined for Mary in the course of the development of doctrine, especially her freedom from original sin, entail her removal from the struggles of life.

Retrieving the Historical Woman

Working out this proposal requires that we critically remember Mary with her own concrete story. This woman shares with the vast majority of people, women in particular, the circumstance that most of their historical life has been little recorded in official versions of important events. Our main sources for her life are the gospels of the New Testament, which carry early Christian depictions of her words and deeds in the context of their witness to Jesus Christ. How to read these texts? Today, the field of feminist biblical hermeneutics is vigorously developing methods that tease out the significance of women mentioned in patriarchal texts and discover new, liberating meaning in their struggles and victories. At the same time, ongoing archaeological discoveries, historical-critical and literary methods, and use of the social sciences and comparative anthropology, which coalesce in the contemporary quest for the historical Jesus, also serve the search for other historical figures. Crafting a theology of Mary in the communion of saints will entail working with all of these scholarly approaches for a glimpse of the historical Galilean Jewish woman. In the process, her socioeconomic, religious, and cultural difference from ourselves will become overwhelmingly clear.

The gap between her world and ours can be bridged, cautiously, by the notion of "solidarity in difference," developed in political and feminist theology to describe the optimum relationship between persons in situations that differ. Both words in the phrase are crucially important. More than simple association with other like-minded people, solidarity has an edge. It is a type of communion that forges deep connection between people in such a way that the sufferings and joys of one become part of the personal concern of others and a spur to transformative action. In situations of tremendous injustice, solidarity among the oppressed themselves leads to actions that resist, hope, and celebrate even in the midst of suffering. For those not directly affected by the particular situation, solidarity is expressed in conversion toward those who suffer, not just being affected emotionally by their pain but choosing to be responsible by joining the struggle for life. In the process, a liberating community of common interest is created. A fascinating aspect of solidarity that makes it useful for this project is that it can also create an alliance between the living and the dead. By emphasizing the common character of human destiny and its unfulfilled promise, solidarity stretches backward through time to affirm that the dead, even the most insignificant and wiped out, are important in their lives, which thereby encourages the living who are still struggling to bring about a more beneficial future. Women struggling for equal human dignity today are tapping into huge reserves of energy by discovering links with women of previous generations. Identifying parallel experiences of suffering and victory under civil, ecclesiastical, and multiple other oppressions that weigh them down, they touch spirit to spirit and draw strength to continue the struggle. For Christian faith, the communion of saints is a symbol of this solidarity that transcends time. Placing Miriam of Nazareth in this community creates a graced connection between her life and our own.

At the same time, there is a danger in the practice of solidarity. Without critical analysis of their own social location, persons of dominant groups tend to project their own way of being in the world onto everyone else, thus erasing the actual suffering of those who differ. African American theorists were the first to level this critique at the tendency of women in the majority race and class to overlook differences among women, assuming their own experience to be universal and folding others into their descriptions. In Australia the aboriginal womanist voice rings with the same critique.[21] By so doing, majority women ignore their own position as oppressors, the complex power relations between privileged and nonprivileged women, and their complicity in the racial stereotyping of men of oppressed groups. From the standpoint of women in poor, marginalized, and oppressed communities, a universal, nonproblematic solidarity is tantamount to a stifling manipulation of their truth, while racism and classism perdure uncontested in the hearts of their white, middle-class sisters. Thanks to this critique, and despite some backsliding, feminist liberation theologies now attempt to hold themselves accountable to differences among women's situations and practical concerns worldwide, appreciating the fact that for the sake of both truth and justice, as Lisa Cahill writes, "the experience of privileged, educated women, those with a voice in politics or the academy, should not merely be projected onto the lives of other women who differ by class, race, ethnicity, or even historical era."[22] The challenge now becomes to respect the full play of women's diversity, summed up in the notion of difference, a concept that is an intense focus of contemporary feminist theorizing.

Shawn Copeland notes how unfortunate it is that the term "difference" rings with negative connotations in our culture, where it points to the presence of a factor disruptive to the harmony of the community and labels those to be avoided or treated with suspicion and disdain.[23] By contrast, feminist critical theory maintains that difference is an existential principle that honors the integrity of the person by giving full play to her historical concreteness. There is no ideal, archetypal "woman." There are only real women whose lives are embedded in various bodily, interpersonal, economic, political, and social relations in historical times and geographic places, for better or worse. When acknowledged within a relationship of solidarity, difference, far from being a regrettable obstacle to community, can be a creative, enriching, community-shaping force. Rather than construing otherness in a hierarchical rank of better and worse, feminist theory envisions that we can learn to grant equal worth to all persons in their concrete difference. Honoring difference cares for life in all its uniqueness and celebrates the rich, radiant combinations that constitute women as well as men and children as images of God. Community then comes about not as the result of suppressing differences and homogenizing everyone into sameness, but by respecting and celebrating persons in all their differences within multiple larger narratives and actions for the common good. The poet Audre Lorde evokes this truth with her koan-like words: "Difference must not be merely tolerated, but seen as a fund of necessary polarities between which our creativity can spark like a dialectic. . . . Difference is that raw and powerful connection from which our personal power is forged."[24]

With this understanding, we guard against a major pitfall that bedevils retrieval of the historical memory of Mary within the communion of saints, namely, erasing her cultural difference. As Bernadette Brooten points out, "A twentieth-century Palestinian Muslim woman may live in greater historical continuity with a second-century Palestinian Jewish or Christian woman than does a North American Christian or Jewish woman."[25] As with the whole company of the saints, what each woman suffered and accomplished, what each one meant for the hope and self-understanding of others in her world, cannot be repeated and may even strike us as strange. Likewise, the present situation with its possibilities and terrors has never existed before. The category of "solidarity in difference" works to prevent memory from making women of old, Miriam of Nazareth included, into merely mirror images of ourselves. It promotes instead appreciation rather than rejection of the otherness of their ways. Creative action in the Spirit can then spring from this deep, nonviolent connectedness.

Retrieving the Human Woman

Working out this proposal also requires that we grant full credence to Mary's genuine engagement in human life. The glorifying and maximalizing tendencies apparent in much traditional thought credited her with supernatural gifts that effectively removed her from the human condition. These proclivities have taken the doctrine of the Immaculate Conception, which declares that Mary was conceived without original sin, to mean that she lived a life like that of Adam and Eve in the garden of paradise before the fall. She had special privileges that enabled her to negotiate the troubles of life effortlessly in a world whose historical struggle was not her own. Exempt from human passions, preserved from temptations, especially those of a sexual nature, immune from wrestling with issues, spared ambiguity when it came to decisions, always in full possession of her wits, clearly knowing God's plan for herself and her son and more than willing to carry it out, she moved through life with unearthly ease. The one allowable exception is the sorrow she felt at the cross, but even here, it is said, she willingly sacrificed her son for the redemption of the world. In this interpretation Mary's uniqueness dehumanizes her. She was perfect. Cocooned in a bubble of privileges, her very humanity is bleached of blood and guts.

A more promising avenue opens up when we realize that being conceived without original sin does not mean being conceived in a vacuum. The opposite of sin is grace, and the Immaculate Conception means that Mary was uniquely blessed at the outset with the gift of grace, God's own self-communication. She was enveloped from the beginning in the love of God. One German phrase for the December 8th celebration of such mercy felicitously captures this meaning, calling it "the feast of the be-gracing of Mary." Working this out in categories of theological anthropology, Rahner points out the ramification that whatever Mary has ultimately reveals something of God's way with all human beings. Her own situation as first of the redeemed in Christ anticipates the gift of grace offered to all humankind in the incarnation. "We too are those who are called, who are enveloped from beginning to end by God's power, love, and fidelity to us even in what is most individual and our own."[26] In its broadest reach the Immaculate Conception means that God takes the initiative to surround the life of all human beings with redemptive love and unrepentant fidelity. The point is, while this doctrine speaks in the language of the absence of sin, in essence it is all about the presence of grace.

Mapping the meaning of grace in contemporary Catholic theology, one is struck by how clearly it holds up *uncreated* grace as of first importance. This is in marked contrast to the neoscholastic theology of the preconciliar era, which dealt primarily with *created* grace. The latter refers to a gift

given to the creature by God, especially sanctifying grace, a habit or quality infused into the human soul that removes the stain of sin. By contrast,
uncreated grace, as the term suggests, refers to God's own self-communication offered as gift to human persons: "grace is first and foremost God's
self-communication and presence to human existence."[27] In grace the
mystery of the living God who is infinitely gracious becomes present not
as origin of the world and not as incarnate Word but as Spirit dwelling at
the heart of human existence. Put more biblically, "the love of God has
been poured into our hearts by the Holy Spirit who has been given to us"
(Rom. 5:5).

The change of focus from created to uncreated grace, from grace being
first and foremost a spiritual "substance" to grace being God's own self-
communication, completely reorients thinking. Rather than grace being a
measurable quantity that connects human beings to God, it is the interpersonal gift of the Spirit of God herself at the heart of existence; in
Rahner's inimitable phrasing, "The Giver himself is the gift."[28] Rather than
something that can be rather easily lost by sin and regained by repentance,
grace remains as God's permanent offer of love and thereby of salvation to
the creature, an offer that cannot be extinguished by the grossest sin.
Rather than something extrinsic added on to natural human life, grace is
constitutive of the human condition, meaning that God's presence as offer
of salvation is historically part of human existence. Therefore, rather than
grace being scarce or available only within the Christian sphere, grace is
universal, offered always and everywhere to all people thanks to God's universal saving will. Rather than something ethereal that cannot be experienced, grace can be tasted indirectly through the mediation of created
things and events. Rather than diminish or subvert the wholeness of
human nature, grace enhances and fulfills it through union with the living
God who is the goal of all creation including the human heart. Finally,
rather than detaching people's interest from the world on the assumption
that a dichotomy exists between divine interest and earthly matters, grace
turns persons toward the world as the locus of God's presence and, given
the drama of redemption, the place that really does matter in the end. This
gives importance to all things human: joys and sufferings, the body and
sexuality, relationships of intimacy and community, creativity and intellectual effort, formation of beneficial social structures, struggle and resistance against oppressive forces, and action for long-term peace, justice,
and the integrity of creation.

The major effects of this shift in the "cartography of grace"[29] continue to reverberate throughout all of theology and ethics, not least in reflection about Mary. The "singular grace" which, according to the doctrinal definition, Mary received at her conception refers to what the community affirms to be God's self-communication, which is unfathomable. Since grace humanizes rather than dehumanizes, since in Rahner's equation "nearness to God and genuine human autonomy grow in direct rather than inverse proportion,"[30] then Mary's relationship to the Spirit creates her as a free, fully human being. She has to accomplish her life in the midst of the struggles of history, not angelically outside them. And since when did God's love ever preserve anyone from struggle? Rahner again makes the point: "The fact is, we often think holiness and absence of sin incompatible with ordinary life on this solid earth, where people laugh and cry, are born and die. We think holiness, when it actually exists, must take a 'heavenly' ethereal form, or at least can only prosper far removed from the sturdy everyday world of the ordinary human being, perhaps behind the walls of a cloister."[31] To the contrary, the grace of God plunges us into the heart of the world. Hence Mary's life was a real human journey. She searched, she felt anxious, she did not understand everything, she had to find her way from stage to stage of her life's passage.[32] Viewed from the outside, hers was a really commonplace and obscure life, that of "any average woman in any odd corner of a small country, far from the great stream of history, of civilization, and of politics."[33] Life did not treat her gently. She lived through the common human lot, "tears and tedium, distress and bitterness, agony and death, joy and light, courage and greatness, a whole long and always unprecedented human life."[34] Thérèse of Lisieux pointed to this truth when she pondered why she loved Mary. It was not because the mother of God received exceptional privileges that would remove her from the ordinary condition, "ravishings, miracles, ecstasies," and the like, but because she lived and suffered simply, like us, in the dark night of faith.[35] For all his marian maximalism, Boff likewise does not hesitate to involve Mary in all the existential contradictions of this life:

> Of course, to believe that Mary, by mystery's design, is without sin is not to believe that her life was a bed of roses. She partook of the blind, seemingly meaningless character of human existence. To say that she is immaculate does not mean that she did not suffer, that she was never troubled, or that she had no need for faith and hope. She was a daughter of earth, albeit blessed by heaven. She had human passions. Everything authentically human was present in her.[36]

To profess that Mary is graced in a special way is not to deny this but to affirm, in view of her vocation to be the woman through whom God became a child of earth, that God's personal, living presence was given to this woman of the people from her beginning.

This interpretation of what the Immaculate Conception does *not* mean finds a strong buttress in contemporary developments in christology. Here biblical scholarship and post-neoscholastic philosophies have opened up new awareness of the truly human reality of Jesus Christ. Rather than being an abstract individual with an *ersatz* human nature, he is "a real, genuine, limited human being with his own experience, an obedient human being, like us in all things except sin."[37] Despite his many gifts he needed to grow in self-awareness, discerning his vocation through his own historical experiences. His ministry and death were not preprogrammed but the result of decisions freely if not always easily made—recall the temptations in the desert, the agony in the garden, the cry of abandonment on the cross. His life was not playacting. Now it becomes harder to maintain a "Superman" model of Jesus' life that would see him as a mild-mannered worker in wood and stone on the outside, with secret, souped-up divine powers on the inside, as if his human mind and will were not utterly affected by his social location in history. All this is affirmed as a way of honoring, not denying, the powerful Christian belief in the Wisdom of God incarnate and casting it in an undeniably salvific mode: "For because he himself has suffered and been tempted, he is able to help those who are tempted.... For we do not have a high priest who is unable to sympathize with our weakness, but one who in every respect has been tempted as we are, yet without sinning" (Heb. 2:18 and 4:15).[38]

If this is the way the presence of God in nature and grace works in the case of Jesus, whom doctrine affirms as hypostatically united to the Word, then how much more so in the case of Mary, who is doctrinally always completely human. Deep relationship to God did not erase her humanity. Firmly rooted in history, this first-century woman lived with all the limitations and difficulties that being human inevitably entails. John Paul II's repeated references to Mary's own need for religious faith bear this out: her life was a pilgrimage of faith; she gave herself to God's word in the "dim light of faith"; like Abraham she had to "hope against hope"; though the mother of Christ, she was in contact with the mystery of his truth only through a "veil," having to be faithful even through the "night of faith."[39] In other words, even where it is most religiously crucial, she struggled through without extra advantages. Patricia Noone's humorous comment is particularly apt: Mary did not have the doctrine of the Immaculate Conception framed and hanging on her kitchen wall, assuring her that she was sinless and free from error.[40] Appreciating this historical slant, I would add a theological point: even if she did, it would not lift her feet off the ground. Understood as the personal, living, self-communication of God's Spirit to Mary at the outset of her life, the Immaculate Conception does not extract her from the challenges that come with life on this planet. Rather, in its peculiar, time-conditioned way, it fundamentally asserts the living God's self-gift to this woman who is called to a special vocation in salvation history. In so doing, it signals that when it comes to God's intent, grace is more original than sin.

To sum up: I propose a pneumatological interpretation of Mary, the historical, graced, human woman, that remembers her as our companion in the communion of saints. Entirely particular, lived out within the constraints of first-century patriarchal society, her life with its concrete details in no way functions as culturally normative for women's lives today, lives racing along in a world she never dreamed of. But the memory of her partnership with God through the power of the Spirit can create liberating energies for justice, especially given her low estate as poor and as female. In all her difference, Miriam of Nazareth abides in the circle of disciples as our sister, a poor woman of the people to whom God has done great things; a young Spirit-filled Jewish woman finding her joy in God; a woman vulnerable to violence in a patriarchal setting; a friend of God who made her own difficult choices with courage; a prophet whose word announced the awesome changes God's coming would bring about in this world; a God-bearer who had divinity dancing under her heart in developing human flesh; a married woman who with her husband toiled hard to provide for their family; a woman with a questioning mind who pondered what God was doing in the midst of her life; the mother of the itinerant preacher Jesus, terribly worried about his ministry; a middle-aged woman whose agonized grief over the public execution of her firstborn connects her with legions of bereaved women; an elder in the budding community of the church. She kept faith. We remember her. We connect her story with our own amid the searching narrative of the human race in its history of suffering and hope. We thereby find courage to enact the critical dream of God for the world. The wager I am making at the outset is that interpreting Mary in relation to the Spirit as a graced, concrete historical person amid the company of saints in heaven and on earth crafts a theology capable of promoting action on behalf of global justice and liberation, particularly empowering to the flourishing of women, coherent with elements of biblical, classical, and conciliar teaching, and productive of religious sense for our time.

6

***

Precedents

The danger of painting history with large brush strokes is that one omits particular distinctions and nuances, thereby ignoring the plurality and ambiguity inherent in any tradition and risking distortion. However, given the immense sprawl of the marian phenomenon, the search for precedents for this book's project makes such large brush strokes necessary. Aware of the distinction between popular devotion, reflective theology, and official doctrine, I am focusing here on theology, or the systematic ideas about Mary and her role that shaped prayer and preaching.

Painting a big picture, I postulate that over the two thousand years of western Catholic Christianity, thought about Mary fell into two roughly different patterns. During the first millennium, especially in its earlier centuries, theology, if it attended to Mary at all, understood her significance to lie largely within the economy of salvation centered on the mercy of God given in Christ through the Spirit. By contrast, the second millennium, especially in its later centuries, saw an increasing tendency to divorce Mary from this context, resulting in ever more rarified reflections on her privileges, powers, and glories. While the second millennium's isolating tendency can be found in the first, and while at its best the second millennium preserved an integrated view of Mary, these two patterns describe recognizably distinct patterns of marian theology in each era.

Continuing with large strokes, I submit that at the Second Vatican Council, the distinctive patterns of the first millennium and the second millennium came into conflict with each other. The first millennium won. Occurring as it did practically at the start of the third Christian millennium, the council's teaching points the way toward new interpretations of Mary more in accord with ancient patterns of belief while tempered by

114

contemporary intellectual assumptions, struggles, and spiritual practice. In this perspective, the immediate precedent for my proposal is Vatican II, whose major decision to integrate teaching on Mary into the document on the church opens a door through which feminist reflection can pass.

The First Millennium

The proposal to interpret Mary as a woman within the company of believers comes with an ancient pedigree in scripture, liturgy, and early Christian theology. None of these sources is created from an explicitly feminist stance; each in fact bears the stamp of the patriarchal context in which it was created. When interpreted with a feminist hermeneutic with its movements of both suspicion and remembrance, however, these sources turn out to be precedents that provide backing in the tradition for the theological placement of Mary among other women and men made holy by the Spirit.

The New Testament stories that mention Mary form a primary source from which all later interpretation arises. Whether seeing her along with Jesus' brothers in a negative light outside the circle of disciples as Mark does, or placing her in a genealogy of Jewish and Gentile ancestors as Matthew does, or presenting her as a woman of faith as Luke does, or symbolizing her at Cana and the cross as John does, the gospels mention her as part of the messianic coming of God's salvation. In this she does not stand alone but is one of many characters whose free participation is important for the total message of the gospel. Luke in particular sees Mary as a Spirit-filled woman deeply connected to the people of Israel and the emerging Christian community of disciples. The last Lukan depiction of Mary places her in the upper room along with 120 women and men disciples and the brothers of Jesus, all in prayer awaiting the coming of the Spirit. The last Johannine depiction of the mother of Jesus sees her joined in relationship to her sister, Mary the wife of Clopas, Mary Magdalene, and the disciple whom Jesus loved, forming one community born of the cross. In each gospel, Mary's particular relation to Jesus as his mother is explicitly mentioned. Her history is no one else's history. At the same time, in both literary and theological terms, her story is woven into the gracious work of the redeeming God along with the others present at the birth of the church. In the biblical view Mary is found within the great cloud of witnesses, a basic precedent for our proposal.

From the early centuries onward, the liturgy has addressed prayer to the trinitarian God according to a clear pattern: "to the Father through the Son in the unity of the Holy Spirit." In the age of persecution under the Roman empire, the community on earth began to think that the martyrs in heaven joined their eucharistic praise of God. Ever since, the central eucharistic prayer has made mention of the host of people who have died in Christ and whose memory swells the chorus of the church's worship. In its many permutations, this mention evokes mutual kinship between the people gathered on earth and the community in heaven. To cite texts currently in use in the Catholic Church: the first Eucharistic Prayer, which itself is based on the ancient Roman canon, twice remembers the saints in heaven. The first time, we pray in union with Mary; her husband, Joseph; certain apostles and martyrs who are called by name; and "all the saints." The second time, the prayer continues, "For ourselves, too, we ask some share in the fellowship of your apostles and martyrs, with John the Baptist, Stephen, Matthias, Barnabas, Ignatius, Alexander, Marcellinus, Peter, Felicity, Perpetua, Agatha, Lucy, Agnes, Cecilia, Anastasia, and all the saints." The sense arises of a whole community of God-seekers linked through time, praising the living God together. The mother of Jesus is part of this group. Eucharistic prayers of more recent vintage are replete with this same insight. The texts of the Mass of Reconciliation pray to the triune God: "Help us to work together for the coming of your kingdom, until at last we stand in your presence to share the life of the saints, in the company of the Virgin Mary and the apostles, and of our departed brothers and sisters whom we commend to your mercy" (I); and, "You have gathered us here around the table of your Son, in fellowship with the Virgin Mary Mother of God and all the saints. In that new world where the fullness of your peace will be revealed, gather people of every race, language, and way of life to share in the one eternal banquet with Jesus Christ the Lord" (II). Liturgical prayer places Mary in the company of the believers, living and dead, providing another precedent for our proposal.

In light of what was to come later in marian theology, the relative silence of the first three Christian centuries is remarkable. Most theologians do not even mention her. Even more striking, there was in those centuries no public, official veneration of Mary. The church celebrated feast days in honor of the martyrs who had witnessed to Christ even to the shedding of their blood, thereby encouraging faith in the rest of the people. Since Mary was not a martyr, she did not receive the community's regard in this formal way.

The main vehicle for driving theological attention to Mary in those years was the growing discussion about the identity of Jesus Christ. In that increasingly heated debate, ideas about her maternity were pressed into service to defend first the humanity and then the divinity of the Messiah. The earliest christological heresy, docetism, held that the body of Jesus was not true human flesh but only appeared to be so. Seeking to honor the transcendent dignity of God by protecting divinity from contact with the material world, this view argued that Jesus' body was a kind of camouflage that allowed God to be seen and heard on earth, but it was not the same stuff of which Adam and Eve and their descendants were made. To counteract this idea, which strikes at the very reality of the incarnation, theologians turned to Mary. They evoked her historic pregnancy to ensure the human authenticity of Jesus' body. One docetic group, the Valentinians, had advanced the notion that Jesus passed through Mary the way water passes through a tube: two different substances, one not affecting the other.[1] In contrast to this view, the Apostles' Creed incorporated the phrase that Jesus was born *ex Maria virgine*, "*of* or *from* the Virgin Mary," that is, out of her body. He is made from the same human stuff she is. Consequently, he is in solidarity with the rest of humanity according to the flesh.[2]

Once the divinity of Christ had been formally confessed at Nicaea in 325, conflict flared up over how to understand the unity of human and divine natures in the one person of Jesus Christ. In one corner, the school of Antioch endorsed a moral view of the unity of his two natures, seeing Jesus Christ as the human being in whom the divine Word dwells, similar to the way God dwells in the temple. While presenting a rather weak view of unity in Christ, so that he could be said to act at times through one nature (hungry in his humanity) and at times through his other nature (working miracles through his divinity), this christology had the advantage of preserving the distinction of natures and thereby guaranteeing Jesus' genuine humanity. In this school the preferred title for Mary was *Christotokos,* or Christ-bearer, meaning that she was mother of the human being who is indwelt by the Logos and who is thereby the Christ. In the other corner, the school of Alexandria argued for a stronger, ontological form of union in which the divine Son of God personally united himself to human nature. While safeguarding the unity of natures in the person of Christ, this notion tended to dilute his humanity, seeing it as somehow mixed with or swallowed up by transcendent divinity. In this school, the passionately preferred title for Mary was *Theotokos,* or God-bearer, meaning that she was mother of the one who is personally the Word of God. Although the essence of the controversy was christological, the marian title itself bore the brunt of the dispute. When the Council of Ephesus in 431 opted for the title *Theotokos*, it spread like wildfire, keeping its original form in the East and being transmuted into the more colloquial "Mother of God" in the West. According to most scholars, the impetus from this council allowed the development of the marian cult to go public in the church. Although discourse about Mary had been in play to express christological truths, it opened up the later trajectory where attention was focused on Mary in herself.

The difference between East and West as these centuries progressed is significant. Numerous instances of fervent, enthusiastic reflection and imaginative interest in Mary originated in the eastern, Greek-speaking church. The western Latin-speaking church, by contrast, displayed a sobriety rather more parallel to the gospels and the earliest eastern theologians. Time after time when these marian creations of the East arrived in the West, they quickly took root and flourished. But in the early centuries the West did little to generate fervent, poetic ardor, thinking instead about Mary largely in relation to the mystery of Christ and the community's life of grace. One good example is the fifth-century preaching of Augustine. Nothing if not complex, his view of Mary is intertwined with his doctrinal positions on sin and redemption as well as his dubious philosophical idea of passive feminine nature and the role women should play. Interestingly enough, he refrained from using the title *Theotokos* for fear the people would confuse Mary with the Great Mother Goddess of Mediterranean religions, the Mother of God who is herself divine. On the subject of Mary's relation to other Christians, however, he established a vivid connection that provides another precedent for my proposal. He clearly preached that Mary belongs to the community of believers: "Mary is holy. Mary is blessed, but the Church is something better than the Virgin Mary. Why? Because Mary is part of the Church, a holy member, a quite exceptional member, the supremely wonderful member, but still a member of the whole body. That being so, it follows that the body is something greater than the member,"[3] the whole body which has Christ as its head. In this light, her relationship to Jesus as his biological mother is important to the Christian confession more because of the faith with which she bore him than because of her maternity itself. Take the scene where Jesus' mother and brothers stand outside asking to speak to him while Jesus, inside, replies that "whoever does the will of my Father in heaven is brother and sister and mother to me" (Matt. 12:46–50). Augustine argues that Mary's faith obviously qualifies her to be his mother. Indeed, "it means more for her, an altogether greater blessing, to have been Christ's disciple than to have been Christ's mother."[4] Feminist interpreters flag the danger here of disparaging women's sexual activity, which Augustine saw as a violation of female integrity leading to an impairment of virtue; virginity was much preferred as the path of a holy life.[5] But ironically, his emphasis on discipleship over biological maternity, when read today, has the effect of relieving the traditionally strong emphasis on motherhood, linked with Mary, as the sole vocation of women. Furthermore, it makes Mary's vocation accessible to all in the church. Augustine preached on the same text: "we do have the nerve to call ourselves the mother of Christ."[6] Why? Because by being heavy or pregnant (*gravida*) with belief in Christ, by carrying him in our hearts full of love, we bring forth the Savior into the needy world.

The theme of Mary's participation in the story of salvation through her mothering of Jesus and her own faith and discipleship was parsed in similar ways by a number of other theologians in the early Christian centuries. By keeping our gaze fixed steadfastly on theology I have, of course, neglected other dynamic factors that also shaped the first millennium's marian tradition. Chief among these was popular piety, a veneration not confined to simple people, the *rudes*, but shared by priests and bishops as well. Historian E. Ann Matter makes the wise observation that "the practice of the pious often takes its own course and can sometimes be strong enough to draw theological theory after it. This is the case with devotion to Mary; in no other realm of Christian theology does theory so closely, and it may even be said, so unwillingly, follow practice."[7] The point for our interest, however, is the way early Christian theology in the West configured itself to scripture and liturgy in situating Mary in the midst of the community rather than above it, seeing her as one among many notable models of faith including the apostles and martyrs. This pattern has led a number of scholars to characterize western marian theology in the first millennium as "objective," insofar as it did not require enthusiastic personal devotion to Mary but honored her along with other saints in the spacious framework of biblical and creedal faith.[8] A quite different mood takes over in the second millennium, when a more "subjective," emotional type of relationship increasingly glorifies Mary in her own right, especially her ability to obtain and dispense mercy.

The Second Millennium

New factors at work in the church, particularly the growing juridical character of church office, an increasingly severe penitential system, and a corresponding remoteness of the risen Christ in medieval theology and art caused a noticeable shift in the West's theology of Mary during the second millennium. Given the human propensity to sin and the ecclesiastical apparatus that confronted the sinner, the possibility of gaining eternal salvation was thought to be exceedingly difficult to achieve; the torment of hell beckoned. In this situation the mother of God came to be seen as a particularly potent help to sinners, a heavenly power who because of her maternal heart would take the sinner's side. Since she was also the mother of the Judge who was bound to honor her with filial piety, she was uniquely positioned to persuade him to save poor sinners. As this trajectory spun out, marian reflection became detached from the gospel story of salvation history, proceeding in an isolation that grew more intense as the millennium progressed.

The idea of Mary as mediatrix is a case in point.[9] In earlier theology the idea of Mary as a mediator had barely been mentioned. When it was, it was rooted in her singular role in the incarnation whereby the Son of God became a human being. Having given her free consent in faith, she conceived him in her body and, through her physical pregnancy and childbirth, delivered to the world its Savior. Thus she was understood to be the means by which God came to earth, the female "mediator," so to speak, of Christ's saving presence in history. Now, however, her mediation began to function in reverse to effect sinful humanity's going back to God. As the theologian Peter Damien wrote, "Just as the Son of God has deigned to descend to us through you, so we also must come to him through you...."[10] This insight found expression in the popular images of Mary as the "neck" connecting Christ with his body the church, and as the "aqueduct" through which the graces of Christ flow. With eloquent rhetoric Bernard of Clairvaux preached that it is God's wish that we venerate Mary with great tenderness, for God "wills us to have everything through Mary"[11]—a line that would be quoted in the marian teaching of later popes and would become a classic axiom in the literature of mariology. True, he goes on, the Father has given us Jesus as our efficacious Mediator; he is our merciful brother, made of our flesh. But we might tremble to approach him, for he is also God of awesome divine majesty. If we wish to have an advocate with him, let us have recourse to Mary, for she is wholly sweet and gentle, full of mildness and mercy. The Son will hear his mother, the Father will hear his Son, and so we will all receive divine favor.

A fearsome edge was given to this mediating role of Mary by emphasis on Christ the Just Judge. Being the mother of the Judge as well as of the ones on trial, Mary could soften the heart of her Son and obtain mercy for sinners, undeserving though they be. The epitome of the felt contrast between Christ and Mary was expressed in an influential sermon by an unknown author, thought until the twentieth century to be Bonaventure: "The Blessed Virgin chose the best part because she was made Queen of Mercy, while her Son remained King of Justice; and mercy is better than justice."[12] Mary, then, was a potent protector of her clients, warding off the just anger of Christ. Given her power to influence even Christ the Lord, she was also credited with being able to protect people from the attacks of the devil and the earthly misfortunes of famine, plague, and war. In the fifteenth century, Bernardine of Siena trenchantly summed up the general perception:

> Every grace which is communicated to this world has a threefold procession. For from God to Christ, from Christ to the Virgin, from the Virgin to us, it is dispensed in a most orderly fashion. . . . I do not hesitate to say that she has received a certain jurisdiction over all graces. . . . They are administered through her hands to whom she pleases, when she pleases, as she pleases, and as much as she pleases.[13]

Theologians today note how Mary regrettably replaces the Holy Spirit in this divine bestowal of grace. But given the prevailing understanding, it is little wonder that devotion to Mary blossomed in a profusion of prayers, hymns, cathedrals, pilgrimages, poems, miracle stories, dramas, songs, images, and practices in an outpouring that is impossible to codify.

The Reformation in sixteenth-century Europe happened when theology and piety were at a low ebb. Marian devotion was by turns sentimental and superstitious, filled on the one hand with a coy, simpering virgin, beautiful but not sacred, and on the other with a powerful mother who promised salvation despite the lack of ethics in one's life. The situation had deteriorated to the point where, according to Laurentin, "repelled by a desiccated intellectualism, people sought life on the imaginative and sentimental plane. Throughout this period of decadence, popular enthusiasm for the Blessed Virgin never faltered, but the adulterated fodder it was nourished on consisted of trumpery miracles, ambiguous slogans, and inconsistent maunderings."[14] The Reformers' criticism was largely justified, and the reforming Council of Trent called for correction of abuse. Over time, however, Protestant leaders, who focused on Christ alone as the mediator between God and sinful humanity, thought that Catholic reform did not go far enough. In the spirit of the day, a war psychology developed, with each punch met by an ever stronger counterpunch. Among Catholics, devotion to Mary became a badge of identity; polemic against those who did not honor her was elevated into an act of fealty; a virtue was made of aggressiveness in promoting her glories. The centuries that rolled on from that split in the western church saw positions polarize. Regarding Mary, Catholics developed a severe case of fixation, while Protestants developed a severe case of amnesia.

In the seventeenth century, new marian feasts, titles, institutions, and forms of piety blossomed; specialized literature running to thousands of volumes appeared in profusion. This was the existential setting for the origin of the scholarly discipline that technically came to be called "mariology." The term itself was coined by Nicholas Nigido in his treatise *Summa sacrae Mariologiae* written in 1602. Inspired by the rational approach of the age of the Enlightenment, this treatise began with a basic principle, Mary's maternity, and from it deduced as corollaries all manner of glorious privileges that accrued to her person.[15] This type of mariology, which spread rapidly, took to itself the piety of the day and gave it a theoretical basis. The effect was to cut thought about Mary off from the rest of theology, especially treatments of Christ, salvation, the Holy Spirit, and the church, which in any event had lost their creative edge. Thus, as Patrick Bearsely writes, "we have a picture of a vigorous mariology growing luxuriantly in an otherwise impoverished theological garden."[16]

This river crested in the nineteenth and twentieth centuries with the so-called marian movement, an upsurge in enthusiasm marked most strikingly by papal proclamation of two marian dogmas, the Immaculate Conception (1854) and the Assumption (1950). Themes of Mary's universal mediation of God's grace and her protection of the sinner resounded in the writings of theologians, spiritual guides, preachers, and popes. Leo XIII, for example, devoted eleven of his forty-two encyclicals to the subject of Mary.[17] New expressions of honor proliferated, including apparitions and pilgrimages to marian shrines such as Lourdes and Fatima. Religious orders dedicated in her name blossomed—Laurentin counts sixty-five founded in the hundred years following 1835.[18] Militant lay associations such as the Blue Army and the Legion of Mary attracted millions of members. Consecrations, crownings, medals, scapulars, holy pictures, and itinerant statues became ubiquitous. Marian journals and scholarly societies proliferated, along with marian congresses on the national and international levels; there were over seventy such meetings in the ten years following 1947.

In terms of systematic theology, mariology was by now a clearly marked independent subject founded on the principle of Mary's maternity and governed by a set of rules: the rule of *singularity* (Mary is unique); the rule of *analogy* (in her own way Mary parallels Christ in all things); the rule of *eminence* (Mary surpasses other Christians in all things so that *de Maria numquam satis,* which loosely translated means "about Mary one can never say enough"); and the rule of *suitability,* expressed in the axiom derived from Duns Scotus, *potuit, decuit, fecit,* or God "could have, should have, and therefore did" do great things for his mother. The result was a view of Mary as the unique, immaculately conceived virgin mother of God par excellence, graced with perfect virtue, the totally obedient, humble handmaid who was also the Queen of Heaven with power to intercede for our salvation, and who was assumed body and soul into heaven. Internally, the Achilles heel of this pattern of thought was its isolation from theology as a whole; mariology had indeed gone off on its own track Externally, it lacked resonance with modern forms of thought and spirituality. However, filling a great need, it flourished.

VATICAN II: CLASH OF THE TITANS

Eve of the Collision

After 1950 a split occurred between those who wished to go on making new conquests for Mary with more titles, privileges, and dogmatic definitions and those who desired to renew marian theology and devotion by a return to the original sources. The latter position was the result of three movements that had started up earlier in the twentieth century, namely, the biblical, liturgical, and ecumenical renewals. Originally opposed by the hierarchical church, these movements were now beginning to bear fruit. Reading biblical books according to the integrity of their genre rather than proof-texting, the biblical movement brought the good news of God's gracious ways in salvation history once again to the forefront. Promoting prayer to the trinitarian God by the worshiping community, the liturgical movement placed the Eucharist at the center of the church's public life, aligning Mary and the saints as part of the praying community. Opening dialogue with separated brothers and sisters, the ecumenical movement brought reforming intuitions to light and allowed Catholics to hear how deviant marian maximalism sounded to Protestant ears. In addition to these three movements, impetus for reform also came from Catholic scholars who for some decades had been returning to the sources of early Christian theology and its more gospel-oriented approach to Mary. Each of these developments in its own way reestablished the powerful truth that salvation comes copiously from God through Jesus Christ and reaches us even now through the power of the Spirit. Each one positioned Mary back into the community of believers.[19]

One early skirmish gave a portent of things to come. During this decade theologians involved in writing traditional treatises on mariology got embroiled in a controversy over what they called the "fundamental principle" of their discipline. Most of the major players argued that Mary's maternity, the role she played as mother of God, should provide the guiding idea for all subsequent privileges and powers. They expressed this principle in various ways, favoring her divine motherhood, her universal motherhood of the whole Christ including head and members, her physical motherhood, her spiritual motherhood, or her bridal motherhood. Taking issue with his colleagues, Karl Rahner proposed that grace rather than maternity should be the founding idea of marian theology. Speaking "simply and soberly," he reminded his listeners of the reality to which Christians entrust their lives: the living God gives human beings a gift of grace that justifies and forgives. This grace is not a created gift, however, but God's own self-communication, which comes to human beings and so influences them that they freely become ready "for the whole glorious infinite life of the triune God to enter the poor heart of this tiny creature."[20] From God's side this is God's love for human beings. From our side, this is love for God, which also in the teaching of Christ includes love for neighbor. Christian life chiefly consists "in our receiving the whole divine life by the power of God's grace, with faith and love, into the depths of our heart in such a way that it extends and redounds to a blessing for others who by our side and like us are to receive the one and only salvation from the eternal God."[21]

Placing Mary in this context, Rahner sees her as an actual realization of this mystery. She receives God's saving, merciful grace and, as part of human history, as "entirely one of us," she accomplishes her own life story. This story takes on a unique importance for our salvation in view of Jesus Christ, whom she conceived by the free consent of her faith and the physical reality of her motherhood. Chosen by God to carry out this role, she is gifted with grace commensurate with her task. In the process, she realizes in herself what faith says about the fullness of grace and salvation radiating in service to others. Mary is the figure who actually typifies the meaning of grace with unsurpassed holiness and dignity. "Yet what Mary has must in the ultimate resort be ours too. We too are to become what she is,"[22] namely, those who hear the word of God and act upon it with all our heart. The living God who self-communicates through Jesus Christ in saving grace, concludes Rahner, is the ultimate reality. This idea should organize and ground our reflection, which would integrate Mary back into theology.

On the eve of the Second Vatican Council the expansive trajectory of the second millennium was clearly coming into tension with more sober facets of the first. In the parlance of the day that served to crystallize the contrasting schools of thought, the second-millennium marian movement position was called maximalist. Its mariology was labeled *christotypical* because it envisioned Mary as an altogether special creature whose privileges paralleled those of Christ. By contrast, the position marked by return to the first millennium in the biblical, liturgical, and ecumenical movements coupled with the patristic renewal was called minimalist. Its mariology was labeled *ecclesiotypical* because it envisioned Mary as herself simply the recipient of grace and a special member of the community of the church. As characterized by Laurentin, christotypical mariology was spiritually mystical in tone, driven by love, focused on the glories of Mary, full of emotional fervor, and dedicated to seeing Mary as the neck connecting the head and members of the body of Christ. Ecclesiotypical mariology was critically rational in tone, driven by a search for truth, focused on Jesus Christ, full of clear-sightedness regarding the needs of the modern world, and appalled by the neck metaphor. Behind each position lay prior theological commitments centuries in the making that commanded deep loyalties. Given the success of the nineteenth and twentieth centuries in glorifying Mary, it is little wonder that going into the council marian enthusiasts looked forward to placing another jewel in the crown of the

mother of God by having the council declare as dogma that she was mediatrix of all graces. Just as insistently, those who were leading the renewal
movements in view of the modern world wished to brake mariological
exuberance and restore a gospel orientation. Their clash was the wildest,
most emotional fight of the whole council.

Clash of the Titans

Should the teaching on Mary be dealt with in the schema on the church
or not? This seemingly simple and straightforward question was the occasion of a bitter dispute in which the titanic differences between the two
millennia came into open conflict.[23] The issue was joined during the second session of the council in autumn 1963. Obviously, those promoting
the glories of Mary opposed the move to include, supporting instead a separate document that would give Mary due regard as superior to the church.
Those in favor of inclusion thought it would be more ecumenically prof-
itable as well as in keeping with the main theme of the council itself to
check exaggerations by bringing Mary back into the theology of the church.
National characteristics played a role in this division, with Spanish, Italian,
and Polish personalities favoring the maximalist heartfelt, enthusiastic
strategy, while German, English, French, Belgian, and Dutch tempera-
ments tended toward a more biblically based, theologically rigorous out-
look. During discussion the atmosphere became explosive. Laurentin
describes it as almost violent.[24] The privileges party denounced the move
to include as a plot against Our Lady, using passionate accusations and
sentimental appeals to make their case. The reform party rejected the char-
acterization of their idea as a devious plot, arguing that veneration of Mary
could be all the more ardent if it were based on a more enlightened foundation. The whole assembly was pervaded with distress.

To reach a decision in a calmer, more fully informed manner, a plenary
session debate was arranged. Cardinal Rufino Santos of Manila spoke for
the "separate schema" party and Cardinal Franz König of Vienna for the
"inclusion in the church" party. Marshaling the best arguments for their
positions, they gave presentations whose difference could hardly be exag-
gerated. Santos gave ten arguments in favor of a separate schema. These
included the theological argument that, given her relations to the Trinity,
Mary has a position of priority with regard to the church beyond the level
of the laity and hierarchy; the pastoral argument that the faithful would see
her inclusion in the church as reduction and loss; and the practical one

that the constitution on the church as already composed had no place where she might be harmoniously added. König in turn articulated four reasons why teaching on Mary should be incorporated into the schema on the church. These included the theological one that Mary belongs there because she is a type of the church, prefiguring its eschatological fulfillment; the pastoral one that the faithful were being encouraged to purify their devotion to Mary and get back to essentials based on scripture; and the ecumenical one that an ecclesiotypical mariology made possible a conversation with the Oriental and Protestant traditions. The issue was joined, and not just on the intellectual level. As Gérard Philips observed, while "both speakers maintained a remarkably high level of thought, the general mood was anything but dispassionate."[25]

In the days between this debate and the vote of the assembly, the atmosphere grew ever more tense. Partisans of each position distributed pamphlets, duplicated materials, and propaganda booklets and engaged in dirty tricks to promote their side. "A Ukrainian bishop distributed pamphlets in front of the Aula; the Spaniards distributed printed leaflets everywhere; Roschini produced a brochure; people were talking of a battle for and against the Madonna; Balić distributed a lengthy booklet printed by the Vatican Press in the form of a schema,"[26] the latter implying that what was actually his own tract was an official statement. Because he circulated a note favoring inclusion, Abbot Butler was violently insulted in the conservative daily newspaper *Il Tempo*. Spearheading the mariology of privileges party, Balić roundly attacked the noted theologian Yves Congar, who had criticized "galloping mariology," accusing him of being a dishonest Catholic. The simple question of placement developed into a bitter melodrama.

On October 29, 1963, the vote was finally taken. It was the closest vote of the council: 1,114 in favor of incorporating marian teaching into the schema on the church, 1,074 against. The motion passed with a legitimate and sufficient majority of forty votes, but if only twenty bishops had declared differently it would have been a tie. The vote was met with stunned silence, "a moment of dazed amazement."[27] Accustomed as they were to deciding issues with near unanimity up to that point, the bishops were terribly dismayed. How could it be that the mother of God, in whose womb the fundamental union of God and humanity was achieved, had become the source of such great division?

Commentators on this vote note that, seen theologically, the mentality of nonhistorical, authoritarian orthodoxy accompanied by a piety that focused on the world to come was outvoted by the forces for renewal that called the church to enter into history and engage the social and political implications of the gospel. Seen politically, the curialist representatives of the "Age of Mary" had lost to the northern European alliance, which advocated dialogue with the modern world. My own view holds that what happened was a kind of seismic upheaval in which the strained, bulging theological earth shifted back to realignment with the pattern of the first millennium. It is important to note that one year, numerous drafts and amendments, and many arguments later, the final version of the Dogmatic Constitution on the Church (*Lumen Gentium*) with the marian schema firmly ensconced as its last chapter was affirmed in solemn assembly with only five negative votes.

FROM MEDIATRIX TO MODEL

The heated and far from academic atmosphere that surrounded the vote on placement made it difficult to write a text that would satisfy both sides. Controversy continued; a series of drafts succeeded one another as each side vied to influence official teaching. The christotypical group continued to urge the council to solemnly define the dogma that Mary is mediatrix of all graces who is closely engaged in the work of redemption as associate of her Son, or at least to declare the doctrine that she is mother of the church. On the other side were those who urged that the cause of unity would be hindered by new dogmas; what was needed was to learn to utter the name of Mary, woman of faith, as part of the vision of the church. Out of the "spirited clashes," "angry speeches," "fiercely emotional debates," and "great conflicts" that marked discussion of the penultimate draft, the final text crafted a middle ground that despite compromises still managed to restore Mary to a first-millennium pattern. Entitled "The Role of the Blessed Virgin Mary, Mother of God, in the Mystery of Christ and the Church," it offers precedent for the proposal we are pursuing here in both its placement and its content.

As to placement, the Constitution on the Church opens with the ringing proclamation that "Christ is the light of all nations," or *lumen gentium* (§1). Radiant with this light and reflecting it the way the moon does the sun, the church helps to shed this light on the world by proclaiming the gospel to every creature. This, then, is the foundational relationship which constitutes the very essence of the church: Christ the Redeemer and the church as the assembly of all those who believe in him and witness him to the world. Subsequent chapters consider aspects of this community on earth: the church moving through history as the pilgrim People of God, the episcopacy and clergy, the laity, the call of the whole church to holiness, and the religious orders. But the reality of the church is not exhausted here, in those who are still alive at any given moment; one does not leave the church by dying. Therefore, the constitution goes on to consider the faithful dead, those "friends and fellow heirs of Jesus Christ" (§50) with whom the living form one community. Then within this context of the whole church, living and dead, the constitution discusses Mary, a preeminent member of the church and faith-filled mother of Jesus Christ, once a pilgrim on earth herself and now with God in glory. Be it noted that this placement is a precise delineation of the program to develop a theology of Mary amid the communion of saints.

As to content, the marian chapter returns to biblical and early Christian sources to sketch out Mary's significance in relation to Christ and the church. First, it tells the story of her life in relation to Christ by running together in a harmonious narrative various gospel stories. Emphasis is placed on her maternity, by means of which the Redeemer entered the world, and her faith, which led her to respond creatively to the call of God in different situations. The dynamism of her life is said to lie in the way she advanced in her "pilgrimage of faith" (§58) from the announcement of Christ's birth to the upper room at Pentecost. Ultimately this pilgrimage led her into the glory of God. The reality of her life, then, is intertwined with the great events of the coming of salvation. The struggle between the two schools of thought can be seen by the "nevertheless" structure of many paragraphs. For example, the document states that Mary's unique role in salvation as mother of the incarnate Redeemer gives her a special relationship to the triune God (christotypical). "At the same time, however, because she belongs to the offspring of Adam, she is one with all human beings in their need for salvation" (ecclesiotypical, §53). United with her Son in the work of salvation from his birth to her presence at his side in heaven (christotypical), she nevertheless did not understand his reply when she found him in the temple but pondered it in her heart (ecclesiotypical, §57).

Besides relating Mary to Christ, the chapter also positions Mary as a member of the church. Here the council bit the bullet in the vexatious mediatrix dispute which had continued to simmer. It carefully declared that "the Blessed Virgin is invoked in the Church under the titles of Advocate, Auxiliatrix, Adjutrix, and Mediatrix. These however are to be so understood that they neither take away from nor add anything to the dignity and efficacy of Christ the one Mediator. For no creature could ever be classed with the Incarnate Word and Redeemer" (§62).[28] Instead of a doctrinal definition, the title Mediatrix is relativized here in three ways: it is placed in a row of other titles; it is set in the context of piety rather than doctrine, thus being descriptive of practice rather than prescriptive; and it is hedged about with christological reservations. In place of Mary as mediatrix, the council reached back to early Christian theology and emphasized the idea that Mary is a model of the church: "As St. Ambrose taught, the Mother of God is a model of the Church in the matter of faith, charity, and perfect union with Christ" (§63). As a model, she signals what the church is called to be at its spiritual best. This idea also shapes the document's final point about venerating Mary. Avoiding false exaggeration as well as narrow-mindedness, people should remember that "true devotion consists neither in fruitless and passing emotion, nor in a certain vain credulity. Rather, it proceeds from true faith, by which we are led to know the excellence of the Mother of God, and are moved to a filial love toward our mother and to the imitation of her virtues" (§67).

Critics of the marian chapter note the inadequacy of its biblical exegesis, which merges all marian texts together without regard for genre or author and which conflates biblical narrative with later dogmatic statements, as if one could indeed write a biography of Mary. Another serious weakness is the chapter's self-absorbed character, neglecting as it does to place marian theology in dialogue with the modern world, a move central to the council's most significant documents.[29] The chapter is also criticized for its almost complete lack of robust pneumatology, an absence that causes functions of the Holy Spirit to be attributed to Mary's maternal mediation. And there is no use of the liberating mariology creatively developed by the church of the poor. Asking what was at stake for women in the fiercely emotional conciliar debate, Anne Carr commends the placement of Mary within the wide framework of the whole economy of salvation, which makes possible a new connection between Mary and women. At the same time, however, the text idealizes this one woman, overuses the language of perfection, sees her as a model of receptivity to God's grace but not of agency and power, uses the harmful Eve–Mary dichotomy, and employs the language of subordination.[30] Kari Børresen points out the fundamental problem that "the female still represented humankind in its subordinate relation to the male, Christ."[31] Nevertheless, as Carr acknowledges, it is an "amazing thing" that Catholicism affirms that a woman is an authentically religious figure on the community's spiritual horizon.

On balance, by returning to original sources and checking the isolating trajectory of the second millennium, the council advanced the renewal of marian theology for the third millennium. In particular, the council's conscious, hard-won choice to include its teaching on Mary within the doctrine of the church, thus connecting her once again to the whole communion of saints living and dead, signals a new point of departure. Working in this reconfigured landscape, the theological investigation under way in this book relies on the council's basic decisions as precedent.

One aftermath was unexpected and leads to the last precedent I will claim. After the council, interest in things marian rapidly diminished in industrialized countries. On the one hand, theology became intensely occupied with questions of Christ and faith in God along with the social, moral issues arising in the modern world. The torrent of mariological writings slowed to a trickle. Assessing the worldwide picture twenty-five years later, Stefano De Fiores demonstrated that traditional mariology had run into a deep crisis, both its method and content having been passed by. Amazingly, even those few who continued to write in this field ignored the council's approach: "not one of the postconciliar mariological manuals adopts the methodology indicated by the Council."[32] On the other hand, among priests and laity, the council's reorientation of Catholic spirituality along the lines of scripture and the Eucharist began to take root. As a result, the superabundant marian devotions that had so marked the preconciliar era quietly imploded. The council had intended that these devotions be reformed, not that they be eliminated. But disappear they did, to the extent that one scholar could even refer to "the wreckage" of postconciliar devotion to Mary.[33] One might wonder at the very least why the conciliar breakthrough regarding Mary as model of the church did not catch the imagination of the faithful. It is a case study in the truth that solving an internal contest between two elite groups in the church does not necessarily translate into engaging the religious interest of the wider community grappling with faith in a rapidly shifting cultural context.

"TRULY OUR SISTER"

Ten years after the council, aware that traditional veneration of Mary was in steep decline, Paul VI penned an apostolic letter *Marialis Cultus* to encourage renewed marian devotion according to conciliar norms.[34] Recognizing that changes in social behavior, literary and artistic expressions, and the communications media have influenced the religious spirit in our time, he acknowledged that certain pious practices that not long ago seemed suitable are now being rejected. He does not promote these devotions because they are linked with social and cultural patterns of a past age. But rather than allow honoring Mary to wither because devotional forms show "the ravages of time," Paul VI remarkably called upon the whole church to act creatively to renew these forms in accord with contemporary sensibilities:

> This shows the need for episcopal conferences, local churches, religious families, and communities of the faithful to promote a genuine creative activity in proceeding to a careful revision of expressions and exercises of piety directed toward the Blessed Virgin. We would like this revision to be respectful of sound tradition and open to the legitimate desires of today's people. (§24)

To speed along the process, Paul VI set forth four guidelines based on the teaching of the council. These guidelines would enable the faithful to appreciate more easily Mary's connection to the mystery of the church and "her pre-eminent place in the communion of saints" (§28), and so enable them to renew devotion in a creatively faithful way. In my view the fault line between the two millennia becomes radically clear if one compares these four papal guidelines with the four principles noted above that governed the construction of preconciliar mariology. We leap from the principles of singularity, analogy, eminence, and suitability to biblical, liturgical, ecumenical, and anthropological criteria.

First, instructs this letter, veneration of Mary should have a *biblical* imprint. This does not entail merely making skillful use of certain relevant texts but steeping devotion to Mary in the great themes of the Christian message of salvation. Next, practices of piety that honor Mary should also be *liturgical*. This means that they should flow from and lead back to the prayer of the Eucharist and harmonize with the liturgical seasons, Advent and Christmas being especially suited. Third, honoring Mary should also be *ecumenical*, that is, rooted in a sound scriptural basis and clear about the centrality of Christ. Desiring full communion in faith among all Christ's disciples, the church desires that in devotional life "every care be taken to avoid any exaggeration which could mislead other Christians about the true doctrine of the Catholic Church" (§32). Fourth, and particularly pertinent to feminist reflection, renewed devotion to Mary should also be *anthropological*, that is, closely attuned to the human sciences that chart the changed psychological and sociological conditions in which modern persons, especially women, live. Paul VI's description is accurate:

> In the home woman's equality and co-responsibility with man in managing the family are being justly recognized by laws and the evolution of customs. In the sphere of politics women have in many countries gained a position in public life equal to that of men. In the social field women are at work in a whole range of different functions, getting daily further away from the restricted surroundings of the home. In the field of learning new possibilities are opening up for women in scientific research and intellectual activities. (§34)

As a consequence, he surmises, contemporary people, and women in particular, feel alienated from Mary because traditional piety presents her as a "timidly submissive woman or one whose piety was repellent to others" (§37), a woman whose life was bounded by ever-so-restricted horizons. One would think he had read the previous chapters of this book. This picture, he goes on to say, was formed by previous generations who drew on their own cultural norms regarding women, norms that are not eternal. While rejoicing at the long history of marian devotion, the church "does not bind herself to any particular expression of an individual cultural epoch or to the particular anthropological ideas underlying such expressions" (§36). Rather, the task now is to employ our own awareness, name the problems honestly, and offer an attractive presentation suitable to this age.

Jump-starting the task, Paul VI describes Mary as a strong and intelligent woman, one who had the wits to question back when the angel addressed her, one who experienced poverty and suffering, flight and exile. In the midst of these troubles she consistently gave active and responsible consent to the call of God, made courageous choices, and worked to strengthen the faith of others. Rather than being submissively pious, "she was a woman who did not hesitate to proclaim that God vindicates the humble and the oppressed, and removes the powerful people of this world from their privileged positions" (§37). In the most quoted passage from this letter, the pope then declares that far from endorsing the particulars of Mary's own life as exemplary, the church proposes her to the faithful as an example to be imitated:

> not precisely in the type of life she led, much less for the socio-cultural background in which she lived and which today scarcely exists anywhere. Rather,

she is held up as an example for the way in which, in her own particular life, she fully and responsibly accepted God's will (see Lk 1:38), because she heard the Word of God and acted on it, and because charity and a spirit of service were the driving force of her actions. She is worthy of imitation because she was the first and most perfect of Christ's disciples. (§35)[35]

In other words, the social location of this woman in first-century Galilee is not determinative for women's ways of being and acting in the world today. What has a permanent, universal, exemplary value is the way she walked the path of her own life before God, which can instruct and inspire people's own creative responses in this new era. We can be inspired by her example because we are all human together. Mary is "one of our race," "a true daughter of Eve," indeed "truly our sister, who as a poor and humble woman fully shared our lot" (§56).

This apostolic letter ends with a sustained reflection on the value of the rosary, a gospel-inspired prayer that fits the four guidelines. Its quiet pace and lingering repetitions concentrate the mind and allow for contemplative attention to the mysteries of salvation. Even here, however, a vital point is emphasized: "We desire at the same time to recommend that this very worthy devotion not be propagated in a way that is too one-sided or exclusive. The rosary is an excellent prayer, but the faithful should feel serenely free toward it" (§55). Since it is a matter of spirituality, people are led by the Spirit to pray in different ways, which must be respected.

Paul VI's four guidelines presented so persuasively to the church deal primarily with concrete expressions of devotion. Because of the organic connection between spirituality and theology, I think they also form a precedent for the project at hand. If these guidelines can serve to orient prayer in a right direction, then they can also direct thought. Along with the biblical, liturgical, and early Christian theological precedents from the first millennium and with the precedent of the late second millennium council whose teaching these papal guidelines seek to apply, they give backing to the theological direction of this book, namely, a theology of Mary whose unifying vision lies in interpreting her as a friend of God and prophet within the circle of all those who seek God, the company of saints living and dead.

PART 4

Picturing a World

7

⸙

Galilee: The Political-Economic World

PICTURING A WORLD

In the companionship model of the communion of saints, remembering the story of a person's graced history in ways that empower our life today assumes primary importance. The task now becomes to explore that history in the case of Mary. A problem immediately arises. In terms of a rolling series of life incidents and her own psychological responses to them, materials that would go to make up the usual kind of biography, we know very little. In this Mary has much in common with the vast number of human persons, poor women in particular, whose lives are lost in the mists of unimportance. It is true that the Christian gospels paint portraits of Mary as the mother of Jesus, weaving glimpses of her story into key moments of their proclamation of the good news of salvation. With clear theological interest, Mark associates her with neighbors and family members who do not understand and even reject Jesus' ministry; Matthew and Luke dwell on details of Jesus' birth; John alone brings her onto the scene at the wedding in Cana and again at Jesus' death; and in a move important for later tradition, Luke also places her in the post-resurrection company of Jesus' women and men followers gathered in Jerusalem to await the outpouring of the Spirit. When analyzed critically, each of these portraits provides a small tethering point. Given the nature of the gospels, however, the authors' main interest is neither historical nor focused on this woman in her own right, and much is omitted.

Sensing this, later apocryphal writings sought to satisfy the curiosity of the popular Christian mind by filling in the gaps left by the canonical gospels. The *Protoevangelium of James*, the most influential of these writings, informs the reader that the parents of Mary were named Joachim and Anna; that they were old and childless; that when Anna gave birth to the girl she said, "My soul magnifies the Lord"; that they dedicated her in the temple at the age of three, where the priest "placed her on the third step of the altar, and the Lord God put grace upon the child, and she danced for joy with her feet, and the whole house of Israel loved her."[1] The story goes on that Joseph, an older widower with children from his previous marriage, was chosen as her husband when a dove flew out of his staff; that when Jesus was born, all motion on earth stopped for a moment, birds stopped flying in mid-air, and a bright cloud overshadowed the cave. Shortly thereafter Mary underwent a gynecological exam that proved the marvel of her virginity after childbirth. The midwife had reported to Salome that a virgin had given birth. Like Thomas at Easter, Salome demurred, "Unless I put forward my finger and test her condition, I will not believe." She did so and her hand shriveled, but was healed when she touched the child.[2] Scholars do not consider the *Protoevangelium of James* and other such texts, written in the second and later centuries, to contain historically reliable testimony. They are a combination of Christian apologetic, doctrinal reflection, and fabulous imagination. At substantive points they mirror issues that troubled the church in those centuries, such as the struggle over women in ministry, but they add little historical information about Jesus or other first-century persons beyond what is given in the canonical gospels.

Is there another avenue that will lead to understanding? At a minimum, we know that Miriam of Nazareth was a Jewish woman, married and a mother, living in Galilee in the decades before and after the year "1," by which the Western calendar now divides the eras. Thanks to contemporary scholarship, this small handful of facts opens a sizable window.

Since the 1980s, scientifically conducted archaeological excavations have produced a veritable explosion of information about ancient Galilee in Roman times. This painstaking work uncovers the material culture of the place, which in turn helps scholars assess what life was like: settlement patterns, agricultural practices, religious affiliations, economic forces, cultural influences, incidents of violence. Jonathan Reed, a key practitioner of this art at the Galilean city of Sepphoris, points out that unlike literary texts, which intentionally set out to tell a story or make a plea from a definite point of view, archaeological evidence uncovers not only the intentional witness of public architecture but also many unintentional witnesses to everyday life in antiquity. "Sherds from pots and pans, hidden coins, discarded kitchen scrap—all afford a glimpse behind closed doors of antiquity."[3] Even here, of course, interpretation of the data is affected by the questions the researcher is asking and the models employed to frame an answer. What results is not a set of naive "pure facts" but inferences drawn from the material evidence. Still, archaeology is providing a new window into this place and time.

Scholars have married this knowledge to other disciplines to amplify their understanding of the social world of Galilee. The very idea that Galilee is a distinct region with its own history and viable subculture to be investigated is itself relatively recent.[4] Studies of cross-cultural anthropology that analyze the relations between different social classes, including gradations among the poor, now combine with studies of how the economy worked in Galilee during the Roman empire. This knowledge connects with literary, political, military, and historical sources to help reconstruct a general picture of its village society. For many scholars, a strong motivation driving this investigation has been the desire to picture the environment in which Jesus and his followers make historical sense, both before and after his violent death. While disagreeing vehemently about specifics, no scholar dealing with this material seriously doubts that first and last Jesus was a Galilean villager living out a Jewish vocation, as the titles of recent works suggest: Jesus the Jew, a marginal Jew, a Mediterranean Jewish peasant, Jesus and Judaism, Jesus' Jewishness, the Galilean Jewishness of Jesus, Jesus of Nazareth, King of the Jews.[5] The result has been an unprecedented number of studies of the Jesus of the gospels in the light of all this concrete evidence about his historical context. Yet another motivation driving this research is the desire to depict the later social world of Galilee in which rabbinic Judaism arose after the disastrous Jewish revolts against Rome starting in 66 C.E.[6]

This wealth of knowledge about the ancient land of Palestine can be put to work to illuminate the life Miriam of Nazareth actually lived. Our knowledge about her history as a specific human person may be minimal. But we are now in a position to draw a concrete picture of the world she inhabited and to allow this picture to shape our imaginations of the warp and woof of her life. Doing so focuses attention beyond immediate Jesus research in at least two ways. Insofar as Miriam of Nazareth was alive before him, probably from twelve to fifteen years prior to Jesus' birth, this investigation includes the situation of those years, especially the traumatic events surrounding the death of Herod in 4 B.C.E. when she was a young adult. Given the importance of gender, our exploration also raises the question of what it was like to be a woman in this Galilean world. Once anchored by this historical context, our dialogue with gospel portraits of her faith can then yield understanding with fresh concreteness. As a first step, this chapter will scan economic, social, and political features of the world she inhabited.

THE LAY OF THE LAND

As the northern part of the ancient land of Palestine, Galilee forms its own distinct, landlocked region. One adjective repeats over and over again in ancient and modern descriptions: fertile. Josephus, the first-century Jewish historian, writes, "The land is everywhere so rich in soil and pasturage and produces such variety of trees, that even the most indolent are tempted by these facilities to devote themselves to agriculture."[7] John Dominic Crossan depicts the 470 square miles of Lower Galilee as "rich with grain and cereal on valley floor and with vine and olive on hillside slope."[8] This lush farmland does not cover the whole region, however, for Lower Galilee, the focus of our attention, is crossed by a series of rugged hills. While some hills rise up abruptly from the plain, making good spots for fortresses, the general pattern is a series of four continuous ranges marked by sharp ridges and curving basins that march across the land in an east–west direction. In between, dotted with farming villages, are the broad, fertile valleys. The growing season is long and allows for three harvests, thanks to the rainy, temperate season in winter coupled with the dry, sunny season in summer. When the rains begin each October bringing wild flowers to bloom in profusion, the landscape is nothing short of beautiful. At the eastern edge of the region, the land suddenly sinks into a huge basin that contains the Sea of Galilee, a freshwater lake that flows into the Jordan River. The lake, river, and their surrounding lands are all below sea level, part of that great cleft in the earth's crust that runs from Lebanon into Africa, where it is known as the Great Rift Valley, the place of the emergence of the human species. Since the Galilean lake is below sea level, the weather around it is subtropical, relatively dry, and almost always warm. Here, too, grew a wealth of plants including, according to Josephus, "the walnut, a tree which delights in the most wintry climate . . . , palm trees which thrive on heat, and figs and olives which require a milder atmosphere. . . . Not only has the country this surprising merit of producing such diverse fruits, but it also preserves them: for ten months without intermission it supplies those kings of fruits, the grape and the fig."[9]

Nazareth, the place where Miriam lived, was a relatively small village located on the slope of a broad ridge in southern Galilee. It could nestle up the hill because the rock was soft and porous, which allowed for springs of water to gather and flow even at some altitude. As Crossan observes, "The village of Nazareth, then, at an elevation of over a thousand feet and with its single ancient spring, is exactly what the terrain dictated. But that, of course, isolated the village off the beaten track."[10] Most of the hard remains uncovered there by archaeology have to do with farming: olive presses, wine presses, cisterns for water, millstones for grain, holes for storage jars. From this it is inferred that "the principal activity of these villagers was agriculture. Nothing in the finds suggests wealth."[11] Scholarly estimates of the population have varied widely. Based on the carrying capacity per head of the surrounding land and also on the location of tombs, always placed outside residential areas, a likely number would be 300 to 400 people. They would consist of peasants who worked their own land, tenant farmers who worked land belonging to others, and craftspersons who served their needs. It should be noted that this Jewish agricultural village was only three to four miles from the growing, gleaming Herodian city of Sepphoris, built on a 325-foot ridge to the northwest. A walk of only an hour or two separated them, but Nazareth was off the main road that funneled most people to this administrative center. The identity of the village as an agricultural hamlet of little consequence would seem to be borne out in the literary record. The Hebrew scriptures do not mention Nazareth, nor does Josephus, who names forty-five villages in Galilee, nor does the Talmud, which refers to sixty-three Galilean villages.[12] As Richard Horsley observes, "Judging from its somewhat out of the way location and small size, it was a village of no special importance."[13]

This was a multilingual world. Latin was the native tongue of the Romans; Greek was the *lingua franca* of the educated, business, and ruling classes throughout the empire and had made massive inroads in Palestine; and Hebrew was the ancient language of the Bible, heard when the Torah scrolls were read and their fine points debated. In the households and villages of Galilee, the ordinary, everyday language was Aramaic.[14] This is borne out in snippets of Aramaic which appear so strikingly in the gospels: *talitha koum* (young girl, arise, Mark 5:41); *ephphatha* (Be opened!, Mark 7:34); *abba* (father, Mark 14:36); and *elōi, elōi, lema sabachthani* (My God, my God, why have you forsaken me?, Mark 15:34). The gospels were written in Greek decades after Jesus' lifetime, but these expressions point to the substratum of Jesus' Aramaic speech embedded in memory. It would seem, in addition, that Galileans spoke Aramaic in a style distinct from the people in the great city of Jerusalem. During Jesus' trial a bystander accosts Peter in the courtyard saying, "Certainly you are one of them, for your accent betrays you" (Matt. 26:73). All evidence points to the fact that, along with her neighbors, the peasant woman Miriam of Nazareth spoke Aramaic with a Galilean accent.

In agricultural Lower Galilee there were about two hundred villages ranging in size from tiny hamlets of a few dozen people to larger towns of a thousand or more. Most, like Nazareth, held several hundred. Archaeological evidence indicates that free-standing, beautifully furnished single-family houses such as those found in wealthy cities like smallish Sepphoris and grand Jerusalem were virtually nonexistent in these villages. Rather, excavations make clear that dwellings were small and clustered together. Each family occupied a domestic space or "house" of one or two small rooms. Three or four of these dwellings were built around a courtyard open to the sky, forming a compound similar to those found in some peasant communities in warm climates even today. Circled together around a courtyard, the space between their outer walls filled in with a thick stone wall, the units formed a secure living space. There would be a single entrance, able to be closed off by a door, which opened onto an alleyway. Regarding these passageways or "streets" that ran crookedly around the domestic enclosures in one village, Reed notes that "none had channels for running water or sewage, which must have been tossed in the alleyways. Instead, the roads in Capernaum bend at the various clusters of houses, and were made of packed earth and dirt, dusty in the dry hot seasons and muddy in the short rainy seasons, but smelly throughout."[15]

The walls of the one- or two-room family dwellings were built of native stone, either black basalt or white limestone, held together by a mortar of mud and smaller stones. Doorways were framed in wood and most likely hung with straw mats or curtains for privacy. Floors were made of packed earth. The absence of roof tiles and stones shaped as arch or vault pieces leads scholars to conclude that the roofs were thatched, constructed of thick bundles of reeds tied over beams of wood, most likely covered with packed mud for additional protection. Reed observes that in the two versions of the story of Jesus healing the paralyzed man whose friends let him down through the roof, "Luke's 'through the tiles' (5:19) is less appropriate to the actual milieu than Mark's more probable 'they dug through the roof' (2:4), which made no sense in Luke's urban setting where roof tiles were common."[16]

The enclosed family rooms were used for sleep and sex, giving birth and dying, and taking shelter from the elements. In the unroofed, common courtyard, inhabitants of the domestic units, most likely an extended family or close kinship group, shared an oven, a cistern that held water, and a millstone for grinding grain, indicating that this was the kitchen where food was prepared and cooked in the open air. Domestic animals also lived here. The people of the village as a whole shared larger food-preparation facilities such as a threshing floor, olive press, and wine press. The diet was mainly grain and olive oil with some fruits, vegetables, and wine filling out nutritional needs, along with occasional milk products if one had a flock of sheep, or fish if one lived near the lake. Living at a subsistence level, households by and large grew their own food, did their own building, and sewed their own clothes from cloth that they spun and wove, mostly woolen cloth from sheep.

The domestic architecture of Galilean village homes indicates that these agricultural peasant communities occupied the lower rung of the social and economic ladder. Poverty with its accompanying illness, infant mortality, and short life expectancy would be a fact of life. Comparing the material finds in the region's villages to those in the city of Sepphoris, Reed makes a telling observation by noting what is *not* present in the villages. Missing from first-century Capernaum are defensive walls and any civic buildings in public spaces. There is no major paved road through the village, no agora or marketplace, no shops or storage facilities, no plaster, mosaic, or fresco decorations. There are no signs of private wealth such as imported wine vessels, perfume bottles, finely decorated containers, or even simple glass.[17] This is typical of the villages in the region. In Nazareth, too, the material culture proves to be simple and more than modest. From the early Roman period there are no paved streets, no public buildings, no public inscriptions, no marble or mosaics or frescoes:

> The fact that so little has been found leads to the conclusion that the houses themselves were rather poorly made of fieldstones and mud, with thatched roofs and coverings over caves. The entire area seems to have been preoccupied with agricultural activities. On the outskirts of the village, traces of terracing have been found, as has evidence of a vineyard tower. Inside the

village, wine-pressing vats with straining depressions, fermenting vats, and
depressions to hold storage jars, along with grinding stones and silos are
complemented by simple locally made pottery and household items, without any trace of imported or fine wares from the earlier periods. There are
no luxury items of any kind.[18]

Reed concludes that the pejorative question in John's gospel, "Can anything good come out of Nazareth?" (1:46) seems apt: "It was a small Jewish village, without any political significance, preoccupied with agriculture
and, no doubt, taxation."[19] For most of her life, Miriam of Nazareth lived
in this village.

ECONOMIC STRUCTURES

In addition to archaeology, scholars employ the social sciences including
economic anthropology, modern rural sociology, and peasant studies to
gain a clearer picture of the economic life of Galilee. As a province within
the vast world of the Roman empire, Galilee was part of a traditional
agrarian society in which land was the primary source of wealth. Hence
control of land and its products constituted a central political question.
Characterized by use of the plow, agricultural production in this society
depended primarily on human and animal energies. The low-level tech-
nology combined with meager energy resources resulted in generally low
yields. As Douglas Oakman comments, "this means that as a rule there is a
very narrow margin between what can be harvested and what is needed by
the majority of agriculturalists for food, seed, or animal fodder. There
might be just enough, but not much more."[20] The harvest, however, did
not belong completely to the Galilean growers to use as they needed. Since
they were part of the Roman empire, a goodly portion of the fruits of their
labor, adequate but not superabundant to begin with, did not remain
among those who toiled on land and lake but was siphoned off to support
a small ruling elite. Technically, then, Galilee was a *peasant* society, meaning not only that most people worked the land but also that their productivity was extracted for the benefit of rulers without an equivalent
economic recompense. The basic economic structure of this society, in
sum, was that of a redistributive network. "This means that taxes and rents
flowed relentlessly away from the rural producers to the storehouses of
cities (especially Rome), private estates, and temples."[21] The little "surplus"

that might exist from such subsistence farming was taken by the ruling groups to support their cultured lifestyle. More often than not there was no such surplus, placing the rural population on a narrow margin between subsistence and famine.

One of the most useful and influential analyses of this system has proved to be the model of traditional agrarian society developed by anthropologist Gerhard Lenski. Synthesized from his study of a number of agrarian societies across different cultures and historical periods, this model charts how wealth is distributed in such an economic order. When interfaced with archaeological and literary evidence, it can illuminate the structure of the economic world inhabited by Miriam of Nazareth as well as her consequent position on the social scale.

According to Lenski's model, agrarian societies have basically two classes, upper and lower, with an enormous gap between them. Within that division there are distinct classes as depicted in this chart, with upper class on the left:

ruler	
governing class	peasant class
retainer class	artisan class
merchant class	unclean and degraded class
priestly class	expendable class

The ruler was really in a class by himself, with proprietary rights to property, water, and crops throughout his domain. The governing class, comprised of the nobility and members of court as well as lesser officials, surrounded the ruler's administration with an ambience of power and glory. Although comprising about one percent of the population, these two top classes were awash in the wealth of the national income: "the governing class and ruler together usually received not less than half."[22] The retainer class was made up of scribes and bureaucrats as well as military personnel, about 5 percent of the population; they supported and defended the ruler and governing class, making their very existence possible. The wealthy merchant class and the priestly class rounded out the ranks of the privileged, allied as they were with the governing class. Overall the upper class comprised about 10 percent of the population. Most often they lived in urban communities.

On the other side of the chasm was the peasant class, numerically the largest group of all. Peasants were the fundamental engine of production, working the land, either their own little plot or the estates of wealthy landowners. "The burden of supporting the state and the privileged classes fell on the shoulders of the common people, and especially on the peasant farmers who constituted the majority of the population; . . . the great majority of the political elite sought to use the energies of the peasantry to the full, while depriving them of all but the basic necessities of life."[23] Even these necessities could be sacrificed. If the harvest did not produce sufficient surplus, the extracting knife of the governing class's tax machine could cut into what peasants needed for sheer survival. The artisan class (including, be it noted, carpenters), consisting of around 5 percent of the population, had a lower median income than the peasants; lacking land, they could not rely on a steady supply of food. The two groups did overlap, however. In the villages farmers could engage in artisan work especially during the brief winter; artisan families may also have worked a plot of land. The unclean and degraded classes were those separated from the mass of peasants and artisans by circumstances of birth or occupations such as prostitution. Finally, with the most terrible circumstances of all, was the expendable class, about 5 percent to 10 percent of the population. "These included a variety of types, ranging from petty criminals and outlaws to beggars and underemployed itinerant workers, and numbered all those forced to live solely by their wits or by charity."[24]

The social stratification based on wealth described in this model was not absolute, but, given the relative power of the upper classes and the relative powerlessness of the lower, downward mobility was much more frequent than upward. Lenski's observation on the whole setup alerts us to the dynamic at work: "One fact impresses itself on almost any observer of agrarian societies. . . . This is the fact of *marked social inequality*. Without exception, one finds pronounced differences in power, privilege, and honor associated with mature agrarian economies."[25] One to two percent of the population, backed up by force, takes half of society's annual agricultural production; a tiny minority of elites controls the vast majority, extracting from them the fruits of their industrious labor. The relationship is not genuinely reciprocal: aristocrats live off peasants. While the former may claim to be providing law, peace, and protection in return, peasants have no choice but to submit to the exploitation of their land and productivity. Or, we should say, they do have a choice, either to submit or revolt, which explains the recurrence of peasant rebellions exploding throughout history.

Applying this economic lens to the first-century villages of Lower Galilee, including Nazareth, we see that these were peasant villages characterized by subsistence farming. Archaeological field surveys have found only minor variation in the size of individual plots. "This relative uniformity in families' holdings suggests a limited economic stratification among villagers (no extremely wealthy villagers) and a relative uniformity of land use."[26] Food was their primary product. Each village produced and consumed grain, wine, and oil, working through all stages of production from planting to harvesting to processing. They also wove their own clothing, tanned leather to make sandals, and engaged in other crafts necessary to maintain the households. Except for metal instruments and tools, they were basically self-sufficient. The fabric of village life involved a network of interrelationships. Not only did the whole village share common equipment for processing the harvest, and not only did households share common kitchens for cooking it, but their economic life at a subsistence level also entailed numerous interactions such as borrowing and lending implements, helping out in each other's fields, repairing a home, midwifing, attending to the sick, and other contingencies. If something was needed by someone else, local householders bartered among themselves, making exchanges in goods rather than coins, for example, three loaves of bread for a basket of figs. No archaeological or literary evidence points to Galilean villages' having craft workshops, stores, or a small market. This was not a market economy such as we know in capitalism. Rather, the villagers were linked to the soil "in terms of day-to-day drudgery and all seasons cultivation in order to procure the necessities of life and meet their various obligations."[27]

As the wife of a village *tekton*, the Greek word used in the gospels to designate a carpenter, stonemason, cartwright, and joiner all rolled into one, Miriam of Nazareth belonged to this peasant world and, using Lenski's model, to the lower bracket of the artisan class. In addition to carpentry work the family probably also cultivated some plot of land for basic foodstuffs. This might explain why many of the images in Jesus' parables are taken from farming rather than carpentry.[28] Referring to Jesus in words that might just as well apply to Joseph, John Meier paints a lucid description of what being a *tekton* entailed:

> Some of Jesus' work would have been carpentry in the narrow sense of the word, i.e., woodwork in constructing parts of houses. But in Nazareth the ordinary house would have had walls of stone or mud brick. Wood would be used mostly for the beams in the roof, the space between beams being filled in with branches along with clay, mud, and impacted earth. The people of Nazareth could not have afforded the use of wood to build whole

houses, or even the floors in them. However, doors, door frames, and locks or bolts were often made from wood, as at times were the lattices in the (few and small) windows. Beyond carpentry in this sense, Jesus would have made various pieces of furniture.... Thus, while Jesus was in one sense a common Palestinian workman, he plied a trade that involved for the ancient world a fair level of technical skill. It also involved no little sweat and muscle power. The airy weakling often presented to us in pious paintings and Hollywood movies would hardly have survived the rigors of being Nazareth's *tekton* from his youth to his early thirties.[29]

We need to guard against romantic images of the carpenter shop, for being an artisan in an agrarian society like that described by Lenski did not give one the same economic and social standing that being a skilled carpenter in an advanced, industrial market economy like our own bestows. Consulting an ancient "lexicon of snobbery," Ramsay MacMullen found *tekton* among the slurs the literate upper classes could throw to disparage someone of plebeian origins.[30] When the gospels record Nazareth's derision over Jesus' teaching, the villagers latch on to his work as a basis to brush him off: "Is this fellow not the woodworker (*tekton*), the son of Mary?" (Mark 6:3), or in Matthew's version, "Is this fellow not the son of the woodworker?" (13:55). Luke seems to find any mention of woodworking offensive, dropping it altogether and changing the jibe to, "Is this fellow not the son of Joseph?" (4:22). In any case, neither Jesus' parents nor his work gained him any automatic respect. The family was a village family of the artisan class, no more respectable than anyone else. They belonged to the poor, who had to work hard for their living. It is true, as Meier argues, that theirs "was not the grinding, degrading poverty of the day laborer or the rural slave."[31] But it is equally misleading to compare, as Meier does, their economic status, however hazily, to "a blue-collar worker in lower-middle-class America."[32] The analogy does not work because there was no middle class. The family of Miriam of Nazareth lived on the economic underside of a two-sided system.

Recall that in a mature agrarian society, the upper classes extract their wealth from the labor of the lower ones. During the period of Roman occupation, which covers Miriam of Nazareth's lifetime, Galilean villagers were triply taxed. They had to pay the traditional tithe, or 10 percent, of the harvest for support of the temple and its priesthood in Jerusalem, though some scholars question whether this was completely enforceable in Galilee at this point. They were also required to pay tribute to the Roman emperor, plus taxes to the local Jewish client-king through whom Rome ruled by proxy. These monies were skimmed off as a certain percentage of the villagers' crops, flocks, or catches of fish. The peasant communities worked intensely hard just to stay afloat, but the power of the governing class to extract payment ground them down. Drained of resources during these years, many fell into increasing indebtedness to the wealthy. As a result, they lost their land and became truly impoverished. In this context, Jesus' proverb rings bitterly true: "I tell you that to everyone who has, it shall be given, but from the one who has not, even what he has will be taken away" (Luke 19:26). The poverty and hunger in Galilee acted as a spawning ground of first-century revolts against the repressive Roman occupation and the taxation it engendered. Miriam of Nazareth labored in this world of social stratification marked by great disparities in wealth, power, and privilege. Her life is typical of that of countless women throughout the ages who experience civic powerlessness, poverty, and the suffering that results from low status and lack of formal education.[33]

To show the theological relevance of this kind of economic analysis, I digress for a moment to the interpretation of marian doctrines worked out by Brazilian theologians Ivone Gebara and María Clara Bingemer. The Immaculate Conception and the Assumption carry the memories of other generations, they write, and true though they be, their relevance is not immediately apparent today on a continent marked by the suffering of millions of poor people. Yet these doctrines carry a liberating impulse and can be made to work as allies in the struggle for life. For the *Immaculata* venerated on our altars is the poor Mary of Nazareth, insignificant in the social structure of her time. This Mother of the People bears within herself the confirmation of God's preference for the humblest, the littlest, the most oppressed. "The so-called Marian privilege is really the privilege of the poor."[34] Similarly, believing in Mary's Assumption means proclaiming that the woman who gave birth in a stable among animals, who shared a life of poverty, who stood at the foot of the cross as the mother of the condemned, has been exalted. "The Assumption is the glorious culmination of the mystery of God's preference for what is poor, small, and unprotected in this world." It sparks hope in the poor and those who stand in solidarity with them "that they will share in the final victory of the incarnate God."[35] To understand these doctrines aright, we cannot forget that they talk of God exalting a woman who lived in poverty and anonymity. As Mary sang in the Magnificat, they reveal the ways of God whose light shines on what is regarded as insignificant and marginal.

POLITICAL RULERS

In addition to situating Miriam of Nazareth in a particular geographic place and economic system, we can also situate her in a political time. Scholars are generally agreed that Jesus was born around the year 4 B.C.E., if not a few years before that in 6 or 7 B.C.E.[36] Given the detail that he was "her firstborn son" (Luke 2:7) and the custom that young women married at the age of menstruation when their bodies were able to bear children, she was then most likely in her early teens. This locates her own birth in the second decade before the year "1" as we now count time, around 20 B.C.E. The death of Jesus, by then in his thirties, took place at Passover on the watch of Pontius Pilate, the Roman prefect who ruled Judea from 26 to 36 C.E. Say it was around the year 30. Small bits of evidence indicate that Jesus' mother was still alive at that point. She would have been getting on in years, facing old age according to the life expectancy of the poor in that era. We have no idea how old she was when she died.

This rough time frame of her life span makes it possible to know who the political rulers of the land were during her lifetime and to picture the impact of their public actions on her life and that of her family and neighbors. Under the general Pompey, the Roman empire had conquered the land of Palestine in 63 B.C.E. Thus, during her lifetime the Jewish homeland was an occupied, colonialized territory under imperial control. This does not mean that there were Roman soldiers stationed in every village or visibly spread throughout the countryside. The major concentration of troops for the region was in Syria just to the north, where four legions plus cavalry stood in readiness to be deployed as needed. In emergencies these forces could and did come south to Palestine to restore order. Over on the Mediterranean coast in the Herod-built city of Caesarea, the Roman governor immediately responsible for Palestine had a garrison of three thousand troops. In addition, in the major city of Jerusalem a small contingent of soldiers was permanently garrisoned in the Antonia Fortress next to the temple. During the three major Jewish religious festivals, when pilgrims by the thousands streamed into the city and gathered at the temple, the Roman governor and his troops would march in from the coast to bolster this small brigade (this explains Pilate's presence in the city when Jesus was put to death).

The visible absence of occupying troops in Galilee, however, did not indicate the absence of Roman rule. As we have seen, Rome exacted monetary tribute from the conquered land of the Jews. Their governing policy kept the occupied populations pacified, working, and paying, while allowing enough freedom for the exercise of their traditional customs so as to prevent open revolt. To carry out this program, Rome customarily appointed client-kings from the conquered population, rulers who were charged with keeping their own people under control. If they failed, the Roman method called for a military response including wholesale burning, slaughtering, and enslaving, carried out with a level of violence calculated to terrorize the surviving populace into submission. This policy of indirect rule through native aristocracies backed up by Roman military might brought three generations of the Jewish Herod family to power. Each is mentioned in the Bible. At least the first two and perhaps the third affected the life of Miriam of Nazareth.

Herod the Great

This client-king came to power in 37 B.C.E. and ruled until his death in March or April of 4 B.C.E.[37] Miriam of Nazareth was born and grew up under his reign. Politically savvy about how to deal with the Romans, Herod was a cruel tyrant at home and ruled with an iron fist. The people hated him. The incident recounted in Matthew's gospel of Herod's killing all the male children under the age of two in Bethlehem, even if not strictly speaking historical, fits with the way he was remembered. His brutality was matched by a love of luxury. He advertised his own magnificence by making grand, monumental statements in stone. A master builder, he launched enormous, grandiose construction projects the remains of which can still be admired. Archaeological excavations are uncovering the port city of Caesarea, which he founded and dedicated to the emperor Caesar Augustus. This project alone entailed developing a deep harbor, building a theater, temple, hippodrome, and other public structures, capped with a huge statue of Caesar visible from far out to sea. To stand here on the ornate balcony of Herod's palace cantilevered over the blue Mediterranean, and to imagine him entertaining guests as the sun sinks into the sea, is to glimpse a luxurious lifestyle that was the complete opposite of that of the Galilean villagers. This Jewish client-king also created smaller cities such as Gaba and Agrippias; rebuilt the important city of Sabaste; built the fortress-residence Herodion, where he was finally buried; and refortified and lavishly furnished numerous strong bastions for himself, such as the one at

Masada, still impressive for its water-delivery system, its mosaics, and its magnificent view high over the desert and the Dead Sea. Above all, in Jerusalem Herod embarked on a massive project to expand and rebuild the temple complex, the sacred center of Jewish worship. The plans for redesigning its outer walls and courtyards and reconstructing its inner sanctum in the Hellenistic Roman style were so massive that they took nearly eighty years to complete. Part of the western wall, enormously strong and showing beautiful craftsmanship, is now a center of Jewish pilgrimage and prayer.

Somebody had to pay for all of this—the construction, the lavish court life, the costly gifts, and of course the royal army. This king of the Jews found the resources he needed through increasingly heavy taxation. In Galilee he took the already existing town of Sepphoris and, although he did not live there, fortified it as the center from which to tax the countryside. Pressure to pay was intense; collectors showed up at the village threshing floors to scoop up the king's portion; no one escaped. To the peasants in the villages the already burdensome triple tax load became next to unbearable as Herod's portion was jacked up. They were being squeezed dry, tipped over from subsistence living into penury and loss of family land. "The indebtedness of small farmers and expropriation of their land are hallmarks of this Roman epoch. Hence one can speak of a regular process of pauperization."[38] This created a climate for rebellion. People yearned for a messianic king like David who would have the good interests of the people at heart.

When Herod died in 4 B.C.E., resentment exploded in revolt all over Palestine. In Galilee the insurrection was led by a popular leader named Judas, whose father had been killed by Herod many years before. According to Josephus, "Judas, son of the brigand-chief Ezekias . . . when he had organized a large number of desperate men around Sepphoris in Galilee raided the royal fortress; having seized all the weapons stored there, he armed all his followers and made off with all the goods that had been seized there."[39] Facing widespread uproar, the Romans responded with brutal efficiency. The Roman legate Varus marched down from Syria with three legions and numerous auxiliary troops and quashed the uprising. In Jerusalem, Josephus notes, they crucified "two thousand" Jewish men outside the city walls.[40] In Galilee they recaptured Sepphoris and, in Josephus's succinct summary, "burned the city and enslaved its inhabitants."[41] Recent excavations at Sepphoris do not as yet show any evidence of fiery destruction from this period. Scholars surmise that Josephus used Sepphoris as a proxy for the surrounding villages, which would have been leveled to punish the rebels among their inhabitants. Villages were burned; people were sold into slavery. Horsley points out that, "in the villages around Sepphoris such as Nazareth the people would have had vivid memories both of the outburst against Herod and the Romans, and of the destruction of their villages and the enslavement of their friends and relatives . . . the mass enslavement and destruction would have left severe scars on the social body of the Galilean village communities for generations to come."[42] Living in Nazareth, Miriam would have been around fifteen or sixteen years old at the time, a young married woman with a new baby. She obviously survived the damage inflicted on her neighborhood by brutally efficient, rampaging Roman legions. Did she hide with other village women in a cave in the Nazareth ridge as the tidal wave of violence came sweeping down? What terror, what loss from deaths, rapes, and looting had to be coped with? How much rebuilding absorbed their energy when psychically they were at a low ebb and materially they had so little to begin with? Sad to say, the wretched wars of the late twentieth and early twenty-first centuries, reported in the press and shown on television, leave little work for our imagination. Watching village women over the years in Vietnam, El Salvador, Bosnia, Indonesia, Congo, Afghanistan, and elsewhere flee, hide, be injured, all the while trying to protect their children from forces intent on their destruction conjures their courage and suffering in real time. The world of Miriam of Nazareth was no stranger to such violence and social disruption. "From the Roman point of view, the slaughter of people, devastation of towns and countryside, and enslavement of able-bodied survivors after the rebellions in 4 B.C.E. and the widespread revolt in 66 C.E. were all pointed attempts finally to terrorize the populace into submission."[43]

Herod Antipas

Once they had crushed this popular Jewish insurrection, the Romans carved up Herod's kingdom among his three sons. Archelaus received Judea and Samaria, the southern and central regions, respectively; Herod Philip was given the far north territories; and Herod Antipas became ruler of Perea to the east of the Jordan River and Galilee in the north.

"To be Antipas was to be sorely disappointed."[44] Thus does Crossan ruefully describe the frustration of this ruler at being named tetrarch or ruler of only a part of a country, and his all-too-human efforts to become full-fledged king of all Palestine like his father. In all his long reign from 4 B.C.E. until he was deposed by the emperor in 39 C.E., he never succeeded. Like his father, Herod Antipas ingratiated himself with the Roman emperor not only by collecting and funneling the required monetary tribute but also by grand building projects. First he focused on Sepphoris, damaged in the peasant uprising and Roman reprisals. Making it his capital city, he launched a huge construction project designed to fortify and beautify Sepphoris "to be the ornament of all Galilee,"[45] in Josephus's memorable phrase. Twenty years later and twenty miles away on the shore of the Sea of Galilee, he founded a brand new capital city named, in typical client fashion, after the new Roman emperor. As Josephus describes it, "The Tetrarch Herod, inasmuch as he had gained a high place among the friends of Tiberius, had a city built, named after him Tiberias, which he established in the best region of Galilee on Lake Gennesaritis."[46] What is most interesting for our purpose of picturing Miriam's world is to observe the impact of these burgeoning cities on the surrounding countryside. Politically, these cities were aggressive symbolic statements celebrating the power of Rome. Galilean people who under Herod the Great had been governed from a distance now had the Roman client-ruler and his entourage present in their territory for the first time, breathing down their necks, so to speak. Most villages were no more than a day's walk from either Sepphoris or Tiberias. Insofar as these Herodian centers represented the alien cultural and religious values of the empire and the willingness of some hellenized Jews to collaborate with that system, they were intrusions into the traditional loyalties of the villagers. Economically, too, the heavy demands for money to finance the building and for foodstuffs to feed the residents of these growing cities made increasingly onerous demands on the productive peasantry. As tetrarch and not king, Antipas was ambitiously drawing on a much more limited economic base than his father had. Tensions between town and countryside inevitably grew strong.

Archaeological excavations at the ruin of Sepphoris got under way in the 1980s and as of this writing are still in progress. Architecturally it has the earmarks of a good Roman-Hellenistic city: fortified city walls, a large paved main street (the ruts made down the middle by the wheels of heavy carts are still visible), planned side streets, colonnaded and roofed sidewalks lined with shops, a water-delivery system and a sewer system, a palace that served as the residential and administrative seat of power, an armory, a large basilica used as a court or market, a theater (whose date is fiercely contested) and, in addition to other public structures, affluent private homes with fresco and mosaic decorations, cosmetic items, and fine tableware. The population can be numbered around 8,000 to 10,000 persons. The majority seem to have been Jewish: witness the presence of numerous *miqva'ot,* or pools for ritual purification according to the Torah, along with the archaeological absence of any temple to the Roman gods, the absence of large public statues, and the absence of human images on the coins Antipas minted (the first commandment of Moses forbade graven images). At the same time, Roman and other Hellenistic representatives of the empire engaged in business, government, and the military would also reside in this administrative city, giving its population an ethnically mixed character. Excavations have been much more limited at Tiberias because, unlike the ruin of Sepphoris, it is a still lively, inhabited town hostile to efforts at disrupting contemporary life to get at older layers of civilization. Literary records describe Herod Antipas's palace there as luxuriously constructed but decorated with images of animals in an alien fashion. Government and military officials lived lavishly nearby. The city's position on the lake near trade and pilgrimage routes made it a bustling commercial center. It should be noted that these were not great cosmopolitan cities but minor provincial capitals. Nevertheless, their cosmopolitan population and display of wealth and power set them clearly apart from the "country people" in the Galilean villages that surrounded them.

Since the Sepphoris excavations began, a number of intriguing questions have arisen that have yet to find a settled answer in scholarship. Why is Sepphoris, such a big important place and so close to Nazareth, not mentioned in the New Testament? Why is Tiberias named only once in passing (John 6:23), though it is not far from the lake village of Capernaum where Jesus centered so much of his ministry? Why is neither city mentioned as a stop on Jesus' itinerant ministry around Galilee? Perhaps Jesus avoided these cities to avoid coming into contact with Herod Antipas, "that fox" (Luke 13:32). Antipas had already arrested John the Baptist and, at his infamous birthday party, had him beheaded. Rather than walk precipitously into the line of fire, some think, Jesus directed his message of the kingdom of God away from the two cities and toward the poor where they lived and worked. There is the added consideration that rather than espousing the values of the urban elites, Jesus consistently criticized the accumulation of wealth and what it did to the soul. Recall his comparison of the rich with John the Baptist, the greatest person ever born of woman: "What then did you go out to see? Someone dressed in soft robes? Behold, those who put on gorgeous apparel and live in luxury are in royal palaces" (Luke 7:25). The implied sharp criticism of the Herodian court indicates that Jesus knew of their existence but opposed their ethos in favor of God's passion for the farmer, the vinedresser, the poor widow, the shepherd, the children, and other peasant folk of the Galilean villages.

More speculative questions surround the "hidden" years of Jesus. As a village *tekton* did Miriam's husband Joseph get a job in the rebuilding of Sepphoris? Did her son Jesus? Nazareth was a one- or two-hour walk from Sepphoris, and they could have commuted. Unlikely say others; as a conservative Jewish family they would have avoided the Gentile culture of the city. No, comes the rebuttal; Sepphoris was a basically Jewish city even if open to Roman influence. Did the young Jesus at least visit the city? If so, he may have been more cosmopolitan than the gospels portray him. The controversy over the date of the theater, whether built during or after Antipas's reign, engages this same issue. Did Jesus ever go to the theater? If so, he was a hellenized man exposed to international urban culture. No, argue others; the theater was built late in the first century, and besides, entertainments were mounted for Antipas's scribal retainers, administrative officials, and other elite city personages. The last people welcome there would be the lower social classes from the outlying villages. Trying to picture the world inhabited by Miriam of Nazareth, we do not have to settle all these questions. From a historical perspective, the most distinctive feature of Galilean life during her adult years was the political-economic impact of the rebuilding of Sepphoris and the founding of Tiberias.[47] Enough to know that she lived in a poor village while nearby this beautiful city was going up, perched on a hill like a little bird, with the function of administering Miriam's village in a new and disruptive way.

Let us focus attention on this circumstance more carefully, to make sure we appreciate its significance. The two cities, Sepphoris and Tiberias, were culturally worlds apart from the Galilean villages. The inhabitants differed not only in dress, language, and lifestyle but also in wealth and power owing to the basic political-economic system in which they functioned. The cities were centers from which Herod Antipas orchestrated the gathering of taxes and supplies, passed onto Rome its share of the tribute, and used the rest to enhance his reign. The village communities formed the economic base of the two cities, providing tax monies for their massive and prolonged construction and food to feed their inhabitants. If this were a market economy the cities' needs might, just might, have worked to benefit the small landowners, provided they could grow more than they required and go into the city markets to sell the surplus. But this was a situation of subsistence farming in an agrarian economy. The villagers were basically poor, living on the edge between hunger and satisfaction of nutritional needs. And now here were these two Roman-Hellenistic royal cities whose powerful presence was tipping the people from subsistence farming to commercialized farming, a scene that repeats in our own day when global development disrupts the livelihood of indigenous populations. Horsley's description of the result is illuminating:

> Subjection to these heavy demands for tribute, tithes, and taxes by three different levels of rulers would almost certainly have affected the Galilean villagers' economic and social life adversely. Peasant plots were traditionally barely large enough to provide a subsistence living for a family of five or six as well as meet the dues imposed from above. The peasant producers had first to meet the demands for taxes and then to live until the next harvest on what was left. Tithes, and apparently tribute and royal taxes as well, were taken right from the threshing floors. Conceivably over one-third of their crops may have been taken with the combination of the three different demands. With insufficient food to live on until the next harvest, many would have found it necessary to borrow. . . . The viability of the peasants' tenure on traditional landholdings was thus seriously and steadily undermined by the imposition of heavy tax burdens.[48]

Taxes might also be paid in goods other than crops, but the outcome was the same. In the case of fish and fish sauces, for example, Herod contracted fishing rights to brokers who in turn leased them to village fishers who, in addition to monies needed for nets and boat repair, were now also indebted to these "publicans" for their rights to fish. Not much was left for villagers to consume. In the case of woven cloth, Marianne Sawicki notes that the cities' demands extracted this fruit of women's labor from their village kinship circles and drained it off into the empire's economy, thus turning "womenpower into imperial wealth and might."[49] However taxes were paid, social elites were extracting materials and monies that the peasantry could ill afford. Exploitation is not too strong a word to name the situation. Borrowing led to debt, which led to land being confiscated by creditors, which led to independent farmers becoming tenant farmers, which might ultimately lead to loss of land altogether, with persons reduced to penury as day laborers, bandits, or beggars. Scripture scholars suggest that this situation is credible as the immediate context in which to understand the ministry of Jesus with his compassion for the poor, the scandal of his association with tax collectors, and the emphasis in his parables and aphorisms on wealth and poverty, moneylending, wages, and debts.

Some scholars such as John Meier, E. P. Sanders, and Paula Fredriksen argue that under Herod Antipas the economic situation was not all that dire. They point to the fact that there was indeed no peasant uprising during his reign. Others such as Richard Horsley, Jonathan Reed, and John Dominic Crossan make the case that the heavy economic burden created pressures that progressively disrupted traditional patterns of Galilean village life. Even Sanders agrees that the peasantry were "hard pressed," even oppressed, by heavy taxation administered from the cities.[50] As Reed explains judiciously,

> It is not necessary to envision an extreme crisis in Galilee—peasant life in antiquity was difficult enough and need not be exaggerated. It is, however, important to stress that Antipas' urbanization of Galilee [the economic strain that his building of Sepphoris and Tiberias placed on the rest of Galilee] began a process in which the latter state was perceived as worse than the former by the vast majority; in other words, the peasants' relative state of deprivation, not their poverty in any absolute terms, is the decisive factor."[51]

To fast-forward in time: hostility to the two cities from which they were ruled and taxed, expressed in small uprisings, finally erupted in a major peasant insurrection in the year 66 C.E., the beginning of the disastrous general Jewish revolt against Rome. Speaking of Sepphoris, Josephus recounts:

> The Galileans, seizing this opportunity, too good to be missed, of venting their hatred on one of the cities which they detested, rushed forward with the intention of exterminating the populations, aliens and all. Plunging into the town they set fire to the houses, which they found to be deserted, the terrified inhabitants having fled in a body to the citadel. They looted everything, sparing their countrymen no conceivable form of devastation.[52]

In Tiberias, too, the anger of the landless spilled over into violence: "Jesus, son of Sapphias, the ringleader of the sailors and destitute class, joined by some Galileans, set the whole palace on fire expecting, after seeing that the roof was partly of gold, to obtain from it large spoils. There was much looting. . . . Jesus and his followers then massacred all the Greek residents in

Tiberias. . . ."[53] The countryside's long pent-up resentment against these two cities, nurtured over two or three generations of being depleted by taxation, is summed up by Josephus: "For they had the same detestations for the Tiberians as for the inhabitants of Sepphoris."[54] This loathing did not spring up overnight.

It is doubtful whether Miriam of Nazareth lived long enough to experience this repeat of the peasant uprising and violent Roman suppression that had marked her youth. But we can picture the ways her life in Nazareth was affected by the processes that led to such fierce fighting. Her village was not immune from the increasing debt-load that disrupted traditional patterns of village life. Did neighbors or friends lose their land? Did young acquaintances become socially uprooted and violent? Did the "downward spiral of indebtedness"[55] affect her own household in some way? Did they go hungry after paying their taxes? Did her kin utter prayer to God to "give us this day our daily bread, and forgive us our debts " with a terrible concreteness? Historically Miriam of Nazareth lived in a peasant society in a rocky, troubled time. Whatever the situation in her immediate family, the political-economic pressures of Roman administration through client rulers ground down the village poor to which she belonged and only got worse over time.

Pontius Pilate

In Judea, the misrule of Archelaus, Herod the Great's son, resulted in this province coming under direct Roman rule in 6 C.E. Instead of being administered by a Jewish client-king, Rome appointed a colonial governor called a prefect, later a procurator, to take the helm. Pontius Pilate was the fifth such Roman governor. He oversaw affairs in Judea from 26 to 36 C.E. before being himself removed for excessive violence, culminating with the slaughter of unarmed pilgrims gathered on Mount Gerizim in Samaria. The first-century philosopher Philo of Alexandria describes Pilate's personal character as being of an "inflexible, stubborn, and cruel disposition," and his government as being marked by "venality, thefts, assaults, abusive behavior, and his frequent murder of untried prisoners."[56] Brutal and insensitive to Jewish religious convictions, his rule provoked repeated public protests from large numbers of Jews, many of whom died as a result of his armed response. One particular Jew who "suffered under Pontius Pilate" was Miriam of Nazareth's son, who came under the Roman governor's direct power by going to Jerusalem for the feast of Passover. During Jesus' trial, in Luke's version, Pilate hears that Jesus is a Galilean:

> And when he learned that he belonged to Herod's jurisdiction, he sent him over to Herod, who was himself in Jerusalem at that time. When Herod saw Jesus he was very glad, for he had long desired to see him, because he had heard about him, and he was hoping to see some sign done by him. So he questioned him at some length; but he made no answer.... And Herod with his soldiers treated him with contempt and mocked him ... then he sent him back to Pilate. And Herod and Pilate became friends with each other that very day. (Luke 23:6–12)

As far as Miriam of Nazareth, a unknown woman from a peasant village, would have been concerned, the friendship between these elite personages, the tetrarch from Galilee and the governor from Rome, was forged over the tortured body of her firstborn son.

Herod Agrippa I

A third-generation Herod, named Agrippa, grandson of Herod the Great, succeeded his uncle Antipas in Galilee in 39 C.E. Before he died prematurely in the year 44, Agrippa had become king of all the Jews of Palestine, like his grandfather before him. If Miriam of Nazareth was still alive, whether she returned to her village in Galilee or, as some think likely, remained with the circle of Jesus' disciples in Jerusalem, a Herod was again in power. The violence continued. This time it was directed against the post-resurrection circle of Jesus' disciples, among others. "Herod the king laid violent hands upon some who belonged to the church. He killed James the brother of John with the sword" (Acts 12:1–2). James and John were sons of Zebedee, fishermen on the Sea of Galilee who had followed Jesus. Now James lay beheaded. To close this chapter, let us perform a thought experiment. In Matthew's account of the death of Jesus, all the male disciples "forsook him and fled" (26:56), but the women disciples who had followed him from Galilee looked on while he was crucified. Among these was "the mother of the sons of Zebedee" (27:56). The sons ran, the mother stayed. Did this unnamed but faithful woman stay in Jerusalem after Jesus' death? Can she be counted among the women who formed part of the group of believers depicted in the upper room before Pentecost, praying for the Spirit? This is not unthinkable, especially if she was widowed. Perhaps the account of Herod's killing of James leaves us with this last picture of Miriam of Nazareth: the old mother of a crucified boy consoling the mother of a newly murdered son.

———————————

Using archaeological, social-scientific, and literary sources to picture the world that Miriam of Nazareth concretely inhabited is not easy. The limitation of our sources, the inevitable disputes among scholars over the sources that do exist, and the enduring tendency to project our own experience in an advanced industrial society back upon the first century leaves us with a portrait framed by "probably" and "presumably" and "most likely." One thing, however, emerges from the ambiguities, and this is the social location of Miriam of Nazareth in an economically poor, politically oppressed, Jewish peasant culture marked by exploitation and publicly violent events. Commenting on how the ruling classes of medieval European Christendom who patronized art and literature had turned the mother of Jesus into one of themselves, the pioneering biblical scholar John L. McKenzie noted, "About Palestinian housewives they knew nothing; if they had, they would have found her like the maids of their palace kitchens or the peasant women of their domains. They were not going to hang pictures of these humble common folk on their walls or sing hymns praising their beauty or virtue."[57] Therefore, before they could venerate Mary, they had to extract her from her own historical life and turn her into the ideal woman, a high-class gentlewoman like themselves, "Our Lady." Carrying out the proposal to honor this woman in the communion of saints, our path is distinctly different. Far from being a member of the upper class in Sepphoris, let alone in medieval France, the actual historical person was a woman of the peasant society of Galilee. Here her concrete reality in this social context intrigues us as the locus of her encounter with God. The next chapter continues to build a picture of her world in terms of its religious dimension.

8

⁓

Second Temple Judaism: The Religious World

ON BEING JEWISH

As the picture of the political-economic world of Galilee has already made clear, Miriam of Nazareth was a Jewish woman. This is meant not only in the ethnic sense that she was born into the people who trace descent from Abraham and Sarah, but also in the religious sense. Her faith in God was shaped by the covenant forged at Mount Sinai, nourished by dramatic Jewish narratives of God's saving deeds in history, and expressed in the prayers, festivals, rituals, and ethical observance of Torah characteristic of this religious tradition. At first glance this view may seem strange to the Christian imagination, which for centuries has depicted Mary as a leading member of the Catholic Church, on earth and in heaven. It should be noted that placing her in the Christian community is not without basis insofar as Luke depicts her praying with the circle of Jesus' disciples assembled in Jerusalem after his death, awaiting the Spirit. While this community indeed developed into a church separate from Judaism and can even be called the "early" church, it was in those early decades still a recognizably Jewish group. Picturing the religious world inhabited by this woman of the peasant-artisan class, then, leads us to center our vision on her enduring Jewish identity.

Diversity was a hallmark of the pre-70 C.E. Jewish religion. In addition to the core population in Palestine, there were Greek-speaking, hellenized Jews living in major cities throughout the Roman empire. In Palestine itself, political and economic differences separated rural Galilee, ruled by a lay aristocracy, from Judea with its urban center Jerusalem, a temple state ruled by a priestly aristocracy. Different groups including Pharisees, Sadducees, and Essenes among others contended for the true interpretation of

162

Jewish tradition with a ferocity that can only be compared to "the full-throated feuds of family dissent."[1] For all of this documented pluralism, however, the Jews were a single people. No matter where they lived they were distinguished from their neighbors by the binding power of a common religious culture, a clearly definable religious orientation that was protected by Roman imperial decrees.

At the center of this religion is a profound relationship between the people and the one God, the incomparable Creator of the Universe, who acts in history to redeem and to save.[2] The biblical confession of faith that expresses this conviction is sung or recited with deeply felt conviction: *Shema*—"Hear O Israel the Lord our God, the Lord is one; and you shall love the Lord your God with all your heart, and with all your soul, and with all your strength" (Deut. 6:4–5). Feeling compassion, knowing what they were suffering, this God of their ancestors had led them out of bondage in Egypt. Even more, the Holy One had entered into covenant with them, choosing them as a "treasured possession" (Deut. 14:2) and promising them land and a future full of hope: "You shall be my people and I shall be your God" (Jer. 30:22, paraphrasing Lev. 26:12). The sacred gift of the Law, *Torah*, functioned at the heart of this relationship. With its life-shaping commandments, including the famous Ten, and its identity-giving features such as observance of the sabbath, food laws, and male circumcision, it gave definite shape to the people's life with God. Over time the broad and deep stream of Jewish religious tradition came to include the prophets with their passionate calls for justice, the psalms with their cries of thanksgiving, lament, and praise, and a growing narrative of divine involvement in their history of success and suffering. This was a religious world of revelation and redemption, of calls to repentance and renewal, and of hope for the future. In the first century, messianic hope was neither uniform nor universal, but it was certainly well established and articulate. It was linked to the coming of the kingdom of God, desire for which increased in proportion to desperation of Roman occupation.

Jewish faith enjoyed a concrete geographic focus, the temple in Jerusalem, rising up in new splendor under Herod's building plan. The God of the universe whose spirit pervaded the whole world dwelt in this place in a particular way. Here the daily priestly ritual of prayer, animal sacrifice, and burning of incense was enacted; here people offered their own sacrifices in repentance and thanks to God; here thousands thronged during festivals, joyfully reaching the goal of their pilgrimage; here every Jewish

male was to send an annual one-half shekel tax for upkeep. This locus of
divine presence, however, focused only part of Jewish observance. Day in
and day out, ordinary life was affected by Torah piety with its prayers and
practices and its summons to the righteous life in the light of the covenant.
In home and village the rhythm of the week was blessed by sabbath observance from sundown Friday to sundown Saturday, a time of rest and
prayer perhaps accompanied by attendance at synagogue. The annual calendar marked the seasons with feasts that could be observed locally. In
first-century experience this religion was not a privatized individual matter but was embedded in the social life of the community.

Recent archaeology has turned attention anew to one aspect of concrete
observance, namely, the purity laws. Numerous *miqva'ot* are dug into the
bedrock all over the land of Israel. These are pools or relatively narrow
tanks with plastered walls into which one descends by a series of steps.
Many such pools are built into the temple complex, mute witnesses to
great numbers of Jews who used them on their way to the altar. They are
found in the homes of the wealthy in Jerusalem, Sepphoris, and elsewhere.
In the poorer villages one pool, usually located near the olive press or other
public spot, would served the whole community. These constructions are
meant for immersion in water. According to the Law, certain actions or
contacts cast a person into a state of ritual impurity, making one unfit to
approach the temple and its altar dedicated to the all-holy God. One might
contract impurity, for example, through contact with human corpses or
lepers, or through bodily processes such as ejaculation, menstruation, or
childbirth. Scripture, which delineates these circumstances, also prescribes
the remedy. Immersion in water and then waiting a set period of time,
sometimes accompanied by sprinkling with ashes or offering sacrifice, rec-
tified the situation. It is important to note that neither economic class nor
gender made one more or less ritually impure. Paula Fredriksen points out
that "the fussiest Pharisee, the highest high priest, would be neither more
nor less impure after sexual intercourse than the scruffiest Galilean fisher-
man"; and again, "a healthy adult Jewish female would incur impurity on
a regular basis, through menses; but so would her husband, through his
own semen."[3] Furthermore, since the principal function of ritual purity
was to regulate access to the temple, these laws had less stringent effect on
the daily life of persons living far from Jerusalem. They certainly did not
keep women from participating in synagogue services. Against Ben Witherington III and others who interpret the purity laws as having fiercely lim-

ited women's participation in the public sphere, Amy-Jill Levine acerbically notes, "Society did not shut down during their menstrual cycles."[4] Perhaps for contemporary Christians the most vital point to appreciate is that being in a state of ritual impurity, which scripture assumes will occur as a matter of course, is not equivalent to being in a state of sin. "Purity enables proximity to holiness," Fredriksen explains; "an impure person—a menstruant, a leper or a mourner—is not thereby a sinner, nor is a pure person necessarily righteous."[5] Rather, as part of the warp and woof of honoring the transcendent holiness of God, the purity rituals enact a person's dedication to the God of Israel: "For I am the Lord who brought you up from the land of Egypt, to be your God; you shall be holy, for I am holy" (Lev. 11:45).

One cannot do justice to this complex faith with such a brief description. The point is that a relatively clear combination of belief and practice identified the Jews as following a particular religious path, even when they were widely scattered in the cities of the empire. This was the religion of Jesus, which he never repudiated, and of his family, including Miriam of Nazareth. Theirs was an observant Jewish household that lived their faith in the one God of Israel in the daily rounds of ordinary life in Galilee, in sabbath rest and prayer, and, occasionally, in festival pilgrimages to the temple in Jerusalem. Understanding the deeply Jewish roots of Miriam of Nazareth's piety is critically important to the integrity of her historical life. As Norman Pittenger points out, her faith was not shaped by the devotion to Christ characteristic of the post-Nicene church; "inevitably and naturally, she remained in her own time and place."[6]

One other time-conditioned element needs to be added to this picture. In the first century, the Jewish religion in the land of Israel was on a collision course with Roman imperial might. Passionate belief in one God whom no graven images could capture clashed with the strange god now brought into the land—Caesar, the emperor, full of power, glory, and divinity. Herod the Great had a golden eagle, a symbol of Rome, enshrined over the main gate of the temple. Two students in a suicidal act tore it down in the uprising after Herod's death. There were repeated protests over Pilate's attempt to display imperial standards with their connotations of a different god. Voices were raised "articulating the feeling of distress among the people that they now had a foreign 'lord and master' in addition to their one true master, the God of Israel."[7] Roman religious belief, which was inseparable from Roman political practice, continually violated the religious sensibilities of devout Jews. In an economic sense, too, the increasing impoverishment of the peasantry had religious ramifications. Rooted in the belief that the land ultimately belongs to God, the Bible holds out a strong vision of justice. The tradition of the sabbatical year and the jubilee year, when debts are canceled and land restored to its rightful inhabitants, carries this ideal even if observed in the breach. John Dominic Crossan makes the case that far from being a superficial element, the notion that God was committed to establishing justice on earth pervades the whole tradition. When Jews prayed to God to "give justice to the weak and the orphan; maintain the right of the lowly and destitute; rescue the weak and the needy; deliver them from the hand of the wicked" (Ps. 82:3–4), they were appealing not only to divine mercy but to what had been revealed as the very character of God. Jewish resistance to Roman rule, then, was more than a people's generic resistance to a state of oppression. In both religious-cultural and economic-political senses, the lordship of Caesar conflicted in a particularly poignant way with traditional Jewish religious loyalties.[8] When the clash finally broke into the open in 66 C.E., Caesar triumphed. Little that was recognizable was left of the central institutions of ancient Judaism.

IN GALILEE

Among scholars there is ongoing dispute over just how Jewish the village residents of Galilee actually were. A history of warfare starting in the eighth century B.C.E. had decimated the ten tribes of Israel that had settled in the north, leaving Galilee open for foreign inhabitants. In addition, Roman rule coupled with the building of Herod's two cities had imported Hellenistic culture to the province. How deep did this overlay of pagan culture extend? Based on diggings in village households, Jonathan Reed argues for an indigenous Jewish population: "wherever archaeologists have excavated, Jewish religious indicators permeate Galilean domestic space in the Early Roman Period."[9] Pointing to the material culture left by first-century residents as evidence, he lists four archaeological indicators of Jewish religious identity: numerous *miqva'ot* used for ritual immersion; stone vessels made of soft limestone rather than clay, also tied to a concern for ritual purity; ossuaries or bone boxes, indicating the Jewish burial practice of collecting and reburying a corpse's bones after the flesh has decomposed;

and a diet without pork, which information is gleaned from analysis of those human bones. The first three of these have been found in Nazareth. When you couple this evidence from private life with the absence of pagan cultic shrines in the public setting, it seems right to conclude that the people of Galilee in the north shared the same socialized patterns of religious behavior as the Jews of Judea in the south.[10]

One relevant structure that archaeology might be expected to turn up but which is almost entirely missing is the synagogue. The remains of one have been found in Gamla, a village near Capernaum, and possibly one or two more. But constructed synagogues as a whole in pre-70 C.E. Galilee are absent (so far). Given the Jewish character of the region, this is vastly puzzling; it is equally curious in view of the gospels' picture of Jesus of Nazareth preaching and healing in the synagogues of Galilee. Scholars explain that while our imagination conjures up a building when we hear the word synagogue, the original Greek term *synagōgē* means an assembly or a congregation of people. It is similar to the word "church," which, though it now usually denotes a building used for Christian worship, originally in Greek, *ekklēsia*, referred to the assembly of persons consecrated by baptism: the people are the church. So too, the synagogue in first-century Galilean villages was the local village assembly: the people were the synagogue. A concrete form of social life that conducted community business, the synagogue could meet in an open space, a public square, under the trees, or in a private house. Entitling his chapter on this matter "Before Synagogues Were Buildings," Horsley suggests some of the purposes of these assemblies. They functioned as means of local self-government, decided disputes in sessions like a local court, watched over tax revenues, announced lost property, collected charity, celebrated events of local significance, and dealt with other community affairs. In this context they also functioned as an assembly of the people for religious purposes. On the sabbath the people gathered to read Torah, recite it, interpret it; they offered prayers of praise and petition to the Holy One of Israel, and took care of other religious business. They would also gather together throughout the year to observe fast days and celebrate religious festivals.[11] In a word, in Galilee the synagogue was usually not a building dedicated to religious observance but a concrete form of social life consisting of an assembly of village people who shared a common faith.

In Judea as well as in the Diaspora outside of Galilee, the assembly (synagogue) was more likely to construct a building (synagogue) to use as a community center and locale for religious activities. Writing of Jews in the cities of Asia Minor, Josephus notes that such communities "had an association of their own in accordance with their native laws; and they had their own place, in which they decide their affairs and controversies with one another. . . . [At this same place] they gather together with their wives and children and offer their ancestral prayers and sacrifices to God."[12] Luke's Acts of the Apostles, written at about the same time, likewise declares, "For in every city, for generations past, Moses has had those who proclaim him, for he has been read aloud every sabbath in the synagogues" (Acts 15:21). Here we see the synagogue in an urban setting as a building, similar to its meaning today. Recall, however, that the Galilean villages engaged in subsistence farming were poor; their inhabitants were also relatively small in number. Their synagogues were simply themselves, assembled as a social grouping.

A significant factor with regard to women's status in the synagogue lay in the absence of a priesthood in Galilee, the priests being centered in the temple in Jerusalem. Without the practice of sacrifice with its accompanying requirement for ritual purity, which restricted the access of women, local custom could prevail. Consequently, the Galilean villages conducted their public communal activities with local leaders and "without restrictions on women's participation beyond those indigenous to the patriarchal peasant family."[13] Presumably, male heads of households would chair village assemblies, lead synagogue services, and conduct the proceedings of the local court. But women would be included among those assembled and would contribute to the public business according to popular custom. Celebrations of the life cycle such as circumcisions, marriage feasts, and funerals would also entail the participation of women according to local tradition. Thus the synagogue was not an all-male affair. This understanding is borne out by the discovery that there is virtually no archaeological or literary evidence from this period to suggest that Jewish men and women had segregated seating in synagogues, with women in balconies or separate first-floor areas. In addition, Bernadette Brooten's pioneering research into inscriptions on synagogues in the Diaspora indicates that some women served as principal officers of local congregations.[14] Horsley's conclusion seems apt:

> While women as leaders in Galilean village assemblies should not be ruled out, pending inscriptional evidence from archaeological explorations, this seems unlikely for patriarchal village communities in Galilee. What seems

highly likely, however, given the evidence from diaspora communities and the portrayal of young women as well as young men running to the assembly in the Book of Judith, is that women participated actively in Galilean village assemblies.[15]

Let us depict in an imaginative way the religious life of a typical Galilean family, placing Miriam of Nazareth in this setting. Everyday piety was anchored by two institutions, the family household and the public assembly or synagogue.[16] The environment of the home formed the primary setting for the worship of God. Here personal prayer ascended to God in the morning and evening. Here children were instructed in the Law. Here the purity laws regarding food and sexual intercourse were kept. And here the sabbath was observed in rest and prayer. The *Shema*, quoted in part above, recapitulates these defining aspects of Jewish life:

> Hear O Israel, the Lord our God, the Lord is one. And you shall love the Lord your God with all your heart, and with all your soul, and with all your might. And these words which I command you this day shall be upon your heart. You shall teach them diligently to your children and shall speak of them when you sit in your house, and when you walk by the way, and when you lie down, and when you rise up. (Deut. 6:4–5)

Praying twice a day was common practice. The phrase that enjoins remembering God's word "when you lie down and when you rise up" led to the practice of reciting the *Shema* itself twice a day in the home, at dawn and in the evening. People could certainly pray more often, and no doubt did, encouraged by scripture and the example of biblical characters to bless God for many divine gifts, to offer thanks, and to petition for help in time of need. Home-schooling children in the commandments "when you sit in your house" was abetted by the rhythm of the week, with the sabbath regularly focusing attention on the word of God. On this seventh day when even God rested, no fields were worked, no weaving was done, no business was transacted. Women baked bread and cooked other foods the day before, keeping them warm on a fire lit before sunset on Friday, thereby opening up time and space for their own reflection on the word of God written "on your heart." In subsequent centuries it became customary for the leading female of the family to welcome the sabbath by lighting the sabbath candles and for the male head of household to bless bread and the cup of wine at the joyous evening meal.[17] Whether this custom was followed in first-century Galilee is difficult to say. In any event, Miriam of Nazareth would make sabbath preparations and join with her family for sabbath rest and prayer.

Here the second institution, the synagogue, plays a role, all indications being that villagers from different households assembled for public reading of the scripture and prayer. Special attention was paid to the five books of Moses, the *Torah*, but the scrolls of the prophets and other writings were also heard. The point of such weekly reading and its accompanying instruction, explains Josephus, was that the people might "listen to the Law and obtain a thorough and accurate knowledge of it."[18] Paula Fredriksen makes the important observation that the synagogue, precisely through its emphasis on public reading, diminished the need for literacy along with the monopoly a literate elite might exercise when approaching the sacred text. The individual Jewish man or woman did not have to be capable of reading in order to be involved in interpreting scripture. "Hearing the Law at least once a week, completing the cycle of the Torah time and again throughout one's life, provided text enough. The bible, through community study, permitted the growth of a kind of secondary literacy, whereby Jews could be very familiar with a text without necessarily being able to read."[19] This secondary literacy fostered personal involvement with the word of God. People could discern its meaning in the light of their own life experience and could exercise their individual flair in interpretation. Without doubt it also forged the historical identity of the Jewish community as a whole, everyone sharing a basic sacred text. In this setting Miriam of Nazareth heard the word of God over and over again and participated according to local custom in the synagogue's deliberations.

Gathered at home with family members carrying out their sabbath rituals, and gathered with other villagers in "synagogue" listening to scripture readings, participating in instruction, offering prayer, and probably joining in the singing of psalms, a Nazareth family entered into the centering peace of the sabbath week after week. They would then return to the everyday grind, taught not only to bless God but also to deal lovingly with their neighbors. The Law commands them not to kill, steal, commit adultery, or lie. The biblical laws of charity also mandate generosity to the poor. During the harvest, farmers should leave gleanings of grain for the hungry to pick up; and "you shall not strip your vineyard bare, or gather the fallen grapes from your vineyard; you shall leave them for the poor and the stranger: I am the Lord your God" (Lev. 19:10). The same goes for olives. The faithful Jew is commanded not to oppress others, not to hate, not to bear a grudge, to care for those in need, and to watch out especially for the most vulnerable in their midst, the widow and the orphan. The Torah summarizes all the commandments that should govern their relations in the one memorable law: "you shall love your neighbor as yourself: I am the Lord" (Lev. 19:18).

This is a way of life meant to be interiorized, written on the heart and observed with gratitude because one's deepest spirit is in tune with the graciousness of God. E. P. Sanders rightly argues that fundamental to Jewish piety is the view that God's gracious gift, which Christians call grace, precedes the requirement of obedience. Scripture narratives teach this over and over: God creates the world and blesses its yield before giving the commandment not to eat from one tree; God freely chooses Israel and redeems the people from Egypt before giving the Law on Sinai.[20] Torah itself is cause for gratitude because it sets forth a sure path by which one can walk as a faithful covenant partner. Faithful, abounding in kindness, wishing not to condemn and destroy, calling to repentance, displaying abundant mercy, surrounding the people with loving care, the God of Israel was gracious to the thousandth generation. In the midst of long days of hard work and the multiple relationships of her life, a village woman's spirit could soar with joy in such a saving God as this. Picturing Miriam of Nazareth's religious world, it is not enough to say that Jewish belief and practice formed a mere "background." Loyal to the traditions of her ancestors, she inhabited this faith foursquare. Our memory risks multiple distortions if we forget the deeply Jewish roots of her own piety.

GOING UP TO JERUSALEM

The Jewish calendar punctuated the daily work and sabbath rest of the Galilean villages with annual festivals. Rooted in ancient agricultural rituals, these feasts took on added depth of meaning as they narrated and celebrated foundational events in Israel's history. Normally these feasts were kept in the home, where special foods such as lamb and unleavened bread along with special prayers and songs during the meal told the story to the next generation. But there was another option, to go to Jerusalem. While several lesser feasts were sprinkled throughout the year, three major ones were the occasion for pilgrimage. Passover/Pesach in the spring commemorated the people's liberation from bondage in Egypt; Pentecost/Shavuot

in early summer gave thanks for the giving of the Law on Sinai; and Taber-
nacles/Sukkot in early fall remembered the people's post-exodus passage
through the desert when they lived in tents or makeshift booths of
branches. These three festivals saw Jews by the thousands from both home
and abroad travel to Jerusalem to offer sacrifice in the presence of God.
Picturing the religious world of Miriam of Nazareth places her at the center of planning and celebrating these feasts with members of her household. It also puts us on the road to this magnificent sanctuary.

Scholars debate how many of the Galilean peasant population would
have been able to make this trip, and how often. Since the distance to be
covered is about eighty miles, the journey took roughly four days to one
week by foot each way, less if one rode by donkey. Another several days
would be spent in and around Jerusalem for the purification and sacrificial rituals. Their economic situation made it unlikely that they could
afford the expenses of such a trip repeatedly, let alone take time off from
their fields in spring and summer when their work was most productive.
In addition, the festivals were, first of all, family affairs, primarily celebrated in the home. Nevertheless, Jerusalem, the City of David, was the
lodestone of Jewish history, and its temple was the only place where ritual
sacrifice could be offered. It is likely that Galileans went back and forth for
the pilgrimage festivals, but not in great numbers. Some families may have
gone once in their lifetime; some once a year. The total was probably hun-
dreds for each feast.[21]

They traveled in groups, camping out along the way. The usual route
took them east to the Sea of Galilee, then south along the flat valley of the
Jordan River. Once near Jerusalem they would begin to climb out of the
great rift, up, up through the Judean hills, singing hymns to God until they
glimpsed the walls of the temple at the edge of the holy city. Jerusalem is
south of the region of Galilee, but speaking colloquially the people went
"up" to Jerusalem both because of the climb required and the way this
exertion became a physical metaphor for the ascent to God:

> I rejoiced when I heard them say, "Let us go to the house of the Lord!"
> And now our feet are standing within your gates, O Jerusalem.
> Jerusalem, built as a city with compact unity:
> To it the tribes of the Lord go up, according to the decrees of Israel,
> To give thanks to the name of the Lord. (Ps. 122:1–4)

The goal of pilgrimage was to arrive at the temple in order to offer sacrifice to God. Recall that Herod the Great had expanded the area occupied

by the temple on a vast and lavish scale. It was now an enclosure of some thirty-five acres, most of it unadorned, expansive space open to the sky. One archaeologist has estimated that twelve soccer fields could fit neatly within its borders.[22] The outer walls of the complex were beautifully constructed of dressed limestone blocks, some weighing two to five tons; even today the huge remaining stones of the western wall glow golden in the late afternoon sun. The great open space of the Temple Mount was organized like a series of nesting boxes, with the open-air altar of sacrifice and the enclosed Holy of Holies at the very heart of the complex. Worshipers first entered the temple up a monumental stairway, through a triple gate, and then up a long tunnel that emptied them into the outermost and largest of the plazas, the Court of the Gentiles. This enormous area could hold tens of thousands of people. It was open to the public, except for those who were unclean according to the Torah. Here everyone mingled; civic affairs were conducted; money-changers and sellers of birds clustered along the walls in the shade provided by huge colonnaded porticos. This Court of the Gentiles was separated from the next section by a four-foot high balustrade posted with warning notices to foreigners not to proceed further. Moving through a gate in the railing, Jewish pilgrims entered the Court of the Women, "open," as Josephus describes, "for worship to all Jewish women alike, whether natives of the country or visitors from abroad."[23] Here is where the women stopped. Jewish men continued into the next open area, the smaller Court of the Israelites. This rectangular space was set off from the next Court of the Priests by a low stone railing. It was in the priestly court that sacrifice was actually performed. Its most notable accoutrement was a huge altar with a roaring fire where choice portions of the sacrificed animals were burned, the smoke going up and returning them to God. Josephus's description of the Court of the Women indicates that it had an elevated gallery or balcony, which is a good thing; otherwise the women would not have been able to see over the heads of men in the next court to what the priests were doing.

At the far end of the Court of the Priests beyond the altar was a tall, 150-foot high, beautifully constructed two-room stone sanctuary—along the lines of a free-standing chapel—with golden doors. This was the inner sanctum where the holy God of Israel dwelt in a special sense. Its outer chamber held a gold seven-branched menorah with continually burning flames, a gold table for the showbread, and a small altar for burning incense. The inner chamber, separated by a veil, contained, stunningly, "nothing whatever."[24] In the temples of Greece, Egypt, and Rome this is where the statue of the deity would reside. But Israel's God, the incomprehensible, invisible Creator and Redeemer of the universe, had no cult image. Into this empty Holy of Holies the high priest alone entered once a year on the Day of Atonement. Otherwise, it was inviolate. This unspeakable "nothingness" signifying the unimaginable plenitude of the Holy One was at the center of the entire Jewish faith.

The observable action of worship, both on a daily basis and massively so during pilgrimage festivals, took place in the Court of the Priests. In common with other religions at the time, Jews offered animal sacrifice to their God in addition to grain, oil, and first fruits. Doves and pigeons, lambs, rams and bulls were killed to atone for sin, to give thanks, or to remove the impurity of childbirth, according to the norms laid down in the Torah. As in many ancient societies, blood had a sacred character. It was the seat of life and so belonged to God alone, the author of life. Shedding it in this majestic setting, yards from a flaming altar, after due preparation, in accord with the Law, with personal prayer and awareness of divine presence, was a religiously meaningful act charged with awe and mystery. In the Court of the Israelites, Jewish men would approach the railing with their animals; on the other side the priests, working in shifts, would receive and sacrifice them. If a woman came without a male companion, one of the Levites, a secondary order of priests who performed essential auxiliary services, would ferry her offering from the Court of Women to the priests. Sanders's description of the scene is illuminating:

> The work of the priesthood proper, put in terms of tasks known today, was a combination of liturgical worship and expert butchery, mostly the latter. The priests heard confessions and accepted sacrifices and offerings in the name of God. They slaughtered animals and birds and flayed (skinned) the animals and cut them up for distribution. They sprinkled or poured blood on and around the altar. They put the principal fatty pieces on the altar, ... separating the remaining parts for their own use or that of those who brought the sacrifices.[25]

An ancient observer adds the detail that the priests who carried pieces of flesh to the altar to be burned exhibited "a wonderful degree of strength. For they take up with both hands the limb of a calf, each of them weighing more than two talents [175 lbs.], and throw them with each hand in a wonderful way on to the high place [of the altar] and never miss placing them on the proper spot."[26] It is clear from this description that the priests were physically fit. Since only priests were allowed in the sacrificial area, they also had to do all the menial tasks such as carrying firewood, stoking the large open fire, and washing down the whole area every evening. They worked barefoot. To enable them to move nimbly, "the sleeves of their tunics were tightly laced around their arms, and they wore breeches for greater modesty."[27] By the end of their shift they would be spattered with blood.

In addition to the sacrifices brought by pilgrims, the temple priests also conducted daily morning and evening sacrifices on behalf of the community, accompanied by a prayer service during which they recited portions of scripture and burned incense. Music for these rituals that opened and closed the day was provided by the Levites. Their hymn book was the Book of Psalms written on heavy scrolls, which they held while they sang, standing on a platform outside the Court of the Priests. They clanged cymbals and blew trumpets as the music required. In all of this, according to *Aristeas*, "Everything is carried out with reverence and in a way worthy of the great God."[28]

In our mind's eye, let us follow a family coming up to Jerusalem for one of the feasts.[29] Arriving after several days' trek from Galilee, they and their neighbors join the throngs who set up camp outside the city walls. Or if they have relatives in the city they lodge with them; or they rent space, perhaps a flat rooftop. The afternoon before offering sacrifice the adults immerse in a public *miqveh* and abstain from sex that night. In the morning, leaving their baby and toddler with a relative, the couple with their older children head for the temple. After purchasing a lamb in the colorful market below the great walls, they enter by the beautiful, majestic gates, emerging into the Court of the Gentiles. There under the far portico they buy a basket with two doves, inspected and approved, for the woman's offering after childbirth. Under a brilliantly sunny sky they cross the expansive Court of the Gentiles and come to the balustrade that warns foreigners to go no farther. Assuring one of the Levites on duty of their status, they enter the Court of the Women. While the woman with her daughters climbs the stairs to the gallery, her husband and sons go right through into the Court of the Israelites. The woman finds a Levite to take her birds to a priest. She keeps an eye on their progress and watches while they are sacrificed. Meanwhile, another Levite helps the man lift his lamb up, suspending its forelegs, breast, and head over the low railing that marks off the priestly sanctuary. A young priest approaches. Placing his hand upon the lamb's head and uttering a prayer, the man bares its neck to the blade. Quickly slashing the arteries of its neck, the priest collects the gush of red blood in a basin, then walks over and splashes it around the base of the flaming altar. He comes back to retrieve the animal's carcass, removing it to a section of the court where he will flay and butcher it. In the interim the womenfolk above and the menfolk at ground level are silent with their own thoughts, musings, prayers. A short time later the priest returns with the result of his handiwork. The man takes the pieces of lamb, offers thanks, gives a portion to the priest, then leaves with the remainder. Meeting back outside the Court of Women, the couple and their children cross the massive outer court and walk down from the temple together. They head back to their campsite with thanksgiving in their hearts after this far-from-routine, close encounter with the all-holy God. Joining up with their extended household, they prepare for the evening's feast.

Imagining such a family grouping celebrating with their lamb at the Passover meal, Paula Fredriksen describes the evening scene. Tired though the adults may be, the excitement of the exodus story eventually grips them all. "Slavery—then freedom; Pharaoh—but Moses! God's strong arm and mighty hand, leading them out, out past the sea, out into the desert, out to the Jordan, finally into the Land. The songs and laughter of other households mingled with their own; all Jerusalem sang its prayers of praise as the sounds of the feast ascended up the valley, up the hillside, up into the starry silver night, the huge full moon, up, up, to the throne of God himself."[30] Just such a scenario of ritual sacrifice and joyful family feasting would have comprised part of the religious world in which Miriam of Nazareth participated.

On these occasions, danger was always present. Not only did Roman soldiers stand guard, observing the pilgrims from their fortress built flush to the side of the Temple Mount. Not only could the spirit of national redemption carried in the festivals awaken strong resistance to the imperial occupying power. Not only could the Court of the Gentiles get so crowded with people from all over the world that incidents of "rabble rousing," meaning rebellion, easily broke out, bringing a swift and violent response. There was indeed tension in the air on the Temple Mount, should a pilgrim from Galilee choose to notice it. But more profoundly, the political role of the temple priesthood cast their leadership into alliance with the foreign occupiers rather than their own people. Like the client-king in Galilee, the high priest of the temple ruled as proxy for Rome in Judea.

Appointed or removed by the Roman governor and accountable to him, the high priest was responsible for the orderly public operations of the temple, the city of Jerusalem, and the wider region. He commanded a brigade of several thousand temple guards, who also served as Jerusalem's police force. He oversaw the collection and expenditure of the wealth accumulated from the offerings of pilgrims, the donations of the rich, and the temple tax paid by Jews even in the Diaspora. The tight combination of political, military, and financial power with religious power, therefore, positioned the Jewish high priest as a key instrument in Rome's designs. Like it or not, he had to preside over the acquiescence of his people or they would suffer severe Roman retaliation and he, of course, would lose his own wealth and standing. When John's gospel depicts the high priest Caiaphas arguing in the case of Jesus that it was expedient to do away with one troublemaker rather than have the Romans come and destroy their holy place and their cities (John 11:47–50), he was but exercising the administrative judgment proper to his role. Miriam of Nazareth was to suffer much from this political arrangement.

On balance, people who lived in the villages of Galilee spent very little of their lives going on pilgrimage to Jerusalem, celebrative though these trips were. Their faith in God was lived out in home and village synagogue, far from priestly hierarchy, sacrificial rituals, or the religious separation of the sexes. Observance of Torah, daily prayer, weekly sabbath, and celebration of the festivals in their times and seasons embedded their covenant relationship with God in the social rhythms of their agrarian communities. From this distance, the northern biblical tradition of prophets who criticized the temple and its burnt offerings in favor of letting justice for the poor roll down like a mighty stream would have resonated to a great degree.

JEWISH CHRISTIANS / CHRISTIAN JEWS

Scripture's last glimpse of Miriam of Nazareth in terms of her chronological years depicts her in Jerusalem in the circle of the disciples awaiting the Spirit. After naming Peter, John, James, and other men disciples, the text continues, "All of these with one accord devoted themselves to prayer, together with the women, and Mary the mother of Jesus, and his brothers" (Acts 1:14). Though the women are unnamed, the reference is most likely to those women disciples whom Luke, the author of Acts, had already depicted in his gospel as following Jesus in Galilee, coming up with him to Jerusalem for the feast of Passover, and becoming key witnesses to his death, burial, empty tomb, and resurrection. These included "Mary Magdalene and Joanna and Mary the mother of James and the other women with them" (Luke 24:10). Numerous people unknown to us formed part of this circle: "the company of persons was in all about a hundred and twenty" (Acts 1:15). When during the feast of Pentecost/Shavuot the Holy Spirit came upon "each one of them" in wind and tongues of fire, they launched the mission that would spread the good news throughout Judea and from there to the wider Hellenistic world. A core group stayed in Jerusalem as a kind of headquarters for the movement while others began to travel.

The scholars who wrote *Mary in the New Testament* judge that placing Miriam of Nazareth in this core Jerusalem community is "a tradition which should be accepted as reliable."[31] Since Luke does not place the mother of Jesus in the earlier crucifixion scene and is silent about later details of her life, the fact that he affirms her by name in the midst of this post-resurrection group of Jesus' followers is not most likely haphazard but reflects a community memory that she was there.[32] Working with this judgment, our last step in picturing the religious world of Miriam of Nazareth entails looking at the early years of the community gathered in Christ's name in Jerusalem.

This group is labeled in various ways: the early church, the mother church, the early Christian disciples, primitive Christianity. They carried forward into history the living memory of the life, death, and resurrection of Jesus, imbued with the growing belief that he was the Messiah of God, the conviction that lies at the heart of the Christian faith. Looking back, we see that they were already the church in its beginnings. Part of the difficulty with such terms as church and Christianity, however, is that they tend to obscure the fact that this was a group of Jews who did not think of themselves as a church separate from Judaism. Rather, they were Jews who joyfully proclaimed that in Jesus the Messiah, God's promise of redemption, which Judaism had long cherished, was now being fulfilled.

Let us depict this community of women and men disciples in Jerusalem in the thirties and forties, the first decades after Jesus' death. By all observable measures they continued to cling to their ancestral Jewish faith, most notably by worshiping in the temple. After Jesus ascended into heaven, the last words of Luke's gospel leave us with this picture: they "were continually in the temple blessing God" (Luke 24:53). In the period after the Spirit descends in wind and fire, a dramatic incident in the temple calls their group to the attention of the temple authorities. "Now Peter and John were going up to the temple at the hour of prayer, the ninth hour," when they passed a man lame from birth who begged alms every day "at that gate of the temple which is called Beautiful" (Acts 3:1–16). "Seeing Peter and John about to go into the temple," he asked for money but, wonderfully, received instead the gift of healing. "And leaping up he stood and walked and entered the temple with them, . . . praising God." When a crowd of people gathered around them "in the portico," Peter and John begin to preach that in Jesus, God was fulfilling the promise made to Abraham. "And as they were speaking to the people, priests and the captain of the temple guard" came up and arrested them for "teaching the people and proclaiming in Jesus the resurrection from the dead." Not every detail of this account may be accurate, but it shows in summary fashion how this early community was perceived. They were observant Jews, filled with the Holy Spirit, who worshiped the one God in the temple, prayed the *Shema* morning and evening, followed the food and other purity laws, and obeyed Torah in the spirit of the covenant. Speaking of this early community, historical studies have brought about a scholarly consensus that "there is no reason to doubt the ongoing Jewish identity of the followers of Jesus and their loyalty to the institutions and basic convictions of Israel."[33]

What marked them off from their neighbors was their relationship to Jesus of Nazareth. Following him in his lifetime, agonized over his death, they now experienced him risen and present in their midst in a radically new, transcendent mode of existence. The righteous sufferer vindicated by God dwelt among them anew by the power of the Spirit. Ransacking their scriptures for ways to express his significance, they gave him many titles, including "Christ," the Messiah or anointed one. By so doing they placed Jesus squarely at the center of the God of Israel's saving activity in the world, hidden and mysterious, yet present and living. The crucified Jesus is risen! Jesus is the Christ! Far from causing them to leave their religion, this conviction was cause for joy. For the messianic hopes so alive in the Jewish tradition were now being fulfilled: God was acting to bring new life to the tortured world. This in fact was the very conviction that led them to stay in the city rather than return to life as they knew it in Galilee. Jerusalem was where the apocalyptic consummation of the world was expected to take place. Time was short. The kingdom of God was near. Jesus, who had been exalted to the right hand of God, would return soon to judge the world. He was already sending the eschatological Spirit upon his followers. Shaped by Isaiah's prophecies, Jewish hope envisioned even the Gentiles being converted. "The word of the Lord goes forth from Jerusalem" (Isa. 2:40), and when it is victorious the Gentiles will stream toward the holy city for the final day of the Lord. To hasten that day, the disciples sent members forth on mission.

This Jewish community of believers-in-Jesus also developed certain rituals that identified them as a particular movement within Judaism. As a ritual of initiation they adopted baptism, after the manner of the Jewish community of Essenes at Qumran and John the Baptizer. And, on a regular basis, they celebrated a common ritual meal, which became recognized early on as a prominent feature of their community. These gatherings took place out of public view in private homes, later called "house churches," rented or opened by owners for the occasion, thus carrying on the tradition of Torah piety lived out in a domestic context. Some scholars now make the case that some house churches were led by women, even in Jerusalem, where Mary the mother of John Mark hosted a gathering for prayer (Acts 12:12).[34] The ritual meal was an important setting for the developing tradition. During it they remembered what Jesus had done at table on the night before he died. They cried out with longing, *Maranatha*, Lord come, in anticipation of the messianic banquet in the kingdom that was fast approaching. Luke's idyllic snapshot captures both what would later disappear and what would grow into a central sacrament: "And day by day, attending the temple together and breaking bread in their homes, they partook of food with glad and generous hearts, praising God" (Acts 2:46–47).

Christianity came into being as this kind of small movement within the Jewish faith. It did not spring full-blown into the world complete with the scripture, liturgy, creed, doctrine, moral code, and governing structures that were known to a later age. These things evolved over time. The movement surged from its rural roots to urban headquarters, from Palestinian to Diaspora Jews, and from the Aramaic language of the first disciples to the Greek language of the wider world. The disciples' preaching soon attracted Gentiles, a few at first and then a torrent. Tensions then arose within the core community over this windfall. Should new Gentile male converts have to be circumcised? How carefully should the Gentiles observe the food laws? In addition to these disputes over Torah observance occasioned by the spread of the good news to non-Jewish populations, more tensions flared at home between this group of messianic Jews and others such as Pharisaic Jews, who found their ideas deviant. The believers-in-Jesus became part of the full-throated family feud of intra-Jewish strife so typical of the pluralistic first century. Still, while harboring a tremendous newness, they saw themselves embedded within the Jewish people bound to God in covenant.

We do not know how long Miriam of Nazareth remained with this community. Perhaps she lived out her years in Jerusalem; the Church of the Dormition there claims to honor the place where she fell asleep in the Lord. Perhaps she went back home to Galilee, an old widow living in an extended household. Tradition has it that she went to the city of Ephesus with John the apostle and evangelist; the Church of St. Mary there also honors the place where she died. There is simply no historical evidence. Picturing the world of her old age in Jerusalem, however, is possible to do, given what we know about that community. Coherent with their Galilean roots, they were poor in material possessions. The need to take up a collection to alleviate the real poverty of the mother church is consistently emphasized later by Paul in his letters (Gal. 2:10; 1 Cor. 16:1–4; Rom. 15:25–26). Together they went daily to the temple at the hour of prayer, where incense and song enhanced the sacredness of sacrifice. They broke bread in their homes with glad and generous hearts in memory of Jesus, with joy in his presence in the Spirit, and in anticipation of his return. They preached vigorously in anticipation of the last day. The point is that for decades, the original community springing from Jesus belonged to the Judaism of the land of Israel on the basis of their own self-understanding, lifestyle, social membership, and geographic anchoring. They certainly developed theological positions that increasingly differentiated them from other Jewish groups. Still, they preserved their Jewish identity, as did the mother of the Messiah in their midst.

Flashing forward one more time, we see that the separation of this group from their fellow Jews was a long and complex process. There was no single moment of divorce but a series of crises that stretched well into the second century. In *The Partings of the Ways*, biblical scholar James D. G. Dunn proposes that at least three significant controversies inched the believers-in-Jesus out onto their own path: debate over the temple and its sacrifice, with Paul for example writing to the baptized in Corinth, "Do you not know that *you* are God's temple and that God's Spirit dwells in you?" (1 Cor. 3:16–17); the controversy at Antioch in the middle fifties that resulted in the boundary markers of circumcision and food laws being waived for the Gentiles; and most especially the ongoing growth of christology, which resulted in Jesus being confessed as the divine Word of God and Wisdom-made-flesh.[35]

While these Christian Jews were evolving in their own way, a terrible event took place that also redefined the Jewish religion itself. Starting in 66 C.E. violent rebellion against the Roman occupation spread like a brush fire across the land of Israel. The might of Rome responded in typical fashion with slaughter, devastation, and enslavement. The climactic moment came in 70 C.E., when the Romans finally destroyed Herod's magnificent temple. Paula Fredriksen's dramatic rendering of Josephus's account catches the terror:

> Jerusalem was burning.
>
> The fire fused with the dry August heat. A thick mass of sounds and smells signaled the end of the siege—stone and burning timbers crashing, soot and dust everywhere, the screams of victim and victor, the dense mix of sweat, blood, and fear from the bodies of the living, the stench from the unburied dead. Above, the white-blue bowl of heaven arched, remote and unmoved by the huge confusion below. Rome's legions, furious, implacable, consumed the ravaged Lower City. . . .
>
> Even the beautiful white-and-gold Temple to the God of the Universe, the heart of the city and of the far-flung Jewish nation, finally succumbed to the devouring flames. The intense heat melted precious metals; even limestone burned and burst. The huge stone expanse of the Temple courtyards choked on carnage and confusion as priests, soldiers, terrorists, and civilians all surged toward the sanctuary, the Holy of Holies. In the austere emptiness of this innermost chamber abided the earthly presence of God. . . . Now it too perished; and in their grief, defying Rome to the last, two priests—Meir ben Belgas and Joseph ben Dalaeus—flung themselves into its fires and so perished with it. The entire mountain that it had crowned . . . was so "enveloped in flames from top to bottom," an eyewitness later wrote, that it "appeared to be boiling up from its very roots." . . .
>
> In the heat of the Roman assault, with frenzied legions surging about them and the Temple collapsing in ruin, some six thousand Jews, a mixed crowd of men, women, and children, managed to climb to the roof of the last colonnade in the outer court. . . . The soldiers, undeterred, fired the columns. None escaped.
>
> The Upper City capitulated. Titus ordered everything razed to the

ground. One legion remained behind; the rest moved off. Survivors trickled away in their different directions to slow death or servitude in Egypt, Asia Minor, or Italy. The massive gold table and menorah from the sanctuary, together with a captured scroll of the Law, made their way to Rome, spoils of the war. What was once Jerusalem stood at the smoking epicenter of a blasted landscape. The surrounding territory, devoured by Titus' need for war machines, had been stripped of trees for miles around. Hill and countryside, once green, now denuded, gave way to inevitable erosion. It was Rome's way with rebels. They make a desert, a Roman historian commented later, and they call it peace.[36]

Imagine trying to keep a religion alive after this shocking disaster, with its central and only place of worship completely ruined, its functioning priesthood destroyed, and its people scattered from the holy city, which was no more than charred ruins. Would the Jewish religion now join so many others that have disappeared into the dustbin of history? Rabbinic Judaism was the brilliant response. Centered more than ever on home and local synagogue, honoring a clearly defined scripture, observing Torah in terms of the righteous life, and led by rabbinic teaching authority, this new form of Judaism coped with the loss of temple, priesthood, and ritual sacrifice by transforming the heart of Jewish covenant faith into a newly "portable" form. In this tumultuous context, preserving a people's identity meant drawing careful boundary lines. Before, the followers of Jesus had offered one colorful option within pluralistic Judaism along with the Pharisees, Essenes, and other definable groups. After 70, you were either with the mainstream or you were out, especially if you held such a widely dissident view that Jesus was the Messiah. Bitter infighting ensued as the two groups gradually and in different places separated and mutually excommunicated each other; the believers-in-Jesus left, were put out of the synagogue, or removed themselves. The gospels were written in this climate and reflect the acrimonious state of relations in their aspersions against "the Jews."[37] Meanwhile, the rabbinic strategy worked to consolidate Jewish tradition and keep it alive and thriving in entirely new circumstances.

By the end of the second century, two great world religions had moved into their separate trajectories: Christianity and rabbinic Judaism. Where once there was the ancient Jewish religion, there were now two offspring. At this point in the literature, metaphors abound. While the temple was still standing, Paul, the Pharisaic Christian Jew, had used the olive tree: Gentiles who came to believe in Jesus were branches of a wild olive tree cut and grafted on to "share the richness" of the cultivated, deeply rooted olive tree of Jewish faith (Rom. 11:17). After the split, forgetting Paul's teaching that "God has not rejected his people" (Rom. 11:2), Christians used the metaphor of succession to imply that they had inherited the richness which the Jews had lost.[38] By contrast, Dunn, drawing on contemporary historical studies, suggests that we think of pre-70 Judaism as a broad stream with diverse and often conflicting currents; then "two strong currents began to carve out divergent channels for themselves." Using the science of genetics, he also suggests that "the major strand that was to become Christianity pulled apart on a sequence of key issues from the major strand that was to become rabbinic Judaism."[39] Given the bloody history that now haunts the two communities, Alan Segal proposes the most challenging metaphor, which if adopted would help to chart a different future: born of the same parent, rabbinic Judaism and Christianity are twin siblings.[40]

This thumbnail sketch, though not without nuance, has necessarily compressed a complex process into a single story line. Something of the same thing happened in subsequent centuries as Christians condensed the story of their evolution into the single narrative of the church's being founded by the direct word and deed of the historical Jesus during his lifetime. The documented evidence, however, seems to be much more interesting. Not the single act of Jesus of Nazareth alone but, under the impact of his life, death, and resurrection, the guidance and inspiration of the Holy Spirit in multiple minds and hearts amid the decisions of history created and continue to create the church into being. This history completes the framework of the religious world of Miriam of Nazareth. Since it is exceedingly doubtful that she lived until 70 c.e., let alone after that terrible year, it is fair to conclude that she lived out her later life as a Jewish believer who continued to trust in the God of Israel through whose mercy she had borne the child now seen to be the Messiah who would soon return: Miriam of Nazareth, on the cusp of the divide between two world religions.

9

Women: The Social-Cultural World

A PERNICIOUS CONTRAST

As a rural Galilean Jewish woman, known in the social roles of virginal girl, married wife, hard-working nurturing mother, and older widow, Miriam of Nazareth was also shaped by her society's laws, customs, and expectations regarding the respective roles of women and men. To round out the picture of her world, we turn to contemporary accounts of the daily lives of first-century Jewish women as these can be gleaned from ancient sources. Adding this sketch to the political, economic, and religious lines already on the canvas will complete the picture of Miriam of Nazareth's historical world, which in turn will form the historical matrix for interpreting the biblical scenes in which she appears.

An important question plagues the work of how to interpret the relevant sources. In an effort to demonstrate that the new religion of Christianity was superior to the older Judaism in its attitude toward women, some researchers have resorted to a questionable ploy. Describing first-century Judaism in unrelievedly patriarchal terms, they then compare this with the enlightened, open approach of Jesus toward women. Instead of acknowledging that "patriarchy is not particularly Jewish and that Jesus was interpreting his critical views in the light of the prophetic and eschatological horizon of Jewish faith itself,"[1] this strategy of overblown contrast is patently unfair. It depicts a highly misogynist Jewish society, and then puts into high relief Jesus' liberating interactions with women made all the more remarkable, it is said, insofar as he departed from the demeaning customs of his day. He called women to be his disciples; he spoke to women in public places such as the well and the roadside; he shared table companionship with women disciples as well as prostitutes; he allowed a woman with an issue of blood to touch him, thus becoming unclean himself, and so forth. In all of this, the argument goes, he was rejecting Judaism and bringing the freedom of the "new law" to the oppressed situation of women. The early church, the claim continues, attracted so many women precisely because they understood and desired the emancipating possibilities that lay in being a Christian rather than a Jew. "Oppressed, repressed, suppressed, and therefore depressed by patriarchal socio-cultural controls," Amy-Jill Levine ironically mocks, "Jewish women of course were attracted to the 'community of equals' of the Sophia-Christ."[2] Obviously, the greater the contrast that can be drawn, the more successful such a strategy turns out to be. Latch onto certain derogatory statements and customs of first-century Judaism that subordinate women; highlight certain emancipatory words and actions of Jesus that value women; then pull both out of context and compare. *Voilà!* It is no surprise that the Christian heritage appears in a more favorable light. If we were to follow this method, we would describe the early life of Miriam of Nazareth as burdened with the insults of patriarchy until her later years, when the redemption wrought by her son began to have an effect on her status. But this is hardly the case.

There are two problems with the strategy of contrast, one ethical, the other intellectual. Regarding the first, the contrast promotes a thinly veiled anti-Judaism, which is a defect that has long marred the history of Christian theology. Sensitive to the ravages of anti-Semitism and hearing this argument from within their own tradition, Jewish feminist scholars of religion were the first to raise this moral issue. Judith Plaskow's essay "Christian Feminism and Anti-Judaism" sounded the alarm, analyzing how, as a consequence of its stereotyping of patriarchal Jewish religion, "feminism is turned into another weapon in the Christian anti-Judaic arsenal."[3] Furthermore, naming Judaism as a primary source of Christian women's oppression not only feeds a pernicious prejudice but also prevents Christianity from taking responsibility for its own sexism, which indeed inheres at all levels of its own traditions. "Blaming the Jews" for patriarchy sets up a scapegoat. Its dynamic defames one group in order to privilege another. But in light of patriarchy's historic habit of accusing women from Eve onward for the evil in the world, Susannah Heschel poignantly observes, "if there is any single most important point promoted by feminism, it is to cease the projection of evil onto others."[4] As recent scholarly discussion makes clear, neither respect for the Jewish religion nor the promotion of the human dignity of all women is served by this disreputable strategy.[5]

In addition to ethical justice, historical accuracy is another casualty of this ploy. For one thing, it usually entails a use of sources from a later period to describe the situation of women earlier on. Those who cite rabbinic sayings that restrict and demean women customarily quote from the Mishnah, assembled around the year 200 C.E., or the various Talmuds, assembled in the fifth to sixth centuries, to establish the role of women in Jesus' time. This is a scholarly mistake because these compilations of Jewish teachings and legal opinions are the product of a later historical period and thus are not reliable evidence for conditions in first-century Judea and Galilee. While some of these passages do reflect first-century conditions before the temple was destroyed, most reflect the situation after the Roman war when rabbinic Judaism was taking shape and gaining authority. Plaskow makes the insightful suggestion that the talmudic writings ought to be compared not with Jesus or the gospels but with their true contemporaries, the church fathers of the second to sixth centuries, an exercise that would leave "neither Christians nor Jews much room for self-congratulation. Rather, what is immediately striking is the similarity between the two traditions— in both, the developing association of women with sexuality and the fear of women as temptress."[6] Even were one to use the Mishnah and the Talmud ever so carefully as sources, in all fairness one should cite the stories and sayings that are beneficial to women along with those that disparage. These works contain multiple voices; one must establish which represent normative opinion and which exist only to be contradicted.[7]

Rather than retroject later conditions reflected in the Talmud into the first century, historical research does better to consult sources contemporaneous with Christian origins. In the process, one must be careful to distinguish between what women were actually doing and the history of men's attitudes and writings about women, especially regarding points where the latter intruded into their world. Feminist scholarship makes clear that statements *about* women that emanate from a male-centered thought system do not correspond to historical reality, where the complex fullness of women's existence actually goes forward and contributes. Taking these considerations into account, researchers are discovering that within the patriarchy common to the whole ancient world, Judaism displayed a surprising diversity. There were differences between the conditions of women living in the Diaspora and in the land of Israel itself; differences between women in rural and urban areas; differences between rich and poor women; and differences among women aligned with the various groups in the first century, such as Essenes, Pharisees, the Baptist's disciples, and the Jesus movement. Such diversity makes it almost impossible to deliver a monolithic judgment about the status of first-century women in this extended community. The variety of Jewish women's experiences makes it not at all evident that Jewish women in the first century were more oppressed than early Christian women, whether Jewish or Gentile. Indeed, both shared the limitations and diverse opportunities that existed in the ancient Greco-Roman world.[8]

On the positive side, both literary and nonliterary sources bring to light the presence of liberating trends within the Judaism of this time. The Book of Judith, composed around the second or first century B.C.E., depicts a heroine who possesses great wealth and commands authority in the community. Being both wise and brave, she executes a risky maneuver that saves Israel from a fierce foe, earning the praise of the people, who thank God exuberantly for her actions. Other popular apocryphal works written around roughly the same time feature similarly self-directed women whose response to revelatory experiences of the holy God of Israel impacts their community and its future. Examples include the role of Rebekah in *Jubilees,* Aseneth in *Joseph and Aseneth,* and Job's wife in the *Testament of Job.*[9] Thus, the picture was not totally bleak when Jesus arrived. With some irony Ross Shepard Kraemer argues that Jesus' own conduct toward women, rather than distinguishing him from first-century Jewish men, opens a window on what was considered acceptable rather than alien behavior, especially since the gospels carry no explicit outside criticism of his being accompanied by women disciples. Indeed, the gospels show us that the presence of Jewish women in a variety of public venues was taken for granted. "Precisely because we are dealing with the attraction of Jewish women to a new Jewish charismatic leader [Jesus], and to a movement around that leader that consists virtually, if not entirely, of other Jews and expresses itself wholly within the broader framework of first-century Judaism,"[10] early Christian writings themselves may be a source of information regarding the situation of women in Judaism.

A variety of archaeological remains, papyrus letters, legal documents, and durable inscriptions on stone and marble demonstrate women's presence in communal life and even allow us to hear their voices. We have already seen that evidence for segregated seating in the synagogue is virtually nonexistent, making it no longer impossible to imagine that women could have served in liturgical functions. Bernadette Brooten's original study of synagogue inscriptions analyzes nineteen Greek and Latin carvings in which women bear the titles "head of the synagogue," "leader," "elder," "mother of the synagogue," and "priestess." These encomiums indicate that some women served in important administrative leadership in at least some synagogues, mostly in the Diaspora.[11] We would love to know more than we do about these female synagogue leaders, but their very presence subverts the old Judaism-versus-Christianity ploy. Other inscriptions pay tribute to women who gave donations for the building or decorating of synagogues, demonstrating that some Jewish women also amassed wealth and deployed it for the benefit of their community. Ross Kraemer's compilation of epigraphs from cemeteries and a wide variety of other venues allows further glimpses into women's activities across a wide societal expanse.[12] In addition to being leaders in synagogues, financially independent landowners, businesswomen, and owners of their own homes, some women acquired religious education and even devoted their lives to the study of Torah.

There is no doubt that first-century Judaism, in tune with the rest of the ancient world, had its patriarchal, androcentric mores and that many, even the majority of women, were legally disadvantaged and powerless. There is also no doubt that, as a result of this, we suffer from a paucity of data about Jewish women's lives both in Palestine and in the Diaspora; Brooten's image of women's history as prehistory and of women's historical research as detective work is unfortunately apt.[13] The sources we do have make clear, however, that no homogeneous definition will fit all groups. Like their non-Jewish sisters in the empire, Jewish women in the first century engaged in a broader range of activity than that suggested by a narrow patriarchal stereotype. In the turbulent years leading up to the first war with Rome, women in Palestine may well have had more than the usual opportunities to assume nontraditional roles. "Certainly the data suggest that one can find models for the leadership positions held by women in the early church both in Jewish and non-Jewish communities, and probably in classes of Roman and Jewish women who shared, at least in part, similar power and opportunities."[14] If some women in the Judaism of this period were powerless but some were leaders, if some were legally disadvantaged but some enjoyed certain rights, then the Jesus movement, insofar as it embodied new visions of human equality and new opportunities for women's leadership, can be seen as carrying forward liberating trends present in Judaism itself. Comparison should then be made not between Jesus and Judaism but between, on the one hand, the Jesus movement as one among several prophetic emancipatory movements in Judaism and, on the other hand, entrenched systems of domination in antiquity that crushed human beings. "Only if one recognizes the egalitarian forces in Judaism can one . . . argue that Jesus as a Jew was egalitarian."[15]

This discussion underscores the importance of method when picturing the cultural world that Miriam of Nazareth inhabited, including the parameters imposed by gender. The all-too-easy contrast of Christianity against Judaism will not serve our purpose. Rather, we seek to discern the actual contours of the gendered world Miriam inhabited in her Galilean village.

MARRIAGE AND FAMILY

In Palestine at this time, as indeed for most of human history, young people entered into marriages arranged by their families. The unions were most often negotiated by the couple's fathers or between the bride's father and her future husband, though in Galilee mothers may have had a say about daughters' marriages; widows could take a more active role in their own remarriages.[16] According to contemporary Roman law, the minimum age of marriage for girls was twelve, for boys fourteen. Jewish practices were comparable, so that marriage for a girl usually took place at or just before puberty, usually between the ages of twelve and thirteen. This not only allowed maximum use of her childbearing years but also served her father's ability to guarantee her virginity, a heavy cultural and economic duty as required by law and custom. Schalom Ben-Chorin relates that this age remained so customary that when the modern state of Israel set the minimum marital age at eighteen, "among Yemenite Jews this met with total incomprehension."[17] Without knowing any details of when, where, or how, we can surmise that Miriam married Joseph at this (to us) young age.

According to Jewish custom at this time, marriage was a process that took place in two stages.[18] The first stage was the betrothal. This involved a formal exchange of the couple's consent to marry, made in the presence of witnesses and accompanied by the payment of the bride price from the bride's family to the groom. Unlike our culture's practice of getting engaged, betrothal constituted a legally ratified marriage even though the girl would remain in her own family's home for about one more year. After betrothal the two persons were henceforth husband and wife. The man had legal rights over the young woman. Any infringement of his marital sexual rights could be punished as adultery; their union could be broken up only if he initiated a formal procedure of divorce. Betrothal also gave the girl the status of a married woman for many purposes. She was called the man's wife and could become his widow. In a year's time the second stage occurred with the transfer of the young woman physically from her family home into her husband's family home, a formal move accompanied with some ceremony. They now shared bed and board. He assumed responsibility for her financial support, and they began to have sexual relations. Both Matthew and Luke reflect these marriage customs when they depict Mary's pregnancy beginning while she was betrothed to Joseph but "before they began to live together" (Matt. 1:18), that is, before the second stage of their marriage took place. Knowing the baby wasn't his, Joseph's initial decision to divorce her rather than complete their marriage with the home-taking made legitimate use of one of the options open to him. But note that he was going to divorce her, not break their engagement: they were legally married.

By the fourth century the idea became popular that Mary had taken a vow of virginity prior to getting married, a vow that Joseph had pledged to honor. The oldest mention of this theory in the East is from Gregory of Nyssa in 386. In the West it spread through the teaching of major figures such as Jerome, Ambrose, and Augustine, becoming a classic position. The context for this idea was the new spread of asceticism, including lifelong virginity as a path of sanctity that replaced martyrdom. Numerous women flocked to orders or monasteries where they could live a celibate life. As we have seen, reflecting the new ideal of holiness, the belief intensified that Mary remained a virgin all her life, even after the birth of Jesus. To ensure this, it was proposed that she made a vow of virginity as if she were a nun. Given our historical and literary knowledge of first-century Galilee, however, such a vow is "totally implausible," as Brown argues. "In our knowledge of Palestinian Judaism, there is nothing that would explain why a twelve-year-old girl would have entered marriage with the intention to preserve virginity and thus not to have children. . . . This theory really only makes sense in subsequent Christianity where the virginal conception, plus the virginity of Jesus and Paul, have led to a re-evaluation of celibacy."[19] Some scholars have pointed to the reputed practice of celibacy among some of the Essenes at Qumran or among the Therapeutae, a respected group of Egyptian Jews, as evidence that Mary could have made that vow. But "such celibacy practiced in an ascetic, quasi-monastic community withdrawn from the mainstream of Palestinian life throws no light whatsoever on the supposed resolve of virginity made by a young village girl *who had entered matrimony.*"[20] We are discussing here not the doctrinal teaching about Mary's virginity but the plausibility that she took a vow of virginity along with her marriage vows. This is not attested in scripture nor, since it involves her historical intentions, is it accessible without a letter, diary, or other documentation. Given contemporary knowledge of Palestinian marriage customs, the likelihood of such a vow distinctly fades.

Once Miriam did transfer into the household of Joseph, she most likely would have become part of an extended family. About their household arrangements we have no concrete information, but it is virtually certain that they did not live in the modern type of nuclear family ideally comprised of two parents and their offspring. In rural Palestinian villages, survival was closely linked to the hard labor and expertise of a whole family unit. In view of all the skills necessary for economic well-being, the efforts of a conjugal pair alone would hardly be sufficient. While complex and changing, households ordinarily consisted of multigenerational groups of people linked by marriage and descent. "A senior couple would have resided with their adult sons, their unmarried daughters (for daughters left home upon marriage), their sons' spouses, their grandchildren, and perhaps also an orphaned niece or nephew or a widowed sibling."[21] Calling to mind the typical domestic architecture of Galilean villages, we can envision one or more extended families sharing a compound with common walls, courtyard workspaces, water cisterns, ovens, and rooftop areas. They would lend tools, utensils, and food materials back and forth; there is some evidence from later in the first century that families living next to each other would share a meal on sabbath or holidays. Life would be characterized by interrelationships within "a network of social units" incorporating the nuclear families embedded in the extended family along with "courtyard neighbors, neighbors of the same alley, and fellow villagers."[22] In this setting the segregation and seclusion of women, typical of higher-status families, was hardly possible. Nor did the family homestead function as a private space for living distinct from the public sphere of work. Rather, the family was a working group and its domicile a nexus of social and economic relations. Lack of privacy was a constituent feature of life. Miriam hardly had a room of her own.

Joseph, Husband of Mary

As a married woman, Miriam's relationship with her husband would be a highly significant element of her life. Very little, however, is known about her life partner or their marriage. Historically he would appear to be a faithful, Torah-observing Jew who supported his family as a *tekton*, a worker in stone and wood, of the artisan-peasant class. The critical factor, according to the gospels, lay in the way he offered the protection of legal paternity to her firstborn son whom she conceived in what appeared to be dubious circumstances. While hard for us moderns to understand, the custom of declaring paternity had a strong force in this culture. When a man acknowledged a child as his own, that in fact made him the legal father. Joseph's action regarding Jesus came as a saving grace, providing a home and long-term provision for this young mother and her child. (Once in a discussion group in Harlem I heard a woman declare that the church should preach less about Mary and more about Joseph, "because he raised that boy like his own kid, which he wasn't.") Together Miriam and Joseph formed a family unit, carried out parental responsibilities of nourishing and teaching, and participated in household and village life. From the fact that he does not show up in any later scenes of the ministry which do record the presence of Jesus' mother along with his brothers and sisters, scholars deduce that sometime before Jesus reached the age of thirty Joseph died, leaving his wife a widow.

The portrait of Joseph in the infancy narrative of Matthew's gospel adds depth of character by modeling him on the image of Joseph in the book of Genesis, he of the coat of many colors.[23] Not only are they both sons of men named Jacob, but also both dream dreams and go into Egypt. Just as the original Joseph is called a "man of dreams" or specialist in interpreting dreams, the husband of Mary four times receives revelation in dreams which he acts upon in a life-saving manner. And just as the first Joseph goes down to Egypt, setting the stage for the escape drama of the exodus, so too Joseph of Nazareth flees Herod's murderous wrath by taking "the child and his mother" into Egypt, from which they come forth in a way symbolic of Moses' journey. Through it all, the later Joseph is characterized as a "just man," meaning upright, honorable, trustworthy, a faithful Jewish observer.

Both Matthew and Luke present a genealogy for Jesus, the former tracing his ancestry down from Abraham, the latter back to Adam and thence to God. Different though their theologies are, they both sound an important note by placing Joseph squarely within the lineage of the house of David. By publicly, officially, and formally accepting the child as his own, Joseph gives Jesus a Davidic heritage that becomes part of the foundation of his acclamation as Messiah in later Christian reflection. One long-standing debate has roiled over the different names the two genealogies give to Joseph's father. According to Matthew, "Jacob was the father of Joseph, the husband of Mary" (Matt. 1:16), while in Luke's version Joseph is "the son of Eli" (Luke 3:23). This leads Brown to query half in earnest, "Did Jesus have too many grandfathers?"[24] Neither genealogy is necessarily historical, their function being not to present strict biological kinship but to illuminate a theology of God's providential design that promises and brings about the Messiah in the history of Israel. In our project of picturing the world of Miriam of Nazareth, these lists lead us to understand that she did indeed have in-laws including a father-in-law, whatever his name.

The lack of historical knowledge about the person and career of Joseph permits only sober speculation about the relationship between Miriam and her husband. The old axiom regarding arranged marriages—marriage comes first, love later—would be in force here, with no extant information about the quality of their love. In a thriving conjugal partnership spouses mediate to one another the very love of God. Through loving acceptance of each other's deepest selves, joy and delight in their differently unique ways, and forgiveness of fault, they bring forth in each other the grace of secure confidence from which their love spills over to others beyond their immediate circle. This outflowing love of the partners in turn mediates the very love of God to the world.

Such a relationship demands generosity in the give-and-take of daily events and decisions, a fundamental self-giving that partakes at times of deep asceticism. In the process of sharing life together, the partners mature both as a unit and as individuals, becoming strong in wisdom, age, and grace through the healing power of shared love. Miriam and Joseph were married for at least twelve years, according to chronology of when Jesus was lost and found in the temple in Luke's gospel. Did they share a love like this, or remain somewhat distant in kind mutual regard, or did they aggravate each other? How did they handle the inevitable tensions of everyday living? Did his voice gladden her heart, her presence quicken his spirit? Or did the exhaustion of work and anxiety of child-rearing dilute their affection? Was she cast into deepest grief at his death, or resigned, or relieved, or filled with ambiguous feelings of all three? We will never know. Some thinkers point to the loving, compassionate qualities of the adult Jesus and deduce that his character would be most likely to emerge from a household of the same caliber—the apple does not fall far from the tree. Others speculate that in simple human terms Joseph, whom the historical child Jesus would have literally called *Abba*, served as the concrete reference for the gracious God of compassion whom Jesus called by the same name. Despite the paucity of details, the historical picture of Miriam's world as a woman must grant her the legitimacy of her marriage and her husband.

Brothers and Sisters of Jesus

An historical picture of the Galilean household that the adult Miriam inhabited needs to account for the persons whom the gospels call Jesus' brothers and sisters. Some of them appear early in Mark's gospel, with parallel accounts in Matthew and Luke, when Jesus' mother and brothers show up outside the house where he is teaching and ask to speak with him. In John's gospel his mother and his brothers go down with him to Capernaum after the wedding at Cana. After the resurrection they are present again in the upper room, where the company of Jesus' disciples awaits the Spirit. In subsequent years, James "the brother of the Lord" (Gal. 1:19) becomes a leader of the Jerusalem church. The most extended entry about the brothers and sisters comes in the scene where Jesus returns to his own village to teach in the synagogue on the sabbath. As Mark relates the event, many people of Nazareth took offense at him, wondering where he got all this wisdom. They said, "Is not this the carpenter, the son of Mary and brother of James and Joses and Judas and Simon, and are not his sisters here among us?" (Mark 6:3). Matthew adapts the Markan version slightly to focus on his father's trade and expand the number of sisters, having the villagers say, "Is not this the son of the carpenter? Is not his mother called Mary? And are not his brothers James and Joseph, Simon and Judas? And are not all his sisters here among us?" (Matt. 13:55–56).

Who are these four brothers and the multiple "all his sisters," unfortunately not named, as is all too customary in androcentric literature? In the first five centuries of the church, as Mary's virginity was increasingly seen as having lasted her whole life, there were some bitter disputes about this question. John Meier notes that during these early centuries, "different views on this question were held by various Christians, who were not formally excommunicated by the church of their day for their differing positions."[25] Recent decades have seen a revival of controversy in the light of contemporary biblical scholarship, attitudes about sexuality, and feminist interest in a holistic image of Mary. Three positions existed in the early church; these roughly correspond to positions taken by Christian churches today.

1. The brothers and sisters are the children of Mary and Joseph, born after the birth of Jesus. From Hegesippus in the second century through Helvidius in the fourth, a number of thinkers including Tertullian took the position that these children were siblings in the normal sense. They appealed to texts in the gospels that point to Mary's having children after Jesus was born, especially Luke's statement that "she gave birth to her first-born son" (Luke 2:7), implying that others followed, and Matthew's comment that Joseph, waking from his dream, took Mary as his wife "but he knew her not until she had borne a son" (Matt. 1:25), implying that sexual relations came later. Neither of these implications is necessary. A woman who bears only one child can always call this child her firstborn; not having sex *until* a child is born tells us nothing about marital relationships after. Still, the sense of the texts points in that direction. The ecumenical team of *Mary in the New Testament* notes that, while these two gospel writers do depict the virginal conception of Jesus by the power of the Spirit, they do not propose Mary's perpetual virginity. Indeed, if we combine Matthew's "until" with his texts on Jesus' mother, brothers, and sisters, "a likelihood arises that according to Matthew's understanding Joseph did come to know Mary after Jesus' birth and that they begot children."[26] In other words, this is what the gospel writer thought. The fact that the brothers are consistently paired with the mother of Jesus in later gospel scenes also needs explanation if they are not her own children. "If they are Jesus' cousins, are they Mary's nephews who are taking care of their widowed aunt? If they are Jesus' half-brothers, now that Joseph is dead, is Mary responsible for these, his children by a former marriage?"[27] Neither scenario seems likely. Aware that the perpetual virginity of Mary after the birth of Jesus is not a question raised directly by the New Testament, Protestant thinkers since the Enlightenment have generally tended to assume that these children belong biologically to Mary and Joseph. In this scenario, Jesus would be the oldest in a family of at least seven children: "a large family, a small income."[28] The biblical evidence leads German feminist scholar Uta Ranke-Heinemann to level the scathing critique that tradition's anti-sex, anti-woman bias has actually robbed Mary of her own children: "And so she was disallowed her children, with the exception of her one son, Jesus. They were taken away from her and, at first, declared to be the children of a fictitious first marriage of her husband, Joseph."[29] Still, the gospels leave room for debate about this position on the parentage of the brothers and sisters: Mary is never called their mother.

2. The brothers and sisters are Joseph's children by a previous marriage. Appearing first in the apocryphal gospel the *Protoevangelium of James* in the mid-second century, this view was still being endorsed by Epiphanius in the fourth. The salient passage in the *Protoevangelium* occurs after the high priest, guided by a sign from heaven, chooses Joseph to be Mary's husband. Joseph protests, "I already have sons and am old, but she is a girl" (9.2).[30] Assured that he should obey the Lord rather than think of his own circumstances, Joseph agrees to the marriage, bringing his children with him. In this interpretation, the brothers and sisters mentioned in the gospels are Jesus' stepbrothers and stepsisters. They are not Mary's natural children; rather, she is their stepmother. Picturing the household of Nazareth in this framework, Jesus would be the youngest of at least seven children, with four older stepbrothers and at least two older stepsisters. The ecumenical team of authors of *Mary in the New Testament* cautions that the *Protoevangelium* itself is not a reliable historical document on most other details; consequently it does not inspire much confidence on this matter, widespread though this view was in the early church. It is still the favored explanation of Orthodox Christianity.

3. The brothers and sisters are actually Jesus' cousins. This view, first championed by Jerome in the fourth century, originally held that the children were born either to Mary's sister or to Joseph's sister or brother, thus allowing not only Mary but also Joseph to remain forever virgin. With no attempt to specify the relationship, the idea that the brothers and sisters were cousins became widespread in western Christianity during the Middle Ages. Functioning in support of the doctrine of Mary's perpetual virginity, the "cousins" position was adopted by the Roman Catholic Church and remains the official teaching of the church. Philological analysis gives some support. The Greek term for brother, *adelphos*, which normally means blood brother in the natural sense, can also mean kinfolk or relative. More broadly still, it can also designate members of the same tribe, clan, or nation. In the New Testament, Christians are called "brothers" over one hundred times in the sense of members of the same religious group, as preachers even today might begin a homily with "my brothers and sisters in Christ." According to this position, it is in one or other of these senses that the gospels use the words *adelphoi* (brothers) and *adelphai* (sisters) of Jesus' relatives.

Contemporary biblical scholars raise doubts about this argument, pointing out that there is a perfectly good Greek word for cousins, *ane-*

psios, which appears elsewhere in the New Testament (Col. 4:10) and which Paul and the gospel writers could have used if that is what they really meant.[31] Furthermore, while the Septuagint, the Greek translation of the Hebrew Bible, did indeed translate the Hebrew term for "cousin" or "relative" with the Greek word for "brother," the authors of the New Testament were not translating but writing in the language they used every day. In their Greek, *adelphos* means brother or half-brother in the flesh, a sharing of parentage. All other passages in the gospels that use "brother" or "sister" to describe family relationships use the terms in this sense of shared parentage rather than "cousins"; recall the Zebedee brothers James and John, the sisters Martha and Mary, their brother Lazarus, and Andrew with his brother Peter. There are the added problems that the use of "sisters" to designate cousins is exceedingly rare, and that "there is no instance of the use of brothers or sisters for more remote kinsmen and kinswomen when the words accompany an enumeration of names,"[32] as occurs with the gospel list of the names of Jesus' brothers. Prescinding from faith and on purely historical and philological grounds, exegete Meier judges that in the case of New Testament language about Jesus' relatives, "the most probable opinion is that the brothers and sisters of Jesus were true siblings."[33] Other scholars such as John McHugh, however, defend the opinion that these children were born to Joseph's sister but brought up by Joseph after his brother-in-law died.[34]

What interests me here is the historical point that all three of the interpretations described above, including the official Catholic "cousins" position, militate against Mary mothering a one-child family. The cousins, or four brothers and all the sisters, did not just appear when Jesus was thirty years old. The manner of their appearance in Jesus' public life indicates relationships of long standing, leading even some proponents of the cousins position to think that they formed part of his family during his years of growing up. Even if these cousins did not live in the immediate household but perhaps shared a courtyard, their repeated presence yoked to the mother of Jesus in the gospels indicates a closeness of multiple children in this blended family. This means that during her own adulthood Mary engaged in a great deal of direct or indirect parenting of a large brood. Along with the physical labor involved, this entailed all the reserves of energy and intelligence required in good child-rearing. When these other children are taken into account, the romanticized picture of an ideal "holy family" composed of an old man, a young woman, and one perfect child does not hold up. There is a lot of noise, a lot of mess, a lot of work, a lot of conversation, perhaps a lot of laughter. Leo Gafney takes this insight into an interesting sideline. Musing on the gospels' picture of Jesus' public skill in speaking, confidence in debate, and ease with people of all description, he queries how Jesus of Nazareth might have developed such qualities. Being at dinner throughout his youth "with nine or ten family members heatedly discussing politics, religion, the law, the prophets— might this also have played a role?"[35]

Shifting to Mary's later years, which she may well have spent as part of the post-resurrection Jerusalem community, scripture indicates that not only were the brothers present at Pentecost but that one of them, James, assumed an important leadership role in the new community. Paul mentions him in his letter to the Galatians: "I went up to Jerusalem to visit Cephas and remained with him fifteen days. But I saw none of the other apostles except James the brother of the Lord" (Gal. 1:18–19). Known in later tradition as James the just, this man was dedicated to a conservative form of Torah piety. He felt that all who were baptized into Christ had to be circumcised first, a conviction that caused Paul, working among the Gentiles, no little grief. Ironically, this devout Jewish brother of the Lord was executed in the year 62 C.E. by the high priest Ananus on a trumped-up charge of flouting the Law. As Josephus tells it, Ananus "called a meeting of judges and brought into it the brother of Jesus who is called Christ, James by name, and some others. He made the accusation that they had transgressed the law, and he handed them over to be stoned."[36] The phrase "brother of Jesus" in this text is an extrabiblical witness to the view that the two were perceived to be blood brothers, because Josephus, writing history and not theology, certainly knew the word for cousin and had no religious point to make by not using it. James met a violent end, as did his more famous crucified brother. We do not know, but it is doubtful that Mary was still alive to mourn this final cruelty.

EVERYDAY LIFE

In the villages of Galilee, surviving as they did through intensive agriculture, it was not efficient for both men and women to develop expertise in all aspects of daily work. In the division of labor by gender that developed, women's economic, maternal, and religious roles intertwined in a series of activities requiring vast investments of time and considerable expertise. In an essay on women's lives in the villages of Palestine that draws on archaeology and social analysis of economic systems as laid out above in chapter 7, Carol Meyers describes the scope and kinds of responsibilities shouldered by village women throughout a typical year.[37] These are analogous to the work of women in communities of subsistence agriculture in many parts of the world even today, where women and men participate in the chores of food production in equal measure. Picturing the world Miriam of Nazareth actually inhabited with her extended family household, we can envision her engaged in some or all of these tasks: producing, processing, and preserving food, making clothing, teaching, training, and caring for children.

The work of providing food was a major factor in women's daily schedule. Even families of craftsmen like Joseph the *tekton* cultivated a plot of land for basic foodstuffs, including grains (mostly wheat, but also some barley), olives for oil, and grapes for wine. A kitchen garden near the compound would supply legumes, vegetables, and leeks, while orchard trees producing figs, dates, and nuts supplemented the basic diet. Most families kept a number of small animals, mostly sheep and goats but perhaps also some cows. These provided dairy products, occasional meat, and skins and wool for making clothing. While women worked in the distant fields at planting and harvest times, the usual locale of their daily work was closer to home to accommodate child care. "The gardening work—cultivating fruit trees, vines, vegetables, and herbs as opposed to field crops—occupied a significant portion of women's outdoor time. Those commodities were grown in plots adjacent to the living quarters, which made it easier for women to tend to both children and crops."[38]

Once picked, some foodstuffs needed to be preserved for long-term storage. The plethora of storage jars and pits uncovered in Galilean village compounds testifies to the work that went into transforming harvested crops into forms that would not spoil and would be available out of season. "Women were responsible for many, if not most, of these food preservation tasks. They did much of the threshing, drying, pounding, and pitting of foodstuffs to ensure a year-round food supply."[39] Other foodstuffs needed to be prepared for immediate consumption. Grain, the dietary mainstay, required a series of time-consuming operations to become edible. It had to be soaked, milled, and ground; then the flour had to be mixed with yeast, set to rise, and baked. This daily work was unceasing, since bread was the main staple of the family diet, the true "staff of life." In addition, olives had to be pressed for oil, grapes fermented, and milk, where available, processed into yogurt or cheese. Routine care of the domestic animals stabled in the courtyard or nearby was also women's responsibility.

And then there was the actual meal preparation. Jacob Neusner observes that women's work of providing nourishment to their families, when done with the intent of observing the Torah's dietary laws, gained an added point of honor. By preparing food in accord with these requirements, "women gained a central role in the correct observance of the rules governing cultic cleanness. . . . It follows that women now enjoyed the power to secure sanctification."[40] Women's work of feeding gained yet further importance in Jesus' parable about making bread, a process he no doubt observed innumerable times during his years of growing up: "The kingdom of heaven is like leaven which a woman took and hid in three measures of meal, til it was all leavened" (Matt. 13:33). In Luise Schottroff's analysis, the large amount of flour reflects common practice whereby bread was made in one batch for several families sharing a single courtyard oven. A woman would leaven one-third of the dough, let it rise overnight, and then knead in the rest and bake the loaves. In the parable this women's work becomes a picture of God's work of renewing and saving the world. "Her hands which knead the bread dough become transparent for God's actions. . . . Bread and God, the hands of a woman baking bread and the hands of God, are brought into relation."[41] The point of the parable in Jesus' telling is that in the eschatological situation in which he and his disciples live here and now, the leaven has already been worked in, the reign of God is already at hand, so wait with calm but eager anticipation. But the image that equates this women's work with divine activity takes on added resonance in a situation of poverty, where the product of mixing flour with water and kneading in leaven is the raw material of life itself: "give us this day our daily bread." Baking bread, seeing that their people actually have food to eat, women symbolize, and Mary would have actually enacted, the life-giving power of God.

Another whole arena of women's labor was the provision of most items of clothing used by the family. While men most likely sheared the sheep, women engaged in the time-consuming and complex tasks of carding and spinning thread, weaving the cloth, and sewing the garments. Resembling the homespun garb of American colonial or frontier days, the resulting clothing would be sturdy but not elegant nor highly ornamented. In addition to textile production, women's hands probably also made baskets used as containers and pottery for household needs, firing the pots communally. Only metal implements and tools had to come from outside the village. All of these life-supporting contributions to the family household absorbed most waking hours of a woman's day. "The time required for indoor, courtyard, and outdoor work, with some seasonal variation, was surely more than ten hours a day."[42] The degree of technological skill required for most of these tasks, furthermore, points to a high level of sophistication both in planning and execution. Some of the work was certainly repetitive, but the overall pattern of accomplishment involved skill, experience, and organizational prowess.

This high level of responsibility and expertise affected women's parenting role. While help would be available from older children, grandmothers, and childless aunts present in the household, a mother was primarily in charge of the care of small children. Rather than compete with her other workday obligations, this care was subsumed into the routine of daily tasks, the children being present where the mother was working. "With more of a woman's time than a man's being spent within the household and its contiguous gardens and courtyards, women spent more time than did men with children of both genders. Until boys were old enough to accompany their fathers . . . and keep up with their strenuous activities, they along with their sisters were cared for mainly by their mothers."[43] In the absence of any formal institutionalized education, women socialized young children. They created the atmosphere breathed in by these young lives. They transmitted to them the culture, beliefs, and values of their Jewish heritage. Meyers points out that this educative task is not visible in scripture, which gives the impression that a cadre of elders and sages exercised a male monopoly on teaching traditional practices and beliefs. "Yet the day-to-day interactions of mothers with children in the household were of foundational significance in passing most aspects of Israelite culture from one generation to the next."[44] As women aged in multigenerational households, their role as mothers also included managing the duties of those junior to themselves, be they older children, daughters-in-law, or nieces. The multiplicity of tasks required to keep the family alive could not be done by one woman alone. Thus, senior women in an extended family assumed managerial responsibility. "They not only taught younger family members . . . how to perform certain tasks; they also assigned jobs and saw that they were accomplished."[45] As a consequence of her success in fulfilling the roles assigned to females in running a complex household, a woman was likely to share strong parental authority with her husband. Their partnership made life possible. Religious observances in the home carried few gender-based restrictions. As organizers of family celebrations of religious feasts, women contributed to the spiritual life of the whole household. Their own prayer could be carried out morning and evening; they sat together with their menfolk and children in the synagogue assembly. While it is not likely that they led synagogue services in Galilee (unlike some places in the Diaspora), some women did perform publicly during funerals, composing and reciting traditional laments for the dead.

From these descriptions of village life, Carol Meyers draws out interesting implications for the status of rural women. The importance, intricacy, and time-consuming aspects of women's work meant that village women exercised control over critical aspects of household life. Rather than their lives being governed by Western dichotomies of female submissiveness and passivity in relation to male aggressiveness and action, they may well have achieved a more relatively balanced form of social unity with men in household settings. They may well have had a say, for example, in arranging marriages, especially for daughters. Girl children, too, were valuable in view of the array of tasks facing female members of a household. Thus the sense of girls being disadvantaged may not have been all-pervasive. It is undoubtedly true that Israel was a patriarchal society with patrilineal descent and male control of economic resources along with legal and political power. Still, our growing knowledge of the social reality of the village in settings of subsistence agriculture tempers the judgment that women were totally oppressed.

> Indeed, the household context of women's lives was so rich in its relational and occupational dynamics that the category "woman" was of little significance. Women were mothers, daughters, sisters, wives; they were also bakers, cooks, weavers, managers, teachers, worshipers, and so on. All these roles involved some combination of social, economic, and biological functions. Only when separated from households might sexuality, and thus the category "woman," emerge as a salient factor in their identity.[46]

Such a situation in fact developed in urban settings, where female enclosure and other restrictions were observed in upper-class households, which no longer functioned as self-sufficient economic units.

All the evidence points to the fact that Miriam of Nazareth, wife of a carpenter in the farming village of Nazareth, lived the bulk of her childbearing years along the rigorous lines described here, engaged in the labor of maintaining a Jewish household in a rural village overlaid with the economic pressures of dominant Roman authorities and their Herodian client-kings. Once she was widowed, her situation would have become economically more precarious, depending on the composition of her household and the ability of others to assume her husband's share of the life-sustaining work. If in her older years she moved to Jerusalem, as seems indicated by Acts, she would have left country life behind and transitioned to urban customs, which involved, at the very least, less manual labor but more segregation by gender, beginning with temple worship.

It seems odd to emphasize this, but so much Christian art from medieval times on has depicted Mary beautifully dressed and living in a palace, upper-class room, or monastery, that our memory needs to be refreshed about the fact that her historical life was shaped by the limits of her time, place, and class. One other aspect where this is the case is literacy. Medieval European art created by and for the upper classes often depicts Mary absorbed in reading. What was Mary doing when the angel came? She was reading a book![47] The book is scripture, and the artist thereby skillfully symbolizes her piety and her readiness to write the next chapter of the divine plan of salvation by mothering the Messiah. In the context of the economic and cultural analysis presented above, however, such literacy is highly unlikely. Numerous studies put the literacy rate in the Roman empire at or below 10 percent. In Pompeii, for example, that thriving first-century Roman town destroyed by Mt. Vesuvius, whose excavated homes, courtyards, and frescoes show a high standard of culture, it is estimated that 2 to 3 percent of the 100,000 people were literate.[48] As Meier points out, "the ability to read, and even more the ability to write, lengthy works in any language was a relatively rare skill in the Greco-Roman world, a skill restricted largely to scribes and an intellectual elite . . . the vast majority of ordinary people were functionally illiterate."[49] As in the rest of the empire, so too in Palestine: literacy was concentrated in the political and cultural elite, who formed a small percentage of the land's inhabitants. Nor is this situation peculiar to ancient times. John Dominic Crossan observes that in a cross-cultural perspective, peasants almost by definition are illiterate. Studies in the twentieth century bear him out: in India in 1921, the illiteracy rate was 90.5 percent; South Africa in 1921: 90.3 percent; Egypt in 1927: 85.7 percent; Turkey in 1927: 91.8 percent; Afghanistan, Iran, Iraq, Saudi Arabia before 1950: above 90 percent in each case.[50]

Some would argue that the Jewish people had more reason than others to promote the ability to read insofar as their religious tradition revered the Torah and the prophets, sacred texts which were written on scrolls, copied, and publicly read. Certainly, there was a cadre of people for whom this was true, most notably the scribes and the Pharisees. But in the Galilean peasant villages living at a subsistence level, it seems highly unlikely that many people were literate. Jonathan Reed points out that the fact that no inscriptions have yet been found in village excavations also points to an illiterate population.[51] Even if some young boys were instructed to read and write for religious purposes (highly debated), the chances that peasant girls were afforded that opportunity are minimal. Low literacy rates, however, did not hamper success in everyday life. We who live in a culture inundated with the written word in books, newspapers, magazines, and computers, to say nothing of video images, can hardly imagine how effective an oral culture can be. Oral exchanges passed on technical knowledge such as agriculture and navigation as well as historical knowledge of the great deeds of the past. Songs, stories, and poems, recited from memory, communicated cultural knowledge. In the home parents taught their children the sacred traditions of their people as well as key prayers and rituals. In village festivals the tradition of the people would be ritualized and expressed.[52] Though she was hardly likely to be reading a book when the angel came, or at any other time, Miriam of Nazareth, like illiterate peasant women everywhere, could participate in a rich cultural and religious tradition through the power of the spoken word in an oral culture.

We have not spoken yet of Miriam of Nazareth's physical appearance, but it has become obvious that not only are the blond hair and blue eyes typical of so much European and North American art inappropriate, but so too is the delicate, unworked physique of a privileged, teenage beauty queen. Art critics note that Renaissance portraits depict women with exquisitely beautiful features whether they were actually beautiful or not, because of the philosophical principle that great beauty implies lofty virtue and, conversely, that spiritual beauty shows itself in physical ways. Given this convention that beauty adorns virtue, artists also painted Mary along the lines of the most ideally beautiful women they knew. These depictions, however, are not accurate, and our culture has altogether abandoned this correlation. "Getting tumbled in a wave of neo-Platonic fantasizing about how outer shape mirrors inner essence—'For Soule is Forme, and doth the Bodie make,' wrote the poet Spenser in 1596—may be great for the figure and complexion when court painters like Botticelli . . . are watching, but it's not so good for documentary truth."[53] Was Miriam of Nazareth beautiful? Perhaps. Perhaps not. Along with the women of her class and ethnic heritage, she had Semitic features, Mediterranean dark hair and dark eyes. Given her everyday life, she also would have had a muscular body shaped by the routines of hard daily labor. Poet Kathleen Norris identifies the need for artists today to produce more work that envisions Mary as a strong peasant woman "capable of walking the hill country of Judea and giving birth in a barn,"[54] a woman with a robust physique both in youth and in old age.

The project of questing for the historical Mary has entailed using the spade of archaeology, the measuring tools of social science, and the quill of ancient authors, all interpreted by contemporary scholars, to construct a picture of the world she inhabited. My purpose has been to describe first-century Galilee with its political-economic, religious, and social conditions in order to picture the actual historical world that Miriam of Nazareth inhabited. The discipline of historical work has required that the past be allowed to stand in all its differences from our own era, rather than erasing that strangeness. I am not interested in this picture simply for historical reasons, however, but am motivated by a theological interest. It is my conviction that remembering Mary as a distinct friend of God and prophet within the communion of saints can generate rich religious meaning in the contemporary church. Picturing her world is the first step in shaping a critical memory within the Christian community that can open up a liberating future. The second step is reading scripture, in particular the scenes in which Mary appears. As we do so, the circumstances pictured above come forward not as mere historical background but as the warp and woof of the world in which the revelation of God took place. For it is precisely in this economic, political, and cultural setting, living out her Jewish faith as a peasant woman of the people, that she walked her journey of faith with enormous consequence. It is precisely to such a woman that Sophia-God has done great things, pouring out divine favor on a marginalized, illiterate villager and calling her to participate in the work of redemption. It is precisely such a woman who rejoices in God and sings prophetically that God is coming to overturn oppression in favor of the poor of the earth. Reading the gospels within the matrix of her actual world is one way to ensure that the way we remember her releases the power of the God of life.

PART 5

Mary in the Communion of Saints

10

℃

The Dangerous Memory of Mary: A Mosaic

THEOLOGICAL MEMORY

Crafting a theology of Mary means seeing the significance of her person and her vocation within the *logos* of faith for our time. Thus, our quest goes beyond historical research to explore the memory of Mary within the great cloud of witnesses made holy by God's Spirit, seeking the import of her story for faith and its practice, including the practice of women and the church's practice regarding women. In keeping with this book's modest proposal, I envision the magnetic center of this memory to be Mary as a woman of Spirit. The presence and power of the Holy Spirit of God, Spirit-Sophia, surround her particular, concrete life, fraught with moments of intense joy and suffering along with stretches of unremarkable, graced dailiness, calling her ever forward. Walking by faith, not by sight, she composes her life as a friend of God and a prophet, one who actively partners the divine work of repairing the world. Her life gives us "lessons of encouragement" not in the sense of laying down precise tracks that other believers in God must necessarily walk. As is obvious from the previous chapters, the circumstances of her actual life can never be repeated. But the style and spirit of her responses reverberate through the centuries to encourage the practice of discipleship in today's different cultural contexts. This is more than giving example. In solidarity with her in the one community of grace, contemporary people experience the impetus to face up to their own encounters with the Spirit and go forward with the best of their faithful wits. This experience receives a critical edge when we remember Mary within women's experiences of historical and religious domination and their struggles to resist and be free. Then the vital memory of this woman empowered by Holy Wisdom challenges, consoles, and sparks hope in present-day contending against ancient patterns of injustice, itself a work of salvation.

How do we remember her? Keeping the findings from archaeology, the social sciences, and ancient history and literature in view and now reframing them in a theological context, this stage of our inquiry turns to scripture as a primary resource. Composed over many decades after Pentecost, the books of the New Testament bear the early church's witness to what God has done in Jesus Christ for the salvation of the world. Rooted in history, these are profoundly theological writings. Within them there are at least thirteen scenes where Miriam of Nazareth, identified either by her own name or as the mother of Jesus, speaks, takes action, or is described as an essential part of the action.[1] In probing these scenes for the theological memory of Mary they carry, I will employ two areas of scholarship as primary tools, namely, modern biblical studies and feminist hermeneutics. Each provides assumptions and methods that shape this theological interpretation of her memory.

Modern biblical scholars hold a fairly solid though not uncontested consensus that the canonical gospels came into being in three stages, starting with the life, death, and resurrection of Jesus of Nazareth witnessed by his disciples, moving to the oral preaching of the early church, and peaking with written composition of the gospels by the evangelists in view of the needs of their churches. While there is some dispute about chronology, a fairly broad agreement also exists that Mark wrote first in the seventies; a decade or so later Matthew and Luke adapted his work, adding sayings of Jesus from a common source (Q) along with their own diverse materials; and John composed last toward the end of the first century, using his own original sources. Since most of the marian material appears in the first two chapters of Matthew and Luke, the genre they used there known as infancy narratives comes in for special attention. Obviously there were no apostolic eyewitnesses to the events of Jesus' conception and birth, nor did these events enter into the early kerygma of the church, which focused on the paschal mystery. The provenance of these infancy stories is a skein of small strands of oral tradition, colored by pigment from narratives from the Hebrew Scriptures, which the evangelists wove into imaginative, theologically powerful scenes that proclaim the identity and mission of Jesus the Christ. Composing these narratives last after the main body of their gospels had been written, but placing them first, Matthew and Luke in effect created christological overtures that sound all the themes that will show up later in their gospels.[2]

One of the major achievements of modern biblical scholarship is the clarity with which it emphasizes that these gospels are all faith documents. All four gospels have as their purpose to announce the good news of salvation coming from God in Jesus through the power of the Spirit, and to bring this story to bear on the spiritual and practical needs of a particular community of believers. Their intent is not simply historical or biographical but missionary and community building: to provide the church with witness to God's gracious mercy in Jesus and to provide guidance for walking in the "Way" according to the Spirit. Consequently, all the gospel writers read the post-resurrection situation back into the ministry and origin of Jesus, interpreting the traditions they received about his words and deeds in light of what they now knew to be the marvelous, God-given outcome of the story of his defeat. They chose certain memories, omitted others, paraphrased his words, and interpreted his healings, companionable suppers, and conflicts so as to grapple with the meaning of his identity and mission. Knowing that post-Easter faith in Jesus as Messiah, Lord, and Savior shaped the gospels' presentations, as did the current challenges and conflicts faced by the different local churches which were the intended audience, biblical exegetes encourage an appreciative approach to the diversity of the gospels. Rather than trying to harmonize their different theological perspectives, let alone concrete points of narrative, we need to understand that each evangelist's voice is important.

Traditional mariology achieved a synthesized view of Mary by harmonizing the diverse gospel texts into a smooth-running narrative of her life, sometimes even rounding things out by adding the postbiblical doctrines of the Immaculate Conception at the beginning and the Assumption at the end.[3] New methods bring new results. Departing from centuries of literal exegesis, a contemporary approach precludes writing a historical biography or psychological study of Mary. In place of such a unifying schema, we acknowledge and honor the fact that the gospels have distinctly different views of Mary, reflecting the evangelists' diverse theologies of world history and understandings of Jesus, and the needs of the local churches in which they wrote. Drawing on these various gospel portraits, consequently, does not produce material for a complete biography but gives different glimpses, snapshots, vignettes, or brief portrayals of incidents in Mary's life, scenes already interpreted as part of each gospel's testimony of faith in God. The biblical portrait of the Galilean Jewish mother of Jesus is shaped by the needs of proclaiming the gospel and is laced through with faith interpretation in the light of Christ's resurrection. It is already a theological memory.

The field of feminist interpretation, working with these standard biblical methods, raises the further critical question of gender bias in both composition and interpretation of texts. The gospels, while part of inspired scripture in the church, are also marked by the sin of the society in which they were crafted, including acceptance of slavery, violence, and patriarchy. They were written by educated men who apparently did not suffer directly from these abuses and whose work tends to erase the experience of those who did. Recall the classic statement in Matthew's account of Jesus feeding the multitudes. The story concludes: "And those who ate were about five thousand men, not counting women and children" (Matt. 14:21).[4] Surely this is not because their appetites were so small as to be unworthy of mention; it is because their persons were unimportant. In the view of the world held by ruling men, such persons literally did not count. This pattern holds true throughout the Bible: the presence and creative activity of women are consistently omitted, played down, or criticized by the patriarchal orientation of the authors. We read these texts, furthermore, through a history of translation, commentary, and preaching shaped by the clerical culture of the church that has given rise to interpretations oppressive to women, including the construals of Mary that women resist today. A venerable axiom would have it that the Bible is the word of God in the words of men. All too true.

To free up the word of God so that it stands in alliance with the flourishing of women, a wide variety of exegetical methods of interpretation come into play. A recent compendium of these methods collected by Elisabeth Schüssler Fiorenza brings together two centuries of women's biblical scholarship under the rubric of *Wisdom Ways*.[5] Questioning the biased point of view of the authors and making the strategic move of placing women at the center of attention, such methods break through inherited patriarchal understandings that run so deep as to be taken for granted. *Corrective* methods seek to remedy uses of the Bible that prohibit women's equal rights by showing that both testaments, if understood correctly, authorize women's full participation in the world. *Historical reconstructive* methods seek to recover forgotten traditions about women, both their accomplishments and the memory of their struggles and defeats, by working with an angle of vision that makes the marginalized visible and their silences audible. *Imaginative* interpretive methods use midrash, storytelling, song, dance, and prayer to bring out the emancipatory potential of the text in dialogue with the emotions of the interpreters. Within these three overarching methods, a rich array of steps can be employed, dance steps that interpret the text according to Wisdom's ways. A hermeneutics of experience consults women's personal and political experiences of the text in order, if necessary, to read "otherwise." A hermenutics of social location critically analyzes the workings of power, both oppressive and liberating power, in the text, its tradition, and its contemporary readers. A hermeneutics of suspicion queries and demystifies structures of domination that are internal to the biblical text and its traditional interpretations. A hermeneutics of critical evaluation makes judgments about the ethical quality of biblical teaching in light of women's human dignity. A hermeneutics of creative imagination generates utopian visions of female emancipation, for what we cannot imagine cannot take place. A hermeneutics of reconstruction retrieves the hidden histories of women, tracing clues buried in the text that indicate they were active subjects of history. And a hermeneutics of transformative action for change explores avenues and possibilities for changing relations of domination inscribed in the text and in everyday life, being particularly accountable to women who struggle at the bottom of the pyramid of discrimination. Like the woman of the gospel looking for her lost coin, these methods search diligently "for submerged meanings, lost voices, and authorizing visions"[6] that will inspire religious imagination for a different future. These methods have already guided the work of retrieving the kind of liberating theology of Mary seen above in chapter 2, and they will be in play in the sections ahead.

One example is worth a thousand words of description. Luke's story of Martha and Mary hosting Jesus in their Bethany home offers a good illustration of feminist hermeneutics at work. Since Luke's infancy narrative is the main source of the image of Mary the mother of Jesus in Catholic tradition, discussion of this passage also flags problems we will face in the Lukan section ahead. To begin with, feminist scholars highlight the enormous ambiguity in Luke's treatment of women. On the positive side, he is interested in affirming women in his mostly Gentile community and educating them in the Christian way. Hence he includes more stories about women than any other gospel. Indeed, throughout subsequent centuries Luke's gospel has played a key role in the development of women's spirituality and Christian self-understanding. On the negative side, however, he is interested in presenting this new religion in a pleasing, nonalarming way to educated readers in the Roman empire. Hence, to defend it from the charge that it threatens society's patriarchal social conventions, Luke hands public leadership in the church to men and tends to silence the women in his stories, stifling their prophecy, diminishing their leadership, and casting them into socially acceptable, obedient roles. Recall how when Jesus' parents present him in the temple, two elders come forth to bless him. Simeon utters a canticle that is still recited as part of the night prayer of the church. Anna the prophet, however, is given no words or speech, even though Luke reports that "she gave thanks to God and spoke of [the Messiah] to all who were looking for the redemption of Jerusalem" (Luke 2:38). We hear the man speak, but not the woman. This paradigm persists right through Luke's Acts of the Apostles, where the Spirit is poured out upon the whole community, "your sons and your daughters" alike (Acts 2:17, citing Joel 2:28), but the stories that follow tell only of the sons who preach and prophesy, not the daughters. While the presence of women prophets, apostles, and missionaries is alluded to, we never hear their voice.

Knowing this pattern alerts us to the dynamic at work in the Martha-Mary scenario (Luke 10:38–42). Luke has Jesus praise the choice Mary makes to sit at his feet listening to his words, thus establishing her role as a disciple. This is a valuable affirmation; but he also has Jesus rebuke Martha for her active service, telling her that Mary has chosen the better part. Preachers have traditionally seen here a contrast between the active and contemplative life, with Jesus giving his blessing to the latter. Feminist scholars detect a different message. The Greek text describes Martha's work with the word *diakonia*, or service, a term that elsewhere epitomizes the mission of Jesus and describes a variety of leadership ministries in the early church. We are not talking about housework here. Within this text lies buried the memory that Martha the "deacon" was a leader in the early church. Confirmation for this idea comes from John's gospel, which depicts Martha as the spokesperson for the christological faith of the community. She rather than Peter utters the community's pivotal confession that Jesus is "the Christ, the Son of God, the one who is coming into the world" (John 11:27).[7] Martha and her sister Mary were originally close friends and disciples of Jesus and, in their different ways, ministers in the early Christian church. Because of his political concern about outsiders' perception of social disorder in the community, however, Luke attempts in this story to denigrate Martha's leadership role. He encourages respectable women to choose "the better part," which consists in receptive listening alone.

In her study of Luke's gospel, Barbara Reid argues that rather than try-ing to rescue this text in itself, the best approach to this story today is to recognize the late-first-century historical situation it reflects. Women were active in many ministries. Concerned about the community's acceptance in the wider society, some men wanted to stop this and return women to traditional gender roles. "It is important to know that the Lukan approval of silent, passive women is only one side of the early Christian debate," she advises. The other side is represented by John's gospel, which "understood Jesus to commission all Christians, women as well as men, to express their faith in the performance of all manner of deaconal ministries."[8] Recogniz-ing Luke's patriarchal bias, readers today need to challenge his prescrip-tions of gender roles and uncover the hidden history of women's ministry buried in this story. "Choosing the better part would be to read with new eyes against Luke's intent."[9]

Mary Rose D'Angelo concurs that Luke-Acts, while not denying that women are engaging in Spirit-filled ministries, is written with the intent "to change that practice, to restrict the participation of women to the bounds of discreet behavior," making Luke's portrayals of women "at once a means of edification and of control."[10] Still, when informed by contem-porary critical methods and by the concerns of women, the historically ongoing process of interpretation in the community of believers allows for new, liberating messages to escape even against Luke's intention. Exploring the oppressive dynamics of this gospel, so powerful because done so artis-tically, Jane Schaberg challenges the reader to approach this text with an ambivalence commensurate to its own: enter into the text to appreciate it, and stand apart from it in order to assess its truth and helpfulness. In terms of women's struggle for equality, Luke is a "formidable opponent" bent on legitimating male dominance in the Christianity of his day. However, "once the negative side of this ambivalent tradition is recognized and worked with, the reader is freed in relation to the text. What is positive and promising in Luke's Gospel can be explored with enthusiasm and even respect."[11] When women find their voices and query the text from the depth of their struggles, their reading may even bring to light egalitarian traditions preserved in the sources of this gospel. Wrestling with the text to gain its blessing, like Jacob with the mysterious angel (a favorite metaphor for the work of feminist biblical interpretation), women discover meanings that nourish their discipleship in this new age. In D'Angelo's felicitous observation, "Like many another Christian author, Luke may have reckoned without the subversive potential of telling women stories of themselves."[12] The story of Mary of Nazareth is one such story. Even though Luke presents her in positive fashion in his infancy narrative, she subsequently sinks into silence along with the rest of the women in the gospel and Acts. If we are to seek out the liberating power of her memory in alliance with women's struggle for true human dignity, we need to connect her with other women then and now and tell her story subversively.

I submit that the work of crafting a mosaic provides a productive metaphor for the work that lies ahead. Unlike a coherent sweep of line that shapes a traditional painting, a mosaic is made up of small fragments of colored stone or marble, called tesserae in the language of art. Each sliver alone is no more than a spot of color or a minute marking. Working according to a pattern, artists inlay these chips in plaster or cement. Assembled together they display a picture or intelligent design, ever more clearly the further back you stand. But it is always possible to move in again and see the individual bits of stone. Like chips of a great mosaic, the marian texts of scripture are discrete images that do not form a complete picture on their own. They are glued into the story of Jesus, which itself presumes the whole biblical sweep of God's gracious history with the world from creation to final redemption, together with its narration of human responses through sin and suffering, fidelity and joy, lament and praise, the struggle for righteousness and profound thanksgiving. They are also refracted in contemporary women's experiences of the Spirit of God in different global locations, women whose conversation with biblical texts generates new angles of vision. Constructing this mosaic, we allow what scholars call the "worlds" of the biblical text to interact to create a living, liberating memory. We attend to the world *behind* the text, or the actual historical world that Miriam of Nazareth inhabited, as explored in the previous three chapters; the world *of* the text, which is the theological view of Mary crafted by the gospel writers as they proclaim salvation in Jesus the Christ in their own time and place; and the world *ahead* of the text, or the ongoing struggle of women today for full participation in every dimension of life. We study tesserae, then, these individual theological memories of Mary, as flashes of color that form part of the texture of the story of the living God's engagement with the flesh and matter of the world, including in our day the uprising of women into full humanity. The goal is a multi-faceted, living, memory-image of Mary within the cloud of witnesses that shares in the quality of "danger" insofar as it awakens resistance, births wisdom, and inspires hope for the flourishing of women, indeed of all human beings and the earth, as beloved of God.

OUTSIDE
(MARK 3:20–21 AND 31–35)[13]

The first tessera for this marian mosaic comes from the earliest gospel, Mark. The story is set in the lake village of Capernaum, where Jesus has begun a ministry of preaching and healing that is drawing large, enthusiastic crowds. Hearing of this, "his own," also translated as his family or his relatives, set out to seize him and bring him home to Nazareth because they think he has lost his mind. Mark fills in the time it takes for them to arrive with a hostile exchange between Jesus and some scribes from Jerusalem, who accuse him of being in league with Satan. As that dispute winds down, Jesus is told that his family has arrived: "your mother and your brothers are outside, asking for you." Tension fills the air. Instead of rising at once and greeting them as custom and law requires, he emphatically "rejects,"[14] "repudiates,"[15] "disowns"[16] his family using characteristic Jewish dialogue: Who are they?

> "Who are my mother and my brothers?" And looking around on those who sat about him, he said, "Here are my mother and my brothers. Whoever does the will of God is brother and sister and mother to me."

Jesus' words are rife with new vision. Blood ties do not guarantee a place in his community of disciples, but loving and acting on behalf of the reign of God do. The blessedness he offers is open to anyone who wants it, without distinction of sex or gender, infertility or maternity, physical kinship or family connections, so long as they seek the will of God. As Mark structures it, the scene draws a strong contrast between Jesus' biological family and a new kind of inclusive community, the eschatological family called into being by shared commitment to doing the will of God. According to this criterion, the mother and brothers of this popular preacher-healer stand outside, not inside with his disciples. Jesus "emphatically distances himself from his blood family."[17] In their stead, "looking around on those who sat about him," he visually and verbally embraces the people in the house, who, unlike his family, do not think he is beside himself nor possessed of a demon. These are his true kin, the authentic family of God. They replace his natural family in importance.

Biblical scholar Joanna Dewey points out that Jesus' redefinition of kinship "is extremely radical in its first-century context,"[18] especially for women. The eschatological family depicted here is not patriarchal, not ruled by or even defined by a male head of household. There are no fathers. Even Jesus himself does not assume patriarchal authority but interprets himself as a brother and a son to all in the group. Women are redefined as his sisters and mother. In place of obedience to husband and father, they owe fidelity only to God in a community built up not by subservience but by nurturing and collegial relationships. In this context Mark's gospel goes on to depict a cast of strong women who interact dynamically with Jesus in ways that benefit themselves and also challenge and change him. Consider the Syro-Phoenician woman, fighting for her daughter, who teaches this Jewish prophet to think more inclusively about his mission (Mark 7:24–30); the unnamed woman who prophetically anoints his living body for burial, receiving the encomium that "wherever the gospel is preached in the whole world, what she has done will be told in memory of her" (Mark 14:3–9); and the women disciples from Galilee whom the gospel describes during the passion as looking on, watching, and seeing—classic verbs describing those who bear witness (Mark 15:40, 47).[19] By contrast, the mother of Jesus here is a foil for authentic discipleship.

This negative portrait is strengthened by a later Markan scene that depicts Jesus' rejection when he does go back to preach in his home village of Nazareth. Responding to the neighbors who take offense at him, the son of Mary says, "A prophet is not without honor except in his own country and among his own kin and in his own house" (Mark 6:4). The scene gives support to the contention that Jesus' own natural family neither understood nor honored him, a tradition that, even though Mark emphasizes it the most, appears also in other gospels. These family tensions and Jesus' sharp disengagement from his mother and brothers during his ministry have good claim to a historical root. Remembering that after Easter Mary shared the faith of the earliest Christian community, the ecumenical team of *Mary in the New Testament* reasons that "since she was from the first a member of the post-Easter community, it is unlikely that her earlier misunderstanding of her Son is simply a creation of Mark or of the tradition he repeats; for it is hard to believe that such a misunderstanding would

have been attributed to the believing mother of the risen Lord if there had
been no basis for such an attribution. The basis seems to have been that, in
fact, she did not follow Jesus about as a disciple during the ministry."[20]

It is instructive to watch how Matthew and Luke edit this scene according to their own interests. Toning down the rejection a bit, Matthew omits
the information that Jesus' family has come to seize him because they think
he is beside himself. They just show up. However, Matthew still describes a
strong contrast between natural family and disciples in Jesus' rhetoric and
gesture: "Who is my mother and who are my brothers? And stretching out
his hand toward his disciples, he said, Here are my mother and my brothers . . ." [Matt. 12:46–50]). By contrast, Luke shifts the whole event into a
positive mode (8:19–20). Not only does he too omit the damaging information about the family's motivation for their trip, but by omitting the
question "Who are my mother and my brothers?" and the replacement
answer "Here are my mother and brothers," he drops the outside–inside
contrast. While the criterion for belonging to the community of disciples
is the same, namely, hearing the word of God and acting upon it, Jesus'
mother and brothers now meet that criterion. Any implication that the
family is hostile or does not understand is avoided. Instead, they are
counted among the disciples. Biblical scholars desiring to defend the good
name of Jesus' family point out that there is nothing in Mark's original scenario that would *prevent* mother and brothers from becoming part of the
eschatological family, *eventually*. Still, in the Markan account they are
clearly "outside."

Traditional mariology that glorified Mary never knew what to do with
this text and as a consequence largely ignored it. In my judgment, it is an
irreplaceable antidote to distortions of the tradition as well as a contribution to the memory of Mary in its own right. Here Jesus' mother and
brothers arrive as a family and are disowned together. Whether these boys
are her natural children, stepchildren, or nephews, their close association
in this crisis places her in maternal relationship to more than one child.
Here, too, the relationship between mother and her firstborn son is
strained, pouring cold water on the multitude of traditional sentimental
reflections about Jesus' relationship with his mother. Psychologically, to
reach maturity men cannot stay fixated on their mother but must move
out to form relationships within their own peer group. We see a healthy
development in this episode.

A feminist interpretation does not seek to change Jesus' critical attitude toward his family, but sees Mary in a different light. Standard commentaries on this passage hold that at the very least Jesus' mother and brothers misunderstood him. Perhaps they did, this being an instance of a truly gifted person soaring beyond the vision and expectations of a typical family. It might just as well be the case, though, that they understood him only too well and sought to forestall what they saw as inevitably disastrous consequences. Parents whose children take risks to follow their dream in dangerous situations know the feelings well: the fear, the pride, the effort to protect. In Miriam of Nazareth's case, as one Jewish writer observes, "This son . . . roams around through the country and creates unrest. He does things that are dangerous: danger threatens from the Jewish authorities and from the hated occupying power of the Romans. He puts *the whole family at risk*."[21] Making this trip, the unnamed mother of Jesus gives the lie to passive obedience as the key to her nature. Who better to have organized such a family expedition? In response to his behavior, which not only "rejected village norms for eldest sons"[22] but also opened the door to disaster for himself and his kin, she and his brothers took action that they considered to be for his own good. They set out to fetch him home. Propelled by the Spirit to follow his own calling, however, Jesus meets their initiative with his own. He moves on without them.

In her feminist analysis of evil, ethicist Nel Noddings criticizes classical notions of evil that have equated it with sinful disobedience to the patriarch and his representatives, human and divine. Such an understanding, she argues, is not adequate to women's experiences. When women are consulted, it becomes clear that evil is defined as that which harms or threatens to harm them and those they love. Chief among the basic evils, considered phenomenologically, that women experience are useless, intractable pain along with the failure to alleviate it; separation or neglect of relation; and helplessness along with the mystification that sustains it. By contrast, moral good and the virtues that promote it are best expressed in an ethic of care that gives powerful impetus to building and remaining in loving relations.[23] Continuing this kind of analysis, Sara Ruddick points to three great interests that govern the actions of those who mother the young: preserving the life of the child, fostering its growth, and shaping an acceptable child. Rather than follow the dictates of law and society were these to threaten the young, maternal thinking issues in ethical action to preserve and protect, regardless.[24] In this light, a feminist perspective espies the exercise of female power in the action of Miriam of Nazareth, who, no stranger to Roman violence and the havoc it could wreak on human lives, goes to persuade her child out of the line of fire. I am reminded of an essay in the *New Yorker* after John F. Kennedy Jr. died along with his wife and her sister while piloting a small aircraft. While she lived, Jacqueline Kennedy Onassis disapproved of her son's wish to fly. The lessons, the license, and the new plane arrived only after her death. Moved by sorrow and aggravation at the loss of these promising young lives, the essayist wants to scream on the wind: *Listen to your mother!*[25]

My point is not to undo or reconfigure the events that Christians believe brought about salvation, central to which are the miserable death and surprising resurrection of Jesus the Christ. A whole new appreciative belief in God-for-us welled up historically out of those events. What happened, happened, and in the end we call it grace. In retrieving this Markan scene as a valuable chip for the memory mosaic of Mary, however, we gain a glimpse of a moment in time before these events took place. Full of concern for one she loves, Miriam of Nazareth does not have the New Testament to help her interpret God's designs. Embarking on a mission that ultimately fails, she stands "outside" with an anxious mind and heart, the frustrated, angry mother of Elisabeth Moltmann-Wendel's image, maladapted to the shedding of blood. We should be wary about judging this scene as evidence of lack of faith. The scholars of *Mary in the New Testament* rather sweepingly declare that the event behind this scene took place *before* "the time at which Mary's belief began,"[26] by which they mean more precisely the post-resurrection understanding of Jesus that she shared with the Jerusalem community. While this may be true in a Christian sense, her faith in God did not begin only after Easter, as witnessed by this scene, where her faith is at full pitch. Believing in God, Creator and Redeemer of the world, this Jewish woman partners the divine work of love by seeking to preserve and protect a precious life. No submissive handmaid, her memory moves in solidarity with women everywhere who act critically according to their best lights to seek the well-being of those they love.

IN THE COMPANY
OF THE UNCONVENTIONAL FOREMOTHERS
(MATTHEW 1:1–17)

Turning to Matthew's gospel, we find that the infancy narrative that forms the first two chapters offers four new tesserae for the marian mosaic. The first stone is the genealogy that opens the gospel. This list of ancestors traces Jesus' lineage from Abraham through King David down to Joseph, "the husband of Mary, of whom was begotten Jesus, who is called the Messiah." Locating Jesus deep within the Jewish tradition, it has the purpose of introducing him as the fulfillment of messianic hopes. When this text is read in liturgical assembly, eyes tend to glaze over with the repetition of the "begats," A was the father of B, B was the father of C, and so on, with the heritage passed on by men of mostly unpronounceable names. Raymond Brown proposes the captivating idea that the church needs to read this text during Advent to remind ourselves that just as most of these people were ordinary folk who nevertheless advanced God's plan, so too ordinary people in the church today can contribute to God's coming into the world by fidelity in the midst of everyday life.

In view of seeking the memory of Mary, there is an even more interesting aspect to consider. This genealogy is terribly androcentric, with the lineage passing down through the fathers in orderly progression. The women who did the work of bearing the sons of each generation go largely unnamed, hidden by the patriarchal construct that considers women only vehicles of reproduction rather than historical agents in their own right.[27] Even Mary is subsumed into Joseph's story in this manner. In Matthew's rendering she neither speaks, nor receives divine revelation, nor expresses a point of view. Yet this overall androcentric pattern of history breaks open when the genealogy lists four female ancestors by name and goes on even more dramatically to change the paternity pattern in Mary's case. In Elaine Wainwright's evocative metaphor, the five women together "open a small fissure in the symbolic universe that the patrilineage constructs. Into this fissure can be drawn the memory of all the mothers and daughters who were likewise ancestors of Jesus."[28]

It is a matter of interest that the four named female ancestors are not the revered Israelite matriarchs from Genesis, who would include Sarah, perhaps Hagar, Rebekah, Leah, and Rachel. Instead the text names Tamar, Rahab, Ruth, and the wife of Uriah. These women all found themselves at some point outside the patriarchal family structure, and consequently in danger. Their stories show how in the midst of their precarious situations they took unconventional initiatives to improve their lot. Furthermore, their enterprise becomes the vehicle for advancing the divine plan of redemption. In these instances, as Phyllis Trible says, "the brave and bold decisions of women embody and bring to pass the blessings of God."[29] In the genealogy these four women foreshadow the mother of the Messiah, who found herself in a similarly perilous situation. She belongs in the company of these unconventional foremothers.

"Judah [was] the father of Perez and Zerah by Tamar." A childless widow, Tamar poses as a prostitute by the side of the road to seduce her father-in-law, Judah, who had reneged on his responsibility under the law of levirate marriage to continue his son's line.[30] Her resulting illegitimate pregnancy brings the terrible sentence of death by burning. This is overturned only when Judah finds out about her ruse. Realizing that she had risked her life to continue the family line, he declares, "She is more righteous than I" (Gen. 38:26). She lives and brings forth twins. This is a powerful story of a woman's initiative and loyalty in the face of grave personal danger. As Jane Schaberg interprets the point, "Tamar herself has acted to secure her rights and demonstrate her righteousness. Suspected of bringing death and disgrace, she has in the end brought life,"[31] life in the form of the continuation of Judah's name and of the covenant promise of descendants for Abraham.

"Salmon [was] the father of Boaz by Rahab." A prostitute in Jericho, Rahab shelters the Israelite spies as they reconnoiter the city on their way back to the promised land. They had most likely sought her out initially in her professional capacity. In return for her hospitality and assistance in their escape, she secures a promise of safety for herself and her whole household when the Israelites finally attack. Basically "a survivor in the world of men at war,"[32] this Canaanite woman, though unfaithful to her own people, uses her ingenuity to ensure life for her loved ones along with success for Israel. Motivated by a measure of faith in Israel's God, she enters the list as a foremother in the blessed lineage of the Messiah. Even the New Testament holds her up as a model of faith and good works (Heb. 11:31; Jas. 2:25).

"Boaz [was] the father of Obed by Ruth." This young Moabite woman, widowed, childless, and poor, joins her aged mother-in-law Naomi in the struggle for survival in the patriarchal environs of Bethlehem. She secures a wealthy husband after crawling under his blanket and spending the night with him on the threshing floor, a story that has overtones of trickery and levirate obligation. It also carries a taint of scandal analogous to that of Tamar, who is, tellingly, mentioned by name in the people's blessing after Ruth gives birth to a son (Ruth 4:12). Though there is no clear evidence of seduction, Ruth risks an accusation of harlotry and is praised for taking that risk. She reverses her fortune, restores life to Naomi's line, and brings another measure of Gentile blood into the heritage of the Messiah.

"David was the father of Solomon by the wife of Uriah." This beautiful woman was the object of David's lust. Procuring her for himself, he commits adultery and has her husband killed on the front lines in war. The widow of a murdered man, she becomes pregnant with her lover's child. As punishment for David, this baby dies. Unlike the previous three women, Bathsheba does not at first exercise initiative but seems trapped in this appalling story, where her motives, feelings, rights, and love count for nothing before the power of the king. Her passivity changes, though, when she bears her next child, Solomon. Then as queen she acts to secure the throne for him from a dying David over the rights of an older brother, thereby also ensuring her own status for the rest of her life. As Schaberg points out, this foremother shows that God's providence goes forward overall in what happens in history, if not in every detail of the sordid, heartbreaking story.[33]

Scholars have long sought a common point among these four ancestral women that would link them with the fifth woman named in Matthew's genealogy. One theory, first proposed by Jerome in the fourth century, holds that they were all sinners, in contrast to Mary. This, however, does not seem to be Matthew's point, because in the Jewish piety of the first century these women were looked upon with respect and praised for their deeds. Another hypothesis, popularized by Luther, proposes that they were all Gentiles, thereby indicating the scope of Jesus' redemptive mission beyond the Jewish people. But this is not necessarily the case for Tamar or Bathsheba, nor does it provide a point of similarity with Mary. A number of contemporary thinkers argue that the link among the women consists in the fact that (a) there is something extraordinary, irregular, even scandalous in their sexual activity, (b) which places them in some peril, (c) in view of which they take initiative, (d) thereby becoming participants in the divine work of redemption. Unexpectedly, God works through, with, and in them in a providential way to bring forth the Messiah. Pointing out that "in post-biblical Jewish piety these extraordinary unions and initiatives were seen as the work of the Holy Spirit," Raymond Brown argues that the genealogy presents these women and their actions as vehicles of divine providence, examples of how God moves in and through the obstacle of human scandal to bring about the coming of the Messiah.[34] "Tamar was the instrument of God's grace by getting Judah to propagate the messianic line; it was through Rahab's courage that Israel entered the Promised Land; it was through Ruth's initiative that she and Boaz became the great-grand-parents of King David; and it was through Bathsheba's intervention that the Davidic throne passed to Solomon."[35] Through these unions, in which the woman was often the heroic figure, God carried forward the divine promise and plan. In straitened conditions the foremothers each dreamed of a future and acted to bring it about, thereby partnering God's redemptive work in history. Reading from a critical feminist perspective, Elaine Wainwright underscores the significance of the point that at the outset, none of these women is properly related to a man as wife or daughter. The fact that these foremothers, whether widowed, unmarried, prostitute, or separated from a spouse, exist independently outside traditional domestic arrangements makes them "dangerous to the patriarchal system." As they act, their stories encode aspects of women's power. And "God's messianic plan unfolds in and through such power."[36] Jesus is as much the son of Tamar, Rahab, Ruth, and Bathsheba as he is of Abraham and David.

The presence of these anomalous women in Jesus' ancestry within the history of Israel frames the unconventional image of Mary as Matthew will describe her. In the genealogy she too exists outside the patriarchal family structure as the startling rupture of the patrilineage declares, "Jacob [was] the father of Joseph, the husband of Mary, of whom Jesus was born, who is called the Messiah" (1:16). Something odd is signified here. It is not Joseph who begets but Mary who gives birth. The patriarchal pattern is shattered, but as the foremothers show, "outside" this norm is not an easy place to dwell. Mary became pregnant without having had sex with Joseph, to whom she was betrothed in a legally binding relationship. In the eyes of society her pregnancy is a scandal damaging to the social order since she had not yet lived with her husband. She is vulnerable to the sanctions of the law and liable to receive rigorous punishment. Providentially, her story, like those of the women before her in the genealogy, has an outcome that ensures the birth of a child to carry on the covenant promise. In terms of giving us a picture of Mary's initiative or creative action in the midst of great danger, Matthew disappoints. She is voiceless in his narrative, which focuses on Joseph. Nevertheless, in her precarious predicament, she, along with her predecessors, "becomes the arena of sacred history and the locus where the divine promises to Israel" are carried forward and fulfilled.[37]

It is precisely here, in the image of Mary as a scandalous woman with whom God identifies, that Jane Schaberg finds a powerful biblical theology. In a word, God acts as "one who sides with the outcast, endangered woman and child."[38] Throughout the rest of Matthew's gospel, a stream of characters, from the hemorrhaging woman and crowds of other sick and disabled people to the Canaanite woman agitating for her little daughter's health, from the demoniac of Gadarene to the tax collector Matthew and his socially repugnant friends, will amplify this message first embodied in the genealogy's foremothers and in the mother of the Messiah. Insignificant, illegitimate, defenseless, tabooed people are beloved of God and may become agents of divine action in history.[39] Jesus himself is the most radical instance of this divine compassion. Born of a non-Davidic woman yet messianic king, crucified by the state yet risen and ever present in the Spirit, Jesus illuminates in his life the presence of grace in people and situations branded sinful and shameful. "In a world racked with injustice," observes Donald Senior, "where the lament of promises never fulfilled and the frustration of hopes doomed to despair are the bitter bread of millions, the unconventional dimensions of the gospel portrayals of Mary seem to have more substance and appeal than ever before."[40] Outside patriarchal expectations, looked upon askance by others, in danger for her life, her participation in the birth of Jesus is acclaimed as holy. Her female power is subversively linked to divine power and presence. In company with the four unorthodox women who act in the genealogy, she stands in solidarity with others in tragic or impoverished situations. Her memory bears the revolutionary gospel assurance that the God of Israel, the God revealed in Jesus, God's own Spirit, is with them.

SCANDAL AND THE SPIRIT
(MATTHEW 1:18–25)

The whiff of scandal surrounding Mary in the genealogy becomes full-blown in the next episode, which recounts how she and her husband negotiate her unexpected pregnancy. Although the story is focused on Joseph and says nothing about Mary's action or faith, the "kernel" within the narrative is the female situation of Mary's conception of Jesus through the Spirit without reference to male begetting and the birth of the Messiah in these anomalous circumstances.[41]

Recall that according to Jewish marriage customs of the day Mary and Joseph were bound together in a legally ratified marriage. The text is replete with references to "his wife," "your wife," and "your husband." Before they came to live together, Mary was found to be with child. Joseph knew he could not be the father. Her pregnancy would seem to be the result of adulterous behavior. Being a just man, upright and observant of Torah, he faced a searing dilemma. According to the Law, if a young betrothed woman is found, on first coming to her husband, to have previously lost her virginity, she shall be stoned to death. In the words of Deuteronomy, "they shall bring the young woman out to the entrance of her father's house and the men of her town shall stone her to death because she committed a disgraceful act. . . . So you shall purge the evil from your midst" (Deut. 22:20–27, at 21). The one exception is if a young woman is raped in the open country as opposed to the city, for out there no one could hear her cries for help. Although this dictate was not carried out assiduously in first-century Palestine, its religious judgment on the non-virginal bride would still wield power over an upright man. Mercifully, Joseph decided to divorce his wife quietly, thus sparing her any exposure to public shame, or worse. Just when the couple was on the verge of breaking up, an angel of the Lord appeared to Joseph in a dream encouraging him not to be afraid to take his wife to his home for "the child conceived within her is of the Holy Spirit." Here Matthew inserts a formulaic citation to show that this conception fulfills Isaiah's prophecy: "the virgin shall conceive and bear a son, and they shall call him Emmanuel" (Isa. 7:14). Faithful to his revelatory dream, Joseph completed the home-taking of the pregnant Mary: "he took her as his wife, but had no marital relations with her until she had borne a son; and he named him Jesus." By exercising the father's right to name the child, he acknowledged his wife's son as his own in the legal and public sense. The child born within this marriage will be regarded as his.

This narrative spells out the odd circumstances of Jesus' begetting hinted at in the genealogy. Like the four unconventional foremothers, Mary's situation is irregular. Her pregnancy is suspicious; socially and legally within patriarchal culture there is more than a hint of disrepute. Yet in the midst of this dangerous trouble something holy is going forward. God's Spirit moves amidst the threatening situation to bring about the birth of the Messiah. Both elements together, scandal and the Spirit, produce a tessera colored by the dialectic so characteristic of the gospel whose consummate event is the resurrection of the crucified one.

Historicity

Biblical scholars of all stripes think with more or less assurance that Matthew inherited an older, pre-gospel tradition that something was irregular about Mary's pregnancy. As Raymond Brown delicately puts it, people remembered that Jesus was born too early after his parents started to live together. There is a reasonable likelihood that this was the case, for why would the evangelist invent an embarrassment that he would then have to explain away? While the evangelist emphasizes that despite the scandal this child is the fruit of the action of the Holy Spirit, from earliest times readers have also wondered what the nature of the scandal actually was. Searching for the historical nucleus of the tradition of this too-early birth, present also in Luke's infancy narrative, thinkers from the second century onward have endorsed four different options. First, Joseph was the biological father who conceived Jesus with Mary while they were in the betrothal stage of their marriage. Second, an unknown man seduced Mary and committed adultery with her. Third, a Roman soldier, usually given the name Panthera, forcibly violated Mary, rape not being an unknown behavior in the Roman army. Fourth, it was a physical, biological miracle, the Holy Spirit of God causing the genesis of the child in Mary's womb in the absence of any human biological father. This last position, technically known as the virginal conception of Jesus, became and remains the official teaching of the Catholic Church, giving rise to the ancient appellation of Mary as Virgin Mother.

Contemporary scholarly discussion that attempts to assess the historical validity of each of these options gives them unequal weight. The Joseph-was-the-father thesis was first held by the Ebionites, an early group of mainly Jewish Christians who held that Jesus was not the Son of God from the beginning. Rather, he started his life simply as the son of Joseph, but in the course of time God adopted him as his own Son. This position has little backing in oral or written evidence. Indeed, Matthew's description of Joseph's quandary would seem to omit it out of court. By contrast, the charge of Jesus' illegitimacy by adultery or rape is clearly documented from the second century in both Jewish and Christian sources. It became a mainstay of anti-Christian polemic for centuries and also appears in Christian rebuttals. So well established did the paternity of the Roman soldier become in Jewish circles that simply the reference Ben Panthera, or son of Panthera, was sufficient to designate Jesus without mention of his given name. Raymond Brown and other exegetes argue that there is no way of knowing whether this charge arose before Matthew wrote, so that he was responding to it with the affirmation that Jesus was conceived by the Spirit, or whether in fact it originated as a derogatory interpretation of Matthew's gospel itself.[42]

In an intensely thoughtful, respectful study of this charge, Jane Schaberg proposes that both Matthew and Luke inherited the tradition that Jesus the Messiah had been conceived in an illegitimate manner outside of marriage, along with the theological understanding that the Holy Spirit was in some way present and active in this event. "Both evangelists worked further with this potentially damaging and potentially liberating material," spinning it so artfully and with such theological astuteness that Christians soon became unaware of the illegitimacy that lay behind their infancy narratives. Trying to discern the contours of Mary's original trouble, Schaberg reads Matthew's text as a story "of a dangerous pregnancy outside the structures of patriarchal marriage—a situation as ancient as it is common," with chilling results on women's well-being throughout history. This reading draws the infancy narratives into the shadow of the cross, the larger scandal of the gospel. The good news, as already explored in the genealogy, is that God sides with the outcast, endangered woman and her child. God does this *not* by intervening directly to stop events of human violence and betrayal, to stop rape or conception after rape, but by being present "as one who reaches into that history to name the messiah." Through the creative power of the Spirit it comes about that "this child's existence is not an unpremeditated accident, and it is not cursed; the pregnant Mary is not to be punished." Rather, conceived of the Holy Spirit, this child has a special relation with God. Jesus is the Son of God, come to save his people from their sins. More profoundly than human beings could ever bring about by themselves, this disgrace turns out to be grace.[43]

Schaberg admits that a major objection to her interpretation lies in the fact that we cannot prove that any early Christians read the infancy narratives as affirming an illegitimate conception.[44] Arguing from a historical perspective, Amy-Jill Levine reasons that since Jewish charges of Jesus' illegitimate birth come from a time later than the composition of the gospel, it is unlikely that Matthew was interested in combating them in his opening chapter.[45] While commending Schaberg's exegesis for challenging readers to pay attention to the perspective of women's experience, Barbara Reid demurs, "There is no doubt that her interpretation is possible, but the question remains whether the texts demand such an interpretation"; she is doubtful whether they do.[46] In a similar vein Luise Schottroff, while respecting the healing power for violated women released by this exegesis, writes that "*measured against the texts*, I find that Schaberg's thesis fails to fit. As the text indicates, it was Joseph's mistaken belief that Mary had been seduced or sexually assaulted. Divine revelation corrects this false assumption," leaving us with a story that carries a profound critique of patriarchal dominance and violence.[47] In my view, there is valuable insight in Schaberg's exegesis even if we grant that the critics are correct. She limns so clearly the consequences for a woman of that culture getting pregnant outside patriarchal social norms that even with belief in the virginal conception we begin to see the dangerous dilemma in which Mary was trapped according to Matthew's telling. Until Joseph's dream and his generous response, nothing but public disgrace, endless shame, perhaps a life of begging, perhaps even death loomed before her. The terror of her situation should be allowed once again to fertilize the Christian imagination, which has tended to "wrap Mary in an aura of romantic joy" at finding herself pregnant.[48]

Contemporary persons have vastly differing reactions to this ancient charge of illegitimacy. Brown notes disapprovingly that some sophisticated Christian believers appreciate it as an example of the depths to which Christ descended when he "emptied himself" in becoming human. As an illegitimate son, Jesus would be counted among the outcasts for sure. It is not only worldly-wise Christians, however, who may find something religiously valuable in this interpretation, but women who are victims of sexual assault and all those in solidarity with them. Violence against women is a chief tool in the maintenance of patriarchy, one of whose defining tenets is man's right to woman's body. In traditional societies this right has been codified in law and custom to the extent of allowing honor killings of women pregnant outside of marriage. In contemporary democratic societies the struggle for women's right to the integrity of their own bodies, for the right to say no and be taken seriously, challenges patriarchal privilege at its core. In both situations, physical and psychological violence serves the cause of male domination and the litany of abuse is long and terrible, from witch burning to forcible rape (stranger rape, acquaintance rape, date rape, rape in marriage), from lesbian bashing to sadomasochistic pornography, from domestic abuse to serial murder, and yes, to slitting the throat of a young Tuareg girl found to be pregnant while betrothed.[49] That the Spirit of God would be with a woman who suffered such violence, able to bring good from an inestimably painful situation, embodies the gospel in miniature and is a deep source of hope.

Devout persons unaware of early Christian history, on the other hand, may well find the charge that Jesus was conceived by seduction or rape utterly shocking. Dom Sebastian Moore recounts his own "devastating" experience when he first realized this theory had merit. "I lay awake all night, not even dozing, while a voice in my head kept saying over and over again, 'She's nothing but a whore, and the Church has made her into a Madonna, it's all a huge fake!' I felt my faith draining away."[50] His crisis was resolved only when at a deep level he began to realize that to God "our petty social categories are nothing"; that while we have prettified the story of Jesus' conception, reducing it to something of a fairy tale, its reality points to a woman's faith, terrifying in its totality, in the mystery of God, who speaks from vast silence saying, "My ways are not your ways." We cannot begin to deal with the question of whether the virginal conception of Jesus is to be taken literally, he concludes, until we have recovered its spiritual significance from the travesty which the sexual immaturity of the Christian tradition has made of it, namely, a mother–son pattern from which the phallus is banished. This in turn has "powerfully reinforced the split image of Christian man, sexually dominating and spiritually sexless, and of Christian woman as virgin and mother but never as spouse."[51] While insisting emphatically that a woman who has been raped is not a whore, I find Moore's analysis of the debilitating antisexual ethic that this story of Jesus' conception has buttressed to be astute. It runs on a parallel track to feminist existential if not political critique.

What then of the fourth position, the virginal conception? Critical biblical methods make it difficult simply to assume that miraculous conception by the Holy Spirit is historically the case, though they certainly do not rule it out either.[52] To begin with, there is the troubling fact that there is no explicit reference to the virginal conception outside of the infancy narratives of Matthew and Luke. The astounding silence of the rest of the New Testament, including Paul, Mark, and John, indicates that this belief was not known, or if known, was not considered an important part of Christian kerygma in the early decades of the church. In addition, the infancy narratives themselves are brilliant literary creations embellished with folkloric elements such as astrology, dreams, and visionary messages and enriched with creative adaptations of material from the Hebrew scriptures; their very genre precludes relying on them as accurate renderings of history. The fact that the infancy narratives are replete with post-resurrection titles for Christ indicates, furthermore, that they were composed more with theological intent than with desire for historical facticity in the sense that dominates modern discussion. Then too, in Galatians, Isaac is said to be "born according to the Spirit" without implications for his mother's virginity (Gal. 4:29). As a result of translation issues, furthermore, biblical scholars eschew an appeal to the prophecy of Isaiah to settle the issue of historicity. In its own time Isaiah's text did not point to a messiah but gave the sign of an imminent birth of a child who would illustrate God's providential care for people under threat. In the original Hebrew, the ʿalmâ who will conceive refers to a young woman of marriageable age, perhaps the current queen. The word itself does not primarily signify virginity, a point reinforced elsewhere, for example, in the Song of Solomon, where it refers to young women in the king's harem (Song 6:8; also Prov. 30:19). In the Greek translation of the Hebrew Bible, the Septuagint, ʿalmâ is rendered as *parthenos*, a word that normally does mean biological virgin. Even here, however, the word is not clinically precise, being used twice of Dinah after Shechem has raped her (Gen. 34:3). Most tellingly, the grammatical structure of Isaiah's prophecy points to a virgin who *will conceive*. The future tense implies that the girl now a *parthenos* will get pregnant, presumably in the normal way. Matthew's use of Isaiah's text to explain Jesus' being conceived of the Holy Spirit gives this ancient prophecy an utterly new interpretation in light of his own theology.

To raise the question of the nucleus of Matthew's conception story is to discover that there is no absolutely satisfactory answer on historical grounds alone. Most scholars agree that this evangelist intends to declare the virginal conception in a biological sense, ruling out any human father. Many also hold that this is the tradition he received. But as to what lies behind that tradition at the first stage of gospel formation, contemporary scholarly approaches to the gospels simply cannot settle the issue. Raymond Brown, who argues that both Matthew and Luke think Jesus was conceived without a human father, points out that they were just not interested in the historical facticity of this question with the intensity of our post-Enlightenment minds. In an early essay on the virginal conception, he concluded that "the totality of the *scientifically controllable* evidence," the kind of evidence that stems from eyewitnesses and flows through a traceable tradition without contradiction with other reliable tradition, "leaves an unresolved problem."[53] At the end of his mammoth work *The Birth of the Messiah*, he reiterates this position: "the resurvey of the evidence necessitated by this commentary leaves me even more convinced of that,"[54] namely, that the core evidence in the New Testament about how Mary conceived is inconclusive at a historical level. Similarly, the ecumenical scholars of *Mary in the New Testament* summarize: "we see no way in which a modern scientific approach to the gospels can establish the historicity of the virginal conception (or, for that matter, disprove it)."[55] Consequently, acceptance of the historicity of the virginal conception rests on other grounds, most notably, belief in biblical inerrancy for Protestants or in the teaching of the church for Catholics, both of which authorities squarely maintain the biologically miraculous nature of Jesus' conception.

In reaching their conclusions about the unprovability of the virginal conception, biblical scholars are wise enough to point out that the assent of faith cannot be equated with affirmations of history. The morality of historical knowledge requires that if one asks a question about a historical event, the answer must be arrived at and verified by the canons of the discipline of history itself. The intellectual responsibility of the investigator into history, as into science, lies in respecting this ethic, in all honesty.[56] Faith has to do with a different kind of knowledge, an awareness of God's gracious, saving intent and action in the world, along with trust that this is the ultimate meaning of the universe and of our lives. Biblical proclamation of this belief is carried in the ideas of ancient cultures from which our own culture departs in many instances. Addressing the question of scientific and historical discrepancies in the biblical text, Vatican II taught a clarifying principle. Faith requires that we believe not every literal detail, but what God wanted placed in the scriptures "for the sake of our salvation."[57] Thus, the account in Genesis of creation in six days does not have to be interpreted as historically factual. So long as we believe that God alone ultimately created the world and everything in it, evolutionary theory can explain the origin of species without threatening faith. So too with the gospels. Their point is not to teach scientifically controlled history but to proclaim the good news of salvation coming from God through Jesus in the power of the Spirit and to evoke our life-defining response. In composing his birth narrative Matthew had this purpose clearly in mind. Despite the ambiguity of its history, the theological significance of this narrative of socially irregular pregnancy is the heart of the matter.

Theology

Placed at the opening of Matthew's gospel, the story of Jesus' irregular conception has as its purpose to inform the reader that Jesus is the Son of God. This the evangelist does by employing a motif that recurs throughout the New Testament, namely, that Jesus' divine sonship is revealed through the action of the Spirit. These two go together like fife and drum in a marching band: through the Spirit, Jesus is the Son of God. This belief arose in connection with the resurrection and then was read progressively back into the Messiah's life. The "backwards development"[58] of this christological trajectory can be traced in specific texts. Paul first played this tune in view of the resurrection: Christ "was descended from David according to the flesh and was declared to be Son of God with power according to the Spirit of holiness by resurrection from the dead" (Rom. 1:3–4). Mark next sounded the tune at Jesus' baptism, where the Spirit descends like a dove while a voice from heaven declares, "You are my Son, my beloved; with you I am well pleased" (Mark 1:11). By the latter part of the first century when Matthew and Luke wrote, Christians were affirming that Jesus was the Son of God not only since his resurrection, and not only since his baptism, but from the very beginning of his human life. Both evangelists present this belief through the same music of the Spirit as the divine agent of Jesus' conception. The idea that Jesus was conceived of the Holy Spirit thus pushes affirmation of his divine sonship, already expanded from resurrection to ministry, back to conception and birth. John will extend Jesus' divine sonship back even further, to before his earthly conception, declaring, "In the beginning was the Word . . ." (John 1:1). It will take until the Council of Nicaea in 325 before a clear decision is made about how far back this "beginning" goes, namely, to all eternity.

Begetting through the Holy Spirit, then, is first of all a theological way of describing divine sonship. Jesus is from God. This being the key to the text, scholars are virtually unanimous in ruling out any interpretation that would have the Spirit acting as a male sexual partner to Mary. In the scriptures the Spirit is the agency of God's creative power and presence. Unlike what happens in Hellenistic myths, the Spirit does not function as a male partner in a sacred marriage between a deity and a woman. Indeed in this Matthean story, while the author gives no indication of how the conception actually took place, there is no hint of divine intercourse of any sort and no language that would suggest the birth of a hero after a male god impregnates a human woman. As Brown writes, "there is never a suggestion in Matthew or in Luke that the Holy Spirit is the male element in a union with Mary, supplying the husband's role in begetting. Not only is the Holy Spirit not male (grammatically feminine in Hebrew; neuter in Greek), but also the manner of begetting is implicitly creative rather than sexual."[59] This intuition is borne out in Christian vocabulary, which does not call the Spirit the father of Jesus. Despite a scenario all too frequently entertained by the literal imagination, it is simply not the case that God the Father or his Spirit inseminates Mary. Conception by the Spirit signifies rather that God is the creative origin of Jesus' being. This nonsexual theological interpretation of creation by the Spirit is strengthened when we employ the female symbolism of the Spirit in Jewish, Syrian, and Christian traditions. Rûaḥ, the vivifying power in the universe, "the great virginal, life-engendering mother of all the living," becomes in this instance the "divine mother of Christ"[60] in collaboration with the endangered woman from Galilee. Spirit-Sophia and Mary together bring in the Christ.

In this light, Mary's being with child of, from, or through (ek in Greek) the Holy Spirit affirms Jesus' christological identity in analogy with the resurrection and baptism stories. These, in turn, draw their power from the creation stories in Genesis, redolent with the same pneumatological power. Just as the Spirit of God moved over the chaotic waters and danced a whole world into being, the same creative Spirit moved over the dead Jesus, the unknown Jesus at the start of his ministry, and the womb of Mary to create a new world. Gerhard Delling explains, "As the Spirit of God hovered over formless matter when the miracle of creation took place, so there is a new creative act of God when Jesus is born."[61] In addition to revealing the identity of Jesus as Son of God, the theological significance of Jesus' being conceived by the Holy Spirit now becomes profound. This story signals that God freely takes the initiative in the advent of the Messiah. The Savior's coming depends not in the first place on human decisions but on God's own incalculable desire to be among suffering, sinful human beings in the flesh. Ontologically Jesus' origin lies in God the Most High. His existence has its foundation in God. He is born wholly of grace, wholly of promise, God's gracious gift to humankind. The *novum* of his approach lies in the incomprehensible depths of the mercy of God. That this requires the human cooperation in different ways of a poor Galilean couple at first vastly troubled by the gift does not diminish the power of divine initiative that blesses the world with a new act of creation by the Creator Spirit.

This line of reasoning leads a number of theologians to conclude that neither the New Testament nor magisterium of the church fundamentally teaches that the virginal conception is first of all a miracle of nature. To do that, you would have to argue that Matthew and Luke had this one essential purpose in mind when they were writing their infancy narratives, which they clearly did not. Frans Jozef von Beeck makes the fine distinction that "calling the virginal conception and birth a miracle is a conclu-

sion from the data of faith, not an article of faith in and of itself."[62] Given
the commonly available understanding of the physiological processes
leading to conception in their day, whereby the mother supplied the physical mass, the father supplied the vital spirit that ignites it to form an
embryo, and God supplied the soul, the evangelists told their infancy stories as "missionary theophanies."[63] Using the cultural assumptions of the
day, they intended to say that Jesus was a child of his mother, and hence
fully human, while affirming that God's own holy will is the sole true ini-
tiator of this child who is the world's Savior: "in loving mercy, God and
God alone takes the initiative in having the divine Power and Wisdom
dwell among us as one of us."[64]

Granted that in scripture and the creeds "conceived by the Holy Spirit"
is not in the first instance a biological but an evocative theological statement, our minds, imbued with contemporary scientific knowledge of how
conception takes place, inevitably return to the historical issue and ask
How? Where did the Y chromosome come from? With what sperm did
Mary's egg unite to initiate a new human being? Theologically, the answer
is that in a new act analogous to the creation of the world, the Creator
Spirit created the Y chromosome *ex nihilo* and caused it to appear in
Mary's body without sexual intercourse. As Brown reiterates, "It was an
extraordinary action of God's creative power, as unique as the initial creation itself."[65] Contemporary debate arises when some scholars query
whether this is really necessary. Given the biblical witness to divine modes
of acting whereby divine agency normally works in tandem with human
agency—through secondary causes, in scholastic terminology—the Spirit
of God can be seen to work in and through what happens in the world to
lure it toward fulfillment. Divine and human fatherhood are not necessarily mutually exclusive. The action of God does not have to replace or can-
cel natural sexual activity so as to render the human role superfluous.[66]
Indeed, since sex is God's own good design for procreation, would it not
be more suitable that God use it in this instance?

In thinking this through, it is important to note that the virginal conception is not necessary to account for the sinlessness of Jesus, which is
present in other layers of New Testament tradition that know nothing of
this belief. Later developments will link sex with sinfulness, but in the
infancy narratives there is no trace of antisexual bias that would demean
ordinary conception in marriage as less than holy. Later Christian teaching

will use the virginal conception as imaginative shorthand for the doctrine of two natures, picturing that God the Father gave Christ a divine nature while Mary his mother gave him a human nature. But in orthodox Christian belief Jesus would be God's beloved child no matter how he was conceived because his sonship is eternal and independent of earthly incarnation. Joseph Ratzinger explains this clearly, beginning with the difference between birth stories of heroes in the history of religions and the birth story of Jesus in the gospels:

> The main contrast consists in the fact that in pagan texts the Godhead almost always appears as fertilizing, procreative power, thus under a more or less sexual aspect and hence in a physical sense as the "father" of the savior-child. As we have seen, nothing of this sort appears in the New Testament: the conception of Jesus is new creation, not begetting by God. God does not become the biological father of Jesus, and neither the New Testament nor the theology of the Church has fundamentally ever seen in this narrative or in the event recounted in it the ground for the real divinity of Jesus. . . . According to the faith of the Church the Sonship of Jesus does not rest on the fact that Jesus had no human father; the doctrine of Jesus' divinity would not be affected if Jesus had been the product of a normal human marriage. For the Sonship of which faith speaks is not a biological but an ontological fact, an event not in time but in God's eternity.[67]

A begetting by divine power through the Holy Spirit always remains *analogous* to human begetting and needs to be understood by appreciating the myriad ways Spirit-Sophia works in the world. In this light, the gospel story of the conception of the Messiah by the Holy Spirit places Mary with the life-giving powers of her body at the heart of Sophia-God's approach to the world. Conceived by the Holy Spirit, the Messiah was born of the virgin Mary.

Scandal and the Spirit

The historical and theological issues of Matthew's conception story receive yet another reading in feminist interpretation. The text of Matthew's birth narrative is filled with tension. While on the surface this is a story shaped by patriarchal law, the narrative is encircled by female images, from the creative Spirit evoked by grammar and imagery to the endangered pregnant woman.[68] It features Joseph as the recipient of divine revelation while at the same time honoring a woman's conception of a child outside of patriarchal norms. It underscores the disgrace that surrounds her condition but affirms emphatically that God stands with the endangered woman and her child to the point where they are the fulfillment of divine promise. Feminist insight into both the scandal and the power of the virgin woman fruitful with the Spirit uncovers unsuspected empowerment for women in this story and gives reason to honor the virginal conception in full strength.

This story of illicit pregnancy places Mary in solidarity with women who suffer violence or the threat of violence from patriarchal authority, affirming against all social consensus that God is with them. Even with the emphasis on Joseph's upright and good-hearted actions, Mary is in danger from her irregular pregnancy. When the story opens, she has no guarantee of her own safety. Then as now in patriarchal society, female virginity functions in a masculinist system of exchange which women violate at their own risk. The story resolves the problem by having her husband ultimately offer safety and legitimacy to his wife and the fetus growing within her, thus bringing them back into the male-dominated order upheld by society.[69] At the same time, and here is the major twist, it demonstrates that patriarchal logic fails to do justice to God's ways. Mary is in jeopardy, but God stands with her to fulfill the ancient promise. Her child appears to be illegitimate but is called holy, the one who will save the people from their sins. Bearing the Messiah outside of patriarchal norms, Mary yet moves within the divine plan of salvation. While reverberating with a tone of scandal, the narrative thus subtly challenges the biased social patterns that create the scandal to begin with. In the end, Mary's validation shows that "the reproductive power of woman and her role in the birth of the Messiah are affirmed outside the patriarchal structure."[70] Not only that, but being "outside" is precisely where the encounter with the Holy One takes place. "Mary is a woman who has access to the sacred outside the patriarchal family and its control";[71] in her precarious state she helps to birth the work of the Spirit. Matthew is no feminist, but it would be hard to write a story that more strongly honors the importance to God of a woman at severe risk for violating the expectations of patriarchal marriage. The shadow cast by her scandalous situation connects in hope with oppressed women struggling by the power of God's Spirit to survive patriarchal violence and the threat of violence. Elaine Wainwright proposes that because of the way it speaks to women's situation, this story itself was kept alive in house churches where there was a living praxis of women in leadership.[72]

This tessera also plays into the current retrieval of the meaning of virginity as a symbol of female autonomy. As we have seen, the symbol of virginity does not necessarily refer in the first instance to the absence of sexual experience. Historians of religion have discovered a raft of virgin goddesses who take lovers but are still considered to be virgins in the sense that they are free from male control, not accessories to men or dependent on their protection. To be virgin is to be one-in-yourself, free, independent, unsubordinated, unexploited, a woman never subdued.[73] In this sense, the virginal conception is valuable in bearing a message of revolutionary female empowerment. The virgin Mary's conception of the Messiah without male begetting epitomizes in its own strange way women's strong abilities in collaboration with divine Spirit. The male is excluded. The end of the patriarchal order is announced. In her often quoted "Ain't I a Woman?" speech, Sojourner Truth voices this insight with unsurpassed eloquence. I quote here from the account published in the "National Anti-Slavery Standard" in 1863. After insisting on her own humanity as a woman in the face of dehumanizing experiences of slavery and male prejudice, she continues:

> "That little man in black there, he say a woman can't have as much rights as a man, 'cause Christ wasn't a woman. Where did your Christ come from?" Rolling thunder could not have stilled that crowd as did those deep, wonderful tones, as she stood there with outstretched arms and eyes of fire. Raising her voice still louder, she repeated, "Where did your Christ come from? From God and a woman! Man had nothing to do with him!" Oh, what a rebuke she gave the little man.[74]

This emancipated slave, abolitionist, and independent preacher, illiterate but steeped in wisdom, recognized anti-woman nonsense being spouted by a clergyman and stood up to set the record straight. God and a woman together brought the Messiah into the world. They did so in partnership, divine *rûaḥ* and a woman of low social status collaborating together, without the intervention of men. All the placid, sentimental paintings of madonna and child cannot rob this gospel story of its raw, subversive implications. It supports the integrity of women's spiritual power when they listen to the blowing of the Spirit in their lives. It affirms their abilities to create new, saving possibilities outside of patriarchal structures and in the teeth of reactionary violence. The account of Mary's being with child from the Holy Spirit adds the color of danger to the marian mosaic, tinted with a striking hue of female power in partnership with God.

WISDOM FROM THE EAST
(MATTHEW 2:1–12)

When Jesus was born in Bethlehem a group of magi, number unknown, followed a star from the East to pay homage to this newborn king of the Jews. Their route took them through the capital city Jerusalem, where their encounter with Herod the Great, Rome's client-king of the Jews, filled the palace coterie with alarm. Pushing on, "they rejoiced exceedingly with great joy" when they saw the star stop. "Going into the house they saw the child with Mary his mother, and they knelt down and paid him homage," offering gifts of gold, frankincense, and myrrh. Warned in a dream not to let Herod know where the child was, they went home by another route.

The Christian imagination has long conflated the infancy narratives of Matthew and Luke, but the two are very different at this point. Luke's story begins in the northern village of Nazareth and uses a Roman-ordered census to move Mary and Joseph south to Bethlehem, David's ancestral home and therefore the birthplace of the Messiah. Matthew works in reverse. His account begins in Bethlehem, then brings the family up to Nazareth by a circuitous route laid down by his theological interest, moving them into and out of Egypt. Matthew knows nothing of a census or of birth in a stable, of being laid in a manger, of shepherds keeping watch over their flocks and angels singing. Instead, this family already dwells in Bethlehem, seemingly as long-term inhabitants. A sign that they are settled rather than transient is that they live in a house, a secure residence, which the magi enter when they reach the goal of their quest. There is no scholarly agreement over which account, Luke's or Matthew's, is more factual, if either, but that is not the point. Their intent is to inform us, as their gospels open, of the christological identity of this child, and they go about it in different ways. Three elements color this tessera of the marian mosaic.

The presence of danger from patriarchal law that ran through the story of Mary's conception grows stronger here with the introduction of Herod, who embodies the menace of the state. Recall his tenure as Rome's pointman in Palestine, to whom the interests of his own people mattered little. His ostentatious living, opulent building projects, excessive taxation, and extravagant cruelty laid a more than heavy burden on the peasant population. Would such a tyrant care to hear that there is a contender for his throne? Indeed, the messianic title King of the Jews appears here in its sole appearance outside the passion narrative, where it was nailed to the cross of Jesus. Suffering looms on the horizon.

The presence of wisdom is signaled by the arrival of seekers from the East, knowledgeable about a wisdom tradition that has led them to search for the new liberator. Although pictured as kings in the popular imagination, they are technically magi, a term that referred historically to people engaged in the mystic, supernatural arts. These included astronomers, priestly augurers, fortune tellers, and magicians of varying plausibility.[75] Whichever mode of discernment they used, magi in general carried out the religious function of trying to interpret the will of the gods. Wainwright offers the feminist suggestion that Matthew's magi may evoke the wisdom tradition of scripture with its many points of contact with foreign religion, including female images of God. They could be following the star of Sophia God, a suggestion made more cogent because Holy Wisdom is used to interpret Jesus in key places later in this gospel.[76] In Brown's opinion, the magi represent the wise and learned among the Gentiles who come to believe in Christ. They epitomize "the best of pagan lore and religious perceptivity which has come to seek Jesus through revelation in nature,"[77] that is, through the star. On their journey their wisdom is enriched by the revelation in the Jewish scriptures uncovered by Herod's scribes, and completed by finding the Messiah himself. Like some of the foremothers of the genealogy, they signal that Jesus is destined for Gentiles as well as Jews. Taking a less literary, more political view, Richard Horsley notes that since magi served as priestly advisers to kings in the Roman-occupied eastern territories, they would stand in opposition to the tyranny of the empire. It was not only the Jewish people who resisted Roman rule. Hence their following the star and giving obeisance to a new and different kind of king expresses their hope for liberation from oppressive rule.[78] Jesus is attended by wise ones whose wisdom makes them figures of resistance; their tribute signals the attraction of the coming reign of God, which will bring about salvation as liberation. Whichever interpretation one chooses, the appearance of these exotic strangers is a mixed blessing. It is the first public acknowledgment of the messianic identity of Mary's child, but it brings in its wake a drumbeat of peril. The visit of the magi has drawn the unwelcome attention of the powerful to the existence of this young, vulnerable family.

The presence of the house in this episode signals an ideal for the church. The drama of good and evil being played out between the danger of Herod and the wisdom of the magi focuses on the house wherein is found "the child with Mary his mother." Recognized by her own name and her relationship to the messianic child, Mary along with her husband receives these seekers, their gifts, and their wisdom from the East. Allied with unconventional foremothers, surviving the scandal of an irregular pregnancy, now nurturing a young child, she is linked from the outset to the core of the new thing God is doing in this world. Unfortunately, Matthew gives her no words to say or actions to take. But we can read her presence in this climactic revelatory scene as an "extraordinary inclusion"[79] with subversive implications for women's participation in the Jesus movement. After Jesus' death and resurrection, the primary locale for this movement throughout the first century was the house church. Members of different social classes, races, and genders gathered in houses across the Greco-Roman world to remember, ritually celebrate, and proclaim the good news of salvation in Christ and to test its implications for the way they lived. In this context Matthew employs the "house" as a continuous metaphor for the church. What goes on in the house in various passages of his gospel evokes the ideal for his community, at the center of whose life lay the house church.[80] The magi with their gifts enter the Bethlehem house and find Christ. As a result, relationships are realigned. In terms of class and social status, "aristocrats acknowledge a child, and resources are shared when the rich give to an ordinary Judean family, one which probably represented the majority of Jewish families impoverished by Herodian, Roman, and temple taxation."[81] So too, implies Matthew, should economic resources to sustain life be shared in the house church. In terms of gender, the magi find Mary in the house, named and at the center of the scene. So too, implies the story, visited by the liberating wisdom of Christ, the church should realign old patriarchal patterns of relationship that marginalize women and move to partnership in the following of Christ. Wainwright suggests that this message was heard in house churches where women took active roles, at least "in the Matthean households who did not take offense at such a challenge."[82] Readers today can still hear this radical invitation.

REFUGEES FROM SLAUGHTER
(MATTHEW 2:13–23)

This tessera places Mary at the center of an experience of terror and displacement. Herod stalked the trail of the magi, a menacing reminder that "while the star of the newborn King has shone forth in purity and simplicity, there are those who will seek to blot out that light."[83] In a towering rage Herod sought to kill his newborn rival. Warned in a dream, Joseph took "the child and his mother" and went fleeing by night into Egypt. Back in Bethlehem, soldiers butchered all the male children under two years of age. After Herod died, Joseph, guided by yet another dream, returned with "the child and his mother" to the land of Israel. Warned again in a dream that despotic Archelaus had inherited his father's rule in Judea, Joseph headed the family north to Galilee, where they made their home in the town of Nazareth. Riveting images impress themselves on the imagination: terrible fear propelling escape in the dark from oncoming murder with no guarantee of success; the iron swords, the baby blood, the red pavement stone, the empty look of mothers mute with shock, their piercing wails of inconsolable grief; a young family's life in exile in a foreign land, negotiating strange language, customs, and institutions, all the while carrying memories of horror and a feeling of pain for those who did not escape; the recognition that you can't go home again and the brave setting out in a new direction.[84]

This story lifts up a memory of Mary with her husband and child in agonized solidarity with the millions of refugees struggling to survive in a harsh world even today. War is "pure hell on earth" for civilian victims, reads a letter from the U.N. High Commission for Refugees; those particularly at risk are children, late-term pregnant women, and the elderly. The twentieth century, continuing into the twenty-first, has witnessed "a staggering tide of uprooted people"[85] stretching from Afghanistan to Sudan to Chechnya to Palestine to East Timor to Haiti, a flood of fleeing millions on five continents. Their basic survival is at stake as hunger, dehydration, and lack of shelter and medical care take their toll, along with the trauma of violence, separation from family members, and ongoing fear and anxiety. This is a crisis that does not last only a day but drags on in the chronic poverty of refugee camps and the blockading of hope for the future. "Over 2,000 years ago, Mary and Joseph sought shelter far from their homeland. Today, millions like them continue to search for a safe place to rest," writes the Catholic Relief Services newsletter. "There are few things more traumatic than losing your family's home." Even if home is a modest shack, it is where people come for refuge and rest, the place where they keep their possessions and cooking utensils, the place where they raise their children and keep the family safe. "Losing the home will put a family on a downward slide into deeper poverty and vulnerability."[86] Millions of lives are uprooted this way because of political disaster. In a similar way, Joseph and Mary fled their house and their homeland with their baby for political reasons, to escape the murderous wrath of their country's ruler. Sri Lankan theologian Tissa Balasuriya makes the astute observation that once arrived in Egypt, Joseph would be akin to a migrant worker, a non-national willing to do even the most menial tasks in order to survive. "For many years, Mary along with Joseph would have experienced tribulations by being foreign workers in Egypt. In this, too, she experienced personally the problems which many of the underprivileged people even in rich countries have to face. . . . It is a pity that popular devotions to Mary do not recall her in this experience as a poor, courageous woman."[87]

Later apocryphal gospels sought to make the flight into Egypt into a triumphal procession for the Son of God. Native African lions and leopards in a docile mood led the caravan through the desert: "wherever Joseph and holy Mary went, they went before them, showing them the way and lowering their heads in worship; they showed their servitude by wagging their tails, and honored Him with great reverence" (*Gospel of Pseudo-Matthew* 19.1).[88] Palm trees bent down to refresh the weary pilgrims with fruit; springs of water appeared in the desert. Their arrival showed Egyptian religion with its 365 gods and goddesses to be false: "But it came to pass that when blessed Mary entered the temple with the child, all the idols fell to the ground, so that they all lay on their faces completely overturned and shattered. Thus they openly showed that they were nothing" (*Gospel of Pseudo-Matthew* 23).[89] The respect of the native Egyptians, including their military commanders, followed. Would that every refugee had it so good. Matthew's original text gives no hint of such an easy escape but positions this young family on the road of exile and deprivation.

Even if not historically factual, the narrative of infant massacre and escape to Egypt reflects the historical situation that prevailed in Jewish Palestine under Roman and Herodian rule. Using death and destruction as a means of intimidating people, the imperial occupiers and their client-kings created thousands of refugees. When military action commenced, people were forced to flee from their homes if they wanted to avoid being killed. The text also accurately mirrors the character of Herod, who indulged in well-attested acts of ruthless cruelty. He had three of his own children put to death on various pretexts. To ensure proper mourning at his own funeral, he instructed his soldiers to kill notable political prisoners upon news of his death: "So shall all Judea and every household weep for me, whether they wish it or not."⁹⁰ The brutality gene was passed on to his son Archelaus, who ushered in his reign with a massacre of three thousand people and was so despised for his dictatorial ways that he was finally deposed by Rome. Carnage, upheaval, loss of home and neighbors, children caught in a web of violence, parents in despair—this story was all too intelligible to readers in Matthew's time, and in our own.

By the way the evangelist shapes this sequence, artfully inserting fulfillment citations from the Hebrew scriptures, he inlays announcements about the christological identity of this child into this story of narrow escape from death. Jesus recapitulates the formative history of the people of whom he is the new, redemptive flowering. Recall how Israel went down to Egypt at the instigation of Jacob and there found refuge from famine. Recall the rescue of the infant Moses from the evil intent of Pharaoh to kill the male babies. Recall the liberating exodus of the enslaved Hebrew people from Egypt. "Out of Egypt I have called my son," the gospel quotes the prophet Hosea (Hos. 11:1), referring now to Jesus but harking back to the original exodus of the people who were God's beloved children. Jesus is the king of the Jews in a theological way that Herod never could be.

A second citation positions this family in relation to the violence. Recall how in the course of Israel's history first the northern and then the southern tribes were led away into exile, a state of banishment from which only a minority returned. "A voice was heard in Ramah, weeping and loud lamentation, Rachel weeping for her children; she refused to be consoled, because they are no more," the gospel quotes the prophet Jeremiah (Jer. 31:15), referring now to the Bethlehem mothers but evoking the captivity and deportation centuries earlier of the tribes descended from their ancient foremother. This infancy story thus deliberately echoes the two great paradigmatic events in Israel's history, exodus and exile, connecting the endangered Messiah with the history of the Jewish people. Tellingly, it affirms the manner in which God's salvific power operates, namely, in the midst of and not above the struggles of history. Emmanuel, his mother, and her dreamy, practical husband retrace the biblical pattern of exile and exodus and end up in Nazareth according to God's salvific design.

In an intense and unusual way, there are multiple references to "the child and his mother" throughout this episode. The repetition of this phrase in verses 13, 14, 20, and 21 establishes a powerful connection between mother and child in this situation of peril. Both are threatened.

Mary has already faced down danger from patriarchal virginity laws, but now her life is once again at risk from the brutal power of the state. The vulnerable child being hunted is never alone but is always in the company of his mother, surrounded, the text implies, by her fierce care, which exposes her to the same peril. Jesus here is indeed "Miriam's child."[91] Repeated allusions to her presence, furthermore, keep punctuating the story with a female center of interest which serves to decenter the exercise of male military and political power that governs this narrative. Her character once again opens a fissure in the symbolic universe of patriarchy. "The infant Jesus is located throughout in the presence of the woman Mary, designated in the text as 'his mother' but evocative of those women whose anomalous stories challenge patriarchal family structures."[92] Connected with the genealogy, the continuously named presence of Mary in this scene evokes the power and presence of women in Israel's history and the birth of its Messiah. Empowering hearers of this gospel who struggle for women's full participation in the Christian mission, this interpretation allows those threatened by patriarchal violence to themselves constitute an internal counterthreat to the status quo.

Neither Mary nor the Bethlehem mothers speak aloud or otherwise react to the slaughter of the children. The voice of Rachel weeping resounds in this silence. Long a symbolic figure of the suffering mother, more specifically of the nation mourning its lost peoples, even more precisely of Jewish mothers, whose children were murdered on a mass scale, this ancestral figure enters the story to send up their lament to God. They bond together as she articulates their grief, allowing their outrage to cry to heaven. Her tears and loud lamentation rip still another fissure in this well-ordered text. "It is the raised voice of Rachel that pierces the male world of power, of slaughter, and of divine favor,"[93] rejecting even the divine plan that would rescue one special child but ignore the rest. Her tears gush forth as resistance to such brutality, her shouts as a challenge to this violent way of running the world. Subverting the patriarchal pattern, this "female image of the compassionate, inconsolable mother provides a counterpoint to the extreme violence of the holocaust of the male children at the hand of the male ruler, Herod."[94] Since the later verses of this Rachel poem in Jeremiah depict divine compassion in female imagery as the love of a mother for the child of her womb, Rachel also points to the motherly God who weeps inconsolably in protest with those who are bereaved (Jer. 31:20).[95]

One day the authority of the imperial state will get Mary's son too. His close, heart-in-the-mouth brush with death in infancy will turn all too real in his thirties, and his mother's lament will take a newly sharp, personal turn. The good news of the gospel is that the advent of God focused in Jesus, who is descended not only from Abraham and David but also from the defiantly lamenting Rachel and the threatened, fleeing, defiantly surviving Mary, compassionately overcomes the worst outrage. This is the Christian hope. But given the river of deaths of millions of children due to military and domestic assault and the institutional violence of poverty, "Rachel still weeps in every country of the world."[96] Borrowing phrases from Mary's Magnificat, one contemporary poet imagines her resonating with her grieving ancestor, saying:

> Wail, mourn aloud, sister Rachel ...
> Unleash grief's force, sister Rachel, to change what made you grieve ...
> Unleash grief's force, sister Rachel, the mighty to bring down, the wealthy to chase out, the hungry to fill up ...
> Of your child you are deprived; let no one steal your rage.[97]

ANNUNCIATION: CALL OF THE PROPHET
(LUKE 1:26–38)

As we begin to examine the tesserae painted by Luke, one color runs through them all. Mary is a disciple, not in the historical sense that she accompanied Jesus during his ministry, but in the existential sense that she heard the word of God and acted upon it. This view comes to the fore in an exchange unique to this gospel. Moved by Jesus' preaching, an admiring woman in the crowd raised her voice to cry, "Blessed is the womb that bore you and the breasts that you sucked!" This was a typical Mediterranean expression that praised a mother for the fine qualities of her son. In reply Jesus emphasized qualities of spirit, saying, "Blessed rather are those who hear the word of God and keep it!" (Luke 11:27–28). Some few interpreters think that with the word "rather" Jesus set up a contrast between true believers and his mother. This explanation does not hold up, however, in view of the positive way Luke presents Mary in all other scenes of his gospel. Instead, the intensifier "rather" means yes, what you said is true as far as it goes, but there is more to be said.[98] In effect, Jesus' beatitude echoes that of Elizabeth, who early on had saluted the young woman pregnant with the Messiah with the words, "Blessed is she who believed . . ." (Luke 1:45). In Luke's theology the faith that marks a genuine disciple consists in hearing and acting upon God's word. The next five mosaic stones, taken from his work, present Mary as just such an exemplary disciple in ever varying scenarios.

The annunciation scene, which appears after the announcement of the birth of John the Baptist, depicts Mary with a mood of celebration as a hearer and doer of God's word. The angel Gabriel was sent from God to a young, unlettered woman in Nazareth, a poor village in the oppressed peasant region of Galilee. The girl is betrothed to a man named Joseph, but in accord with Jewish marriage customs has not yet moved into his house to share life together. The heavenly messenger announces God's desire that Mary bear a child who will be great, the Messiah, the holy Son of God. Assured that the Spirit will empower and protect her, she gives her free consent, casting her lot with the great work of redemption in the belief that nothing is impossible with God.

The overarching purpose of this story, as with Matthew's opening narrative, is to disclose to Luke's readers at the outset the truth about Jesus' messianic identity. Using christological titles and language developed by the church after the resurrection, the scene vividly dramatizes the theological point that Jesus did not just become the Son of God after his death (Paul) or even at his baptism (Mark) but is the Son of God from his very conception in this world. At the same time, by making Mary the central character, Luke's text invites reflection on her faith and action in her own right. Indeed, throughout centuries of translation and reflection, no other text has had more influence on the development of mariology, for better or worse. At its worst, the emphasis of some interpreters on the phrasing of Mary's response, "be it done to me according to your word," has led to that ideal of woman as an obedient handmaid, passively receptive to male commands, which women today find so obnoxious. But other interpretations are possible. By examining three facets of this text, namely, its literary structure, language about the Holy Spirit, and the import of Mary's consent, we can draw this rich scene into a liberating memory replete with "lessons of encouragement."

Literary Structure

In this scene Luke deftly combines two conventions of biblical narrative, the birth announcement and the commissioning of the prophet. Both types of stories follow the same literary structure, which in its complete form comprises five standard elements. First, an angel or some other form of messenger from heaven appears with a greeting. Next, the recipient reacts with fear or awe and is encouraged not to be afraid. Third, central to the story, the announcement itself declares God's intent and gives a glimpse of what the future outcome will be. Fourth, the recipient then offers an objection: How so? Fifth, the story ends with a sign of divine power that reassures the recipient. This story pattern is used at significant junctures in Israel's history both to announce the coming birth of a significant child and to describe the call of adult persons into collaboration with God's designs. The scriptures are replete with examples. A birth story: when the Israelites were groaning under a foreign oppressor, an angel of the Lord appeared to a barren woman, wife of Manoah, to declare that she would conceive and bear a son who would deliver Israel from the hand of the Philistines. The dynamism of the structured story line runs on, ending with the sign of the angel ascending in the flame of the sacrificial altar, followed by the birth of Samson, in whom the Spirit stirred at an early age (Judg. 13:2–23). In a similar fashion, the classic birth announcement heralds the coming of Ishmael to Hagar, Isaac to Abraham and Sarah, John the Baptist to Zechariah and Elizabeth, and Jesus to Joseph (in Matthew's gospel).[99] The Christmas morning gospel presents a familiar example in the story of angels appearing to the shepherds, which follows the pattern of appearance, fear and reassurance, message about the birth of the Messiah, and the sign of a babe in swaddling clothes lying in a manger. By using this fixed literary pattern to announce the birth of Jesus to Mary, Luke is linking mother and child to the great sweep of God's gracious history with Israel and heralding the significance of this child in that history.

Luke fuses this function of the announcement story with the second scriptural use of this literary form, which is to call and commission a prophet. One particularly telling example is the story of Moses (Exod. 3:1–14). While he is shepherding flocks in the desert, (1) the angel of the Lord appears to him in a burning bush; (2) Moses takes off his shoes, hides his face in fear; (3) then comes the message: God has seen the misery of the people enslaved in Egypt, has heard their cries, feels what they are suffering, and has come down to deliver them: "Come I will send you to Pharaoh to bring my people, the Israelites, out of Egypt"; (4) Moses' objection follows as the night the day: "Who am I?" too slow of speech; (5) finally, God gives assurance with the indelible words "I will be with you," coupled with a sign in the form of a future promise that, once freed, the people will worship on this very mountain. Here the five-point pattern of the announcement story narrates the moment when Moses, prophet and liberator, enters into his life's vocation. It signals God's intent to deliver an enslaved people, for which task a human being is chosen and for which this person's free assent is essential. Once the die is cast, the presence of God will guide this person through thick and thin, and the community will remember him with gratitude for the ways in which his response brought blessing upon the oppressed people. In the beginning, though, it is a religious encounter that transpires in the solitude of the heart before God: the exiled shepherd, the flaming bush, the prophetic call, the free response, all embedded in the tradition of a community now struggling for freedom.

Another clear instance of this pattern at work is the story of Gideon, set in a time when the people were groaning under conquerors from the land of Midian (Judg. 6:11–24).[100] The angel of the Lord appears under an oak tree; Gideon's fear is met with the classic reassurance, "The Lord is with you"; then comes the message that Gideon is to deliver Israel from the oppressive hand of Midian: "I hereby commission you"; but, objects Gideon, my clan is the weakest of all; nevertheless, "I will be with you," and the sign is fire that consumes his sacrificial bread and meat. The call of other prophets and liberators in the history of Israel often follows this pattern, Jeremiah being another memorable example.

Luke's artistry welds the announcement of Jesus' birth to the call of Mary as a woman commissioned by God. Biblical scholars point out that in this scene she is engaged for a prophetic task, one in a long line of God-sent deliverers positioned at significant junctures in Israel's history.[101] All five elements of the literary convention march in full, vigorous display. The angel appears with the classic greeting "Hail, favored one, the Lord is with you," a formula often used to greet a person chosen by God for a special purpose in salvation history. Mary reacts with a troubled heart and receives the classic encouragement not to be afraid. The messenger announces that she will conceive a child who will be great, son of the Most High, inheriting the throne of David in a kingdom without end. Her objection "How can this be?" is met with the promise that the Holy Spirit will be with her. The promise is underscored with the sign of old Elizabeth's pregnancy. Replete with angelic voice, fear and reassurance, message, objection, and sign, this is a story of Mary being commissioned to carry forward God's design for redemption. The announcement of her impending motherhood is at the same time her prophetic calling to act for the deliverance of the people. She now takes her place "among those prophets called to give word and witness to the hidden plan of God's salvific activity not yet seen by other members of the community of faith."[102] Her affirmative response to this divine initiative sets her life off on an adventure into the unknown future. The divine presence will be with her through good times and bad, and ultimately the community will remember her life with gratitude. In this scene the whole story is captured in its beginning: it is a prophetic vocation story of a Jewish girl and her God, set within the traditions of her people struggling for freedom.

Holy Spirit

At the center of this story lies a powerful declaration of the relationship between this peasant woman and the Spirit of God. In good standard fashion Mary has objected, "How can this be since I do not know man?" The angel replies, "The Holy Spirit will come upon you, and the power of the Most High will overshadow you," and thus the child will be called holy, Son of God. By the fourth and fifth centuries, once church councils had declared the doctrinal identity of Jesus Christ to be that of one person in two natures, human and divine, the Christian imagination interpreted this Lukan text in a literally sexual way. Mary the virgin was somehow impregnated by the Spirit of God, which resulted in Jesus' having a human mother and a divine father; this ensured the truth of his two natures. The difficulty with this interpretation, however, lies partly in the fact that nowhere in scripture is the Spirit's action that "comes upon" and "overshadows" a person analogous to sexual intercourse. Rather, these verbs indicate the presence of God who empowers and protects:

• *Eperchesthai* ("come upon") in Greek literally signifies the coming and going of persons or things such as ships. This rootedness in physical movement in space equips the word to function figuratively to point to the intangible approach of the living God. Carrying the notion of onrushing, overpowering vitality, it tells of divine presence on the move creating something new. A prime example is Jesus' saying in Acts that assures his disciples after his resurrection, "You will receive power when the Holy Spirit has *come upon* you" (Acts 1:8). When this does indeed happen, the women and men of his circle are empowered to preach the good news to the ends of the earth. This same sense of empowerment is well attested in the Hebrew Bible. After Samuel's anointing, "the Spirit of the Lord *came mightily upon* David from that day forward," beginning his march toward kingship (1 Sam. 16:13). Isaiah foretells devastation "until the Spirit *comes upon* us from on high," when a period of blessed refreshment will begin (Isa. 32:15). These and other biblical examples make clear that the Spirit "coming upon" someone is not sexual but creatively empowering in a broader sense. It connotes the approach of the power of God in a decisively new way.

• *Episkiazein* ("overshadow") in Greek literally means to cast a shadow on something. In contemporary Western parlance this may have a negative, ominous ring. In the Middle East, however, where the sun is so strong it can fry your brains, the cooling shadow of a little tree or even the wall of a building is much appreciated. When used in scripture with reference to God, "overshadowing" thus has the positive meaning of manifesting powerful divine protection over a person or even the whole people. The word is often coupled with concrete images such as a moving cloud or sheltering wings under whose shadow persons find refuge, figurative ways of speaking about God's protection from harm. John Calvin thought the cloud was a particularly "elegant metaphor" for divine presence insofar as it conceals as much as it reveals, covering over divine glory with a haze of brilliance.[103] With this nuance, the overshadowing cloud resonates with allusions to the *Shekinah*, the indwelling, saving presence of the Holy One in later rabbinic writings.

Two other instances closely parallel this verb's meaning in the annunciation text. In the exodus story a cloud settles on the tent of meeting that Moses pitched in the desert: "the cloud *overshadowed* it and the glory of the Lord filled the tabernacle" (Exod. 40:34ff.). When the cloud rose, the people followed it and trekked on; when it settled down on the tabernacle, they rested. Casting a shadow by day, shot through with fire at night, "the movement of the cloud directs the journey toward freedom."[104] What is being spoken of here is the presence of God. Signified by the cloud, this presence protects, refreshes, directs, liberates. Again, all three Synoptic Gospels use the same verb in their account of Jesus' transfiguration: "Then a cloud *overshadowed* them, and from the cloud there came a voice . . ." (Mark 9:7; Matt. 17:5; Luke 9:34). As in the Sinai story, the action of the cloud, itself a metaphor of divine presence, brings God close to the scene with gracious, redemptive intent. The voice speaks the same message about Jesus' being the Son of God as was already heard at the baptism, and the two scenes are parallel. The Spirit descends like a dove, the cloud of glory overshadows, and Jesus' messianic identity is revealed.

Overshadowing, then, always means the Spirit of God drawing near and passing by to save and protect. Given this usage, given that neither in secular nor religious language does the word ever function as a euphemism for sexual intercourse, it is clear that the Holy Spirit's overshadowing Mary in the annunciation story is, as Carsten Colpe insists, "the opposite of human procreation."[105] What is being described is not a god impregnating a mortal woman such as occurs in Hellenistic stories of sacred marriage. Luke does not mean that God acts as a substitute male sexual partner. Indeed, Paul can write of Isaac that he was "the child who was born according to the Spirit" (Gal. 4:29) without implying that Abraham's sexual paternity was absent. As the ecumenical authors of *Mary in the New Testament* teach, "the overshadowing of 1:35 has no sexual implication." Rather, the term comes from a tradition "where no sexual import is possible. God is not a sexual partner but a creative power in the begetting of Jesus."[106] Remembering the female imagery used in scripture of the Holy Spirit— rûaḥ, mother, Sophia—further strengthens this philological insight. The Spirit does not mate with Mary.

Hence, the angel does not answer Mary's objection with a satisfactory description of the mechanics of "how shall this be." Joseph Fitzmyer's judgment about what happened historically is the baseline from which all theologizing should proceed: "What really happened? We shall never know."[107] In view of the religious meaning of Mary's pregnancy, however, we know a great deal. The text declares that the creative presence of God's Spirit will be with her. As Schaberg explains, "What is the essence of this second angelic response? It is this: You should trust; you will be empowered and protected by God. The reversal of Elizabeth's humiliation shows that nothing is impossible for God."[108] Recall how in the opening scene in Genesis, the Spirit of God blows like a mighty wind over the dark waters and the world came into being. Just so, in this new moment of the renewal of creation, the Spirit is on the move again. Recall, furthermore, the Easter proclamation that it is by the Spirit that Jesus is raised from the dead and made Son of God in power. Just so, the same life-giving Spirit creates him as Son of God at his conception.[109] The point for our remembering here is that both in its structure as a commissioning story and in its metaphors of the Spirit's coming upon and overshadowing, this scene with its primary christological interest is a theophany. It places this woman in deep, attentive relation to the Spirit of God. Mary belongs in the company of those whom Spirit-Sophia approaches: "From generation to generation she enters into holy souls and makes them friends of God and prophets" (Wis. 7:27). We do not have access to Mary's religious experience, but can simply say that by the power of the Spirit she encountered the mystery of the living God, the gracious God of her life, the saving Wisdom of her people. In that encounter, the die was cast for the coming of the Messiah.

Consent

All of this takes place as a result of God's free initiative. As always in biblical portrayals of divine interaction with human beings, divine freedom does not override created freedom but waits upon our free response, which, in a theology of grace, God has already made possible. Hearing the divine call, Mary decides to say yes. Casting her lot with the future, she responds with courage and, as the next scene of the visitation will show, with joy and prophecy to this unexpected call: "And Mary said, 'Behold the handmaid of the Lord. Be it done to me according to your word.'" Here Luke innovates by adding Mary's verbal consent as a sixth, climactic element to the literary structure of the announcement story, whose design normally has five points whether used for prophetic commissioning or foretelling birth. "In none of the twenty-seven Hebrew Bible commissionings, none of the ten nonbiblical accounts, none of the fifteen other commissionings in Luke-Acts, and none of the nine other New Testament commissionings . . . are the commissioned ones depicted as assenting verbally and directly to their commission," Schaberg analyzes.[110] Luke's innovation is meant to underscore Mary's conscious and active faith as one who hears the word of God and keeps it. Here I am. *Fiat*. Her stance is one that affirms her own identity in the act of radical trust in God, based on a bedrock conviction that God is faithful. Over the centuries many persons have understood and been inspired by this.

In our day, however, Luke's intention is subverted by the language of slavery. In the original Greek of the gospels the word *doulē*, which is usually translated "handmaid," literally means female slave girl; *kyriou* means literally "master" or "lord." The relationship signified by this phrase "handmaid of the Lord" is thus enormously problematic in feminist and womanist theology. As we already criticized, centuries of patriarchal interpretation have labeled Mary's response as submissive obedience and have held up this stance as the proper ideal for all women in relation to men, a view antithetical to women's hopes for their own human dignity. The bias involved becomes clearer by contrast, as Luise Schottroff points out: when Paul uses *doulos* to describe himself (Rom. 1:1), interpreters think of ministry and office rather than of humble obedience.[111] Traditional demands for conformity to patriarchal order and for obedience to male religious authority figures, be they God, husband, or priest, make women shudder before this text and reject it as dangerous to physical and psychological health as well as to a liberating spirituality.

One might argue to the contrary that obedience, which word in fact does *not* appear in the text, comes from the Latin *ob-audire*, meaning "to listen," in this case to listen to the word of God. One might also point out that Luke is here depicting Mary as the ideal disciple, whose chief characteristic is hearing the word of God and keeping it, doing it, acting upon it, responding to it, this being the model for both women and men disciples without distinction. Again, one might take *doulē* in its most literal meaning, a female slave, connect it with the Pentecost story where Mary also appears, and interpret it as an instance of the glorious freedom of the last days when God's Spirit will be poured out upon all flesh, yes, "even upon my slaves, both men and women, in those days I will pour out my Spirit, and they shall prophesy" (Acts 2:18, citing Joel 2:28–32). This interpretation has the advantage of showing how the advent of the Spirit lifts up the lowly, reverses their low estate, unseals their lips, and empowers them to prophesy. Again, one may even translate the term *doulē* not as handmaid or female slave but as the generic "servant," thereby linking Mary to the whole lineage of distinguished faithful servants of God including Abraham and Moses, Deborah and Hannah, culminating with the Servant of Yahweh in Isaiah.[112] But helpful though such moves may be, they do not get at the root of the problem, which is the master–slave relationship, now totally abhorrent in human society and no longer suitable as a metaphor for relationship to God, certainly not in feminist theological understanding. African American women who write theology out of the heritage of slavery and subsequent domestic servitude stress this repugnance even more strongly in unmistakable terms. Slavery is an unjust, sinful situation. It makes people into objects owned by others, denigrating their dignity as human persons. In the case of slave women, their masters have the right not only to their labor but to their bodies, making them into tools of production and reproduction at the master's wish. In such circumstances the Spirit groans with the cries of the oppressed, prompting persons not to obey but to resist, using all their wiles.

Rather than defending this master–slave metaphor as written by Luke in a world where it was not questioned, a more satisfying strategy allows us to criticize it and then look for the liberating reality at the core of Mary's response. Very carefully we peel off the layers of saccharine humility and forced subordination. This young peasant girl discerns the voice of God in her life commissioning her to a momentous task. Exercising independent thought and action, she asks questions, takes counsel with her own soul. In a self-determining act of personal autonomy, she decides to go for it. This is her choice and it changes her life. A woman of Spirit, she embarks on the task of partnering God in the work of redemption. African American theologian Diana Hayes describes Mary's action here as one of "outrageous authority"; standing alone, she yet had enough faith in herself and in her God to say a powerful and prophetic yes.[113] From a Latin American viewpoint, Ana María Bidegain argues that far from signifying "self-denial, passivity, and submission as the essential attributes of women," Mary's consent is a free act of self-bestowal for the purpose of co-creating a new world. In this light, "Mary's humility consists in the daring to accept the monumental undertaking proposed to her by God"; her consent is a free and responsible act, "not the yes of self-denial."[114] In consort with other Asian thinkers, Chung Hyun Kyung emphasizes the risk this decision involved. Mary's initial hesitation was well founded, for her choice turned her world upside down. She was not a heroic superwoman but a village woman of the people, albeit one who was attentive to God's calling, and this calling drew her from her own private safety. "With fear and trembling she takes the risk of participating in God's plan out of her vision of redeemed humanity. . . . Jesus was born through the body of this woman, a liberated, mature woman, who had a mind and will of her own, capable of self-determination and perseverance in her decisions."[115]

Women note that in this scene God speaks directly to Mary, the message not being mediated through her father, betrothed spouse, or priest. In addition, she does not turn to any male authority figure either to be advised or to seek permission regarding what is to be done. Indeed, the setting is not the temple with its priestly cult, where Zechariah earlier received his announcement, but her own lay, female space, in the village. While still operating within a patriarchal text, she is portrayed in terms of her relationship to God independent of men's control, a stance that in itself undermines patriarchal ideology. Poet Kathleen Norris notes how in this scene Mary finds her voice, rather than losing it. Like any prophet, she asserts herself before God saying, "Here am I." This picture of a young woman courageously committing herself in turn "may provide an excellent means of conveying to girls that there is something in them that no man can touch; that belongs only to them, and to God."[116]

Existentially, Mary's response carries with it a fundamental definition of her personhood. Facing a critical choice, she sums herself up "in one of those great self-constituting decisions that give shape to a human life."[117] In a by now classic analysis of the human situation, Valerie Saiving observed that, conditioned as we are by patriarchy, the traditional "temptations of woman *as woman* are not the same as the temptations of man *as man*." Unlike men, women experience temptations that "have a quality which can never be encompassed by such terms as 'pride' and 'will-to-power.' They are better suggested by . . . underdevelopment or negation of the self."[118] Drifting, overdependence on the judgment of others, and self-sacrificing in order to please are but a few examples of feminine traps. The memory that this young woman's decision is not a passive, timid reaction but a free and autonomous act encourages and endorses women's efforts to take responsibility for their own lives. The courage of her decision vis-à-vis the Holy One is at the same time an assent to the totality of herself. Remembering Mary's *fiat* in this light, Dutch theologian Catharina Halkes writes that far from the passivity imposed on women by a patriarchal society and church, Mary's stance is one of "utmost attentiveness and the creativity which flows from it, based on a listening life."[119] Far from being the "proper" attitude of a slave girl, such a grasp of oneself in the world forges a way of integrity in the midst of society's dissipating demands. In the paradigmatic commissioning narrative of the annunciation, encountering God's redemptive grace and empowered by the Spirit, Mary was not *forced* to bear the Messiah. Acting as a responsible moral agent, she made her own choice.

The annunciation is a faith event. Dramatically, this poor, unconventional peasant woman's free and autonomous answer opens a new chapter in the history of God with the world. "It is Mary's faith that makes possible God's entrance into history," writes Ruether,[120] in the sense that henceforth God will be at home in the flesh of the world in a new way. Brazilian theologians Ivone Gebara and María Clara Bingemer note that annunciations keep on happening, bringing into the ordinariness of life a message of God's gracious care and desire to repair the world. Touching the root of our humanity, these messages reveal hidden possibilities within the limits of our existence, revive our hope in the midst of struggle, and summon our energies for creative action.[121] Seen in this light the particulars of Mary's call, unique in that only one woman conceives and delivers Jesus, illuminate the fundamental dynamic of everyone's vocation through the ages. The Holy One calls all people, indeed all women, and gifts them for their own task in the ongoing history of grace. In the midst of family, work, and social life in village, suburb, and city, it begins with an encounter in the solitude of the heart before God: everywoman, the voice, the call, the courageous response, in the context of a world struggling for life.

The disclosive power of the structure of the annunciation story, along with its central elements of the Spirit's presence and the woman's response, place Miriam of Nazareth in the company of all ancestors in the faith who heard the word of God and responded with courageous love. Now like Abraham, she sets out in faith, not knowing where she is going. Now like Sarah, she receives power to conceive by this faith, considering the One who promised to be worthy of her trust. Listening to the Spirit, rising to the immense possibilities of her call, she walks by faith in the integrity of her own person. Inspired by Spirit-Sophia, women who make their own decisions before God claim her into their circle.

VISITATION: JOY IN THE REVOLUTION OF GOD[122]
(LUKE 1:39–56)

Fresh from her encounter with the angel, "Mary arose and went with haste into the hill country" to visit her kinswoman Elizabeth, herself swelling with a pregnancy in her old age. Filled with the Spirit, both women burst into glorious speech. Elizabeth salutes Mary, who in turn sings out a prophetic song of praise to God. Known as the Magnificat from its opening word in Latin translation, this canticle can barely contain her joy over the liberation coming to fruition in herself and the world through the creative power of the Spirit. As noted earlier, classical mariology rarely dealt with this prayer. Its radical depiction of Mary's no to oppression completes her earlier yes to solidarity with the project of the reign of God. By sealing this page of scripture, such theology managed to suppress the portrait of Mary as a prophet and to forestall the upheaval that would ensue from oppressed peoples, including women taking a similar stance. Yet as Schaberg rightly describes, "the Magnificat is the great New Testament song of liberation—personal and social, moral and economic—a revolutionary document of intense conflict and victory. It praises God's actions on behalf of the speaker, which are paradigmatic of all of God's actions on behalf of marginal and exploited people."[123] Evoking the powerful memory of God's deliverance of enslaved Israel from Egypt, it praises God's continuing actions throughout history to redeem the lowly, including the speaker herself and all marginal and exploited people. Rooted in Jewish tradition, Mary stands as the singer of the song of justice of the coming messianic age. Tracing the contours of this scene and its theology from a critical biblical and feminist perspective places a dazzling, unmistakably prophetic tile in the mosaic of the critical remembrance of Mary.

Early church writers already interpreted this scene with a prophetic gloss. Ambrose saw in Mary's hurried journey through the hill country of Judea an analogy to the church's stride across the hills of centuries. He connected both travelers to the itinerant prophet of glad tidings depicted by Isaiah who wrote, "How beautiful upon the mountains are the feet of the messenger who announces peace, who brings good news, who announces salvation" (Isa. 52:7). Ambrose then exhorts, "Watch Mary, my children, for the word uttered prophetically of the church applies also to her: 'How beautiful thy sandaled steps, O generous maid!' Yes, generous and beautiful indeed are the church's steps as she goes to announce her gospel of joy: lovely the feet of Mary and the church."[124] Irenaeus, after showing how Christ became a human being so that human beings might become children of God, depicts Mary's song leading the way for the church's response: "Therefore Mary rejoiced, and speaking prophetically in the church's name she said, 'My soul magnifies the Lord.'"[125] Finding Mary the prophet in this text thus develops an ancient tradition. In our day new dimensions emerge when this text is read with biblical scholarship through women's eyes.

Two Women Meeting

First, the encounter. The house is Zechariah's but he has been struck dumb. No other men are around. Such quieting of the male voice is highly unusual in scripture. Into this spacious silence two women's voices resound, one praising the other and both praising God. This is a rare biblical vignette of a conversation between two women. Despite the overall androcentric literary context, this story is told in an entirely gynocentric manner.[126] The outpouring of the Spirit on Elizabeth and Mary happens in traditionally female domestic space. Women are the actors who hold center stage; women are the speakers who powerfully convey the resounding good news; women themselves embody the mercy of God which they prophetically proclaim. And they do so in the context of meeting and affirming one another.

Both personal and political insights weave their threads into the texture of this scene. In *Just a Sister Away*, African American biblical scholar Renita Weems notes how pregnant women have an almost physical need for the company of others in the same condition to share their fears, find courage, express hopes, and learn practical wisdom about how their bodies are changing.[127] Being singled out as mothers of redemption made Elizabeth and Mary need each other for this and much more. Having resigned herself to living with disappointment over never having had a child, Elizabeth now has to deal with an "unexpected blessing." Mary in turn has to figure out how to live with a blessing that causes more problems than it solves. How explain this to Joseph? This was not how she had planned her life. Each needed to talk with another woman who knew what it meant to grapple with God's intentions. Their mutual encouragement enabled them to go forward with more confidence and joy despite the struggle that still faced them.

Focusing on "the politics of meeting," Tina Pippin sees that by connecting with each other, these two women are empowered to speak with prophetic voices.[128] They meet, and the force of their meeting leads them to proclaim in the midst of their history that God blesses the lowly and overthrows oppressive institutions. Through their discourse they image power by setting forth the political meaning of their pregnancies, namely, hope for the dispossessed people of Israel. Here is a rare glimpse of female reproductive power as both physically nurturing and politically revolutionary. "The two pregnant women beat the drum of God's world revolution,"[129] starting with the option for debased women and then including all the starving, powerless, and oppressed. A pregnant woman is not the usual image that comes to mind when one thinks of a prophet, yet here are two such spirit-filled pregnant prophets crying out in joy, warning, and hope for the future. Clearly this is a picture of Mary that is the complete opposite of the passive, humble handmaid of the patriarchal imagination. Susan Ross envisions yet another way this text is dangerous: it portrays women looking to each other for validation of their authority rather than to men. This experience of female solidarity is unequaled in its ability to support women's struggles for equal justice and care, for themselves and for others.[130] Whether one sees Elizabeth and Mary as "women of Spirit birthing hope,"[131] or as the Spirit-approved "pregnant crone and the unmarried, pregnant bride suspected of adultery,"[132] their meeting is powerful and potentially empowering. It brings the theme of women's solidarity and mutual female empowerment into the mosaic of the memory of Mary.

Elizabeth's Song

This older woman had been faithfully walking in the way of God for many long years. Luke draws her portrait using the paint of the Hebrew scripture's barren matriarch tradition, especially the stories of Sarah, Rebekah, Rachel, Samson's mother, and Hannah, and the symbol of the barren Jerusalem.[133] The parameters of this tradition are patriarchal: a woman's worth resides in her ability to bear sons for her husband and her people. Rooted in their time and place, the biblical writers seem unable to envision any other kind of world, such as one where women would exercise other social functions and equal value would be given to the birth of daughters. Within their own limited context, however, they signal God's compassionate vindication of the lowly with stories of humiliated women being blessed by conceiving and bearing a son. Long childless but called righteous nevertheless, Elizabeth lives such a story. In the annunciation, her pregnancy has already been used as a sign to encourage Mary at her calling. Now, "filled with the Holy Spirit," she greets the younger woman with exuberant blessing.

Seeing deep wisdom in this passage of one woman blessing another, Barbara Reid calls attention to the back story. Earlier when Elizabeth had first conceived she said, "So has the Lord done for me" (Luke 1:24).[134] Compared to her husband's difficult, doubting dialogue with the angel, it is striking how easily she recognizes the grace of God coming into her life. A long life of attentiveness to the Spirit enables her to see that this child is not a gift for Zechariah or her people alone, but signifies God's gracious regard of herself as a loved and valuable person: "so has the Lord done for *me*." Then, sequestered for six months "alone with God and her silent husband," she nurtures the life within her while contemplating the divine compassion she is experiencing. Elizabeth names the grace in her own life so well that when Mary comes calling, she is prepared to recognize and name the grace of another.[135] Her experience of God's fidelity is used to give confidence to another:

Blessed are you among women, and blessed is the fruit of your womb. And why is this granted me, that the mother of my Lord should come to me? For behold, when the voice of your greeting came to my ears, the babe in my womb leaped for joy. And blessed is she who believed that there would be a fulfillment of what was spoken to her from the Lord.

Luke does not give Elizabeth the title of prophet, but "filled with the Holy Spirit" she functions like one. She blesses Mary as a woman in her own right first, then her child, then her faith. Her words echo the praise addressed to other women famous in Israelite history who have helped to deliver God's people from peril. When Jael dispatches an enemy of the people, the prophet Deborah utters, "Most blessed be Jael among women" (Judg. 5:24). After Judith's spectacular defeat of the enemy general, Uzziah praises her, "O daughter, you are blessed by the Most High God above all other women on the earth" (Jdt. 13:18). The scholars of *Mary in the New Testament* caution that the fact such blessings have been invoked upon other women "prevents us from taking it too absolutely, as if it meant that Mary was the most blessed woman who ever lived."[136] The "alone of all her sex" syndrome cannot be inferred from this verse, taken in context. Rather, Elizabeth's exuberant praise shouted with unrestrained joy joins Mary to solidarity with a long heritage of women whose creative action, undertaken in the power of the Spirit, brings liberation in God's name. Moreover, this blessing weds her historic pregnancy to her faith, again depicting her as someone who hears the word of God and acts upon it even in her own body.

Mary remained with Elizabeth for about three months. During that time before the birth of John, Zechariah remains silent. Luke does not depict their time together, but in women's reflection Elizabeth takes Mary in and nurtures her, affirms her calling, nourishes her confidence. Together they chart the changes taking place in their bodies and affirm the grace in their own and each other's lives. Their gladness hails the advent of the messianic age. The support they share with each other enables them to mother the next generation of prophets, the Precursor and the Savior of the world. On balance, the figure of Elizabeth stands as a moving embodiment of the wisdom and care that older women can offer younger ones, who, brave as they are, are just starting out on their journey through life. A Spirit-filled woman, she exudes blessing on others. Preceding Mary in childbirth and in theologizing, her presence assures the younger woman that she does not face the uncertain future alone. Her mature experience sustains the new venture. What emerges with undoubted clarity from their interaction is women's ability to interpret God's word for other women.

Mary's Song

Swelling with new life by the power of the Spirit and affirmed by her kinswoman, Mary sings the Magnificat, a canticle that joyfully proclaims God's gracious, effective compassion at the advent of the messianic age. It should be noted at the outset that as the longest passage put on the lips of any female speaker in the New Testament, this is the most any woman gets to say. Other women have life-changing visions of angels, most significantly at the empty tomb on Easter morning, but while we are told that they proclaim the good news, we unfortunately do not get to hear their own words. The cadences of this canticle stand in righteous criticism against such scriptural silencing of "the lowly." While Luke may silence the voice of Mary Magdalene, Joanna, and others, our interpretation today reads against his intent, to find in Mary's song a protest against the suppression of women's voices and a spark for their prophetic speech. Following the logic of her praise, who can dare tell women they cannot speak?

> And Mary said:
> "My soul magnifies the Lord,
> and my spirit rejoices in God my Savior,
> for he has looked with favor on the lowliness of his handmaid.
> For behold, henceforth all generations will call me blessed,
> for the One who is mighty has done great things for me,
> and holy is his name.
> And his mercy is from generation to generation on those who fear him.
> He has shown strength with his arm;
> he has scattered the proud in the imagination of their hearts;
> he has put down the mighty from their thrones,
> and exalted those of low degree;
> he has filled the hungry with good things,
> and the rich he has sent empty away.
> He has helped his servant Israel,
> in remembrance of his mercy,
> according to the promise he made to our ancestors,
> to Abraham and to his posterity forever.

The Galilean woman who proclaims this canticle stands in the long Jewish tradition of female singers from Miriam with her tambourine (Exod.

15:2–21) to Deborah (Judg. 5:1–31), Hannah (1 Sam. 2:1–10), and Judith (Jdt. 16:1–17), who also sang dangerous songs of salvation.[137] Their songs are psalms of thanksgiving, victory songs of the oppressed. In particular, the song's form and even whole phrases are explicitly modeled on the canticle of Hannah in the book of Samuel. From Hannah's opening lines, "My heart exults in the Lord; my strength is exalted in my God," to her prophetic verses, "The bows of the mighty are broken, but the feeble gird on strength; those who were full have hired themselves out for bread, but those who were hungry are fat with spoil," the parallelism links both women in their vocal response to the peculiar mercy of Israel's God, who graciously chooses to be in solidarity with those who suffer and are of no account in order to heal, redeem, and liberate.

Composed according to the overall structure of a thanksgiving psalm, which first praises God and then lists the reasons for gratitude, the Magnificat has two main stanzas or strophes. The first praises divine mercy to the speaker and the second reflects the Holy One's victorious deeds for the oppressed community. Far from being separate pieces, the two stanzas are linked theologically by a profound sense of God's faithful compassion, existentially by the atmosphere of joy that results in the lives of the liberated, and socially by virtue of the speaker Mary's being herself a member of the oppressed people who experience redemption. The unity in distinction of the two stanzas, one praising God with deep personal love and the other proclaiming God's justice, can be seen to reflect a way of life basic to Jewish and Christian traditions: love of God and love of neighbor in gospel terms, or spirituality and social justice according to the prophets, or contemplation and action in the tenets of traditional spirituality, or mysticism and resistance in the terms of contemporary theology.[138] By attending to the way this canticle resonates with the rich biblical traditions that celebrate God's liberation, we add the prophetic Mary, now singing her song of salvation, to our mosaic.

1. God's mercy to the peasant woman: The canticle begins with a poor woman's cry of joy. Mary's soul magnifies the Lord and her spirit rejoices in "God my Savior." This lyric mood, so characteristic of intimate experience of relationship with God, pervades the Jewish biblical tradition. The psalmist sings: "Then my soul shall rejoice in the Lord, exulting in his deliverance" (Ps. 35:9); the prophet Isaiah encourages: "This is the Lord for whom we have waited; let us be glad and rejoice in his salvation" (Isa. 25:9);

even the natural world is caught up in the gladness: "Let all the earth cry
out to God with joy" (Ps. 66:1). What does it mean to rejoice in God your
Savior? This is not a superficial joy but is written against the whole canvas
of the world's pain. It is messianic joy, paschal joy, aware of the struggle
unto death yet hopeful that the great "nevertheless" of God leads to life. In
the midst of suffering and turmoil, the sense of divine presence in compassionate care offers strength, leading one to be glad that God is great.
Mary *magnifies* God her Savior, which in formal Elizabethan English
means to celebrate the greatness, or sing and dance in praise of the goodness of someone wonderful.[139] Her soul and her spirit do this, meaning her
whole self, her whole being, with body, mind, and strength. Hers are not
the words of half-hearted appreciation. She is caught up, feels herself lifted
up into God's good and gracious will. With a foretaste of eschatological
delight, she breaks forth in praise and singing.

Mary's song is the prayer of a poor woman. She proclaims God's greatness with her whole being because the Holy One of Israel, regarding her
low estate, has done great things for her. The term for lowliness, *tapeinōsis*
in Greek, describes misery, pain, persecution, and oppression. In Genesis it
describes the situation in the wilderness of the escaping slave woman
Hagar, whom God heeds (Gen. 16:11); in the exodus story it describes the
severe affliction from which God delivers the people (Exod. 3:7). Mary's
self-characterization as lowly is not a metaphor for spiritual humility but
is based on her actual social position. Young, female, a member of a people subjected to economic exploitation by powerful ruling groups, afflicted
by outbreaks of violence, she belongs to the semantic domain of the poor
in Luke's gospel, a group given a negative valuation by worldly powers. Yet
it is to precisely such a woman that the call has come to partner God in the
great work of redemption. Just such a woman will mother the Messiah
because God has regarded her, has turned the divine countenance toward
her and let divine pleasure shine upon her. It is not just that God often
chooses unconventional people for a task, not just that Mary is among the
inconsequential poor of the earth, like unlettered women in any poor village on this planet. It is the combination that is revolutionary: God has
regarded *her* precisely as a lowly woman. Her favored status, declared by
Gabriel, Elizabeth, and now herself, results from God's surprising and gracious initiative. Rejoicing follows. Here the background picture of a poor,
first-century Galilean peasant woman living in occupied territory, struggling for survival and dignity against victimization, imbued with Jewish

faith, aptly coalesces with this biblical portrait of Mary, singer of the song of justice in the name of God.

In his commentary on this canticle, Martin Luther sought to place its sentiments squarely at the center of the church's life. Mary's song gives all of us confidence in God's grace, he teaches, for despite our lowliness God has a "hearty desire" to do great things for us too. What we need is faith, trusting in God as Mary did with "her whole life and being, mind and strength." Then we will be caught up in God's good and gracious will, which operates with kindness, mercy, justice, and righteousness. True, this always involves a reversal of values, "and the mightier you are, the more must you fear; the lowlier you are, the more must you take comfort."[140] But just as the Spirit overshadowed Mary, inspiring her joy and fortitude, so too the Spirit imbues us every day with rich and abundant grace to follow our own calling. The important thing to remember is that Mary had confidence in God, finding in God her Savior a wellspring of joy and comfort. "Thus we too should do; that would be to sing a right Magnificat."[141]

2. God's mercy to the oppressed people: What begins as praise for divine loving-kindness toward a marginalized and oppressed woman grows in amplitude to include all the poor of the world. The second strophe of the Magnificat articulates the great biblical theme of reversal where lowly groups of people are defended by God while the arrogant end up losers. All through scripture the revelatory experience of the character of God who liberated the Hebrew slaves from bondage finds ongoing expression in texts that praise divine redemptive care for the lost. In the psalms and the prophets, the Holy One of Israel protects, defends, saves, and rescues these "nobodies," adorning them with victory and life in the face of despair. Proclaiming the Magnificat, Mary continues this deep stream of Jewish faith in the context of the advent of the Messiah, now taking shape within her. The approach of the reign of God will disturb the order of the world run by the arrogant, the hard of heart, the oppressor. Through God's action, the social hierarchy of wealth and poverty, power and subjugation, is to be turned upside down. Jubilation breaks out as the proud are scattered and the mighty are pulled from their thrones while the lowly are exalted and mercy in the form of food fills the bellies of the hungry. All will be well, and all manner of thing will be well, because God's mercy, pledged in covenant love, is faithful through every generation.

In all the gospels, Jesus preaches and acts out this vital message of reversal. The Asian women theologians at the Singapore Conference note with unassailable logic that "with the singer of the Magnificat as his mother, it should not surprise us that Jesus' first words in Luke's account of his public ministry are also a mandate for radical change."[142] The beatitudes encapsulate this message in especially dramatic form: "Happy are you poor ... you who hunger now ... you who weep now. ... But woe to you rich ... who are full now ... who laugh now" (Luke 6:20–26).[143] Through his own death and resurrection this same reversal is embodied in Jesus himself, who becomes the mother lode of God's life-giving mercy for the world. By placing the Magnificat on the lips of Mary, Luke depicts her as the spokeswoman for God's redemptive justice, which will be such a part of the gospel. She proclaims the good news by anticipation, and she does so as a Jewish woman whose consciousness is deeply rooted in the heritage and wisdom of the strong women of Israel. Knowledgeable about the liberating traditions of her own people and trumpeting them with "tough authority,"[144] this friend of God stands as a prophet of the coming age. "The song of Mary is the oldest Advent hymn," preached Dietrich Bonhoeffer, the German theologian killed by the Nazis:

> It is at once the most passionate, the wildest, one might even say the most revolutionary Advent hymn ever sung. This is not the gentle, tender, dreamy Mary whom we sometimes see in paintings; this is the passionate, surrendered, proud, enthusiastic Mary who speaks out here. This song has none of the sweet, nostalgic, or even playful tones of some of our Christmas carols. It is instead a hard, strong, inexorable song about collapsing thrones and humbled lords of this world, about the power of God and the powerlessness of humankind. These are the tones of the women prophets of the Old Testament that now come to life in Mary's mouth.[145]

A dispute about the origin of this canticle sheds light on the material significance of this second strophe. Based on its form and religious content, some biblical scholars think that the song was written by the early church in Jerusalem. Its christology, which interprets Jesus as the Davidic Messiah, has Jewish overtones, and its piety is redolent of the prayer of the *anawim*, a term meaning "poor ones." Raymond Brown argues forcefully that the early church in Jerusalem saw themselves as *anawim*, combining as they did material poverty with temple piety.[146] Along with other canticles in Luke's infancy narrative uttered by Zechariah and Simeon, he believes, the Magnificat formed part of the "hymn book" of this Jerusalem community described at the beginning of Acts. For Luke to place the song on Mary's lips, adding the verse about God's regard for his lowly handmaid, is artistically and theologically apt, given her Jewish faith, her material poverty, and her probable participation in this post-resurrection community of disciples.

To the contrary, other scholars think that the milieu in which the Magnificat originated was not the religious life of the Jerusalem community but the political struggle of the people of Palestine against their oppressors. The song portrays intense conflict. The six central verbs that describe God's help to Israel denote forceful action: show strength, scatter, pull down, lift up, fill up, send away. There are close parallels between this hymn and other Jewish hymns from the period of arduous resistance to imperial rule, including the Qumran *War Scroll* and hymns celebrating the victory of the Maccabees (today's feast of Hanukkah).[147] Richard Horsley argues that the core subject of the song is God's revolutionary overthrow of the established governing authorities who are squeezing the life out of the people, a view made even more cogent when we recognize that "the words and phrases used throughout the Magnificat are taken from and vividly recall the whole tradition of victory songs and hymns of praise celebrating God's victorious liberation of the people of Israel from their oppressive enemies."[148] Correlatively, there are no *anawim* as a spiritual group; the term applies to the people generally, caught in bad and worsening socioeconomic conditions.

It may be that both views are right in their own way. The Jerusalem community may have taken a preexisting victory hymn already in circulation and adapted it for their own use. Brown notes, furthermore, that the first followers of Jesus were Galileans; that Galilee was the spawning ground of first-century revolts against repressive Roman occupation and the heavy tax burden it laid on people's backs; and that there was real poverty among those who became the nucleus of the post-resurrection church. In this setting, the spiritual themes of the Magnificat have real economic and political resonance as the song declares that these poor people are ultimately the blessed ones, not the mighty and the rich who oppress them.

The value of this debate lies in the way it alerts us to the presence of a memory that is truly dangerous. The history of interpretation contains many instances of thinkers who opt to spiritualize this text, to take away its political teeth, to blunt its radical tone by appeal to the eschatological reversal promised for the last day. Rooted in the biblical heritage of Palestinian Jewish society, however, the song's provenance makes clear that it is a revolutionary song of salvation whose concrete social, economic, and political dimensions cannot be blunted. People are hungry because of triple monies being exacted for empire, client-king, and temple. The lowly are being crushed because of the mighty on their thrones in Rome and their deputies in the provinces. Now, with the nearness of the messianic age, a new social order of justice and plenty is at hand. Like the beatitudes Jesus proclaims for the poor and brokenhearted, Mary's canticle praises God for the kind of salvation that involves concrete transformations.

People in need in every society hear a blessing in this canticle. The battered woman, the single parent without resources, those without food on the table or without even a table, the homeless family, the young abandoned to their own devices, the old who are discarded—all who are subjected to social contempt are encompassed in the hope Mary proclaims. Working amid the poor in India, R. J. Raja reflects that Mary portrays the God of Israel, who will "not stop short of subverting all satanic structures of oppression, inhuman establishments of inequality, and systems which generate slavery and non-freedom," including those that debase people on account of their birth, caste, sex, creed, color, religion, tenets, weakness, and poverty.[149] It is precisely in this way that God is established as Savior of the people in the face of human degradation. The church in Latin America more than any other is responsible for hearing this proclamation of hope in a newly refreshed way. The Magnificat's message is so subversive that for a period during the 1980s the government of Guatemala banned its public recitation.[150] Seeing the central point of this song to be the assertion of the holiness of God, Peruvian Gustavo Gutiérrez argues, "Any exegesis is fruitless that attempts to tone down what Mary's song tells us about preferential love of God for the lowly and the abused, and about the transformation of history that God's loving will implies."[151]

This message will not appeal to those who are satisfied with the ways things are. It will also be ignored by those who seek to restore intact some past epoch in the history of culture or religion. Even affluent people of good will have difficulty dealing with its shocking, revolutionary ring. Doesn't God love everyone? Indeed yes, but in an unjust world, the form this universal love takes differs according to circumstance. The language of this canticle makes clear that divine love is particularly on the side of those whose dignity must be recovered. God protects the poor, noticing their tears, while challenging the comfortable and the proud to conversion, to genuine discipleship, even at the loss of their own comfort. The divine intent is not to take revenge and so create a new order of injustice but to build up a community of sisters and brothers marked by human dignity and mutual regard. Only thus is the coming reign of God rendered genuinely historical. Addressing his economically privileged compatriots, John Haught offers a valuable insight. For those who have little, for the destitute and dispossessed, for the wretched of the Earth, for the *anawim* of Yahweh, he writes, there remains only the ever-coming God of the future to sustain their lives and aspirations. "A major part of the message of prophetic religion is that the dreams that arise among the poor are not naive illusions but compelling clues to the nature of the real. . . . Perhaps only by allowing our own lives to be integrated into the horizon of their dreams and expectations, that is, by our own solidarity with victims, can we too make ourselves vulnerable to the power of the future."[152] Rather than legitimate or ignore the miserable circumstances of the afflicted, those who are affluent need to dream with the poor the dream of God's future that their suffering opens up, and thus be transformed themselves. For both poor and affluent, the Magnificat is a vehicle of that dream.

3. Both stanzas together. This is a profoundly theocentric canticle, centering the singer on God's gracious goodness for personal and communal reasons. In Edward Schillebeeckx's inimitable phrase, it is a "toast to our God,"[153] offered in jubilant thanksgiving in the midst of the tragic history of the world. The point for our remembering is that Mary not only sings of God's liberating transformation of the social order in redemptive acts of mercy, but she herself embodies the oppressed people, who have been exalted through God's compassionate action. Like those enumerated in her song, she occupies a position of poverty and powerlessness in her society, and does so with the added oppression that accrues to being a woman of little account. Hence her song puts her in solidarity with other women who strive for life: "Mary appears in its strains no longer as the sweet mother of traditional piety. She is now made to speak in concert with the oppressed wives and the famished mothers of the world."[154] She sings pregnant with hope, bearing the Messiah, embodying the historic reversal she proclaims. Who shall mother the Messiah? Not a well-protected queen, not someone blessed with a bounteous table and a peaceful life, not a well-regarded woman of influence. Indeed, there is nothing wrong with these things; peace and abundant nourishment are among the blessings hoped for in the messianic age. But the world is distorted by sin. People accumulate power and wealth at the expense of others. Suffering is rampant. And the pattern

persists through the generations. Into this unjust situation comes the choice of God, Creator and Redeemer of the world. Hearing the cries of the oppressed, seeing their misery, knowing well what they are suffering, coming down to redeem, the Holy One aims to turn the unjust order of things upside down and make the world right again, being faithful to the covenant promise. In the deepest revelatory insights of Jewish and Christian traditions, there is no other God. Thus God's choice of Mary to give birth to the Messiah is typical of divine action. As Janice Capel Anderson explains, just as "God has chosen a female servant of low estate to bring the Lord into the world and exalted her, so will God overturn the proud, rich and mighty and exalt the pious, hungry, lowly."[155] Read through these eyes, Mary's song of God's victory over the powerful becomes a song about the liberation of the most nondescript poor people on this earth. Imagine the world according to the defiant Mary's Magnificat, invites African writer Peter Daino: a heavenly banquet and all the children fed.[156]

Through Women's Eyes

This visitation scene, with its high point in the Magnificat, garners rich attention in women's theological reflection. Once the analysis of patriarchy is in place, Mary's song of God's victory over those who dominate others rings with support for women in the struggle against male domination as well as against racism, classism, heterosexism, and all other demeaning injustice. "Mary's song is precious to women and other oppressed people," Schaberg writes, "for its vision of their concrete freedom from systemic injustice—from oppression by political rulers on their "thrones" and by the arrogant and rich." Mary preaches, she continues, as a prophet of the poor and those who are marginalized. "She represents their hope, as a woman who has suffered and been vindicated."[157]

The Spirit who vivified Mary and empowered her prophetic voice is the same Spirit who inspires and vivifies women of all ages. Remembering her in the cloud of witnesses, women draw many and varied lessons of encouragement in her company. One of the strongest and most unusual in the light of traditional mariology is the right to say no. "Men toiling in the service of male power interests represent Mary only as the woman who knew how to say yes."[158] Indeed, at the annunciation Mary uttered her yes to the call of God's Spirit, a consent to adventure that has been used so abominably to promote the passive submission of women. Here her *fiat* finds its home in her defiant resistance to the powers of evil. She takes on as her own the divine no to what crushes the lowly, stands up fearlessly and sings out that it will be overturned.[159] No passivity here, but solidarity with divine outrage over the degradation of life and with the divine promise to repair the world. In the process she bursts out of the boundaries of male-defined femininity while still every inch a woman. Singing of her joy in God and God's victory over oppression, she becomes not a subjugated but a prophetic woman.

Catholic women in whose tradition Mary has been a significant figure wrestle with the significance of this canticle for their own subordinate position in current church structures. With no little irony, Gebara and Bingemer cite the homily preached by Pope John Paul II in Zapopán, Mexico, where he pointed to Mary of the Magnificat as a model for those "who do not passively accept the adverse circumstances of personal and social life and are not victims of alienation, as they say today, but who with her proclaim that God 'raises up the lowly' and, if necessary, 'overthrows the powerful from their thrones.'"[160] If this is applied to women's struggle for full participation in governance and ministry in the church, the reversals of the Magnificat become rife with significance for ecclesial life. "How is it possible," Marie-Louise Gubler writes, "to pray Mary's song each night at Vespers without drawing spiritual and structural consequences for the church?"[161] Indeed, Mary's prophetic speech characterizes as nothing less than *mercy* God's intervention into a patriarchal social order. Not only Mary but the women disciples in Luke, "believing sisters of Jesus' believing mother," grasp that God is no longer to be sought in the clouds, as the men of Galilee once thought, but here on earth, in the flesh, in birth, and in a grave, however surprisingly empty. God is to be sought and found in daily encounters with suffering, in tears and in the laughter of the poor, in the hungry of this earth, and in the groaning of creation. "Mary's prophetic song stands at the beginning of all this. How is it, then, that the body of the resurrected one, in the dual sense of sacrament and the church, has ended up exclusively in the hands of men?"[162] Susan Ross's critique spells out the implications. In many ways in the church, the mighty still occupy their thrones; the lowly still await their exaltation. "Women's very real lack of power in the church today stands as an indictment of the power structures as they exist. . . . The scandal of women's exclusion from power cannot be overlooked. Therefore any discussion of the empowerment of women must be juxtaposed with our lack of political and symbolic power and the failure of the leadership of the church to rectify this scandal."[163] In addition to hope against their dispossessed status, women glean from this text grains of encouragement for their own creative behavior. Ruether sees in this canticle an example of a woman becoming a theological agent in her own right, actively and cooperatively figuring out the direction of the Spirit in the crisis of her time.[164] Norris treasures Mary as an original biblical interpreter, linking her people's hope to a new historical event.[165] In the context of hierarchal power that has silenced women's voices through the centuries, Schaberg casts Mary positively as a preacher. Noting the powerful proclamation of the good news that issues from her mouth, she writes, "Without an explicit commission to preach, she preaches as though she was commissioned," that is, with authority.[166] In the struggle against sexism in the church, the great reversals roll on, their tone of judgment and promise resounding in the voices of prophetic women today.

It is above all in the reflections of women in the church of the poor that the profound dimensions of Mary's prophecy become clear. The Puebla Document, issued by the bishops of Latin America, describes the situation: "The poor do not lack simply material goods. They also miss, on the level of human dignity, full participation in sociopolitical life. Those found in this category are principally our indigenous people, peasants, manual laborers, marginalized urban dwellers, and in particular, the women of these social groups. The women are doubly oppressed and marginalized,"[167] not only because they are poor but because they are women in a society where machismo reigns. So described, Latin American women in base Christian communities recognize a striking analogy between their own situation and that of Miriam of Nazareth. Both dwell in poverty as a result of structural injustices in the economic order; both inhabit worlds organized around the idea of masculine superiority and the inhibition of women's gifts; indigenous women suffer added indignities due to their racial heritage and culture. Appreciation grows: Mary is one of us. This context becomes a "sound box" that amplifies the Magnificat.[168] Mary sings this song as a woman of the people, like millions of poor peasant women in Latin America, doubly and triply oppressed, old before their time. God regards her lowliness, as God regards theirs. Pregnant with new life, she cries out for transformation of the old order, as do they. She belongs to the tradition of women who beget their people amid suffering and despair.[169] Who but a strong decisive woman would call down God's justice on the heads of the oppressors of the poor? Her song sets out the game plan of the coming reign of God. It reveals that women fully participate in the mission of announcing and bringing about these redemptive changes. And it keeps hope alive that poor women themselves, the least of the least, will taste justice on this earth according to the promise that God's "mercy is from age to age, on those who fear him." "Mary's song is a war chant," write Gebara and Bingemer with perhaps too much enthusiasm for a military metaphor, "God's battle song enmeshed in human history, in the struggle to establish a world of egalitarian relationships, of deep respect for each individual, in whom godhead dwells."[170] In solidarity with her song, women on every continent find a key source for their spiritual journey and practice of the reign of God.

The multi-hued mosaic chip of the visitation scene gives us an image of Mary, reassured and applauded by another woman, speaking with prophetic authority a liberating hymn of praise. Regarding this canticle, Luther made a wise observation: "She sang it not for herself alone but for all of us, to sing it after her."[171] Doing so places us in intense relationship to the living God, overflowing source of hope and joy, who regards the suffering world with utmost mercy and summons us together into the struggle to build a just and human world.

"AND SHE GAVE BIRTH"
(LUKE 2:1–20)

This tessera shines with the quintessence of both bodiliness and spirituality. Mary's pregnancy ended when she gave birth, an experience that connects her with women around the world who bring forth the next generation of human beings out of their own bodies. The scene in Luke is, after the cross, the most widely recognized image in Christianity. In Bethlehem Mary gives birth to her firstborn son and lays him in a manger; angels sing the revelatory canticle announcing that this child is the Savior, Christ the Lord; shepherds visit, marvel, and return praising God; Mary ponders the meaning of it all in her heart. From much of the great art of the European Renaissance to popular commercial depictions, this birth has been bathed in a golden light commensurate with the glory of God in the angels' song. All too often it has elicited responses that range from deep to shallow sentimentality. More than any other biblical scene it has traditionally played into the ideology that sets parameters around women's lives with the dictate that their one and only God-given vocation is to be mothers. To restore this tessera to its original colors for our mosaic, we look at its elements of lowliness, bloodiness, and thoughtfulness.

Among the Poor

In Luke's story a number of elements flag the difficulty of this birth, starting with the uprootedness of its setting. Joseph of Nazareth leaves home with "Mary his betrothed," who is far along in her pregnancy. Their journey is undertaken because of a decree of the Roman emperor Caesar Augustus that all should be enrolled in their ancestral towns. Biblical scholars, finding no evidence of such an edict in Roman records that would fit the time frame of Jesus' birth, normally conclude that Luke has used an actual registration that occurred later in 6 C.E. and crafted it for his own purposive storytelling.[172] In terms of a marian portrait, the dislocation that this trip requires becomes but the first in a series of signals that this is not a powerful family but one ranked among the lowly. The purpose of the census is to count heads for tax purposes. The Roman emperor can command tribute; the colonized villagers must hustle to obey. Thus does dominating authority ever bestride the earth, pushing around the poor of the land who have little power to change their status, unless they want to take up arms.

Far from home, these expectant parents are depicted in lowly circumstances. With "no room for them in the inn," they take shelter in a cave or stall where animals were stabled. And there "the time came for her to be delivered." In this unfamiliar, uncomfortable situation, she gave birth. It is not a great stretch of the imagination to see Mary and Joseph as transients, "equivalent to the homeless of contemporary city streets, people who lack adequate shelter,"[173] or as marginalized persons pushed to the edge, "like squatters living in the shanty towns of many big cities of the third world."[174] In this setting, Mary, a young woman in a patriarchal society, brought her child into the world in the manner of enormously disadvantaged people, without the security of a home. She wrapped him in swaddling clothes, the traditional Palestinian way of securing a newborn, and laid him in a manger. Mentioned three times in this passage, a manger was a feeding trough for domesticated animals. It could be a movable wooden container or a low curved depression on a rocky ledge.[175] While it served the purpose of cradling a baby, as do cardboard boxes and other such artifacts creatively appropriated by poor people today, its previous use removes any romantic pretense about the ease of this birthing scene. Meanwhile, the first to hear the message were shepherds, themselves a group of laborers of low economic and social rank, busy with their flocks. Commentators point out that the fields around Bethlehem, being relatively dry and sparsely vegetated, are "shepherd country." Proximity to Jerusalem, furthermore, might mean that shepherds worked the estates of the priests, supplying livestock for temple sacrifice. In any event, even if they owned their own flocks, shepherds were poor by definition, ranked among the lowly of Palestinian society. Hurrying with haste to Bethlehem, they "found Mary and Joseph and the baby lying in a manger." The displaced couple, the manger, and the shepherds together form a clear signal: the Messiah comes from among the lowly people of the earth.

She Gave Birth

Luke's laconic "and she gave birth" evokes a female bodily experience of profound suffering that can issue in equally profound joy. For nine months Miriam of Nazareth had been knitting her child together in her womb, sheltering a mystery of unfolding genes, developing tissues, growing movement, aiming toward viability. Now came the moment to deliver. The risk of death in childbirth in ancient Israel, as in any premodern society, was very real. Its occurrence kept the average life expectancy for women to approximately thirty-five years. Whenever possible a midwife and several female helpers were on hand. According to ancient sources, the midwife brought a birthing stool that had "bars for handgrips on each side, a back to lean against, and a crescent-shaped hole cut into the seat through which the infant could pass. In the absence of a stool, the woman was to sit on the lap of another woman who was strong enough to hold her during contractions. The midwife knelt on the floor in front so that she could see both the mother's face and the emerging child."[176] After wiping mucus from the baby's mouth and nose, allowing it to gasp its first breath, and after tying and cutting the umbilical cord, the midwife would bathe and swaddle the baby from head to toe. Then she would assist in the discharge of the mother's placenta.

Was there a midwife in the stable? How long did Miriam's labor last? With what bodily wisdom did she handle the ever-stronger contractions? When did her water break? When did she transition into the final, wrenching stage of active labor where pushing, breathing, and waves of pain fuse into an utterly concentrated moment from which there is no going back? No details are given. But the words "she gave birth" evoke that event of almost cataclysmic stress by which women bring forth new life. The phrase recalls women's pain and strength involved in laboring, sweating, counting contractions, breathing deeply, crying out, dilating, pushing hard while riven to the very center of one's being with unimaginable bursts of pain, until slowly, slowly, the baby's head finally appears and with more pushing the little creature slips from the birth canal, to be followed by the discharge of the placenta, with much bleeding, and then deep fatigue, breasts swollen with milk, and unpredictable hormonal swings. Thinking to honor Christ and his mother, later apocryphal gospels will present a picture of an effortless delivery with Jesus arriving as a ray of light or passing through Mary's womb the way the risen Christ passed marvelously through walls and locked doors (*Protoevangelium of James* 17–19).[177] The authors assume that natural bodily processes are not worthy of the Creator, as if womb and breasts, flesh and bleeding are outside the sphere of the sacred. In the late fourth century, Ambrose would develop the theological meaning of the birth of Jesus with strange new emphasis on the physical integrity of Mary's body. As Mary T. Malone paraphrases, "Nothing of the mother was broken, changed, or altered in this birth."[178] The utter intactness of her body, never penetrated or torn, will come to stand for the purity of the church, sealed against its enemies. Mary's virginity in childbirth will enter into church doctrine as part of her threefold virginity before, during, and after the birth of Christ, a doctrine open to multiple interpretations, as we have seen.

But Luke knows nothing of this idea. "She gave birth" has no inkling of such escape from the human condition. Later generations will honor this woman for the fact that she brought forth and nurtured the Savior; indeed, in faith language, her prophetic mothering is a charism, a gift given by God to an individual for the good of the community.[179] For Luke this religious interpretation does not counteract the idea that Mary traveled deep into the experience common to women who bring forth a new person out of their own bodies, even at risk of their own death. Biblical scholars point out that otherwise the scene that comes next in Luke's gospel, where Mary offers sacrifice after childbirth, would make no sense. She would not need to be purified from uncleanness if this were a miraculous birth.[180] Real blood was shed at this delivery, by a poor woman of peasant society far from home, laboring in childbirth for the first time. And it was holy.

Pondering in Her Heart

In addition to arduous physical engagement, this scene also depicts Mary intensely ruminating over the word of God. After the shepherds leave, having shared what the angels said, "Mary kept all these things, pondering them in her heart." Twelve years later she is described thinking again, after Jesus was lost and found in the temple: "his mother kept all these things in her heart" (Luke 2:51). Both of these scenes have to do with the revelation of the identity of this child. The fullness of his significance is not immediately apparent, and so Mary keeps on mulling things over. To "keep" in the sense Luke uses the word, *syntērein* and *diatērein* in Greek, means to preserve, to remember, to treasure these events. To ponder, *symballein*, means to puzzle out their meaning, to toss things together until they make sense. Experiencing things she does not fully understand, this woman turns them over in her mind, weighs them. As the ecumenical authors of *Mary in the New Testament* write, "This would mean that Mary did not grasp immediately all that she had heard but listened willingly, letting events sink into her memory and seeking to work out their meaning."[181] No mindlessness here. She is trying to interpret her life. She is seeking to understand difficult matters concerning the lives of those she loves. She is hoping to discern how the divine Spirit is moving in their midst. She ponders in order to fathom the meaning and keep on the right path. Following Luke's image of Mary as an exemplary disciple, later generations will see here a woman at prayer, actively contemplating the word of God. Hers is a life in the process of becoming—no final answers yet available.

FULFILLING TORAH
(LUKE 2:21–40)

Every religious tradition observes customs surrounding the birth of a child that welcome the new life and initiate the child publicly into the community. Usually called the "presentation in the temple," Luke's next tessera depicts Mary and Joseph as religiously observant Jews who carry out these rituals after Jesus' birth according to the Law of Moses. With the Messiah now present, the text itself is focused on the manifestation of this child as "a light for revelation to the Gentiles and for glory to your people Israel," two equal dimensions of the one salvation that God has made ready. In this context, we gain a piece for our mosaic by observing how the acting subjects of the text are "the child's father and mother." Here we glimpse Mary, a young daughter of Israel, now decidedly part of a married, parenting couple, growing into the long line of mothers in Israel,[182] celebrating her childbirth in accord with prescribed ritual.

Even though the episode roughly follows common practice, biblical scholars point out that this narrative contains several inaccuracies, such as implying that both parents need to be purified rather than just the mother, she being the only one who had bled in childbirth.[183] This confusion is probably due to the fact that Luke, being Gentile, had a general knowledge of Judaism while being unfamiliar with the intricacies of how customs actually worked. Scholars concerned for gender equality today also raise obvious questions about the particulars of this part of the Law of Moses, such as the higher valuation of male children as seen in their consecration to God, the doubled time for purification made necessary by a female child, and the status of ritual impurity attached to a woman after childbirth.[184] No other episode, however, better portrays Mary and Joseph of Nazareth as active parents committed to the heritage of their ancestors.

Fulfilling the Law

The scene is pervaded with an atmosphere of traditional Jewish piety, with the couple embodying the spirit of religious fidelity.[185] After eight days they circumcise the baby, cutting the covenant into his very flesh in the tradition of Abraham. They name him Jesus. Forty days after his birth, they go up to the temple in Jerusalem to present him to God and to carry out the required ritual of purification. It is not hard to imagine them climbing the great staircase, babe in arms, emerging into the Court of the Gentiles, buying a pair of birds under the portico, heading into the Court of Women, Joseph going forward into the Court of the Israelites, Mary handing over her sacrifice to a Levite, both following the actions of the priest who kills and offers the birds, the great fire roaring on the altar. The sentiments of this young woman's prayer, expressed so clearly in her *fiat* and so powerfully in her Magnificat, find expression in this dramatic moment of ritual offering now that she has delivered her baby. Here the young friend of God called to a prophetic work, who has sung her Magnificat, given birth, and pondered the meaning of it all, carries out with her husband the law of the covenant in ceremonies imbued with their people's profound gratitude for the living God's gracious and liberating care. Depicting so clearly Mary's religious engagement in temple worship according to Torah, this text offers a strong antidote to a remembrance that would erase her Jewish identity and paint her as a Gentile Christian.

Once again these parents are portrayed as among the poor of the land. Leviticus instructs the woman to bring a first-year lamb; but "if she cannot afford a sheep, she shall take two turtledoves or two pigeons, one for a burnt offering and the other for a sin offering; and the priest shall make atonement on her behalf, and she shall be clean" (Lev. 12:8). According to these criteria, their very offering reveals their social location at the insignificant lower ranks of society. Nevertheless, two charismatic older people, emblems of maturity and wisdom, intercept their progress across the great court. Simeon, who is led by the Spirit to show up on this day, and Anna, called a "prophet," who remained always in the temple, joyfully proclaim in this sacred space of Jewish worship that salvation has come in this child. Cradling the baby in his arms, Simeon sings a canticle that praises God for allowing his old eyes to see this coming of redemption to Israel and the Gentiles; now, he prays, he is ready to die. Eighty-four-year-old Anna's response is particularly intriguing. Rather than getting ready for death, she goes to work spreading the good news. We never hear her actual preaching, but are told that she kept on praising God and "speaking about the child to all who were looking for the redemption of Jerusalem." Once again, we get a glimpse of Mary being encouraged to go on with her life's work through the ministry of a woman.

The Sword of Discernment

The tone of the scene changes suddenly as Simeon utters an ominous oracle declaring that a price will be paid. The child will be a sign of contradiction, and as for his mother, "a sword will pierce your own soul too." Soul and spirit stand for the whole self, the heart, the personal 'being' with which Mary proclaimed the greatness of the Lord. What is the meaning of the prophecy that her whole person would be run through with a sword? Long-standing popular interpretation has taken the sword to refer to the sorrow she would experience under the cross when Jesus suffered, died, and then was pierced with a lance. Part of the difficulty with this view, however, is that "there is no evidence that Luke or his community ever thought that Mary was present at Calvary."[186] Her absence from the group who witnessed Jesus' death, burial, and empty tomb, whom Luke indicates were "Mary Magdalene, Joanna, Mary the mother of James, and the other women with them" (Luke 24:10), indicates that in this gospel the sword does not symbolize this particular suffering. Raymond Brown points out that starting with theologians in the early church numerous other meanings of the sword have been suggested, including a scandalized doubt that pervades Mary's soul during the crucifixion, or her own violent death, or she herself being rejected, or her pregnancy being illegitimate, or the fall of Jerusalem which she lived to see, or the word of God, or her enmity with the serpent from the garden in Genesis. Because they are extraneous to Luke's text, these explanations are as implausible as the popular idea that the sword stands for her sorrow at the cross. Drawing on the image of the sword in Ezekiel 14:17, where a sword of judgment passes through the land, Brown suggests that a more plausible interpretation is that for Luke this sword signifies spiritual discernment. Hearing the word of God and keeping it will not happen easily but will require struggle to arrive at wisdom. Miriam of Nazareth will be tested in the depths of her faith. As Reid writes, "What Simeon intimates is that Mary, like all disciples, will experience difficulty in understanding God's word. She was not given automatic knowledge and insight about her son and his mission."[187] In truth, as Norris reflects, far from embodying a passive, submissive femininity, Mary wrestled with the living God as something of a biblical interpreter, hearing, believing, and pondering the word of divine promise even when it pierced her soul like a sword. This is hardly passivity, but faith, the strong faith of a peasant woman.[188]

Blessed Together

Woven through this scene that portrays Mary fulfilling Torah and walking her journey of faith are also distinct threads of her partnership with Joseph. As Luke writes, "they" brought the child up to Jerusalem; "they" offered sacrifice; Simeon encountered "the parents" doing for Jesus what was customary under the law; "the child's father and mother" reacted with awe to his revelatory words. And in a moment little depicted in Christian art, "the child's father and mother marveled at what was said about him; and Simeon blessed them . . . ." What a striking development, the young married couple wrapped in blessing from this wise old elder, prayed over and remembered before God, together. It is not Mary alone who is blessed here, nor Joseph on his own. The two are bonded in marriage, adjusting to the care of a new baby, and divine favor is invoked upon "them" as such. Ambivalence dogs our reflection. Feminist scholars point out that according to the custom of the times, this was an arranged, patriarchal marriage and thus not something that women searching for equality would aspire to today. Furthermore, Mary is here incorporated into a patriarchal text rather than subverting it as in the annunciation and visitation stories. At the same time, in a church tradition that has long ignored Mary's married status in favor of an idealized portrait of the virgin mother and, more to the point, has used that image to relegate married women to subordinate status, it is surely liberating to give Mary back her marriage, to give her back her relationship with the man with whom she shared her life, for better or worse. And to know that this is blessed.

This episode as a whole ends with a summary statement that implies years of partnership in parenting: "When they had finished everything required by the law of the Lord, they returned to Galilee, to their own town of Nazareth. The child grew and became strong, filled with wisdom, and the favor of God was upon him." Jesus grew up not in a vacuum but in the circle of his Galilean family. It is more than likely that at least some of his understanding of God's power to save came from his Jewish parents who, during the decisive years of his growth, taught him about the compassionate, liberating God of the Hebrew scriptures.

LOSING AND FINDING
(LUKE 2:41–52)

In the final scene of the infancy narrative, Luke brings the reader back once more to the temple in Jerusalem twelve years later. After the Passover feast Jesus remains behind, only to be found by his terribly worried parents after a three-day search. Their reunion sets the stage for the high point of the story, where Jesus declares that his primary allegiance is to God's business, to being "in my Father's house." This narrative has all the earmarks of a typical Hellenistic biographical tale in which a childhood incident foreshadows the greatness of the person in adulthood. Its point is christological, borne in the pronouncement of the deep relationship between Jesus the Jew and the God he experiences in a most intimate way. At the same time, both the language and content of the story give us another memory of Miriam of Nazareth in action. From this we glean one more tessera for our mosaic, a complex picture of parenting.

Note that this family is once again depicted as observant of Jewish tradition, traveling up to Jerusalem for the most important pilgrimage feast in the calendar. The firstborn son is now old enough to accompany them, taking another step in growing into his religious heritage. They travel in the company of "their relatives and acquaintances," a typical pilgrimage party of family members and village neighbors sharing the joyful spirit of the festival as well as giving each other safety in numbers. Their return begins "when the feast was ended," indicating they had all observed the full custom of purification, sacrificing a lamb, eating the Passover meal, and observing the days of unleavened bread that followed. One day into the return journey, disaster strikes. Anyone who has ever loved a child in danger can fill in the blanks of this narrative, which overlooks the intervening search and skips to the parents' finding the boy "after three days." Their dramatic reunion after a frantic search is again redolent of Jewish custom. They find Jesus in the temple in the midst of the teachers of the Law, "listening to them and asking them questions," while giving back answers filled with insight. This young man on the brink of adulthood has studied Torah and takes delight in debating it. Give credit to his parents.

Human Anguish

Parenting well, besides demanding an enormous amount of intelligence and energy, places the heart in a vulnerable position. Running through the joy of relationship with children in daily life and through all the milestones of their growth, there is also the background fear that harm may befall these young creatures, injuring them in ways that parents cannot prevent however responsible they may be. The joy and the suffering together are facets of love, which is expressed in the paradoxical mix of relief and anger that parents experience after danger has passed. The confrontation between Jesus and his parents in this story plays out this theme. "When his parents saw him they were astonished; and his mother said to him, 'Son, why have you treated us like this? Look, your father and I have been so worried looking for you.'" The verb Luke uses for worry, *odynasthai* in Greek, connotes severe mental pain or sadness, overwhelming anxiety. Two other scenes where Luke uses this term underscore its heaviness. In the parable of the rich man who ignores the poor man starving at his gate, both eventually die; the rich man cries out to Abraham, "have mercy on me and send Lazarus to dip the tip of his finger in water and cool my tongue, for I *am in agony* in these flames" (Luke 16:24). In Acts, Paul takes leave of the elders of the church in Ephesus; "there was much weeping among them all; they embraced Paul and kissed him, *grieving* especially because of what he had said, that they would not see him again. Then they brought him to the ship" (Acts 20:37–38). The anguish of a soul in hell, the heart-wrenching sorrow of saying a final goodbye—these are analogies for the torment felt by Mary and Joseph looking for their lost boy. It is no wonder that when they find him, her words carry an unmistakable tone of rebuke and reproach accompanying their relief. She corrects him, scolds him, complains about his behavior. Jesus' response in turn, far from being contrite, distances himself from his parents' concern. He reproaches them for searching with such anxiety. Brown points out that Jesus' answer even carries a tone of grief that his parents have understood him so poorly. Intellectually curious about matters religious and enamored of the whole temple experience, this is a village boy discovering his vocation. His calling lies in the service of God, which takes priority over family ties. The world beyond the village beckons.

When Jesus finished explaining himself to his parents, "they did not understand what he said to them." Biblical scholars warn against toning down their incomprehension. It functions in Luke as a narrative necessity because Jesus' divine sonship, while announced from his conception, becomes fully appreciated only in the christology of the post-resurrection church. Before then, scope for pondering and deciding is given to every character in the narrative. This literary reason, based in the actual course of the historical development of Christian faith, can be accompanied by existential interpretation. It is never easy to raise a child. When children are precocious, navigating the waters of parental love and responsibility becomes ever more complex, the more so as they get older. The tension and upset between parents and child in this scene are palpable. The boy went off to chart his own course. The parents did not understand—no idealization possible here.

"Your Father and I"

As in the presentation in the temple, Mary and Joseph are depicted in this story as a full-fledged married couple and parents of this son. The scene begins with their joint action: "Now his parents went to Jerusalem every year at the feast," and ends with Jesus' returning to their common home: "And he went down with them and came to Nazareth, and was obedient to them." In between, the pronoun "they" occurs eight times with the verbs that move the action: they sought him, they did not find him, they found him, they were astonished, they did not understand. In an unusual depar-

ture from patriarchal protocol, this story depicts Mary rather than her husband speaking in the name of both parents when she reprimands their son.
This is odd, because overall in this infancy narrative Joseph acts as the
rightful, legal, even if not actual, father of Jesus. Commentators note the
likelihood that Luke received this temple story, in which Joseph appears
straightforwardly as Jesus' parent, from a source that knew nothing of the
annunciation story or its implied point that Joseph was not the biological
father of Jesus. This literary artist lets the inconsistencies stand, just as in
the coming chapters he will at one point slip in a restriction to paternity—
Jesus began his ministry "being (as was supposed) the son of Joseph" (Luke
3:23)—while at the same time having the Nazareth villagers respond to the
preaching of their native son by exclaiming "Is this not Joseph's son?"
(Luke 4:22) with no qualifications. The point to remember is that Luke
portrays Mary having a partner in parenting, at least for twelve years.
Reflecting on the significance of these years, Indonesian theologian
Marianne Katoppo recalls a cartoon on the wall of the World Council of
Churches' editorial office in Geneva. It depicts an obviously pregnant
Mary and a young Joseph, who says to her, "When you're the Mother of
God, will you still be my Mary?" Underneath, the caption reads: "Do we
ever think that they loved each other? 'Joseph my husband,' 'Mary my wife.'
A child listens. And grows. And becomes the lover of humankind."[189] Mary
and her husband are companions in faith and married collaborators in
child-raising. In this relationship, furthermore, she is no passive partner
but speaks out and takes initiative, as this scene depicts. Together they create a home that nurtures life.

Thinking Mother

In this scene Jesus has reached the brink of maturity, physically and spiritually. In its aftermath he returns to the family fold in Nazareth, not to be
heard from again until he starts his ministry at around the age of thirty.
Once again we are told that Mary "cherished all these things in her heart."
And, as Luke summarizes the years that roll by, "Jesus increased in wisdom
and in stature, and in favor before God and human beings." It takes so
much parenting for this to happen! It takes so much nourishing care for a
newborn to negotiate the hazards of infancy and reach the second year of
life. Even today, in countries with a high rate of infant mortality, the first
birthday is a great cause for celebration. Each year after that brings new
challenges of survival and growth, the whole marvelous panoply of a

developing human being. The person or persons charged with watching over this progress are committed to long-term love in action. So much practical care, providing nourishment, cleaning up, providing clothing for a changing body; so much teaching, encouraging, disciplining; so much holding, providing intuitive psychological support, wiping away tears. So much loving. The summary statements about Jesus' growth cover over the enormous amount of mothering he received, and the fathering, without which he would not have reached adulthood physically, emotionally, and spiritually as the person he became. And through it all Mary of Nazareth kept pondering, kept thinking about the meaning of her life and the lives of those she loved, kept walking her journey of faith with God.

I want to be very careful here, since holding up Mary's motherhood as a model for all women is one of the neuralgic points in traditional mariology. Social customs surrounding the family are undergoing epochal shifts in our day. It becomes clear that not all women want to be mothers, nor need they be in order to be true women. Women who do bear children are finding ways to combine career and family with more or less satisfaction. Some men are staying home to raise their children. In wealthy societies, thanks to longer life expectancy, even women who assume traditional maternal roles will spend more years without children at home than with them. Here is where the principle that the circumstance of Mary's life provides no paradigm for all women bears critical fruit. There are many avenues along which women may rightly live out their human vocation, traditional motherhood being but one. Even if Mary is to function as an exemplar, Paul VI's teaching becomes ever more germane: she is an exemplar not in the particular social conditions of the life she led, but in the way in her own life she heard the word of God and kept it. By implication, responding to this word of God may take many creative forms in women's lives.

The question we are pursuing is the slightly different one of how to remember her in a liberating way in the midst of the community of the church. This episode presents her as a married woman and a mother, thinking, praying, full of initiatives, living out her familial relationships in Nazareth, which village summons up the peasant culture, economic stresses, and political oppression that formed the context of her hardworking life. In this time and place, year in and year out, far from temple, priesthood, and sacrificial ritual, she walked faithfully with her God. Respecting her particularity, we remember her in solidarity with women

everywhere whose life energies literally mother the next generation, and
with all who use their generative powers to nurture and build up healthy
lives in the social and natural worlds.

WINE AT THE WEDDING
(JOHN 2:1–11)

The sounds of feasting fly through the next tessera with robust joy, halt for
a tense spell, then resume with even greater merriment. "There was a wedding in Cana of Galilee, and the mother of Jesus was there. Jesus with his
disciples had also been invited to the wedding." Amid the feasting, dancing, and singing, unfortunately the wine gave out. When the mother of
Jesus noticed and brought this to his attention, he declined to get involved
for "my hour has not yet come." Disregarding his hesitation, she bid the
servants to follow his word, which they did, filling to the brim six stone
water jars with a capacity of twenty-plus gallons each. When the chief
steward tasted the liquid it had changed into excellent wine, a point on
which he complimented the groom. The text itself concludes by pointing
out the significance of this extravagance: "Jesus did this, the first of his
signs, in Cana of Galilee, and revealed his glory; and his disciples believed
in him."

In the view of biblical scholarship, the story of the wedding feast at Cana
has all the earmarks of a popular story or folktale. It originally circulated
to express people's interest in the early, hidden life of Jesus, the finding of
the twelve-year-old boy in the temple probably being another example.
Given the existence of different types of literature in the Bible, Raymond
Brown observes, "there is no reason why, alongside inspired history, one
could not have inspired fiction or inspired popular narrative." Scholarly
techniques determine the literary genre one is dealing with, but for any
story to become scripture, whether historically based or not, it must
become a vehicle of God's message of salvation. "The evangelist is not
responsible for the origin or historicity of the story; he is responsible for
the message it serves to vocalize."[190] As the closing remark of the Cana narrative explains, its main purpose is christological, to reveal the person of
Jesus gifted with the glory of the Messiah. Like virtually every other scene
in the Gospel of John, it does this through rich use of symbolism. Both
wedding feast and banquet are well-known biblical themes that symbolize

the coming messianic days. Abundance of wine is also a consistent figure for the joy of the last days, promised in many prophetic utterances: "the mountains shall drip sweet wine, and all the hills shall flow with it" (Amos 9:13). In this gospel the wine, more than one hundred gallons of it, signifies the abundant gift of salvation for which light, water, and food are other Johannine symbols. The motif of Wisdom's presence in this scene also carries a christological message. In Proverbs Holy Sophia prepares a banquet, inviting people to eat of her bread and drink of her wine. The very act of drinking her wine is a symbol for accepting her message. Those who do so lay aside immaturity and find fullness of life, walking in her way of insight (Prov. 9:1–6).[191] Here in Cana we have Jesus, already revealed in John's prologue as the incarnation of divine Wisdom, providing wine in abundance to drink and eliciting belief from the disciples.

Given this plethora of christic symbolism, it would be surprising if the figure of the mother of Jesus, never given her personal name, did not also have a symbolic function. While affirming this to be the case, scholarly opinion is deeply divided over the significance of her words and actions in this scene.[192] She is an image of the true believer because of her faith in Jesus; no, she has good intentions but imperfect faith, seeing him only as a wonder-worker; no, she is an example of unbelief because she overrode his preferences; well, there is no reference to Christian faith here, but only a portrait of a mother with exuberant belief in the ability of her offspring. Again, Jesus' initial resistance to her request is a rebuke; it is not a rebuke but the Johannine version of the Synoptic saying that hearing the word of God and doing it are more important than physical family ties; it is neither of these but part of the typical gospel pattern of request-resistance-persistence-granting, as can be seen in the second Cana miracle, where Jesus cures the official's dying son only after being repeatedly petitioned (John 4:47–50). Again, the mother of Jesus here is a collective personality, a symbol of the church; no, she is an individual personality with an important symbolic function; no, she is an inessential figure whose function of getting the action rolling could have been filled by anyone else. Mary's presence in this scene ties Cana to the cross, the other Johannine scene in which she appears and where Jesus' hour has now come; no, the two scenes are not clearly related. Mary's function here is either so unique as mother of Jesus or universal as an ideal disciple that it offers little insight regarding women's participation in church leadership roles; to the contrary, her words and deeds offer an intriguing portrait of a woman as leader and catalyst in the mission of Jesus rife with implications for women's empower-ment. Navigating my way through this exegetical minefield, I clarify once again that my purpose is not to adjudicate these disputed interpretations in the rich field of Johannine scholarship, let alone write yet another com-mentary on John. We are seeking answers to the question, How do we remember her? What does this Cana story, this little colored stone tile, con-tribute to the marian mosaic of dangerous memory being constructed here from a liberating, feminist perspective? Taking this narrative as a whole, I glue this tessera in to catch and reflect back the strong light of the two sentences attributed to the mother of Jesus at the wedding.

They Have No Wine

While highly symbolic, this story is surprisingly grounded in the historical reality of the times. About nine miles north of Nazareth, Cana was a simi-lar small village of mostly peasant farmers struggling under Roman and Herodian rule. The wedding celebrated the second stage of marriage, when the bride traveled to her husband's home, often in a quasi-formal proces-sion. A festive wedding supper with friends and relatives followed, some-times lasting through the night into the next day. It is doubtful whether the full week of feasting reported of wealthy urban families could be afforded in the straitened economic circumstances of these villagers. The six stone jars "for the Jewish rites of purification" sound a further authentic note, being found today in archaeological digs in Galilee and interpreted as evi-dence for the Jewish character of the Galilean population. According to levitical purity laws, stone jars were to be used instead of common clay pots because the latter more easily absorbed contamination.

"They have no wine." This was more than an embarrassment to the providers of the feast and the couple whose union was being celebrated, though it was certainly that. It was a concrete, painful reminder of the pre-carious economic situation in which the wedding guests all lived. Acting in a decisive and confident manner, Mary named the need and took initiative to seek a solution. Because she persisted, a bountiful abundance soon flowed among the guests. Feminist reflection espies here the kind of woman whose movements typically run counter to the expectations of idealized femininity. Far from silent, she speaks; far from passive, she acts; far from receptive to the orders of the male, she goes counter to his wishes, finally bringing him along with her; far from yielding to a grievous situa-tion, she takes charge of it, organizing matters to bring about benefit to those in need, including herself. Her words ring with the tones of prophecy, deploring and announcing hope at the same time. From this angle, she stands in solidarity with women around the world who struggle for social justice for themselves and their children, especially daughters. "They have no wine," nor security from bodily violation, nor equal access to education, health care, economic opportunity, nor political power, nor cultural respect because of their race or ethnic heritage, nor dignity due their persons as created in the image and likeness of God herself. Uttering these words, women can be empowered to turn away from socialized lack of self-esteem and docile acceptance of marginalization to engage instead in critical praxis on behalf of their own good. Every step to secure these human blessings, starting with the cry "we do not have it, we should have it," shares in God's own compassionate desire to establish the divine reign of justice on this earth.

As it works out in the churches, wherever an entrenched clerical system wielding specious arguments keeps women from the ecclesial leadership of the altar, the pulpit, and the decision-making chamber, "they have no wine" reverberates with critical hope for women's full participation in the ministries of the church. Where this restricting of women's Spirit-given gifts, as well as the gifts of men who are married to them, consequently renders whole communities deprived of the Eucharist, "they have no wine," literally no consecrated bread or cup of salvation, calls for the old water of outmoded, patriarchal practice to be transformed into renewed and fruitful sacramental life.

Reflecting with the poor in third-world contexts, theologians discover yet further profound insight in this portrait. In Brazil, Gebara and Binge-mer note that in this scene Mary stands among the people, herself a member of the group without wine, and speaks the hope of the needy. And that night the poor community of Cana in Galilee "becomes the place where God's glory is made manifest as men and women drink wine, make merry, and celebrate the wedding feast."[193] The story continues today as the figure of the mother of Jesus accompanies the poor in their ongoing struggle for bread and human rights. In view of the symbolism of the story, her words reverberate with the deep desire people feel today for their own messianic liberation. Her cry as spokeswoman from among the people energizes their hope: "They have no wine, nor peace, freedom, rights, food, housing, jobs, health . . . ."[194] In India a similar reflection places the mother of Jesus in solidarity with people who are humiliated. Then as now, "they have no wine" resonates among the voiceless, empowering those who are marginalized "on account of economic colonialism, colour prejudice, caste distinction, racial discrimination, religious fanaticism."[195] Extrapolating to a global context, Mary's strong impulse to call for relief corresponds to God's own dearest desire, giving us in the Cana story an enacted parable of the coming of the reign of God's hospitality. As part of the dangerous memory of the mother of Jesus, this challenging plea addresses the conscience of the body of Christ today, especially in the richest nations on earth. "They have no wine, no food, no clean drinking water": you need to act.

Do Whatever He Tells You

With these words the mother of Jesus alerts the servants to listen to his word and follow his way. In order to grasp the significance of this point, we need to step back and understand that women play surprisingly significant roles in the gospel of John as a whole, both in the number of incidents recounted and their theological consequence. Filled with the Spirit, they exhibit deeply wise knowledge of Jesus, take steps to support and encourage his mission, and act to witness his message to others. Feminist scholars credit these powerful portraits to the situation of John's church community, where women were "enabled by the communal prophetic experience which made every believer a source of spirit and life," where "leadership and structure . . . [seem] to have been dynamic and charismatic in character," and where despite struggle women exercised apostolic leadership functions.[196] This context in turn shaped John's robust presentation of women's ministerial actions. In addition to the Cana story, where Jesus begins his public ministry in response to the initiative of a woman, the gospel includes numerous others.

• The Samaritan woman, who enters into theological conversation at the well, whom Jesus also addresses as "Woman" and to whom he reveals his messianic identity, acts on her own initiative to bring news of this Messiah to her townspeople. Many people "believed in him because of the woman's testimony" (John 4:39), marking her as a highly successful early missionary to the Samaritans.

• Martha of Bethany, whose word summoned Jesus to the grave of her dead brother, acts as a primary spokeswoman for her community's faith. To Jesus' revelation that he is the resurrection and the life, her confession "you are the Christ, the Son of God, the one who is coming into the world"

(John 11:27) parallels that of Peter in Matthew's gospel, marking her as the leader in this gospel responsible for articulating the community's christological confession.

• Mary of Bethany, anointing Jesus' feet with costly, fragrant ointment and wiping them with her hair, flags the end of Jesus' public ministry. Her faithful love stands in sharp contrast to the betraying heart of Judas, one of the Twelve. Jesus himself discredits male objection to her ministry of anointing with the words "Leave her alone!" (John 12:7). Her deed stunningly anticipates his command to wash one another's feet as a sign of following his path of love, marking her as an exemplary disciple.

• Mary Magdalene, who stood by the cross of Jesus, was first to the tomb on Easter morning, and called Peter and the beloved disciple to witness the emptiness of the grave. Even more striking, she herself was the first among the disciples to experience an appearance of the resurrected Christ. Addressed as "Woman" by the risen Lord, her commission to preach this good news to others was carried out so powerfully, and her words "I have seen the Lord" (John 20:18) bore so unmistakably the technical formula of revelation as the basis of one's witness, that centuries later the church was still calling her *apostolorum apostola,* the "apostle of the apostles."[197] Sandra Schneiders underscores the importance of the Mary Magdalene material in this gospel:

> It shows us quite clearly that, in at least one of the first Christian communities, a woman was regarded as the primary witness to the paschal mystery, the guarantee of the apostolic tradition. Her claim to apostleship is equal in every respect to both Peter's and Paul's, and we know more about her exercise of her vocation than we do about most of the members of the Twelve. Unlike Peter, she was not unfaithful to Jesus during the passion, and unlike Paul, she never persecuted Christ in his members. But, like both, she saw the risen Lord, received directly from him the commission to preach the Gospel, and carried out that commission faithfully and effectively.[198]

Elisabeth Schüssler Fiorenza sums up the result of extensive research into women in the Johannine gospel with the insight that "at crucial points of the narrative, women emerge as exemplary disciples and apostolic witnesses,"[199] and this despite the androcentric nature of the traditioning process itself.

What, then, of the mother of Jesus at Cana? "It could be that this woman too, who knows of Jesus' powers and instructs others to obey him, is to be seen as an apostolic figure," Adele Reinhartz suggests.[200] Jesus calls her "Woman," which seems to place her on the same level as the Samaritan woman and Mary Magdalene, whom he also addressed with this appellation; her actions show that she is of the same mettle. Her instruction "Do whatever he tells you" charges the servants at the wedding to turn believingly to Jesus, and they do so on the strength of her testimony. For the original readers of this gospel in John's ecclesial community, this injunction resonated with symbolic overtones. As with every apostolic exhortation, the grounds for accepting this are not because it comes from Jesus' mother per se, but because it is given by a believing disciple.[201] Without abandoning her relationship as mother of the Messiah, and even while exercising a mother's influence, Mary of Nazareth joins the company of her sisters the Samaritan woman, Martha of Bethany, Mary of Bethany, Mary of Magdala, and a host of other women, remembered and forgotten, as an exemplary woman disciple among other disciples, recognized by the love and apostolic witness to Christ that they give.

This tessera reflects the picture of a celebrative woman calling for more wine at the wedding, a spokeswoman of the hope of the disenfranchised and the poor, and an apostolic witness who leads others to Christ. These images are not mutually exclusive. By overlaying them we gain a powerful memory that gives impetus to women's vocation in church and world in mutuality with men living the Christian faith today in all its complexity.

NEAR THE CROSS (JOHN 19:25–27)

Death. Irreversible, irrevocable, shutting down a person's time forever. Worse when it occurs as the result of an act of violence. Causing unnameable grief in the hearts of those who love and lose another. Worse when the loss occurs as the result of an act of violence. Decisively, incredibly final.

In John's gospel the scene is described in brief shorthand: "standing near the cross of Jesus were his mother, and his mother's sister, Mary the wife of Clopas, and Mary Magdalene." The dying Jesus, seeing his mother and the disciple whom he loved, addressed them both: "Woman, behold your son.... Behold, your mother." From that time on the beloved disciple took her into his home. Then Jesus knew that everything was finished. After crying out his thirst and sipping sour wine, "he bowed his head and gave up his spirit." He died. The subject of countless works of art, this scene conjures up all the anguish and desolation a woman could experience who had given birth to a child, loved that child, raised and taught that child, even tried to protect that child, only to have him executed in the worst imaginable way by the power of the state. It is interesting to note that the gospel never describes Mary holding the body of her dead son when he is taken down from the cross. Yet the artistic image of the *pietà* truly captures the existential tone of inexpressible sadness at the heart of this event.

As with Cana, biblical scholars question whether the scene as written is actually historical or whether its origin lies in the evangelist's symbolic imagination. Jesus' death on the cross is clearly a historical event, mentioned even by Roman and Jewish writers. Similarly, the presence of women at the cross has historical warrants. All four gospels agree that a group of women kept vigil, standing firm in the face of fear, grief, and the scattering of the male disciples. Women standing near the cross or at a distance kept the death watch, their faithfulness a sign to Jesus that not all relationships had been broken, despite his feeling of intense abandonment even by God. The names of the women differ in the different gospel accounts, but the fact that they are mentioned in every gospel eloquently strengthens the argument that their presence at the cross is historically accurate in general outline.[202] What counts against the historicity of this particular Johannine scene of the mother and the beloved disciple are its overt symbolism along with two critical considerations. First, there is no mention in the Synoptic gospels of the mother of Jesus being among the women at the cross. Luke, who places her in Jerusalem with the community of disciples at Pentecost, would likely have named her among the Galilean women if he knew that she was present at the crucifixion. His silence indicates that she was not there. Second, the gospels stress that all the male disciples fled or scattered, which leaves little room for the continued presence of one believing, beloved male disciple. This unnamed beloved disciple, not one of the Twelve, plays a role that is utterly peculiar to John's gospel. He is the witness who guarantees the validity of the Johannine community's understanding of Jesus. Their christological views might be different from those of the petrine churches, but they were still utterly authentic, a point underscored by the way the profound faith of the beloved disciple is frequently contrasted with Peter's stumbling belief.

The symbolic theological importance of the crucifixion scene in John surfaces in the idea that at the end of his life Jesus brought into being a community in the very Spirit that flowed from him on the cross. Two great figures without a name appear, the mother of Jesus and the beloved disciple. Both were historical persons but are not named here because they are functioning as symbols of discipleship. Standing by the cross they are turned toward each other by Jesus' words and given into each other's care. Henceforth they "represent the community of true believers it is Jesus' mission to establish."[203] The formula "Behold" or "Look" indicates that a revelation is to follow, such as John the Baptist's cry "Behold the Lamb of God" (John 1:36) and Pilate's statement "Behold your King" (John 19:14). Beholding each other in a new relationship, the mother of Jesus and the beloved disciple mark the birth of a new family of faith founded on the following of Jesus and his gracious God. The mother/son language indicates that, just as in the Synoptic scene with the mother and the brothers, Jesus is reinterpreting family in terms of discipleship. Many biblical scholars today also note that the symmetry of the beholding between the woman and the man signals that neither is to be elevated above the other. Both are equal partners in the family of disciples, reflecting the Johannine community as a whole where to a great extent "women and men were already on an equal level in the fold of the Good Shepherd."[204] In a word, the mother and the beloved disciple are representative of a larger group, the church. Symbolically Jesus provides a communal context of mutual love and egalitarian regard in which they shall all live after he is gone.[205] Regarding Mary herself, the scholars of *Mary in the New Testament* offer a counterintuitive insight: "Paradoxically, if the scene is not historical and the presence of the mother of Jesus and the beloved disciple reflects Johannine theological inventiveness, that may enhance the importance of Mary for the Johannine community."[206] It is not likely that she would signify the fundamental vocation of the community if they did not already remember her as an exemplary disciple and apostolic witness, an insight supported by having Jesus address her once again as "Woman."

Uncovering the symbolism of the mother/beloved disciple scene in John's gospel leads to rich insight into the theological links between Jesus' death, the gift of the Spirit, and the foundation of the Christian community. In terms of our project, its legitimate designation of Mary as a precious symbolic figure also has the unfortunate effect of deleting her human reality as a historical woman with a crucified son. Even if she did not stand at the foot of the cross, even if she was still in Nazareth, which seems likely, news would have reached her. Then she joined the desolate cadre of women through the centuries who experience the terrible human condition of outliving one's child. There is no speaking this racking sorrow. It is out of the natural order of things. Worse yet, this death itself did not occur in the natural order of things but was violently inflicted, preceded by excruciating torment and carried out with public shame. One never really gets over the pain when someone you love is a victim of violence. *Mater Dolorosa* is not a theological concept or a symbolic image or an archetypal experience, but a real person who got hit one day with the terrible fact that her firstborn son was dead by state execution.

Crucifixion, a particularly cruel manner of killing, was a Roman death penalty reserved for slaves and noncitizens. It was inevitably carried out in cases where people had been involved in revolt against the empire. The notice of Jesus' crime tacked to his cross read "King of the Jews," thus placing him among the dregs of messianic hopefuls who had threatened the political power of Caesar. Thousands of others were dispatched the same way—recall Josephus's account of the crucifixion of two thousand Jewish men during the uprising after Herod's death. From the purely historical point of view, Jesus suffered and died in a broad political context of Jewish suffering and death at the hand of the Romans. Mary in this tessera is a suffering Jewish mother. Her sorrow for her dead son places her in the company of her contemporaries in Galilee and Judea whose children also fell victim to the imperial power of the empire, and in the company of their descendants through the ages, including horrifically those touched by the Christian Crusades, the Russian pogroms, and the Nazi Holocaust, whose children's lives were extinguished. Emphasizing this connectedness of the historical mother of Jesus, David Flusser observes, "She belongs to the countless Jewish mothers who lament their cruelly murdered children. . . . It would not be such a bad Mariology that did not forget these sisters of Mary in the flesh."[207]

This particular, unappeasable pain also places her memory more broadly in solidarity with mothers of children dead by state violence everywhere, for it remains horrifically the case that the life given from women's bodies keeps on being taken away by brutality, war, and terrorism. Asian women strongly identify Mary with today's "mothers who suffer as their children are being massacred and taken as political prisoners for their actions on behalf of justice and love."[208] Calling on her memory, grieving mothers, wives, and daughters find strength in their bitter struggle against state repression and personal despair. Latin American women theologians speak of the "shared Calvary" women suffer with Mary in the civil wars and political repression that feed on their own children's lives.[209] Muslim Palestinian, Bosnian, and Afghani women, mothers of criminals executed in the United States, surviving mothers of Cambodian and Rwandan genocides, the mothers and grandmothers of Argentina's Plaza de Mayo still demanding to know the fate of their disappeared loved ones—all drink from the same cup of suffering. Like them, Mary suffered the anguish of not being able to save her child from the hand of torturers and executioners.[210] The fact that Christian imagination can picture Mary standing with desolated people under all the crosses set up in the world is due to the history of her own very real grief. This memory finds its liberating effectiveness when it empowers the church's women and men to say, STOP IT. No more killing of other people's children. No more war, brutal greed, and tyranny. This is, of course, a utopian wish, a hope for a world shaped according to God's reign which will be a world with no more sorrowing mothers. On the way to this world, the memory of Mary near the cross abides, galvanizing non-violent action to stop the violence as the only appropriate expression of faith.

"ALL FILLED WITH THE HOLY SPIRIT"
(ACTS 1:14–15 AND 2:1–21)

With this tessera we arrive at the center of this book's proposal to enfold Mary into the communion of saints. For here she dwells in the post-resurrection company of Jesus' disciples gathered in the upper room to await the coming of the Spirit. They are all praying, remembering, expecting. This scene appears at the beginning of the Acts of the Apostles, which was composed by Luke as the second volume of his story of Christian origins. While "the first book" he wrote was a gospel that dealt with Jesus' words, deeds, and destiny, this sequel is a companion volume that tells the story of the church and its increasingly successful mission to the Gentiles throughout the Roman empire.

Following Jesus' ascension into heaven from the Mount of Olives, the disciples returned to the upper room in Jersualem where they were staying. The text names eleven leading men in the group, and then continues, "All these with one accord devoted themselves to prayer, together with the women and Mary the mother of Jesus, and with his brothers." Obviously a mixed group of women and men comprised of Jesus' Galilean disciples and some of his family members, "the company of persons was in all about a hundred and twenty." The tessera might end there with Mary at prayer among the followers of Jesus after Easter. She is not mentioned again by name. However, the subsequent Pentecost story opens with the words "they were all together in one place," when the sound from heaven came, and the rush of a mighty wind filled the house, and tongues as of fire "rested on each one of them." While no names are given of members of this group, biblical scholars presume that the "all" refers back to the earlier list of Jesus' disciples and family members in the upper room. Hence Mary is present when "they were all filled with the Holy Spirit and began to speak in other tongues, as the Spirit gave them utterance." As part of the community that was gathered in Jesus' name, this older Jewish woman, marked by the struggles of a hard life, receives a new outpouring of the Spirit of God and raises her voice again in inspired praise and prophecy.

There is good reason for accepting this picture of Mary enfolded into the nascent Jewish-Christian community as reliable tradition. It is highly unlikely that Luke would have cast her as such an exemplary disciple from the annunciation on, someone who heard the word of God and kept it, if the community did not remember her as part of their circle. Furthermore, since Luke does not mention her among the women at the cross, the surprise of her reappearance in the Jerusalem community after Jesus' death and resurrection indicates a historical memory that she was indeed there, at least for a time. The presence of Jesus' brothers, too, is validated by the fact that James, "the brother of the Lord," became a key leader of the church in Jerusalem. This scene is constructed with beautiful artistry. Brown points out that just as Luke begins his gospel by walking the faithful Jews Elizabeth and Zechariah, Anna and Simeon, right out of the Hebrew Scriptures to witness to Jesus the Messiah, so too he gathers three groups from the gospel and walks them into Acts to bridge Jesus' ministry and the later story of the church: Mary, who witnesses to Jesus' infancy, the Twelve who witness to his ministry, and the women who witness to his death and burial (although it should be noted that the women, too, witness to his ministry).[211] Both of Luke's volumes begin with the startling promise that the Holy Spirit will come upon main characters in the story: Mary in the gospel, the community of disciples in Acts. When the Spirit does descend, the result is new birth that comes from God: Jesus in the gospel, the church in Acts. The literary virtuosity of this author, however, does not negate the validity of the memory reflected in his work. Historically, Mary very likely belonged to the early Jerusalem church.

To have a liberating appreciation of this mosaic tile, we must correct a popular distortion. Traditional artistic depictions of Pentecost portray the Spirit descending upon thirteen figures, one woman, Mary, surrounded by twelve male apostles. The product of an androcentric imagination that erases women and insignificant men, this picture hardly does justice to Luke's text with its one hundred twenty persons. These all must be restored to the scene. We need especially to attend to "the women" present in that upper room. They are depicted not as extras but as an integral part of the praying community in Jerusalem. Although they are not named in this passage, biblical scholars assume, reasonably enough, that they are the women mentioned in Luke's gospel account of the passion. There we read that when Jesus died on the cross, "the women who had followed him from Galilee stood at a distance and saw these things" (Luke 23:49). These women were disciples, as the technical meaning of "follow" makes clear. Their function was not that of the idle crowds "gazing at" the spectacle, but that of witnesses who "saw" what happened, as the technical meaning of "see" makes clear. Their role as witnessing disciples continued when Joseph of Arimathea wrapped Jesus' corpse in a shroud and laid it in the tomb: "the women who had come with him from Galilee followed and saw the tomb and how the body was laid" (Luke 23:55). At early dawn on Sunday morning they returned to the tomb with spices and ointments to perform a final, merciful anointing, only to find it empty. Now the legitimacy of the whole Christian message hinges on their observation and interpretation. The women disciples "play an absolutely essential role in the gospel accounts . . . the identity of Jesus' tomb with the empty tomb depends on their testimony."[212] Two dazzling messengers relayed the news of the resurrection, whereupon the women "remembered" Jesus' words. Returning to the city, they announced their discovery "to the eleven and to all the rest." At this point Luke finally names some of the women involved in this momentous revelation: "Now it was Mary Magdalene and Joanna and Mary the mother of James and the other women with them who kept repeating this to the apostles" (Luke 24:10)—a whole cadre of female witnesses to the death, burial, and resurrection of Jesus Christ. In wrenching patriarchal fashion, the women's words seemed to the men "like an idle tale, and they did not believe them" (Luke 24:11). The term for idle tale, *lēros* in Greek, "could scarcely be more condescending," forming the root of the English word delirious.[213] It was as if the women were spouting nonsense, so much delirious humbug. Peter even ran to the tomb and saw that it was empty as the women had said; but he went home "wondering" what was going on, rather than believing in the risen Christ on the strength of the women's testimony—a not unfamiliar scene even today.

When the leader of a messianic movement dies, the movement frequently dies too. In the case of Christianity, however, something happened that changed this local Jewish movement into a worldwide religion. Many factors contributed to this development, but, as Jewish scholar Tal Ilan observes, "the initial momentum seems to have begun with the people who interpreted the events following Jesus' death as a resurrection. The gospels unanimously agree that these people were women."[214] They saw angels where the men saw nothing.[215] Consequently, women were not only extremely instrumental at the most critical moment of Christian history, but the basic creed of Christianity, namely, that after his death Jesus was raised to life, was initiated by women's testimony. They were the first to understand the resurrection faith that is the foundation of the church. Earlier in his gospel, Luke had depicted some of these same women traveling with Jesus around Galilee, including Mary Magdalene and Joanna, the wife of Chuza who was Herod's steward, along with Susanna "and many others" (Luke 8:2–3). This group of women disciples constitutes a moving line of continuity, from Galilee to the cross to the full tomb and the empty tomb and now to the upper room at Pentecost. All this history of these women's vocational choice in response to Jesus, their experiences of following, their brave fidelity, their outspoken witness, and men's rejection of their word, is present in that upper room. Now they are filled with "power from on high" and emboldened to speak out with more power than ever.

The gender inclusiveness of the gift of the Spirit comes to the fore when Peter speaks out to explain Pentecost to the gathering crowd. He quotes the prophet Joel:

> And in the last days it shall be, God declares,
> that I will pour out my Spirit upon all flesh,
> and your sons and daughters shall prophesy,
> and your young men shall see visions,
> and your old men shall dream dreams.
> Even upon my slaves, both men and women,
> in those days I will pour out my Spirit;
> and they shall prophesy. (Joel 2:28–29, cited in Acts 2:17–18)

Feminist insight would expand Joel to include young women having visions and old women dreaming dreams as well. The point is that a sign of messianic times occurs when not only men but women receive the

Spirit; when not only free persons but slaves, even slave women who rank at the lowest rung of the social ladder, pour forth prophetic speech in the power of the Spirit given to them in like measure. This scene, key to the birth of the church, dramatically sounds the opening bell: it has begun. Witnessing to Christ, bearing Christ forward in history, the church is the creation of the Spirit firing up the hearts and loosening up the tongues of even the most insignificant person, moving the whole community to speak and act on behalf of the reign of God. It is interesting to note that this is not the only time the Spirit is given. Later on, in the shock of the first persecution, the early community prayed for courage; "and when they had prayed, the place in which they were gathered together was shaken; and they were all filled with the Holy Spirit and spoke the word of God with boldness" (Acts 4:31).

The text of Acts is a site of conflict. Given this Pentecost beginning, one would expect many stories to follow of women's leadership in preaching and prophesying. Such is not the case. Luke focuses instead on the deeds of Peter and Paul with little regard for women's ministry. Even where women are mentioned, incidentally and sporadically, as building up the church, we never hear them speak. Virtually every woman biblical scholar who deals with Acts makes the same point: the author selected his stories with androcentric interest. Desiring to impress his readers in the Roman empire with the trustworthiness of this new movement, he consistently depicted men in public leadership roles and, in order to conform with the empire's standards, kept women decorously under control in supportive positions. Having eyes mainly for elite men, he fudged women into an insignificant background ignoring the leadership roles they in fact held. "Luke is above all a gentleman's gentleman, and Acts is his book,"[216] is the telling judgment of Gail O'Day, echoed throughout women's exegesis. Consequently, Acts does not contain a representative picture of church leadership in the early decades. It tells only part of the story.

To reconstitute a fuller history, feminist scholars look to a broader spectrum of texts.[217] They read the story of women's discipleship and apostolic witness across the canonical gospels, as we saw in the tessera of John's account of the cross. They take account of the letters of Paul, whose salutations give a vibrant picture of women's extensive participation in ministry, one that stands in contrast to women's marginalization in Acts. Recall Paul's salutation to the deacon Phoebe, leader of the church of Cenchreae; and to Junia, outstanding among the apostles in Rome; and to the wife and husband team Prisca and Aquila, leaders of a house church in Rome; and to beloved Persis, who "worked hard in the Lord" for the same community, working hard being a code phrase for leadership (see Rom. 16:1–16). They also consult second- and third-century apocryphal gospels, which take figures from Jesus' ministry and place them in situations reflective of the later church. One telling incident occurs in the apocryphal *Gospel according to Mary*.[218] The scene opens with Mary Magdalene encouraging the disheartened, terrified male disciples by preaching to them what the risen Lord had taught her. In anger Peter interrupts asking, "Did he really speak privately with a woman and not openly to us? Are we to turn about and all listen to her? Did he prefer her to us?" Troubled at this disparagement of her witness and faithful relationship to Christ, Mary responds, "My brother Peter, what do you think? Do you think I thought this up by myself in my heart, or that I am lying about the Savior?" At this point Levi breaks in to mediate the dispute: "Peter, you have always been hot-tempered. Now I see you contending against the woman like the adversaries. But if the Savior made her worthy, who are you, indeed, to reject her? Surely the Lord knew her very well. That is why he loved her more than us." The story ends with the apostles gaining courage from Mary Magdalene's testimony and going forth to preach. Acting like detectives, scholars piece together these bits of evidence to understand that this incident reflects the second- and third-century conflict over women's ministry as an ascendant male leadership tried to suppress them. Slowly such scholarship is restoring the historical picture of women's leadership in the early church and the ensuing struggle to defeat it.

I have not forgotten Mary the mother of Jesus. But the Christian tradition of art and liturgy has forgotten the Galilean Jewish women with her who were all filled with the Spirit at Pentecost and were moved to invaluable and authoritative ministerial commitments. Reducing them to only glancing significance while focusing on the glories of Mary has robbed the whole church of the full story of its founding and deprived women of their heritage of female leadership in the Spirit. It also lies at the root of the damage androcentric mariology has done to women's spirituality and equal participation in ministry in the church. Here at Pentecost, both historically and in the text of Acts, Mary lives among the women founders of the church as well as the men. She is the mother of Jesus, who gave birth to him in troubling circumstances, taught and nurtured him, and let him go to his destiny with very great love. Other women there, Mary Magdalene,

Joanna, Mary the mother of James, and many unnamed others, are Jesus' friends and disciples who supported his ministry, witnessed his death and burial, and bore the earth-shattering responsibility of being chief witnesses to his resurrection whether the men believed them or not. Each woman brings her own history of relationship to Jesus. None is reducible to the other. With their particular gifts and history, all are vital in different ways. Their believing discipleship and varied leadership roles form a constitutive part of the apostolic church. Mary cannot be separated from the rest of this community. They are all essential to one another. This text does not portray Mary at the center of the community, as mother of the group, or as the one and only ideal member. Nor does it allow her presence to overshadow the distinctive witness and ministry of the other women. Rather, it positions her amid the community as one unique member among other unique members, the whole group living by the power and presence of the Spirit and seeking to bring that warmth and light to the world.[219]

Mary's presence in the Jerusalem community allows for some imaginative questions. What was the conversation like between her and Miriam of Magdala, leading witness of the risen Christ? What stories did she swap with Joanna, who followed Jesus despite having wealth and social prestige to spare? What memories, hopes, and strategies did she share with the other women in this community? Perhaps she lived peaceably as a beloved old woman revered as the mother of the Messiah. Perhaps during the breaking of the bread, when listening to the women and men around the table ponder the meaning of her son's life, death, and resurrection, she shared her own wisdom, such as it was. Perhaps, too, she was an outspoken elder, weighing in with creative opinions about the incipient problems with the Gentiles and supporting the leadership in the community of women such as Mary Magdalene. She may have been concerned about the destitute among them, especially the widows; or caught by the inevitable sadness that never quite goes away after violence; or full of proclamations about what God was doing to set right the world; or encouraging the creative efforts of the young; or on fire with the Spirit in a mystic's old age. All of these scenarios are seriously imaginable.

This final tessera allows us to remember that the life of the historical woman Miriam of Nazareth was indeed a journey of faith, with significance for people struggling to negotiate the challenges of faith today. From her peasant domicile in Nazareth to the house church in Jerusalem, both

of which labored to survive under oppressive economic and political circumstances; from youth to marriage to widowhood; from the birth of her
firstborn to his horrendous death to hearing him proclaimed Lord, Messiah, and Savior—she walked her life's path keeping faith with her gracious
God, the Holy One of Israel. Now she is an older woman wise in the Spirit.
All her years of suffering and joy, danger and risk-taking, questioning and
pondering, anxiety and hope, hard work and sabbath rest, intimate relationships and losses, coalesce in a new quickening. Inconceivable though it
may be, the God of Israel in whom she believed has acted to fulfill the
ancient promise made to her people. All creation is headed for a vivifying
transformation. Death does not have the last word. "Afire with some
unnamed energy,"[220] she like "all of them" is empowered to witness with
boldness, bequeathing a legacy still capable of igniting hearts with hope in
the living God in the midst of a world of suffering.

11

Mary, Friend of God and Prophet

Assembled together, the individual biblical portraits of Mary of Nazareth form a mosaic image of a woman of Spirit. Honed by the historical background of Galilean Judaism and interpreted by women's sensibilities, this mosaic delivers a glimpse of an actual woman, a first-century member of an oppressed peasant society, whose walk with the Spirit at a pivotal moment in salvation history made a unique contribution to the good of the world. Within the overarching picture of God's redeeming action in Christ, each tessera adds a different aspect to the church's memory of her life. Our final task is to weave this living memory into that of the great company of friends of God and prophets which is the communion of saints. In the process, we need to keep doing our God work, understanding that female imagery rightly belongs in our discourse about the divine mystery: the living God herself is our mother of infinite mercy. And we need to keep doing our anthropology work, shucking off gender definitions of the feminine that confine women to subordinate roles. With our flanks thus continually safeguarded, we step back from a close focus on the marian mosaic to espy the sweeping vista of which it is a part.

THE SPIRIT WHO WEAVES CONNECTIONS

The key to our theologizing is this: Mary is a woman of Spirit. She entrusted her life to the utterly gracious reality of the transcendent God ever-present to vivify, renew, and make holy the world. Whether she was taking initiative, rejoicing, criticizing, pondering, suffering, or otherwise finding her way through ordinary days, her loving partnership with Spirit-

305

Sophia inscribes in our history a story of grace. In this she is sister to all who respond to the gift of the Spirit in their own lives, in ways seen and unseen. Together they form the communion of saints.

Classical theology characterizes the Spirit most often as Love, a love that unites while preserving difference. The presence of Spirit-Sophia brings about the fruits of love: blossoming life, engagement against suffering and evil, renewal when things get broken and ruined, and energy for new beginnings. If the first person of the Trinity signifies God as unoriginate source of all, and the second person refers to God who becomes incarnate in history to save, then the third person names the living God who is still here, the ever-coming power of the future acting to bring all things to fulfillment. This she does in many and varied ways. One of her signature works is the creation of community. As Creator Spirit, she vivifies the universe and energizes the community of life with its long, evolutionary development. As Holy Spirit, God's own self-communication in grace, she vivifies human beings with divine life, consecrating them at their core and welding them into a company whose ideal is to walk a godly path, even if they often miss the mark. Dwelling at the heart of the world, Spirit-Sophia empowers profound interconnection between all manner of creatures as history rolls on.

The communion of saints is one of the abiding creations of Spirit-Sophia's artistry. Somewhat abstract in itself, this community comes to birth in a river of holy lives, a great intergenerational company of persons in the matrix of the natural world, itself the original sacred community of life. While the phrase "communion of saints" itself arises in a Christian context and often functions as shorthand for Christians themselves, the Spirit does not limit divine blessing to any one group. Within human cultures everywhere God calls every human being to fidelity and love, awakening knowledge of the truth and inspiring deeds of compassion and justice. Happily, those who respond are found in every nation and tongue, culture and religion, and even among institutional religion's cultured despisers. Indeed, where human participation in divine holiness disappears, the opposite appears: barbarity, cruelty, murder, and unspeakable despair. At its most elemental, then, the communion of saints does not refer to Christians alone but affirms a link between all women and men who have been brushed with the fire of divine love and who seek the living God in their lives. From this angle the symbol of the communion of saints shows itself to be a most inclusive belief. It crosses boundaries, breaking down social lines of division and building up a vastly diverse people by the play of the Spirit through the ages and across the wide world.

A rich metaphor in the biblical book of Wisdom introduces fresh vocabulary for this company. This metaphor is found in a passage that describes the deeds of Sophia or Holy Wisdom, here functioning as a female image of the Spirit of God:

> Although she is but one, she can do all things,
> and while remaining in herself, she renews all things;
> in every generation she passes into holy souls
> and makes them friends of God, and prophets. (Wis. 7:27)[1]

• To be a friend of God is to enter into mutual relationship with God, freely, with trust and affection; knowing and letting yourself be known in honest intimacy; taking time to savor the relationship with its delights and challenges in prayer and contemplation; caring passionately about what God cares about; clinging together even in harsh adversity, even in the dark night; allowing divine presence to be the foundation of your life even when it is experienced as wrenching absence; living with the experiential knowledge that we are, as Jesus said, no longer servants but friends.

• To be a prophet is to raise your voice in criticism against injustice because, being God's friend, your heart loves the world the way God loves it; your imagination sees how it should flourish; when this collides with the social arrangements people make at one another's expense or at the expense of the earth, you are moved to speak out and act in service of the reign of God, thus creating possibilities for resistance and resurrection. In the worst moments, being a prophet also means to comfort others with words of hope, because, in view of God's life-giving power, this pain is not forever. Either way, acting critically or consolingly, being a prophet often entails, as Jesus said, being without honor in your own country and among your own people.

Down through the centuries as Spirit-Sophia graces person after person in land after land, they form together a grand company of the friends of God and prophets, a community of redeemed sinners. This community stretches backward and forward in time and encircles the globe in space, crossing boundaries of language, culture, race, gender, class, sexual orientation, religion, and all other human differences, stretching into eternity. The inmost depth and outermost horizon of this communion of holy ones remains God's Holy Spirit, who vivifies creation, weaves interconnections, saves what is lost, and makes holy the world. This is the way we will think about the communion of saints: it refers to the great and diverse multitude of people who are continually being connected to God and one another in graced relations of friendship and prophecy. Interpreting Mary with her unique history within this great company locates her significance for faith amid multiple relationships of mutuality formed by the Spirit.

Within this pneumatological framework, five dimensions that mark the communion of saints contribute layers of meaning to a contemporary theology of Mary.

THE GRACE OF THE LIVING

The first, irreplaceably important truth is that the communion of saints refers to the graced lives of human beings who are alive today. To call Mary blessed is to recognize the blessedness of ordinary people who are called to participate in the work of God in our own day. If the Christian community in the twenty-first century does not grasp this point, then the proposal to view Mary within the communion of saints loses its foundation and liberating power. You cannot celebrate the work of the Spirit in the life of another person if you do not recognize the Spirit's blessing in your own life. Unfortunately, for many long centuries the consecrated character of the baptized people of God was given short shrift as institutional structures seemed to transfer holiness from the nave of the church up into the restricted sanctuary. Discussions of the saints focused only on deceased paradigmatic figures, who then became the real saints to the detriment of average persons who were never assured that God's grace also made them holy. Patriarchal theology tarred women with the brush of the supposed sinful colors of Eve while exalting the sinlessness of Mary. All these developments woefully shortchange the breadth and depth of the Spirit's strategy, which is to consecrate the whole community in grace and truth.

It was not always this way. The early church understood themselves called together to be a holy people, a theme with deep roots in the Jewish tradition. Inspired by the common waters of baptism and the shared eucharistic meal, they came to realize that the power of the Spirit who had raised Jesus from the dead was forming them into a holy community of disciples. As in the Jewish tradition, their holiness was more than simply an ethical matter, being holy as being either innocent of sin or being morally perfect. Rather, it consisted in being blessed with the very life of God through Jesus Christ in the power of the Spirit. The mission to bear good news into the world arose as an outflowing expression of this core consecration. Early Christians expressed this sense of being a holy community with interesting vocabulary. They called everyone "saints," *hagioi* in Greek, a term that appears over sixty times in the New Testament. Paul's letters witness to the widespread use of this term. "To all God's beloved in Rome, who are called to be saints" (Rom. 1:7), he writes; and, "To all the saints in Christ Jesus who are in Philippi" (Phil. 1:1); and, "To the church of God that is in Corinth, to those who are sanctified in Christ Jesus, called to be saints" (1 Cor. 1:2); and again, "Greet one another with a holy kiss. All the saints greet you" (2 Cor. 13:12–13). This extensive use of "saints" to refer to the church reflects the vigor of the people's sense of their own graced lives.

There was as yet no highly structured sacramental system, ordained priesthood, or monastic life such as would develop in the course of later centuries. Thus there was no assignment of degrees of holiness based on persons' state of life, a practice with terribly damaging effects. Instead, the lay prophet Jesus, who was never in his own lifetime a priest, is the only priest named for the Christian community in the New Testament. Metaphorically speaking, he performed the service of merciful and faithful high priest by his sacrificial death. Everyone else is consecrated in virtue of the grace of the Spirit: "you are a chosen race, a royal priesthood, a holy nation, a people belonging to God" (1 Pet. 2:9). This identity inheres in the community and every person belonging to it without distinction. Since all are baptized the same way into the death and resurrection of Jesus and all have received the gifts of the Spirit, then all share in the holiness of God. This does not level out differences: "there are varieties of gifts but the same Spirit" (1 Cor. 12:4). But these distinctions are not the occasion for the saints to divide themselves in the usual oppressive ways of humankind, subordinating some and elevating others. Rather, the foundation of the community's holiness is Jesus Christ, which point carries a subversive program: "As many of you as were baptized into Christ have clothed yourselves with Christ. There is no longer Jew or Greek, slave or free, male and female; for all of you are one in Christ Jesus" (Gal. 3:27–28).[2] All together and without discrimination, Christians gathered here or gathered there, women and men equally, are a community of saints.

On this score Vatican II made a remarkable breakthrough, retrieving the ancient awareness of the holiness of the whole living community. At the very center of the council's Dogmatic Constitution on the Church (*Lumen Gentium*) lies a chapter entitled "the call of the whole church to holiness." Here it is emphasized that through baptism human persons are put right with God in Christ. Receiving the Spirit, they become sharers in the divine nature. Lest anyone doubt the result, the council says it plainly: "In this way they are really made holy" (§40). This holiness, furthermore, is essentially the same for everyone. There is not one type of holiness for lay persons and another for those in religious life or ordained ministry. There is not one kind of indwelling of the Spirit for office-holders in the church and another for unnoticed, faithful members. Rather, "in the various types and duties of life, one and the same holiness is cultivated by all who are moved by the Spirit of God" (§41). One and the same holiness: this is a radically biblical idea. The church is not divided into saints and non-saints by office or gender or any other marker. Vivified by grace, all women, men, and children are consecrated at the core of their being as part of this community of redeemed sinners. When this Constitution on the Church goes on to treat the subject of Mary, it places her within this company as herself a sharer in the same divine grace.

This, then, must be lifted up as of primary importance: the holiness of so-called ordinary persons including women, sometimes overheard to say "I'm no saint" but in reality called and gifted in the Spirit. This truth also underscores the importance of everyday life as the milieu for living out a holy life. The phrase "heroic sanctity," used in official language as a criterion for canonization, reflects the value given to a certain kind of spiritual achievement attained by intrepid acts. It customarily points to bloody martyrdom, stringent asceticism, renunciation of family and worldly possessions, or lifelong dedication to the sick, the poor, the imprisoned. Noble these titanic acts may be, but praising them in a church that has lost its sense of the holiness of the whole people only serves to reinforce the unsaintliness of most whose lives do not measure up to such epic proportions. Understanding the communion of saints first of all as a company of the friends of God and prophets alive today reclaims the ordinary milieu of grace and the nobility of everyday struggle despite failure and defeat. It locates a holy life not only or even chiefly in mighty deeds, though these may indeed be someone's vocation, but in creative fidelity in the midst of everyday life. Thus is room created, in the living community's acknowledgment of the saving grace so generously poured out on themselves, for appreciating that Mary is blessed among women and men who are themselves blessed.

From generation to generation the great Spirit of God, Holy Wisdom herself, passes into holy souls and not so holy ones and makes them friends of God and prophets. We who are alive today are bearers of this holiness, connected to each other around the world in all our differences. But we do not live forever. At some point, having made our own contribution, we pass through the shattering of death into the life-giving hands of God, to be followed by the fresh young faces of a new generation of saints.

A CLOUD OF WITNESSES

The second dimension of the communion of saints that affects interpretation of Mary is the fact that it includes persons who have died. Given later Christian usage, it is interesting to note that in the New Testament no one who has died is called a saint, that nomenclature being reserved for the living. In short order, however, the living saints began to count the dead as among their own company. Drawing on their Jewish belief that God would raise the dead at the end of the world and witnessing to the resurrection already, in advance, of Jesus who was crucified, early Christians extended membership in their community of saints to those who had died. Teasing out the logic of this early intuition of faith, we see that they forged a certain syllogism. If living persons share in the life of God, and if the dead are likewise still clasped by the living God, then both the living and the dead are united to each other, forged into one community by the same vivifying Spirit. Paul puts this insight succinctly: "whether we live or whether we die, we are the Lord's. For to this end Christ died and rose again, that he might be Lord of both the living and the dead" (Rom. 14:7–9). Thus the idea grew that the community of sinful yet redeemed followers of Christ not only extends across spatial boundaries to include those living in different lands at the present moment, but, as the past recedes, also stretches across time boundaries to include those living in different historical periods. The communion of saints thus expanded to include the dead according to the logic of hope in the fidelity of God.

The Letter to the Hebrews, written in the late first century, presents a key example of how the early church envisioned its relationship with those who had gone before. Writing in a persuasive style, the author reels off a roll call of Jewish ancestors who responded in faith to God's call. Some are mentioned by name: Abel, Noah, Abraham, Sarah, the parents of Moses, Rahab, David, some nineteen persons in all. The litany then expands to include whole groups of people who walked by faith: prophets, those who administered justice, who received promises, who won victories, who were tortured, scourged, stoned, cut in two, who were afflicted and destitute. Finally, having assembled all these people in memory, the author reaches the dramatic high point:

> Therefore, since we are surrounded by so great a cloud of witnesses, let us also lay aside every weight and the sin that clings so closely, and let us run with perseverance the race that is set before us, looking to Jesus the pioneer and perfecter of our faith, who for the joy that was set before him endured the cross, disregarding its shame, and has taken his seat at the right hand of the throne of God. (Heb. 12:1–2)

The dynamism of this passage moves from the narrative of faithful individuals to groups in the past to enthusiastic exhortation for the contemporary community. The movement of the text expresses a strong sense of solidarity between the living and the dead, with the latter surrounding the former like a cloud of witnesses. Commentators note that the background metaphor here refers to a sports arena. Up in the stands a crowd of spectators, each of whom once ran the race, now cheers for those exerting themselves on the tarmac. Here the faithful dead are proposed not as exemplars to be imitated or helpers to be invoked, but as witnesses whose journey encourages those who are still on the way. It is a matter of being inspired by the whole lot of them and the wonderful testimony of their lives to the living God. It is interesting that this lineup penned by a Christian author honors figures who were important in the history of Israel but does not include persons such as Mary Magdalene, first apostolic witness of the resurrection, or Stephen, first Christian martyr, or even Mary the mother of Jesus. Reflecting reverence for the history of God's holy people before the Christian community came into existence, the passage sees its own audience as participants in this tradition now configured in Jesus, pioneer of faith, whose advent does not discredit but rather enhances the history of holiness of his own people.

The community of saints embraces persons who live and breathe at the present moment along with those who have passed into eternal life. The two groups are related by a common life in the Spirit and by a common history of call and response to God amid the ambiguities of human history. As centuries pass by, millions upon millions more join the company of saints in heaven. As in Hebrews, some few are remembered by name; some belong to groups that have made an impact on public life; all too many are untimely dead, their lives ruined in godforsaken incidents of terror, war, and mass death. Most are anonymous. The point is that in their own unique ways, in different times and places, they struggled to be faithful, leaving an imprint in the heritage of life in the Spirit that we inhabit. People alive today who celebrate the feast of All Saints salute this vastly diverse company of the redeemed, which includes also their own beloved dead. It is in this great cloud of witnesses that Mary belongs. Her historical life having ended, she died and passed into the unimaginable, life-giving embrace of the living God. Now she joins the company of loving, faithful people who encourage those still running the race.

PARADIGMATIC FIGURES

Within the great cloud of witnesses, specific persons emerge whose lives embody one or more central values of the faith in a strikingly concrete form. When such persons are recognized by the common spiritual sense of the community, they become publicly significant for the lives of many others. These paradigmatic figures are the persons traditionally and all too narrowly called "saints," though in actuality they are a subset of the whole company. They have no essential spiritual advantage over the rest of the church, who are saints in the biblical sense. All are touched by the fire of the Spirit and called to a life of friendship and prophecy with God, which renders grace a general and constant phenomenon in the sinful church. But certain unique personalities interact with historical conditions to give such outstanding witness that they assume a distinct function in the wider circle of their fellow pilgrims. The direct force of their example acts as a catalyst in the community, galvanizing recognition that, yes, this is what we are called to be. Because Christianity is a way of life, their concreteness leavens and nurtures the moral environment, drawing others to greater commitment according to the dynamic expressed by William James: "one fire kindles another."[3]

Mary is one such paradigmatic figure. As the first dimension made clear, she is first and foremost a real human woman of our history, graced by God with the gift of the same Spirit given to all. The second dimension emphasizes that even though she has now passed from history, she remains connected to the community by the loving fidelity of God who holds even the dead in life. What is surprising about this third dimension, and it is the surprise of the gospel that lifts up the lowly, is her function as a paradigmatic figure in the church. The tether of historical concreteness makes clear that Miriam of Nazareth belonged to the world of the poor who are overlooked in the telling of history: those who lived in the colonial situation of the Roman province of Galilee, in hunger and hard work and oppression, whose villages were fiercely attacked, but who hoped for more. The gospels add theological insight. She bore a poor woman's life with faith in the living God of Israel, believed in a gospel for the downtrodden, found a way to bring forth the Messiah, and journeyed into the new community that spearheaded Jesus' vision to the world. Through it all she was led by the Spirit, the life-giving power of Sophia God, who entered into her soul and made her a friend of God and prophet. Her distinctiveness lies in being the mother of Jesus. No one else has this bodily, psychological, social relationship to the Messiah and, as with all human beings, the relationship is irreplaceably important for both mother and child. All the gospel tesserae note this relationship but do not leave it there. Her own faithful partnership with the Spirit, by which she heard and enacted the word of God, places her in the company of ancestors whose memory the community celebrates and finds challenging. Now she is part of the church's proclamation of the healing, redeeming, liberating salvation coming from God through Jesus, a story which also includes the witness of numerous other women and men. In view of the torrent of misogyny that has flowed from traditional mariology, her historical and gospel specificity with its liberating potential must serve as a criterion for the legitimacy of her paradigmatic status. So anchored, the narrative of her life can teach, inspire, and cheer on the lives of the people of God today. It can defy, protest, and resist active wrongdoing that blocks rather than serves the coming of the reign of God. Across the centuries, kindred spirits find her encouraging their discipleship.

Paradigmatic saints, among them Mary the mother of Jesus, form one vector of the larger reality of the communion of saints. To interpret them in such a way that their memory liberates rather than diminishes the discipleship of others, we must make sure that they stay connected to the whole graced company. By the power of Spirit-Sophia generations upon generations of redeemed persons are joined in a living tradition of friendship with God and compassion toward the world. No one of them alone or no one group, even the paradigmatic saints, can ever monopolize what it means to be holy. "The definition is never complete," writes David Matzko of sainthood. "A single, a few, a dozen lives of the saints will not complete what it means to love God and neighbor or to be in the community of heaven. The definition can be given only by the whole communion of saints."[4] Cheered on by this great, richly varied cloud of witnesses, including the woman from Nazareth, the people of God today run their own lap of the race on the track of discipleship as legacy for future generations.

THE COMPANIONSHIP PATTERN

Over the centuries two different patterns have characterized the relationship between the living and the dead in the communion of saints. The more ancient, biblical pattern is one of companionship whereby the two groups relate as mutual partners in the Spirit. The later, by now more familiar pattern of patronage casts the saints in heaven as benefactors who act as patrons for earthly petitioners. The boundaries between these two models are not absolute. In the companionship model people gladly pray for one another, and in the patronage model some may muster equal regard for one another. However, the overall shapes of the relationships, crudely described as a circle of companions or a pyramid of patrons respectively, are different enough to warrant considering them as two distinct models. A crucially important task for a contemporary feminist theology of Mary is the retrieval of the companionship model of interaction.

The Patronage Model

This pattern of relationship gained influence when the Christian church became an established religion of the Roman empire in the fourth century. Reeling from persecution and seeking to shore up its legitimacy, the church then began to model itself on the structures of empire. Key among these was the institution of patronage, which pervaded both urban and rural life. In sociological terms, patronage is a system of exchange founded on asymmetrical relations between persons of unequal status—the antithesis of friendship between equals. It arises when concentrations of wealth and political power in the hands of the few, coupled with neediness of the many and lack of democratic processes, conspire to create permanent social stratifications. Basic to all patronage arrangements is inequality, marked social and economic inequality accompanied by pronounced differences in privileges and honor. As the system works, the patron does favors for clients, which clients repay with loyalty and the giving of honor.

Given the church's inculturation into this social system, it is perhaps not surprising that patronage began to govern its transactions not only on earth but also with the realm of heaven. By the late fourth century the term *patrocinium* (patronage) was applied to the activity of the apostles and martyrs in heaven on behalf of the faithful. Just as the terrestrial patron is asked to use his influence with the emperor, so now the celestial patron is asked to use his or her influence with the Almighty. These mediators, though subject to God themselves, have their own spheres of influence in descending order and may prove to be benefactors in return for devotions such as prayer, pilgrimage to their tombs, or reverence for their relics. The saints were seen in various ways, writes Stephen Wilson, "as advocates pleading causes before a stern divine judge, as mediators, as go-betweens, as intriguers or wire-pullers at the court of Heaven—all metaphors were used. It is significant also that the saints themselves were arranged in a hierarchy, in both the liturgy and official iconography, with the Virgin Mary as the arch-intercessor through whom petitions of other saints were directed."[5] Such a religious arrangement would not be foreign to those who had grown up in a world pervaded with the patronage system.

The patron–client pattern gained ascendency through the period of late antiquity, becoming the predominant feature of medieval devotion to the saints. Mary the mother of God sat at the pinnacle of influence, able to impact her Son's judgment even over a soul's eternal destiny in heaven or hell. It seems clear that the abuses in the cult of the saints that drew such withering criticism from the Reformers were the result of this patronage model run wild. While the reforming Council of Trent reined in the more egregious offenses, it defended the patronage model as if it were the only possible way to honor the saints. Consequently, ever new patron–client practices became a feature of Catholic spirituality in the post-Reformation period, an exuberance checked by Vatican II. The patronage pattern still waxes strong wherever social and spiritual forces conspire to rob the living community of its identity in the Spirit as a holy people, but wanes with the weakening of those forces. In a study of both earthly and heavenly patronage as practiced in Malta, Jeremy Boissevain observes that "both types seem to have thrived in periods when power was concentrated in the hands of a few, when economic and political uncertainty prevailed, when widespread poverty induced dependency." Because of changing circumstances, he concludes, "In Malta, as elsewhere in Europe, the saints are marching out."[6] I would suggest rather that in our democratic, egalitarian culture the patronage system is marching out. People may be losing their client status, but they do not need to be bereft of their cloud of witnesses.

The Companionship Model

A very different pattern of relationship, found in scripture and early Christian tradition, promotes mutual companionship in Christ between the living and the dead. Already observed in the "cloud of witnesses" passage in Letter to the Hebrews, this pattern perdured through the age of the martyrs in the first three Christian centuries. It can be heard in the account of the martyrdom of the beloved bishop Polycarp:

> Little did they know that we could never abandon Christ, who alone suffered for the redemption of those who are saved in the whole world, the innocent one dying on behalf of sinners. Nor could we worship anyone else. For him we worship as the Son of God. But the martyrs we love as disciples and imitators of the Lord, and rightly so because of their matchless affection for their own king and teacher. May we too become their comrades and fellow disciples.[7]

The living members of the church were partners, companions, comrades, co-disciples with Polycarp and other outstanding exemplars of faith. The martyrs gave their witness; those struggling to live faithfully on earth loved them; and both were encompassed by the saving grace of God on the path of discipleship.

Augustine's preaching over the span of many years provides an extensive vocabulary for the companionship model. "Blessed be the saints in whose memory we are celebrating the day they suffered on," he exclaimed; "they have left us lessons of encouragement."[8] The best lesson they have left us is their actual lives. When we celebrate their memory, the effect is like opening a fragrant flagon of perfume in a small room. Then their witness pervades our community with reassurance and deep hope. While human just like ourselves, they struggled through very severe testing with the help of God. This acts as a beacon of light in our own troubles because God's help hasn't dried up; it flows toward us still. Cherishing their memory, we are inspired to follow in the footsteps of their example. "By passing along the narrow road they widened it, and while they went along, trampling on the rough ways, they went ahead of us."[9] Augustine was aware of how indebted each present generation is to those who went before. The earliest generations of Christians, he thought, deserve special appreciation, for they pioneered a whole new way of life: "When numbers were few, courage had to be great."[10] Since then, many others who believed before us had no idea that one day we would gather in this place, a church of the future praising God: "they weren't yet able to see it, yet they were already constructing it out of their own lives."[11] To realize that we are the heirs of the tradition shaped by such persons makes us grateful and rejuvenates our desire to contribute to this heritage for the next generation. Their adventure of faith opened a way for us, and now we go ahead of others in an ongoing river of companions seeking God. And when our own journey grows hard, we can draw strength from the memory of our forebears' sufferings and victories: "How can the way be rough when it has been smoothed by the feet of so many walking along it?"[12] The communion of saints in this companionship model forges bonds across time that sustain faith in strange new times and places. Surrounded by this cloud of witnesses, we cherish in very different circumstances what they cared enough to live and die for.

An underlying sense of companionship pervades this pattern of relationship. The living and the dead together are a holy people, redeemed sinners, at different stages of the journey. Each one gives and receives what is appropriate, while the whole group of friends of God and prophets is centered on the incomprehensible mystery of divine love poured out in Jesus Christ for the sake of the world. Without ignoring differences, the companionship model structures relations along the lines of mutuality, not hierarchy. To use a spatial metaphor, here the saints in heaven are not situated *between God* and those on earth, with some more and some less powerful in intercessory pull. Rather, they are *with* their sisters and brothers in the one Spirit. It is not distance from God's throne, nor fear of "his" judgment, nor the impression of "his" cold disinterest, nor the need for grace given only in small portions, nor a sense of one's own utter unimportance in the hierarchy of power, nor any other such motivation that impels the community to turn to the saints in heaven. Rather, gratitude and delight in this cloud of witnesses with whom we share a common humanity, a common struggle, a common faith, and a common destiny commend their memory to our interest. We thank God for their victory, learn from their example, and share their friendship on the road of discipleship. Vatican II took this approach when, appealing to the experience of friendship in the church, it taught that "just as Christian communion among wayfarers brings us closer to Christ, so our companionship with the saints joins us to Christ, from whom as from their fountain and head issue every grace and the life of God's people itself" (*Lumen Gentium* §50).

The ancient companionship model offers a road not often taken, but experienced anew by women in their relationship with newly discovered, encouraging foresisters, and they recommend it to the whole church. The living church of women and men now bears the heat of the day; it is their turn to contribute to the repair of the world amid multiple struggles for justice and fullness of life. But solidarity with those who have gone before, including the Spirit-filled Mary the mother of Jesus, releases energies for ongoing fidelity. The relationship among those living on earth and those with God in glory is fundamentally mutual and collegial. They form a circle of friendship centered on the graciousness of the living God.

COMPANIONS IN MEMORY AND HOPE

In the companionship model, the core practice that connects the living with the dead friends of God and prophets is the act of remembrance. This is a very particular kind of remembering. It does not revisit the past in order to dwell there with nostalgic sentimentality. Rather, it brings the witness of past lives forward into the present as challenge and source of hope. Telling the stories of our forebears, it releases the power of their "lessons of encouragement." This is memory with the seed of the future in it. By daring to evoke the suffering, the beauty, the defeats and victories of people who struggled before us, it nourishes our own wavering commitment in the present. By connecting us with their unfinished agenda, it sparks the idea that something more is still possible. By prodding our religious imaginations with concrete examples of love and courage, it releases surprisingly creative energies.

As J. B. Metz has never tired of pointing out, this kind of remembering functions with an edge of danger insofar as it prevents any easy settling-down with an unjust status quo.[13] Instead, by lifting up the discipleship of others it turns our hearts toward those who are suffering and quickens hope that "all will be well," despite the world and the church itself lurching on in such stubbornly unredeemed ruts. In the process, those who are companions in memory become also companions in hope. Recalling those on the far side of death carries with it the conviction that their lives have not been snuffed out like a candle but transformed in the unimaginable glory of God. The living press forward with the unfinished business of caring for the world while those who have entered the vast silence of death but are alive in God become themselves part of the community's vocabulary of hope. This fifth dimension of the communion of saints bears directly on practice. Remembering the saints operates as a practical, critical, liberating force that energizes our resistence and protest, imagination and love.

This practice is connected with the central act that shapes Christian identity, the liturgical memorial of the life, passion, death, and resurrection of Jesus Christ. As with every critical memory, remembrance of the crucified and risen Jesus Christ is "dangerous" in a very particular way. Since God sided with this victim of unjust execution rather than with his judges, this memory subverts the expectation that the powerful will always win. Instead, God is in solidarity with those who suffer, galvanizing hope for salvation. This creates a moral and social force that propels the church out of passivity into active engagement on behalf of all those in agony, in particular those brought low by human injustice. The effective power of this memory with its hope in the future, promised but unknown, has sustained the church's efforts to live with passion and compassion in the world, and continues to do so even now.

Woven into this paradigmatic memory of Jesus Christ are the lives of all disciples and seekers in the Spirit, persons who reveal the face of God while disfigured with suffering, alive with resistance, beautiful with love, compassionate to heal, in other words, all the saints. Their dangerous memory can galvanize the church. The pallid state into which the traditional roster of saints has fallen can be measured by the degree to which the official memory of this company now fails to function in such a life-giving way. Part of the problem lies in issues already identified above: loss of the community's sense of its own holiness; the patriarchal patronage relationship; and the focus on heroic virtue which casts ordinary persons into the shadows. These problems are exacerbated by the system of canonization in the Catholic Church, which since the twelfth century has produced a list of official saints who are mostly male, clerical, celibate, and aristocratic; a group, furthermore, that is created in response to large investments of time and money and thus generally exclusive of lay persons, including women and poor persons.

Groups on the margins of officialdom, however, are rediscovering the power of critically remembering the friends of God and prophets. One striking example comes from the church in Latin America, where in the late twentieth century people drank anew from the crucible of martyrdom. To the litany of the saints, recited now as a roll call of the martyrs—Oscar Romero, Ita Ford, Ignacio Ellacuria, Celina Ramos, young catechists, community workers, and religious leaders of the *pueblos*—the people respond, *"Presente."* This is a multivalent term asking that the saint be present, trusting that the saint is present, and implicitly affirming the life-giving Spirit of God, who makes it possible for the saint to be present. The prayer summons a strong, concrete memory that commits the community to emulating their lives. Circles of women are also pioneering critical memory of the saints as a liberating element in the practice of faith. Through ritual, art, song, and story in the context of prayer, they foster connection with foresisters who walked faithfully and imaginatively with their God. Naming women whose witness was largely erased by patriarchal transmission of Christian culture and celebrating exemplars who encourage greatness of spirit, they experience the power that the companionship model can deliver. "Mary Magdalene went and announced to the disciples, 'I have seen the Lord'; and she told them that he had said these things to her" (John 20:18);[14] "Mary McLeod Bethune, with $1.50 and a prayer, started a school for girls in Daytona":[15] these are memories with the seed of the future in them. Solidarity with such a cloud of witnesses brings strength and comfort in the struggle for greater life and freedom. No atrophied connection, this, but a touching of spirit in the Spirit that empowers and blesses in the face of strong indifference and opposition.

In this context, women have been actively creating a discourse of Mary, friend of God and prophet, from female experiences and especially the lives of poor women. Instead of using her to develop a new theology of "woman" or stressing her stereotypical feminine virtues, this theology opens up space for women to claim their concrete faith history and equal participation in the church. Instead of separating her out as an unreachable paragon, it connects her with the human race, women in particular, seeing her blessedness as a sign of the capacity of all women to bear the image and likeness of God. Positioning her among our ancestors in the faith, it seeks to set loose the power of her critical memory and be enlivened by the lessons of encouragement that flow from her life. *Miriam of Nazareth: Presente!* In a world still structured by patriarchal injustice, the logic of this approach taps the power of her memory to work dangerously against the status quo of women's marginalization. Mary is socially insignificant yet highly favored: this spills over to raise the dignity of other women with minimum worldly power. She is endangered yet God is with her, as with other women who risk or suffer violence at the hands of patriarchal power. She is impoverished, at times homeless, a refugee in a strange land, yet blessed, as are women and their families to whom sinful injustice also denies a full plate and a safe dwelling. Unconventional woman though she be, God has done great things for her, as for others similarly outside the pale. She knows sorrow enough to break a human heart, losing a loved one to violence; yet, hoping against hope "amid the ruins,"[16] she experiences along with the company of disciples the advent of God in the event of suffering itself, bringing life. Together with Mary Magdalene the first witness of the resurrection, Joanna, and many other women, she is filled with the Spirit and speaks out God's word: women who speak with authority in the power of the Spirit today, even at risk of ridicule, are borne up by the Pentecost company of disciples, singly and together. She sings her joy in God because the mighty are brought down and the hungry fed: the revolutionary energy of her words inspires the song to go on in countless hamlets and cities where women struggle against their own diminishment and for the flourishing of the world. Her courageous response to the Spirit's call charts lessons of encouragement for both women and men and nurtures the spirit of the whole community. Faithful to God through all uncertainty, she becomes part of the community's story. Companion in memory, she becomes through solidarity with the struggles of women a companion in hope. She is truly, subversively, our sister.

A PRAYER FOR A SEASON OF STRUGGLE

Throughout the centuries prayer has been one venerable expression of people's regard for Mary. Beautiful antiphons of praise and fierce petitions for help well up through the generations, many not workable in this paradigm of Mary as friend of God and prophet. Aware of the difficulty as he was, Paul VI made a strong case that the rosary, while its origins lay in medieval times, could still function in a beneficial way. The heart of this prayer, he noted, entails meditation on the gospel scenes announced for each decade. Indeed, without this focus the prayer becomes merely repetitive rote. The rosary's repetition of the Hail Mary itself, though, has its own value. In a busy, frantic world, it acts as something of a mantra to quiet and make gentle the mind so that meditation can take place. The two together, external repetition and internal focus, function as an "excellent" way to lift the mind and heart to God. In addition, the portability of the rosary and its adaptability to time and place outside of official church functions commend it to our use.[17]

Creative women are also contributing to the prayerful remembrance of Mary by employing new forms and filling traditional genres with new insights. The Pax Christi "Litany of Mary of Nazareth" addresses her with new encomiums as a marginalized woman, seeker of sanctuary, and mother of an executed criminal.[18] Miriam Therese Winter's feminist lectionary and psalter imaginatively retells gospel stories from the perspective of Mary and other women and composes psalms that lift up women's yearnings to God.[19] Ann Johnson's series of new Magnificats of prophecy, of waiting, of desolation, and of hope sweeps the reader along in the company of Mary to praise the God of Israel.[20] All of these prayers honor Mary not by getting lost in admiration of her virtue but by bringing her in as a companion to the historic search for God's reign, including justice for women, now under way.

In that spirit, I close this book's exploration into Mary as friend of God and prophet in the communion of saints with her own gospel prayer, the Magnificat. While this canticle is a first-century Jewish-Christian hymn, like all good prayers it contains a dynamism that bridges the gap between past and present, between first and twenty-first centuries. A recent study of the use of the biblical psalms in prayer sheds light on how this dynamism works. The psalms of the Hebrew scriptures clearly reflect the ancient religious and cultural milieu in which they were composed. Yet when a community or an individual prays them today, time stretches and becomes fluid. Later generations slip into the role of the Israelites of old, participating in their world and relating to God along the lines of their experience. For example, some psalms recall the historical plight of the Hebrews enslaved in Egypt. These psalms then go on to rejoice in the way God led the people out toward freedom; to wonder at the providential guidance that got them through a dry and trackless desert; and to praise God for entering into covenant relationship with them. Millennia later, the experience of praying these psalms creates a dynamism whereby what God did for "them" becomes what God has done for "us." Rather than leaving these events in the past, the prayer form becomes an invitation to experience

God's gracious acts for ourselves and be transformed into persons of the covenant here and now. Again, after being accused of adultery by the prophet Nathan, David the king cries for mercy beginning with the memorable words, "Have mercy on me, O God, according to your steadfast love; according to your abundant mercy blot out my transgressions" (Ps. 51:1). Communities and individuals who pray that psalm today do not think that they are simply repeating David's plea as though in a theater production. Rather, identifying with his sinfulness, they allow these words of sorrow for a past historical misdeed to flow through the centuries and shape their own repentant relationship to God. The same holds true for psalms of lament, where someone under persecution cries out in agony. Those who pray them now identify experientially with those who suffered in the past and hope for the same help in time of trouble. In each of these examples, the dynamism of prayer connects us, even identifies us, with certain historical figures. But "biblical events refuse to be relegated to the past."[21] The prayer form itself draws us into their religious world and thereby we find ourselves situated in a certain relationship with God in our own day. Unlike past events that are simply reported, these situations remain continually relevant through the experiential connection set up by the dynamic of prayer. The oft-repeated invitation in Catholic liturgy to "say the prayer that Jesus taught us" reflects the same phenomenon, transporting people today into the position of the first-century Galilean disciples where they hallow God's name and ask for daily bread and forgiveness as if no time at all had passed.

In a similar manner, the Magnificat, claimed anew as a prophetic prayer by poor people across cultures and interpreted anew by women as a liberating word, structures a religious world. Like other great biblical prayers, Mary's song refuses to be relegated to the past. Entering into its cadences, the community at prayer identifies with Mary of Nazareth bearing the Messiah, pregnant with hope. We enter into her faith stance and relate to God along the lines of her witness. Time becomes permeable. Her passionate joy, protest, and hope flow through the centuries and become ours. Rather than praising her, we join with her in praising God and the surprising divine compassion poured out on a world run amok. In the process, our relationship to God takes on an intimate, liberating character which energizes action on behalf of justice. "And Mary said," and with her, this woman of Spirit, mother of Jesus, friend of God and prophet, we the community of disciples say:

My soul proclaims your greatness, O my God,
and my spirit rejoices in God, my Savior.
For your regard has blessed me, poor, and a serving woman.
From this day all generations will call me blessed,
for you, who are mighty, have done great things for me;
and holy is your Name.
Your mercy is on those who fear you, from generation to generation.
You have shown strength with your arm.
You have scattered the proud in their hearts' conceit.
You have put down the mighty from their thrones,
and have lifted up the lowly.
You have filled the hungry with good things,
and have sent the rich away empty.
You have helped your servant Israel,
remembering your mercy,
as you promised to Abraham and Sarah,
mercy to their children forever. (Luke 1:46–55)[22]

℮

Notes

CHAPTER 1
FRAGMENTS IN THE RUBBLE

1. The best compendium of this tradition remains Hilda Graef, *Mary: A History of Doctrine and Devotion* (London: Sheed & Ward; Westminster, Md.: Christian Classics, 1990; orig. two volumes, 1963, 1965). Excellent thematic charts of this tradition include: in theology, George H. Tavard, *The Thousand Faces of the Virgin Mary* (Michael Glazier Book; Collegeville, Minn.: Liturgical Press, 1996); in spirituality, Sally Cunneen, *In Search of Mary: The Woman and the Symbol* (New York: Ballantine Books, 1996); in culture, Jaroslav Pelikan, *Mary through the Centuries: Her Place in the History of Culture* (New Haven and London: Yale University Press, 1996). Marina Warner, in *Alone of All Her Sex: The Myth and the Cult of the Virgin Mary* (New York: Knopf, 1976), provides a wealth of historical detail coupled with judgment from a feminist perspective. For a more concise historical and systematic treatment, see Richard McBrien, "Mary," in *Catholicism* (San Francisco: HarperSanFrancisco, 1994), 1077–1121; and "Mary," in *Handbook of Catholic Theology,* ed. Wolfgang Beinert and Francis Schüssler Fiorenza (New York: Crossroad, 1995), 444–72.

2. This is the thesis of Georg Kretschmar and René Laurentin, "The Cult of the Saints," in *Confessing One Faith: A Joint Commentary on the Augsburg Confession by Lutheran and Catholic Theologians,* ed. George Forell and James McCue (Minneapolis: Augsburg, 1982), 279–80.

3. Els Maeckelberghe, *Desperately Seeking Mary: A Feminist Appropriation of a Traditional Religious Symbol* (Kampen, The Netherlands: Kok Pharos, 1991), 42.

4. The careful biblical work done by a team of ecumenical scholars led by Raymond E. Brown, Karl Paul Donfried, Joseph A. Fitzmyer, and John Reumann remains foundational; see *Mary in the New Testament,* ed. Raymond Brown et al. (New York: Paulist; Philadelphia: Fortress, 1978). Two of the most important dialogue studies are *The One Mediator, the Saints, and Mary: Lutherans and Catholics in Dialogue VIII,* ed. George Anderson, Francis Stafford, and Joseph Burgess

(Minneapolis: Augsburg Fortress, 1992); and the Groups des Dombes, *Marie dans le dessein de Dieu et la communion des saints* (Paris: Bayard Éditions & Centurion, 1999).

5. Vatican II, Declaration on the Relationship of the Church to Non-Christian Religions (*Nostra Aetate*) §3. All citations from the Second Vatican Council are from *The Documents of Vatican II,* ed. Walter Abbott (New York: America Press, 1966). For the Islamic view of Mary, see Tavard, *Thousand Faces of the Virgin Mary,* 32–45 ("Mariyam of Arabia"); R. J. McCarthy, "Mary in Islam," in *Mary's Place in Christian Dialogue,* ed. Alberic Stacpoole (Wilton, Conn.: Morehouse-Barlow, 1982), 202–13; and Aliah Schleifer, "Maryam in Morisco Literature," *Islamic Quarterly* 36 (1992): 242–61.

6. Maria Reis-Habito, "Maria-Kannon: The Mother of God in Buddhist Disguise," *Marian Studies* 47 (1996): 50–64; Kwok Pui-lan, *Chinese Women and Christianity* (Atlanta, Ga.: Scholars Press, 1992), 29–64; and Judith Martin, "Theologies of Feminine Mediation," *Journal of Dharma* 6 (1981): 384–97.

7. Vasiliki Limberis, *Divine Heiress: The Virgin Mary and the Creation of Christian Constantinople* (New York and London: Routledge, 1994); and A. Cameron, "The Cult of the Theotokos in Sixth Century Constantinople: A City Finds Its Symbol," *Journal of Theological Studies* 29 (1978): 79–108.

8. Barbara Corrado Pope, "Immaculate and Powerful: The Marian Revival in the Nineteenth Century," in *Immaculate and Powerful: The Female in Sacred Image and Social Reality,* ed. Clarissa Atkinson, Constance Buchanan, and Margaret Miles (Boston: Beacon, 1985), 177.

9. Robert Orsi, *The Madonna of 115th Street: Faith and Community in Italian Harlem, 1880–1950* (New Haven: Yale University Press, 1985).

10. Nicholas Perry and Loreto Echeverría connect the American version of this phenomenon to the broader tradition of militant marianism with roots in Byzantium and Rome (*Under the Heel of Mary* [London: Routledge, 1988]); see also Thomas Kselman and Steven Avella, "Marian Piety and the Cold War in the United States," in *Modern American Protestantism and Its World,* ed. Martin Marty (New York: K. G. Sauk, 1993), 175–96; and Michael Cuneo, *The Smoke of Satan: Conservative and Traditionalist Dissent in Contemporary American Catholicism* (New York: Oxford University Press, 1997), chapter 5, "Mystical Marianism and Apocalypticism," 121–77.

11. Ronald B. Taylor, *Chávez and the Farm Workers* (Boston: Beacon, 1975).

12. See n. 1.

13. John XXIII, *Pacem in Terris* §41, in *The Gospel of Peace and Justice,* ed. Joseph Gremillion (Maryknoll, N.Y.: Orbis, 1976), 209–10.

14. Rosemary Radford Ruether, "Mistress of Heaven: The Meaning of Mariology," in her *New Woman, New Earth: Sexist Ideologies and Human Liberation* (San Francisco: Harper & Row, 1975), 50; to my knowledge this is the earliest sustained feminist analysis of the subject.

15. Margaret Cuthbert, Cape Town, South Africa.

16. Sabina Lopez de Hernandez, Oaxaca, Mexico.

17. Warner, *Alone of All Her Sex,* xxi. The title is taken from a poem by Caelius Sedulius (fifth century):

> She . . . had no peer
> Either in our first mother or in all women
> Who were to come. But alone of all her sex
> She pleased the Lord.

18. Ibid., 338.

19. Mary Hines, *Whatever Happened to Mary?* (Notre Dame, Ind: Ave Maria Press, 2001), 8.

20. Hilda Buhay, O.S.B., "Who Is Mary?" in *Women and Religion: A Collection of Essays, Personal Histories, and Contextualized Liturgies,* ed. Mary John Manan-zan (Manila: St. Scholastica's College, 1992), 55.

21. Cited in Chung Hyun Kyung, *Struggle to Be the Sun Again: Introducing Asian Women's Theology* (Maryknoll, N.Y.: Orbis, 1994), 124 n. 12.

22. Elisabeth Behr-Sigel, "Mary and Women," *Sobornost: Eastern Churches Review* 23 (2001): 25.

23. Ibid., 32.

24. Rosa Maria Gil and Carmen Inoa Vazquez, *The Maria Paradox: How Lati-nas Can Merge Old World Traditions with New World Self-Esteem* (New York: Putnam, 1996), 266; Ten Commandments on p. 8. See also Evelyn Stevens, "Mari-anismo: The Other Face of Machismo in Latin America," in *Female and Male in Latin America,* ed. Ann Pescatello (Pittsburgh: University of Pittsburgh Press, 1973), 89–101.

25. Mary Gordon, "Coming to Terms with Mary," *Commonweal* (January 25, 1982): 11.

26. Rosemary Haughton, *The Re-creation of Eve* (Springfield, Ill.: Templegate, 1985), 119.

27. Paul Tillich, *Theology of Culture* (New York: Oxford University Press, 1964), 53–67.

28. Mary Jo Weaver, *New Catholic Women: A Contemporary Challenge to Tra-ditional Religious Authority* (Bloomington, Ind.: Indiana University Press, 1986), 203.

29. Gordon, "Coming to Terms with Mary," 12.

30. María Pilar Aquino, *Our Cry for Life: Feminist Theology from Latin Amer-ica* (Maryknoll, N.Y.: Orbis, 1993), 159.

31. Ivone Gebara and María Clara Bingemer, *Mary, Mother of God, Mother of the Poor,* trans. Phillip Berryman (Maryknoll, N.Y.: Orbis, 1989).

32. Cunneen, *In Search of Mary,* 14.

33. Diana Hayes, "And When We Speak: To Be Black, Catholic, and Womanist,"

in *Taking Down Our Harps: Black Catholics in the United States,* ed. Diana Hayes and Cyprian Davis (Maryknoll, N.Y.: Orbis, 1998), 113–14.

34. Jeanette Rodriquez, *Our Lady of Guadalupe: Faith and Empowerment among Mexican-American Women* (Austin: University of Texas, 1994), xxi; see also Ada María Isasi-Díaz and Yolanda Tarango, *Hispanic Women: Prophetic Voice in the Church—Toward a Hispanic Women's Liberation Theology* (San Francisco: Harper & Row, 1988).

35. Mary DeCock, "Our Lady of Guadalupe: Symbol of Liberation?" in *Mary according to Women,* ed. Carol Francis Jegen (Kansas City, Mo.: Leaven Press, 1985), 113–41. The question becomes more complex when Christian differences are taken into account: Nora Lozano-Díaz, "Ignored Virgin or Unaware Women: A Mexican-American Protestant Reflection on the Virgin of Guadalupe," in *A Reader in Latina Feminist Theology,* ed. María Pilar Aquino, Daisy Machado, Jeanette Rodriguez (Austin, Tex.: University of Texas Press, 2002), 204–26.

36. "Final Statement: Asian Church Women Speak," in *We Dare to Dream: Doing Theology as Asian Women,* ed. Virginia Fabella and Sun Ai Lee Park (Hong Kong: Asian Women's Resource Centre for Culture and Theology, 1989), 149.

37. Singapore Conference, "Summary Statement on Feminist Mariology," in *Feminist Theology from the Third World,* ed. Ursula King (Maryknoll, N.Y.: Orbis, 1994), 272.

38. From Nancy Fackner and Kathy Britt, C.S.J., Christmas 1987.

39. Pauline Warner, "Mary: A Two-edged Sword to Pierce our Hearts?" *Epworth Review* 18 (1991): 77. After this book had gone to press, a substantial new contribution appeared: *Blessed One: Protestant Perspectives on Mary,* ed. Beverly Roberts Gaventa and Cynthia Rigby (Louisville, Ky.: Westminster John Knox, 2002).

40. Cited in Kathleen Hurty, "Mary, Luther, and the Quest for Ecumenical Images," *Midstream* 30 (1991): 62.

41. Dorothee Soelle, "Mary Is a Sympathizer," in her *The Strength of the Weak,* trans. Robert and Rita Kimber (Philadelphia: Westminster, 1984), 47–48.

42. See the programmatic essay by Elisabeth Schüssler Fiorenza, "Breaking the Silence, Becoming Visible," in *The Power of Naming: A Concilium Reader in Feminist Liberation Theology,* ed. Elisabeth Schüssler Fiorenza (Maryknoll, N.Y.: Orbis, 1996), 161–74.

43. Mary Catherine Hilkert, *Speaking with Authority: Catherine of Siena and the Voices of Women Today* (New York: Paulist, 2001).

44. John XXIII, *Pacem in Terris,* §§39–45.

45. Karl Rahner, "Mary and the Christian Image of Woman," in *Theological Investigations,* volume 19, trans. Edward Quinn (New York: Crossroad, 1983), 217.

CHAPTER 2
WOMEN'S THEOLOGICAL WORK

1. Mary Farrell Bednarowski thus identifies the ambivalent position in which women discover themselves due to being excluded from significant sectors of a religious community to which they deeply belong (*The Religious Imagination of American Women* [Bloomington, Ind.: Indiana University Press, 1999], chapter 2). A particularly readable account of the problematic position of women in Christianity is Karen Armstrong, *The Gospel According to Woman* (New York: Doubleday, 1987).

2. The critical principle of feminist theology articulated by Rosemary Radford Ruether, *Sexism and God-Talk: Toward a Feminist Theology* (Boston: Beacon, 1983), 18.

3. For a survey of feminist theology on all continents, see Rosemary Radford Ruether, *Gender and Redemption: A Theological History* (Minneapolis: Fortress, 1998), chapters 6, 7, and 8. International writings are collected in *Feminist Theology in Different Contexts*, ed. Elisabeth Schüssler Fiorenza and M. Shawn Copeland (Maryknoll, N.Y.: Orbis, 1996); and *Power of Naming* (see chap. 1, n. 42).

4. For feminist theory as it intersects with theology, see *Religion and Gender*, ed. Ursula King (Oxford: Blackwell, 1995); *Horizons in Feminist Theology: Identity, Tradition, and Norms*, ed. Rebecca Chopp and Sheila Greeve Davaney (Minneapolis: Fortress, 1997); Serene Jones, *Feminist Theory and Christian Theology: Cartographies of Grace* (Minneapolis: Fortress, 2000); and *Feminism in the Study of Religion: A Reader*, ed. Darlene Juschka (New York: Continuum, 2001).

5. *The Beijing Declaration and The Platform for Action* (New York: United Nations, 1996), 2.

6. Adrienne Rich, *Of Woman Born: Motherhood as Experience and Institution* (New York: Norton, 1976), 56. See extended definitions in *Dictionary of Feminist Theologies*, ed. Letty Russell and J. Shannon Clarkson (Louisville, Ky.: Westminster John Knox, 1996); and Bonnie J. Fox, "Conceptualizing Patriarchy," in *Feminism in the Study of Religion*, ed. Juschka, 314–33.

7. Gerda Lerner, *The Creation of Patriarchy* (New York: Oxford University Press, 1986), 239.

8. Elisabeth Schüssler Fiorenza, "To Follow the Vision: The Jesus Movement as *Basileia* Movement," in *Liberating Eschatology: Essays in Honor of Letty M. Russell*, ed. Margaret Farley and Serene Jones (Louisville, Ky.: Westminster John Knox, 1999), 127; Schüssler Fiorenza coined the neologism *kyriarchy*. See the sharp critical analysis by M. Shawn Copeland, "Toward a Critical Christian Feminist Theology of Solidarity," in *Women and Theology*, ed. Mary Ann Hinsdale and Phyllis Kaminski (Maryknoll, N.Y.: Orbis, 1995), 3–38; and Elizabeth Spelman, *Inessential Woman: Problems of Exclusion in Feminist Thought* (Boston: Beacon, 1988).

9. Lerner, *Creation of Patriarchy*, 238. See also Joan W. Scott, "Gender: A Useful Category of Historical Analysis," *American Historical Review* 71 (1986): 1053–75; and Jones, *Feminist Theory and Christian Theology*, 22–48. For the contrary idea that sex, too, is socially constructed, see Judith Butler, *Gender Trouble: Feminism and the Subversion of Identity* (New York: Routledge, 1990), esp. chapter 1.

10. Sandra Schneiders, *Beyond Patching: Faith and Feminism in the Catholic Church* (New York: Paulist, 1991), 15.

11. Ada María Isasi-Díaz, *En la Lucha, In the Struggle: Elaborating a mujerista Theology* (Minneapolis: Fortress, 1993), 189.

12. Diverse positions are described by Serene Jones, "Women's Experience between a Rock and a Hard Place: Feminist, Womanist, and *Mujerista* Theologies in North America," in *Horizons in Feminist Theology*, ed. Chopp and Davaney, 33–53; and Anne Clifford, *Introducing Feminist Theology* (Maryknoll, N.Y.: Orbis, 2001), chapter 1.

13. Rita Nakashima Brock, *Journeys by Heart: A Christology of Erotic Power* (New York: Crossroad, 1988); Elisabeth Schüssler Fiorenza, *In Memory of Her: A Feminist Theological Reconstruction of Christian Origins* (New York: Crossroad, 1983); Anne Carr, *Transforming Grace: Women's Experience and Christian Tradition* (San Francisco: Harper & Row, 1988).

14. Cunneen, *In Search of Mary*, 269 (see chap. 1, n. 1).

15. Warner, *Alone of All Her Sex* (see chap. 1, n. 1).

16. Irenaeus, *Adversus Haereses* 3.31.1. See the studies by Walter Burghardt, "Mary in Western Patristic Thought," in *Mariology*, ed. Juniper Carol (Milwaukee: Bruce, 1957), 1:110–17, and "Mary in Eastern Patristic Thought," in *Mariology*, 2:88–100; and Robert Murray, "Mary, the Second Eve in the Early Syriac Fathers," *Eastern Churches Review* 3 (autumn 1971): 372–84.

17. Tertullian, *De cultu feminarum* (The Dress of Women), in *Corpus Christianorum, Series Latina*, volume 1 (Turnholt: Typographia Brepols, 1954), 343.

18. Susan Ashbrook Harvey, "Eve and Mary: Images of Women," *Modern Churchman* 24 (1981): 135; see also Nehama Aschkenasy, *Eve's Journey: Feminine Images in Hebraic Literary Tradition* (Philadelphia: University of Pennsylvania Press, 1986).

19. William Cole, "Thomas on Mary and Women: A Study in Contrasts," *University of Dayton Review* 12 (1975–76): 25–64.

20. Edward Schillebeeckx, *Mary, Mother of the Redemption* (London: Sheed & Ward, 1964), 172.

21. Leonie Liveris, "Time to speak: The voice of feminism in the Orthodox Church," in *Freedom and Entrapment: Women Thinking Theology*, ed. Maryanne Confoy, Dorothy Lee, and Joan Nowotny (North Blackburn, Victoria, Australia: HarperCollins, 1995), 198.

22. Ruether, "Mistress of Heaven," in *New Woman, New Earth*, 36–62 (see

chap. 1, n. 14); also "Mariology as Symbolic Ecclesiology," in her *Sexism and God-Talk*, 139–58.

23. René Laurentin, "Mary and Womanhood in the Renewal of Christian Anthropology," *Marian Library Studies* 1 (1969): 78.

24. Tissa Balasuriya, *Mary and Human Liberation* (Colombo, Sri Lanka: Centre for Society & Religion, 1990), 191, 7; being published as two volumes of *Logos*, vol. 29, nos. 1 and 2. See also *Mary and Human Liberation: The Debate*, ed. Helen Stanton (Valley Forge, Pa.: Trinity Press International, 1997).

25. Kari Børresen, "Mary in Catholic Theology," in *Mary in the Churches*, ed. Hans Küng and Jürgen Moltmann (Edinburgh: T & T Clark; New York: Seabury, 1985), 55.

26. Clarice Martin, "Womanist Interpretations of the New Testament," *Journal of Feminist Studies in Religion* 6 (1990): 41–66; see her "The *Haustafeln* (Household Codes) in African American Biblical Interpretation: 'Free Slaves' and 'Subordinate Women,'" in *Stony the Road We Trod: African American Biblical Interpretation*, ed. Cain Hope Felder (Minneapolis: Fortress, 1991), 206–31.

27. Delores Williams, *Sisters in the Wilderness: The Challenge of Womanist God-Talk* (Maryknoll, N.Y.: Orbis, 1993). See the lucid philological analysis of this term applied to marian texts by Marianne Sawicki, *Seeing the Lord: Resurrection and Early Christian Practices* (Minneapolis: Fortress, 1994), chapter 5, "Son of God's Slavewoman," 95–118.

28. Shawn Copeland, "Wading Through Many Sorrows: Toward a Theology of Suffering in Womanist Perspective," in *A Troubling in My Soul: Womanist Perspectives on Evil and Suffering*, ed. Emilie Townes (Maryknoll, N.Y.: Orbis, 1993), 122.

29. Jacquelyn Grant, "The Sin of Servanthood and the Deliverance of Discipleship," in *A Troubling in My Soul*, ed. Townes, 199–218.

30. Texts in Hilda Graef, *Mary: A History of Doctrine and Devotion*, 48–55 and 77–101 (see chap. 1, n. 1); and Elizabeth Clark, *Women in the Early Church* (Wilmington, Del.: Michael Glazier, 1983). The groundbreaking essay is Rosemary Radford Ruether, "Misogynism and Virginal Feminism in the Fathers of the Church," in *Religion and Sexism: Images of Woman in the Jewish and Christian Traditions*, ed. Rosemary Radford Ruether (New York: Simon & Schuster, 1974), 150–83. See also Peter Brown, *The Body and Society: Men, Women, and Sexual Renunciation in Early Christianity* (New York: Columbia University Press, 1988); Margaret Miles, *Carnal Knowing: Female Nakedness and Religious Meaning in the Christian West* (Boston: Beacon, 1989); and Mary T. Malone, *Women & Christianity*, volume 1, *The First Thousand Years* (Maryknoll, N.Y.: Orbis, 2001), 144–72.

31. Ute Ranke-Heinemann, *Eunuchs for the Kingdom of Heaven: Women, Sexuality, and the Catholic Church* (New York: Doubleday, 1990), 5; she notes that Michael Schmaus in his influential *Catholic Dogmatics* (5:109) argues that this assertion bears witness to "the unanimous teaching of the church" (*Katholische Dogmatik* [Munich: Max Heuber, 1958]).

32. David Hunter, "Helvidius, Jovinian, and the Virginity of Mary in Late Fourth-Century Rome," *Journal of Early Christian Studies* 1 (1993): 70–71. See Ranke-Heinemann, *Eunuchs for the Kingdom of Heaven*, 46–63; and "Notes on Mariology," 340–48; Warner, *Alone of All Her Sex*, 68-78; and Maurice Hamington, *Hail Mary? The Struggle for Ultimate Womanhood in Catholicism* (New York and London: Routledge, 1995), 53–87.

33. Rosemary Radford Ruether, "Mothers of the Church: Ascetic Women in the Late Patristic Age," in *Women of Spirit: Female Leadership in the Jewish and Christian Traditions*, ed. Rosemary Radford Ruether and Eleanor McLaughlin (New York: Simon & Schuster, 1979), 71–98.

34. Peter Brown, "The Notion of Virginity in the Early Church," in *Christian Spirituality*, volume 1, *Origins to the Twelfth Century*, ed. Bernard McGinn and John Meyendorff (New York: Crossroad, 1985), 427–43.

35. Jo Ann McNamara, *A New Song: Celibate Women in the First Three Christian Centuries* (New York: Haworth Press, 1983), 5.

36. Malone, *Women & Christianity*, 1:145. See also Elizabeth Castelli, "Virginity and Its Meaning for Women's Sexuality in Early Christianity," *Journal of Feminist Studies in Religion* 2, no. 1 (1986): 61–88; and Elizabeth Clark, *Ascetic Piety and Women's Faith: Essays on Late Ancient Christianity* (Lewiston, N.Y.: Edwin Mellen Press, 1986).

37. Sydney Callahan, "Mary and the Challenges of the Feminist Movement," *America* 169 (December 18–25, 1993): 14.

38. Susan Roll, *Toward the Origins of Christmas* (Kampen, The Netherlands: Kok Pharos, 1995), 219.

39. Sister Bernard Mncube, "Sexism in the Church and in the African Context," in *Women Hold Up Half the Sky: Women in the Church in South Africa*, ed. Denise Ackerman, Jonathan Draper, and Emma Mashinini (Pietermaritzburg, South Africa: Cluster Pub., 1991), 358–59.

40. James Preston, "Conclusion: New Perspectives on Mother Worship," in *Mother Worship*, ed. James Preston (Chapel Hill: University of North Carolina Press, 1982), 335.

41. Jean Shinoda Bolen, *Goddesses in Everywoman: A New Psychology of Women* (New York: Harper, 1984), 36. See Jennifer Dines, "Mary and the Archetypes," *The Month* (August–September 1987): 288–94.

42. Marianne Katoppo, "Woman's Image of Herself," in *The Emerging Christian Woman: Church and Society Perspectives*, ed. Stella Faria, Anne Vareed Alexander, and Jessie Tellis-Nyak (Ishvani: Satprakashan Sanchar Kendra, 1984), 72; and Rita Monteiro, quoted in *Exploring Feminist Visions*, ed. Frances Maria Yasas and Vera Mehta (Bombay and Pune, India: Streevani; Ishvani: Kendra, 1990), 224–25.

43. Catharina Halkes, "Mary in My Life," in *Mary, Yesterday, Today, Tomorrow*, by Edward Schillebeeckx and Catharina Halkes (New York: Crossroad, 1993), 75.

44. Augustine, *City of God*, trans. Marcus Dods (New York: Random House,

1994), 22–23: "Of the Violence Which May Be Done to the Body by Another's Lust, While the Mind Remains Inviolate" (1.18).

45. Vatican II, Dogmatic Constitution on the Church (*Lumen Gentium*) §64.

46. Chung Hyun Kyung, *Struggle to Be the Sun Again*, 77 (see chap. 1, n. 21), citing Marianne Katoppo, *Compassionate and Free: An Asian Woman's Theology* (Maryknoll, N.Y.: Orbis, 1981), 20.

47. Barbara Jane Coleman, personal correspondence.

48. Harvey, "Eve and Mary," 134.

49. René Laurentin, *The Question of Mary* (New York: Holt, Rinehart and Winston, 1965), 72ff.

50. Elizabeth Johnson, "Mary as Mediatrix," in *The One Mediator, the Saints, and Mary*, ed. G. Anderson et al., 311–26 (see chap. 1, n. 4).

51. Adrienne Rich, *Of Woman Born: Motherhood as Experience and Institution* (New York: W. W. Norton, 1986); and *Motherhood: Experience, Institution, Theology*, ed. Anne Carr and Elisabeth Schüssler Fiorenza (Edinburgh: T & T Clark, 1989).

52. See a good description in Sallie McFague, "God as Mother," in her *Models of God: Theology for an Ecological, Nuclear Age* (Philadelphia: Fortress, 1987), 97–123.

53. Kathleen Norris, *Meditations on Mary* (New York: Penguin Putnam, 1999), 22.

54. Ranke-Heinemann, *Eunuchs for the Kingdom of Heaven*, 346.

55. See the powerful essay endorsing the religious worth of herself as a childless woman by Mercy Amba Oduyoye, "A Coming Home to Myself: The Childless Woman in the West African Space," in *Liberating Eschatology*, ed. Farley and Jones, 105–20.

56. Jean Galôt, *L'église et la femme* (Gembloux: J. Duculot, 1965), 57. See the review of this issue by James Mackey, "The Use and Abuse of Mary in Roman Catholicism," in *Who Needs Feminism? Male Responses to Sexism in the Church*, ed. Richard Holloway (London: SPCK, 1991), 99–116; and Una Cadegan and James Heft, "Mary of Nazareth, Feminism, and the Tradition," *Thought* 65 (1990): 169–89.

57. Megan Walker, "Mary of Nazareth in Feminist Perspective: Towards a Liberating Mariology," in *Women Hold Up Half the Sky*, ed. Ackerman et al., 145.

58. Ruether, *Sexism and God-Talk*, 157; for the whole discussion, see pp. 139–58.

59. Weaver, *New Catholic Women*, 201–11 (see chap. 1, n. 28).

60. Elisabeth Moltmann-Wendel, *A Land Flowing with Milk and Honey: Perspectives on Feminist Theology* (New York: Crossroad, 1985), 194; see also her "Motherhood or Friendship," in *Mary in the Churches*, ed. Küng and Moltmann, 17–22.

61. Sarah Coakley, "Mariology and Romantic Feminism: A Critique," in

Women's Voices: Essays in Contemporary Feminist Theology, ed. Teresa Elwes (London: Marshall Pickering, 1992), 97–110.

62. Mary Daly, *Beyond God the Father* (Boston: Beacon, 1973), 84; see pp. 82–90.

63. Julia Kristeva, "Stabat Mater," in *The Kristeva Reader*, ed. T. Moi (Oxford: Blackwell, 1986), 160–86; see Phyllis Kaminski, "Kristeva and the Cross," in *Women and Theology*, ed. Hinsdale and Kaminski, 234–57.

64. Leonardo Boff, *The Maternal Face of God: The Feminine and Its Religious Expression*, trans. Robert Barr and John Diercksmeier (Maryknoll, N.Y.: Orbis, 1987), 79.

65. Ibid., 13.

66. Elisabeth Schüssler Fiorenza, *Jesus: Miriam's Child, Sophia's Prophet* (New York: Continuum, 1994), 168.

67. Ibid., 174.

68. Els Maeckelberghe, *Desperately Seeking Mary* (see chap. 1, n. 3).

69. Aquino, *Our Cry for Life* (see chap. 1, n. 30); Isasi-Díaz, *En la Lucha: Elaborating a Mujerista Theology*.

70. *Mary according to Women*, ed. Jegen (see chap. 1, n. 35).

71. Mary Grey, "Reclaiming Mary: A Task for Feminist Theology," *The Way* 29 (1989): 334–40; and Patricia Noone, *Mary for Today* (Chicago: Thomas More Press, 1977).

CHAPTER 3
CUL-DE-SAC: THE IDEAL FACE OF WOMAN

1. *In the Embrace of God: Feminist Approaches to Theological Anthropology*, ed. Ann O'Hara Graff (Maryknoll, N.Y.: Orbis, 1995); and Jane Kopas, "Beyond Mere Gender: Transforming Theological Anthropology," in *Women and Theology*, ed. Hinsdale and Kaminski, 216–33 (see chap. 2, n. 8).

2. Thomas Aquinas, *Summa Theologiae*, q. 92, a. 1.

3. Jerome, *Comm. In epist. ad Ephes.* 3.5 (in *Patrologiae cursus completus: Series latina*, ed. J. P. Migne [Paris, 1857–66], 26:567). See Kari Vogt, "Becoming Male: A Gnostic and Early Christian Metaphor," in *The Image of God: Gender Models in Judeo-Christian Tradition*, ed. Kari Elisabeth Børresen (Minneapolis: Fortress, 1995), 170–86; Kari Elisabeth Børessen, *Subordination and Equivalence: The Nature and Role of Woman in Augustine and Thomas Aquinas* (Lanham, Md: University Press of America, 1981); and Eleanor McLaughlin, "Equality of Souls, Inequality of Bodies: Woman in Medieval Theology," in *Religion and Sexism*, ed. Ruether, 213–66 (see chap. 2, n. 30).

4. Aschkenasy, *Eve's Journey*, 13 (see chap. 2, n. 18). See also the programmatic

study by Elizabeth Clark, "Women, Gender, and the Study of Christian History," *Church History* 70 (2001): 395–426.

5. Carol A. Newsom, "Woman and the Discourse of Patriarchal Wisdom: A Study of Proverbs 1–9," in *Gender and Difference in Ancient Israel*, ed. Peggy L. Day (Minneapolis: Fortress, 1989), 142–60.

6. Sarah Grimké, *Letters on the Equality of the Sexes and the Condition of Woman* (1838; New York: Burt Franklin, 1970), 3–4; quoted in Carolyn DeSwarte Gifford, "American Women and the Bible: The Nature of Woman as a Hermeneutical Issue," in *Feminist Perspectives on Biblical Scholarship*, ed. Adela Yarbro Collins (Chico, Calif.: Scholars Press, 1985), 19.

7. Catherine LaCugna, "God in Communion with Us: The Trinity," in *Freeing Theology: The Essentials of Theology in Feminist Perspective*, ed. Catherine LaCugna (San Francisco: HarperSanFrancisco, 1993), 99.

8. Ann Loades, "The Virgin Mary and the Feminist Quest," in *After Eve: Women, Theology, and the Christian Tradition*, ed. Janet Soskice (London: Collins Marshall Pickering, 1990), 168.

9. See the exegesis of Phyllis Trible, *God and the Rhetoric of Sexuality* (Philadelphia: Fortress, 1978), 1–30.

10. These anthropological constants are adapted from Edward Schillebeeckx, *Christ: The Experience of Jesus as Lord*, trans. John Bowden (New York: Seabury, 1980), 731–43; see also Colleen Griffiths, "Human Bodiliness: Sameness as Starting Point," in *The Church Women Want: Catholic Women in Dialogue*, ed. Elizabeth Johnson (New York: Crossroad, 2002), 60–67.

11. The importance of women's difference from each other is delineated in Katherine Zappone, "'Women's Special Nature': A Different Horizon for Theological Anthropology," in *The Special Nature of Women?* ed. Anne Carr and Elisabeth Schüssler Fiorenza (Philadelphia: Trinity Press International, 1991), 87–97; all the essays in this collection contribute excellent insight.

12. Natalie Angiers gives a marvelous tour of female biology (*Women: An Intimate Geography* [Boston and New York: Houghton Mifflin, 1999]).

13. By now classic studies include Jean Baker Miller, *Toward a New Psychology of Women* (Boston: Beacon, 1976); Carol Gilligan, *In a Different Voice: Psychological Theory and Women's Development* (Cambridge, Mass.: Harvard University Press, 1982); Mary Field Belenky, Blythe McVicker Clinchy, Nancy Rule Goldberger, and Jill Mattuck Tarule, *Women's Ways of Knowing: The Development of Self, Voice, and Mind* (New York: Basic Books, 1986); *Embodied Love: Sensuality and Relationship as Feminist Values*, ed. Paula Cooey, Sharon Farmer, and Mary Ellen Ross (San Francisco: Harper & Row, 1987); and especially Catherine Keller, *From a Broken Web: Separation, Sexism and Self* (Boston: Beacon, 1986).

14. Margaret Farley, "New Patterns of Relationship: Beginnings of a Moral Revolution," *Theological Studies* 36 (1975): 627–46; see also *Weaving the Visions: New Patterns in Feminist Spirituality*, ed. Judith Plaskow and Carol Christ (San

Francisco: Harper & Row, 1989); and Katherine Zappone, *The Hope for Wholeness: A Spirituality for Feminists* (Mystic, Conn.: Twenty-Third Pub., 1991).

15. Sara Ruddick, *Maternal Thinking: Toward a Politics of Peace* (Boston: Beacon, 1989); Nel Noddings, *Caring: A Feminine Approach to Ethics and Moral Education* (Berkeley: University of California Press, 1984).

16. Ruether, *Sexism and God-Talk*, 159–92 (see chap. 2, n. 2). The initial trumpet was sounded by Valerie Saiving, whose essay on sin and grace as experienced differently by women and men pioneered this paradigm shift: "The Human Situation: A Feminine View," *Journal of Religion* 40 (1960): 100–112.

17. Boff, *Maternal Face of God*, 2, 18 (see chap. 2, n. 64).

18. Ibid., 54.

19. Ibid., 91.

20. Ibid., 189.

21. Hans Urs von Balthasar, *Mary for Today*, trans. Robert Nowell (San Francisco: Ignatius Press, 1987), 62–63, 74.

22. Hans Urs von Balthasar, *The Glory of the Lord: A Theological Aesthetics*, volume 1, *Seeing the Form*, trans. Erasmo Leiva-Merikakis (San Francisco: Ignatius Press; New York: Crossroad, 1982), 338–65. For insightful analysis, see Walter Brennan, "The Issue of Archetypes in Marian Devotion," *Marianum: Ephemerides Mariologiae* 52 (1990): 17–41.

23. Hans Urs von Balthasar, *Love Alone: The Way of Revelation* (London: Burns & Oates, 1968) 63, with reference to *parastēsai* (2 Cor. 11:2 and Eph. 5:27) and *kecharitomenē* (Luke 1:28).

24. *The von Balthasar Reader*, ed. Medard Kehl and Werner Löser, trans. Robert Daly and Fred Lawrence (New York: Crossroad, 1988), 228 (cited from *Klarstellungen*, 59–64).

25. Hans Urs von Balthasar, "The Marian Principle," *Communio* 15 (1988): 129.

26. Hans Urs von Balthasar, *Theodramatik* II/2, 326, cited in Antonio Sicari, "Mary, Peter, and John: Figures of the Church," *Communio* 19 (1992): 200.

27. Balthasar, *Reader*, 213 (cited from *Der antirömische Affekt*, 115–23).

28. Balthasar, in *Theodramatik* III, cited in Edward Oakes, *Pattern of Redemption: The Theology of Hans Urs von Balthasar* (New York: Continuum, 1994), 262, with clarifying discussion, 250–73.

29. James Heft, "Marian Themes in the Writing of Hans Urs von Balthasar," *Communio* 7 (1980): 127–39. For further analysis of the patriarchal feminine, see Rosemary Radford Ruether, "The Female Nature of God: A Problem in Contemporary Religious Life," in *God as Father?* ed. Johannes Baptist Metz and Edward Schillebeeckx (New York: Seabury Press, 1981), 65; eadem, "Mariology as Symbolic Ecclesiology: Repression or Liberation?" in her *Sexism and God-Talk*, 139–58 (see chap. 2, n. 2).

30. John Paul II, Apostolic Letter *Mulieres dignitatem* (On the Dignity and Vocation of Women), *Origins* 18, no. 17 (October 6, 1988), §6.

31. Ibid., §30. For background, see Richard Leonard, *Beloved Daughters: 100 Years of Papal Teaching on Women* (Melbourne, Australia: David Lovell Pub., 1995).

32. John Paul II, *Mulieres dignitatem* §29. Christine Gudorf presents clarifying background ("Encountering the Other: The Modern Papacy on Women," in *Feminist Ethics and the Catholic Moral Tradition*, ed. Charles Curran, Margaret Farley, and Richard McCormick [New York: Paulist, 1996], 66–89).

33. John Paul II, *Mulieres dignitatem* §§29, 10.

34. Ibid., §26.

35. Ibid., §5.

36. John Paul II, *Theotokos: Woman, Mother, Disciple: A Catechesis on Mary, Mother of God* (Boston: Pauline Books and Media, 2000), 45, 43.

37. John Paul II, Encyclical *Redemptoris mater* (Mother of the Redeemer), *Origins* 16, no. 43 (April 9, 1987): §46.

38. John Paul II, *Mulieres dignitatem* §27 and n. 55.

39. John Paul II, *Theotokos*, 18.

40. John Paul II, *Redemptoris mater* §26.

41. John van den Hengel, "Mary: Miriam of Nazareth or the Symbol of the Eternal Feminine?" *Science et Esprit* 37 (1985): 319–33.

42. Raimundo Panikkar, "The Marian Dimensions of Life," *Epiphany* 4 (summer 1984): 4.

43. John Macquarrie, "God and the Feminine," *The Way: Supplement* 25 (1975): 9.

44. Pelikan, *Mary through the Centuries*, 223 (see chap. 1, n. 1). See also his *The Eternal Feminine* (New Brunswick, N.J.: Rutgers University Press, 1990), especially 101–19.

45. Elisabeth Schüssler Fiorenza, "Feminist Theology as a Critical Theology of Liberation," *Theological Studies* 36 (1975): 623.

46. See the essays in *Sexual Diversity and Catholicism: Toward the Development of Moral Theology*, ed. Patricia Beattie Jung and Joseph Andrew Coray (Collegeville, Minn.: Liturgical Press, 2001).

47. Suzanne Pullon Fitch and Roseann M. Mandziuk, *Sojourner Truth as Orator: Wit, Story, and Song* (Westport, Conn.: Greenwood Press, 1997). The authors present three different versions of this speech (pp. 103–8), with literary analysis of differences between texts (pp. 72–75).

48. Ruether, *Sexism and God-Talk*, 174.

49. Newsom, "Woman and the Discourse of Patriarchal Wisdom: A Study of Proverbs 1–9," 155.

50. Gebara and Bingemer, *Mary, Mother of God, Mother of the Poor*, 1–19 (see chap. 1, n. 31).

51. Irene Zimmerman, "Liturgy," in *Womenpsalms*, compiled by Julia Ahlers,

Rosemary Broughton, and Carol Koch (Winona, Minn.: St. Mary's Press, 1992), 55–56.

CHAPTER 4
CUL-DE-SAC: THE MATERNAL FACE OF GOD

1. These quotations are taken from Teilhard de Chardin's letters, quoted in *The Eternal Feminine: A Study on the Poem by Teilhard de Chardin*, ed. Henri de Lubac, trans. René Hague (London: Collins, 1971), 126 and 125. This chapter is adapted from Elizabeth Johnson, "Mary and the Female Face of God," *Theological Studies* 50 (1989): 500–526.

2. John Paul II, "Letter to Women," *Origins* 25, no. 9 (July 27, 1995): 137–43, no. 3; on the occasion of the U.N.-sponsored Beijing Conference on Women.

3. For this evocative metaphor of mining the marian tradition I am indebted to Lawrence Cunningham, *Mother of God* (San Francisco: Harper & Row, 1982), 103.

4. Hugo Rahner, *Greek Myths and Christian Mysteries*, trans. Brian Battershaw (New York: Harper & Row, 1963), 13.

5. Jean Daniélou, "Le culte marial et le paganisme," in *Maria: Etudes sur la Sainte Vierge*, ed. D'Hubert du Manoir (Paris: Beauchesne et ses Fils, 1949), 159–81.

6. The thesis is explored further in Warner, *Alone of All Her Sex*, passim (see chap. 1, n. 1); Gail Paterson Corrington, *Her Image of Salvation: Female Saviors and Formative Christianity* (Louisville, Ky.: Westminster John Knox, 1992); Joan Chamberlain Engelsman, *The Feminine Dimension of the Divine* (Philadelphia: Westminster Press, 1979), 122–33; Stephen Benko, *The Virgin Goddess: Studies in the Pagan and Christian Roots of Mariology* (Leiden and New York: E. J. Brill, 1993); and R. E. Witt, *Isis in the Graeco-Roman World* (Ithaca, N.Y.: Cornell University Press, 1971), 269–81. Witt concludes his study of the influence of the Egyptian goddess Isis on mariology with the observation that Christians should acknowledge that the roots of their religion were abundantly watered not only by the Jordan but also by the Nile (p. 280).

7. Leonard Moss and Stephen Cappannari, "In Quest of the Black Virgin: She Is Black Because She Is Black," in *Mother Worship*, ed. Preston, 53–74 (see chap. 2, n. 40).

8. Graef, *Mary: A History of Doctrine and Devotion*, 48 (see chap. 1, n. 1). See linguistic analysis of Greek and Latin versions by Gerard Sloyan, "Marian Prayers," in *Mariology*, ed. Juniper Carol (Milwaukee: Bruce, 1960), 3:64–68.

9. *Akathistos: Byzantine Hymn to the Mother of God*, trans. Paul Addison

(Rome: Mater Ecclesiae Centre, 1983); an accessible translation appears in the *Appendix* of Limberis, *Divine Heiress*, 149–58 (see chap. 1, n. 7).

10. "Great indeed, after her brief eclipse, was Diana of the Ephesians"—wry comment of Geoffrey Ashe, *The Virgin* (London: Routledge & Kegan Paul, 1976), 191.

11. Epiphanius, *Panarion* 79.4, 7; see Graef, *Mary: A History of Doctrine and Devotion*, 70–73. Ashe develops the thesis that this sect, with its attractive worship of Mary, was a threatening rival to the developing Catholic Church (*Virgin*, 149–71 ["The Seventy-Ninth Heresy"]).

12. See Jaroslav Pelikan, *The Growth of Medieval Theology* (Chicago: University of Chicago Press, 1978), 158–74; Walter Delius, *Geschichte der Marienverehrung* (Munich: E. Reinhardt Verlag, 1963), 149–70; and Heiko Oberman, *The Harvest of Medieval Theology* (Cambridge, Mass.: Harvard University Press, 1963), 281–322, especially "Mariological Rules" (pp. 304–8).

13. Anselm of Canterbury, "Prayer to St. Mary (3)," in *The Prayers and Meditations of St. Anselm*, trans. Benedicta Ward (New York: Penguin Books, 1973), 121.

14. Psalm 96/97, in *The Mirror of the Blessed Virgin Mary and The Psalter of Our Lady*, trans. Sr. Mary Emmanuel (St. Louis: B. Herder Book, 1932), 254.

15. Ibid., 294–95.

16. For this and the following examples see Jaroslav Pelikan, *Reformation of Church and Dogma (1300–1700)* (Chicago: University of Chicago Press, 1984), 38–50; and Graef, *Mary: A History of Doctrine and Devotion*, 241–322.

17. Gen. 1:2; and Pss. 17:8; 36:7; 57:1; 61:4; 91:1, 4; Isa. 31:5; and Exod. 19:4; Deut 32:11–12.

18. Robert Murray, "The Holy Spirit as Mother," in *Symbols of Church and Kingdom* (London: Cambridge University Press, 1975), 315.

19. Schillebeeckx, *Mary, Mother of the Redemption*, 113–14 (see chap. 2, n. 20); a similar approach is found in Andrew Greeley, *The Mary Myth: On the Femininity of God* (New York: Seabury, 1977).

20. Edward Schillebeeckx and Catharina Halkes, *Mary: Yesterday, Today, Tomorrow* (New York: Crossroad, 1993), 12–42. See Elizabeth Johnson, "Mary and Contemporary Christology," *Église et Théologie* 15 (1984): 155–82, which traces retrenchment in Schillebeeckx's and Rahner's approach to Mary as a result of their immersion in contemporary christology.

21. Thus A. M. Allchin, *The Joy of All Creation: An Anglican Meditation on the Place of Mary* (Cambridge: Cowley Pub., 1984); John Macquarrie, "God and the Feminine," *The Way Supplement* 25 (1975): 5–13; and Catholica-Arbeitskreis der VELKD, "Maria: Evangelische Fragen und Gesichtspunkte: Eine Einladung zum Gespräch," *Una Sancta* 37 (1982): 184–201.

22. Yves Congar, *I Believe in the Holy Spirit*, volume 1, trans. David Smith (New York: Seabury, 1983), especially 159–66; and his *Christ, Our Lady, and the*

Church: A Study in Eirenic Theology, trans. Henry St. John (Westminster, Md.: Newman Press, 1956); René Laurentin, "Esprit Saint et théologie mariale," *Nouvelle Revue Théologique* 89 (1967): 26–42; Heribert Mühlen, *Una mystica persona: Die Kirche als das Mysterium der Identität des Heiligen Geistes in Christus und den Christen* (Munich: Schöningh, 1968), 461–94; and Leon Cardinal Suenens, "The Relation that Exists between the Holy Spirit and Mary," in *Mary's Place in Christian Dialogue,* ed. Stacpoole, 69–78 (see chap. 1, n. 5). But see the feminist critique of Congar by Sarah Coakley, "Femininity and the Holy Spirit?"in *Mirror to the Church: Reflections on Sexism,* ed. Monica Furlong (London: SPCK, 1988), 124–35.

23. Elsie Gibson, "Mary and the Protestant Mind," *Review for Religious* 24 (1965): 397.

24. Boff, *Maternal Face of God,* 93 (see chap. 2, n. 64).

25. Børresen, "Mary in Catholic Theology," in *Mary in the Churches,* 54–55 (see chap. 2, n. 25); Jean Galôt, "Marie et le visage de Dieu," *Marianum* 44 (1982): 427–38; J.-M. Hennaux, "L'Esprit et le féminin: la mariologie de Leonardo Boff," *Nouvelle Revue Théologique* 109 (1987): 884–95.

26. Major collections through the 1990s include *Frontiers of Hispanic Theology in the United States,* ed. Alla Figueroa Deck (Maryknoll, N.Y.: Orbis, 1992); *We Are a People! Initiatives in Hispanic American Theology,* ed. Roberto Goizueta (Philadelphia: Fortress, 1992); Justo Gonzalez, *Voces: Voices from the Hispanic Church* (Nashville: Abingdon, 1992); *Hispanic/Latino Theology: Challenge and Promise,* ed. Ada María Isasi-Díaz and Fernando Segovia (Minneapolis: Fortress, 1996); *Teología en Conjunto: A Collaborative Hispanic Protestant Theology,* ed. José Rodríguez and Loida Martell (Louisville, Ky: Westminster John Knox, 1997); and *From the Heart of Our People: Latino/a Explorations in Catholic Systematic Theology,* ed. Orlando Espín and Miguel Díaz (Maryknoll, N.Y.: Orbis, 1999).

27. Virgil Elizondo, *Guadalupe: Mother of the New Creation* (Maryknoll, N.Y.: Orbis, 1998), 126.

28. Ibid., 127.

29. Virgil Elizondo, "Mary and the Poor: A Model of Evangelizing," in *Mary in the Churches,* 64; and his "Our Lady of Guadalupe as a Cultural Symbol: The Power of the Powerless," in *Liturgy and Cultural Religious Traditions,* ed. Herman Schmidt and David Power (New York: Seabury, 1977), 25–33.

30. Orlando Espín, *The Faith of the People: Theological Reflections on Popular Catholicism* (Maryknoll, N.Y.: Orbis, 1997), 8.

31. Ibid., 9; see especially 6–10, 73–77.

32. Orlando Espín, "An Exploration into the Theology of Grace and Sin," in *From the Heart of Our People,* ed. Espín and Díaz, 121–52, at 150 n. 37.

33. Miguel Díaz, *On Being Human: U.S. Hispanic and Rahnerian Perspectives* (Maryknoll, N.Y.: Orbis, 2001), 125.

34. Elisabeth Schüssler Fiorenza, "Feminist Spirituality, Christian Identity, and Catholic Vision," in *Womanspirit Rising*, ed. Carol Christ and Judith Plaskow (San Francisco: Harper & Row, 1979), 136–48.

35. McFague, *Models of God*, 97–123 (see chap. 2, n. 52).

36. John Paul I, *Osservatore Romano*, September 21, 1978, 2. See the metaphor of God as Mother in Elizabeth Johnson, *She Who Is: The Mystery of God in Feminist Theological Discourse* (New York: Crossroad, 1982), 170–87.

37. Trible, *God and the Rhetoric of Sexuality*, 31–71 (see chap. 3, n. 9).

38. Patricia Fox, "Mother of Mercy: Reclaiming a Title for God," *Listen: Journal of the Sisters of Mercy of Australia* 14, no. 1 (1996): 25–30.

39. Both this and the preceding title are taken from the Litany of Loreto; see also the *Akathistos Hymn* for similar titles.

40. Examples abound in Paule Bétérous, *Les Collections de Miracles de la Vierge en Gallo et Ibéro-Roman au XIII Siècle*, Marian Library Studies 15–16 (Dayton, Oh.: University of Dayton Press, 1983–84); and Johannes Herolt [Discipulus], *Miracles of the Blessed Virgin Mary*, trans. C. Bland (London: Routledge, 1929).

41. Anselm, "Prayer to St. Mary (2)," in *Prayers and Meditations of St. Anselm*, trans. Ward, 110.

42. John Paul II, Encyclical *Redemptor hominis* (Washington, D.C.: United States Catholic Conference, 1979), §22.

43. *A Hopkins Reader*, ed. John Pick (Garden City, N.Y.: Doubleday, 1966), 70–73.

44. Ibid., 56–57. See analysis of symbols that connect Mary with natural life by René Laurentin, "Foi et mythe en théologie mariale," *Nouvelle Revue Théologique* 89 (1967): 281–307.

45. Anselm, "Prayer to St. Mary (3)," in *Prayers and Meditations of St. Anselm*, trans. Ward, 120.

46. "Mary of Nazareth, Sign of God's Liberation," in *Celebrating Women Witnesses* (Cleveland: FutureChurch, 2000).

CHAPTER 5
A MODEST PROPOSAL

1. Wolfhart Pannenberg, "Mary, Redemption, and Unity," *Una Sancta* [Chicago] 24, no. 1 (1967): 62–68.

2. Raymond E. Brown, "The Meaning of Modern New Testament Studies for an Ecumenical Understanding of Mary," in his *Biblical Reflections on Crises Facing the Church* (New York: Paulist Press, 1975), 105. Patrick Bearsley develops Brown's idea in "Mary the Perfect Disciple: A Paradigm for Mariology," *Theological Studies* 41 (1980): 461–504.

3. Brown, *Biblical Reflections,* 107.

✓ 4. Karl Rahner, *Mary, Mother of the Lord,* trans. W. J. O'Hara (New York: Herder & Herder, 1963), 30.

5. Vatican II, Dogmatic Constitution on the Church (*Lumen Gentium*), §63.

6. Vatican II, Constitution on the Sacred Liturgy (*Sacrosanctum Concilium*), §103. The habit of referring to the church with a female pronoun is highly problematic, rooted as it is in the patriarchal masculine–feminine gender system.

7. United States Catholic Bishops, *Behold Your Mother: Woman of Faith,* published in *Catholic Mind* 72 (May 1974): 26–64; citations from §§35 and 111.

8. Max Thurian, *Mary, Mother of the Lord, Figure of the Church* (London: Faith Press, 1963); and Lukas Vischer, "Mary: Symbol of the Church, Symbol of Humankind," *Mid-Stream: An Ecumenical Journal* 17 (1978): 1–12.

9. Rosemary Radford Ruether, *Mary, The Feminine Face of the Church* (Philadelphia: Westminster, 1977).

10. Elizabeth Johnson, "The Symbolic Character of Theological Statements about Mary," *Journal of Ecumenical Studies* 22 (1985): 313.

11. Ibid., 327; see Paul Ricoeur, *The Symbolism of Evil* (Boston: Beacon, 1967).

12. U.S. Catholic Bishops, *Behold Your Mother,* §102.

13. Ibid., §61.

14. Vatican II, Dogmatic Constitution on the Church (*Lumen Gentium*), §68.

15. John van den Hengel presents a good survey of these two options ("Mary: Miriam of Nazareth or Symbol of the Eternal Feminine," *Science et Esprit* 37 [1985]: 319–33).

16. Karl Rahner, "Christianity's Absolute Claim," *Theological Investigations,* volume 21, trans. Hugh Riley (New York: Crossroad, 1988), 176.

17. Vatican II, Dogmatic Constitution on the Church (*Lumen Gentium*), §58.

18. J. N. D. Kelly, *Early Christian Creeds* (London: Longman, 1972), 391, emended for inclusivity; see full discussion on pp. 388–97.

✓ 19. Schillebeeckx, *Christ,* 641 (see chap. 3, n. 10). In this discussion of the creed I am borrowing liberally and with gratitude from his description of the four structural elements of Christian faith (pp. 629–44).

20. Ibid., 641.

21. See essays by Audre Lorde, *Sister Outsider* (Freedom, Calif.: Crossing Press, 1984), especially "Age, Race, Class, and Sex: Women Redefining Difference" (pp. 114–23). See also Anne Pattel-Gray, "Not yet Tiddas: An Aboriginal womanist critique of Australian Church feminism," in *Freedom and Entrapment,* ed. Confoy et al., 165–92 (see chap. 2, n. 21).

22. Lisa Cahill, "Feminist Ethics, Differences, and Common Ground: A Catholic Perspective," in *Feminist Ethics and the Catholic Moral Tradition,* ed. Curran et al., 184 (see chap. 3, n. 32); see, however, the ongoing critique of white racism in feminist thought by Ellen Armour, *Deconstruction, Feminist Theology, and the Problem of Difference: Subverting the Race/Gender Divide* (Chicago: Uni-

versity of Chicago Press, 1999).

23. M. Shawn Copeland, "Toward a Critical Christian Feminist Theology of Solidarity," in *Women and Theology*, ed. Hinsdale and Kaminski, 3 (see chap. 2, n. 8); see also her "Difference as a Category in Critical Theologies for the Liberation of Women," in *Feminist Theology in Different Contexts*, ed. Schüssler Fiorenza and Copeland, 141–51 (see chap. 2, n. 3).

24. Lorde, *Sister Outsider*, 111–12. This idea is developed by Sharon Welch, "An Ethic of Solidarity and Difference," in her *A Feminist Ethic of Risk* (Minneapolis: Fortress, 1990), 123–51.

25. Bernadette Brooten, "Jewish Women's History in the Roman Period: A Task for Christian Theology," *Harvard Theological Review* 79 (1986): 29—an insightful programmatic essay.

26. Rahner, *Mary, Mother of the Lord*, 52. This approach is fruitful for Christian dialogue, as affirmed by Harding Meyer, "The Ecumenical Unburdening of the Mariological Problem: A Lutheran Perspective," *Journal of Ecumenical Studies* 26 (1989): 681–96. Critique of my previous effort to retrieve this doctrine appears in Hamington, *Hail Mary?* 164–66 (see chap. 2, n. 32).

27. Roger Haight, "Sin and Grace," in *Systematic Theology: Roman Catholic Perspectives*, ed. Francis Schüssler Fiorenza and John Galvin (Minneapolis: Fortress, 1991), 110; what follows adapts the points made in this essay in pp. 77–141.

28. Karl Rahner, *Foundations of Christian Faith*, trans. William Dych (New York: Seabury, 1978), 120.

29. This lovely metaphor of mapping grace comes from Serene Jones, *Feminist Theory and Christian Theology: Cartographies of Grace* (see chap. 2, n. 4).

30. Rahner, *Foundations*, 226.

31. Rahner, *Mary, Mother of the Lord*, 78.

32. Raymond Brown gives references to medieval and later thinkers who insisted that Mary's knowledge was not limited; but this is not the testimony of scripture (*The Birth of the Messiah: A Commentary on the Infancy Narratives in Matthew and Luke* [Garden City, N.Y.: Doubleday, 1977], 492 n. 45).

33. Ibid.

34. Ibid., 50.

35. Thérèse of Lisieux, *Pourquoi j'aime Marie* (1887), cited by René Laurentin, "Holy Mary," in *Models of Holiness*, ed. Christian Duquoc and Casiano Floristán (New York: Seabury, 1979), 64.

36. Boff, *Maternal Face of God*, 130 (see chap. 2, n. 64).

37. Karl Rahner, "I Believe in Jesus Christ: Interpreting an Article of Faith," *Theological Investigations*, volume 9, trans. G. Harrison (London: Darton, Longman and Todd, 1972), 166.

38. For a thoroughgoing christology from a historical perspective, see Roger Haight, *Jesus Symbol of God* (Maryknoll, N.Y.: Orbis, 1999); for detailed analysis of

Jesus' human psychology, see Karl Rahner, "Dogmatic Reflections on the Knowledge and Self-Consciousness of Christ," in *Theological Investigations*, volume 5, trans. Karl Kruger (New York: Seabury Crossroad, 1975), 193–215; for summary, see Elizabeth Johnson, "The Word Was made Flesh and Dwelt Among Us: Jesus Research and Christian Faith," in *Jesus: A Colloquium in the Holy Land*, ed. Doris Donnelly (New York: Continuum, 2001), 146–66.

39. John Paul II, Encyclical *Redemptoris mater*, *Origins* 16, no. 43 (April 9, 1987): §§14 and 17.

40. Noone, *Mary for Today*, 62 (see chap. 2, n. 72).

CHAPTER 6
PRECEDENTS

1. Mentioned by Irenaeus, *Adversus Haereses* 1.7.2; see 3.11.3. This dispute is recounted in *Mary in the New Testament*, ed. R. E. Brown et al., 270 (see chap. 1, n. 4).

2. Kelly, *Early Christian Creeds*, 144–46, 332–38 (see chap. 5, n. 18); the phrase "born of the Virgin Mary" was placed into the old Roman creed around 175 C.E.

3. Augustine, *Sermons*, 10 vols., ed. John Rotelle, translated with notes by Edmund Hill (Brooklyn, N.Y.: New City Press, 1990–95), 3:288 (Sermon 72A.7).

4. Ibid., 3:287.

5. Graef, *Mary: A History of Doctrine and Devotion*, 94–100 (see chap. 1, n. 1); Kim Power, *Veiled Desire: Augustine on Women* (New York: Continuum, 1996), 171–211 (part 5: "Mary"); and E. Ann Matter, "Women," in *Augustine Through the Ages: An Encyclopedia*, ed. Allan Fitzgerald (Grand Rapids: Eerdmans, 1999), 887–92.

6. Augustine, *Sermons*, 3:288 (Sermon 72A.8).

7. E. Ann Matter, "The Virgin Mary: A Goddess?" in *The Book of the Goddess, Past and Present*, ed. Carl Olsen (New York: Crossroad, 1990), 81.

8. Leo Scheffczyk, *Das Mariengeheimnis in Frömmigkeit und Lehre der Karolingerzeit* (Leipzig: St. Benno Verlag, 1959).

9. Pelikan, *Growth of Medieval Theology*, 158–74 (see chap. 4, n. 12); Oberman, *Harvest of Medieval Theology*, 281–322 (see chap. 4, n. 12); and Elizabeth Johnson, "Marian Devotion in the Western Church," in *Christian Spirituality*, volume 2, *High Middle Ages and Reformation*, ed. Jill Raitt (New York: Crossroad, 1987), 392–414.

10. Peter Damien in *Patrologiae cursus completus: Series latina*, ed. J. P. Migne (Paris, 1857–66), 144:761; in Graef, *Mary: A History of Doctrine and Devotion*, 207.

11. Bernard of Clairvaux, "Sermo in Nativitate B.V. Mariae (De aqueductu)," in *Patrologiae cursus completus: Series latina*, ed. J. P. Migne (Paris, 1857–66), 183:441.

12. Graef, *Mary: A History of Doctrine and Devotion,* 289.

13. Bernardine of Siena, "Sermo 5 de nativitate B.M.V.," chap. 8, in *Opera Omnia* (Lugduni, 1650), 4:96.

14. René Laurentin, *Queen of Heaven: A Short Treatise on Marian Theology* (London: Burns, Oates & Washbourne, 1956), 60.

15. P. Nigido, *Summa sacrae Mariologiae pars prima* (Panhormi, 1602); see Graef, *Mary: A History of Doctrine and Devotion,* 2:43. The exaggeration associated with this word explains today's preference for the phrase theology of Mary; see Donal Flanagan, *The Theology of Mary* (Hales Corner, Wis.: Clergy Book Service, 1976).

16. Patrick Bearsley, "The Metamorphosis of Mariology," *Clergy Review* 69 (1984): 67.

17. *The Papal Encyclicals: 1740–1981,* volume 2, ed. Claudia Carlen (Wilmington, N.C.: McGrath Pub., 1981).

18. Laurentin, *Question of Mary,* 10 (see chap. 2, n. 49); this book has an excellent analysis of the marian movement and the two opposing mariological tendencies on the eve of the council.

19. Writing at the time of the Second Vatican Council, Laurentin underscores the shock of these retrievals:

It is only necessary to recall the position of the Bible in the life of the Catholic Church thirty years ago. Not only was it neglected, but the opinion was still current in certain Catholic circles that the Old Testament (or even the whole Bible) was on the Index. When I was young I heard this opinion repeated even by priests. Only a little more recently the papers, even the Catholic ones, reported without the slightest upset the words of an over-enthusiastic convert who threw a dagger and a "Protestant Bible" at the feet of Pius XII, saying: "This is the weapon with which I wanted to kill you, and the book in which I learnt my false teaching." At that time, the publishing of Catholic Bibles was at a very low ebb, in sharp contrast with the position among Protestants. What a long way we have come! (*Question of Mary,* 33)

20. Rahner, *Mary, Mother of the Lord,* 35 (see chap. 5, n. 4).

21. Ibid., 35–36.

22. Ibid., 40. The original essay is his "Le principe fondamental de la théologie mariale," *Recherches de Science Religieuse* 42 (1954): 481–522.

23. For complete documentation, see *Commentary on the Documents of Vatican II,* volume 1, ed. Herbert Vorgrimler (New York: Herder & Herder, 1967), especially Gérard Philips, "Dogmatic Constitution on the Church: History of the Constitution" (pp. 105–37); and Otto Semmelroth, "Chapter VIII: The Role of the Blessed Virgin Mary, Mother of God, in the Mystery of Christ and the Church" (pp. 285–96). Also *History of Vatican II,* volume 3, ed. Giuseppe Alberigo and Joseph Komonchak (Maryknoll, N.Y.: Orbis, 2000), 95–98, 366–72, 425–28. Eyewitness accounts are recounted by Karl Rahner, "Zur konziliaren Mariologie,"

Stimmen der Zeit 174 (1964): 87–101; and René Laurentin, *La Vierge au Concile* (Paris: Lethielleux, 1965).

24. Laurentin, *Question of Mary,* 136.

25. Philips, in *Commentary on the Documents of Vatican II,* ed. Vorgrimler, 1:125.

26. Rahner, cited in *History of Vatican II,* ed. Alberigo and Komonchak, 97–98.

27. Laurentin, *Question of Mary,* 137.

28. For details, see Elizabeth Johnson, "Mary as Mediatrix: History and Interpretation," in *One Mediator, the Saints, and Mary,* 311–26 (see chap. 1, n. 4).

29. Mary Hines, "Mary and the Prophetic Mission of the Church," *Journal of Ecumenical Studies* 28 (1991): 289.

30. Anne Carr, "Mary in the Mystery of the Church: Vatican Council II," in *Mary according to Women,* ed. Jegen, 5–32 (see chap. 1, n. 35).

31. Børresen, "Mary in Catholic Theology," in *Mary in the Churches,* ed. Küng and J. Moltmann, 54 (see chap. 2, n. 25).

32. Stefano De Fiores, "Mary in Postconciliar Theology," in *Vatican II: Assessment and Perspectives* I, ed. René Latourelle (New York: Paulist, 1988), 478.

33. Van den Hengel, "Mary: Miriam of Nazareth or the Symbol of the 'Eternal Feminine,'" 320.

34. Paul VI, Apostolic Letter *Marialis Cultus* (Devotion to the Blessed Virgin Mary), in *The Pope Speaks* 19 (1974–75): 49–86.

35. Donal Flanagan notes that this papal invitation to a new vision was made to a mariology in shock, if not in decline, and it has not been taken up to any significant degree ("The Impact of Feminism on Mariology," *One in Christ* 21 [1985]: 75–78).

CHAPTER 7

GALILEE: THE POLITICAL-ECONOMIC WORLD

1. Critical notes and the full text of *The Protoevangelium of James* appear in *New Testament Apocrypha,* ed. E. Hennecke and Wilhelm Schneemelcher (Louisville, Ky.: Westminster John Knox, 1991), 1:426–39; citation from p. 378. For discussion of the apocrypha, see *Mary in the New Testament,* ed. R. E. Brown et al., 241–82 (see chap. 1, n. 4); Beverly Gaventa, *Mary: Glimpses of the Mother of Jesus* (Columbia: University of South Carolina Press, 1995), 100–125, with full text of the *Protoevangelium,* pp. 133–45.

2. *Protoevangelium of James* 19.3 (*New Testament Apocrypha,* ed. Hennecke and Schneemelcher, 1:385).

3. Jonathan Reed, *Archaeology and the Galilean Jesus: A Re-examination of the Evidence* (Harrisburg, Pa.: Trinity Press International, 2000), 19. I also draw here

from *What Has Archaeology To Do with Faith?* ed. James Charlesworth and Walter Weaver (Valley Forge, Pa.: Trinity Press International, 1992); John Rousseau and Rami Arav, *Jesus and His World: An Archaeological and Cultural Dictionary* (Minneapolis: Fortress, 1995); and *Archaeology and the Galilee: Texts and Contexts in the Graeco-Roman and Byzantine Periods,* ed. Douglas Edwards and C. Thomas McCollough (Atlanta: Scholars Press, 1997), especially James Strange, "First Century Galilee from Archaeology and from Texts" (pp. 39–48).

4. A groundbreaking work is Seán Freyne, *Galilee: From Alexander the Great to Hadrian, 323 B.C.E. to 135 C.E.: A Study of Second Temple Judaism* (Wilmington, Del.: Michael Glazier; Notre Dame, Ind.: University of Notre Dame Press, 1980). This present chapter draws especially on chap. 3, "Galilee under the Romans" (pp. 57–97).

5. Geza Vermes, *Jesus the Jew: A Historian's Reading of the Gospels* (Philadelphia: Fortress, 1973); John Meier, *A Marginal Jew: Rethinking the Historical Jesus,* volume 1, *The Roots of the Problem and the Person;* volume 2, *Mentor, Message, and Miracles;* volume 3, *Companions and Competitors* (New York: Doubleday, 1991, 1994, 2001); John Dominic Crossan, *The Historical Jesus: The Life of a Mediterranean Jewish Peasant* (San Francisco: HarperSanFrancisco, 1991) (the debate generated by this work can be followed in Seán Freyne, "Galilean Questions to Crossan's Mediterranean Jesus," in Seán Freyne, *Galilee and Gospel* [Tübingen: Mohr-Siebeck, 2000], 208–29); E. P. Sanders, *Jesus and Judaism* (Philadelphia: Fortress, 1985); *Jesus' Jewishness: Exploring the Place of Jesus in Early Judaism,* ed. James H. Charlesworth (New York: Crossroad, 1996); Bernard Lee, *The Galilean Jewishness of Jesus* (New York: Paulist, 1988); Paula Fredriksen, *Jesus of Nazareth, King of the Jews* (New York: Alfred A. Knopf, 1999). Theological implications of this research are debated by Marcus Borg and N. T. Wright, *The Meaning of Jesus: Two Visions* (San Francisco: HarperSanFrancisco, 2000); and in *Jesus: A Colloquium in the Holy Land,* ed. Donnelly (see chap. 5, n. 38).

6. With interreligious respect, standard academic usage marks the years before and after Christ as B.C.E. and C.E., for "before the common era" and "common era."

7. Flavius Josephus, *Jewish War* 3.42–44. Josephus (37–100 C.E.) was a member of a Jewish priestly family who operated first as a military commander and later as a historian. His writings, while needing critical interpretation, give a fresh and often eyewitness view of first-century events in Palestine. In addition to *Jewish War,* he wrote *Jewish Antiquities, Against Apion,* and his *Life.* See *Anchor Bible Dictionary,* ed. David Noel Freedman (New York: Doubleday, 1992), 3:981–98.

8. John Dominic Crossan, *The Birth of Christianity* (San Francisco: HarperSanFrancisco, 1998), 219.

9. Josephus, *Jewish War* 3.517–19.

10. Crossan, *Historical Jesus,* 17.

11. Ibid., 16, citing Eric Meyers and James Strange, *Archaeology, the Rabbis,*

and Early Christianity: The Social and Historical Setting of Palestinian Judaism and Christianity (Nashville: Abingdon, 1981), 56.

12. "From Jewish literary texts, then, across almost one thousand five hundred years, nothing" (Crossan, *Historical Jesus*, 15).

13. Richard Horsley, *Archaeology, History, and Society in Galilee: The Social Context of Jesus and the Rabbis* (Harrisburg, Pa.: Trinity Press International, 1996), 110; see this work for further descriptions and excellent maps.

14. For the following discussion, see the lucid presentation by Meier, *Marginal Jew*, 1:255–68; Horsley, *Archaeology, History, and Society*, 154–75; Freyne, *Galilee from Alexander the Great to Hadrian*, 144.

15. Reed, *Archaeology and the Galilean Jesus*, 153. For good description of these houses and their significance, see Marianne Sawicki, *Crossing Galilee: Architectures of Contact in the Occupied Land of Jesus* (Harrisburg, Pa.: Trinity Press International, 2000), 13–22.

16. Reed, *Archaeology and the Galilean Jesus*, 159.

17. Ibid., 148–60.

18, Ibid., 313–32.

19. Ibid., 132.

20. Douglas Oakman, "The Countryside in Luke-Acts," in *The Social World of Luke-Acts: Models for Interpretation*, ed. Jerome Neyrey (Peabody, Mass.: Hendrickson, 1991), 155.

21. Ibid., 156.

22. Gerhard Lenski, *Power and Privilege: A Theory of Social Stratification* (New York: McGraw Hill, 1966), 228. I am following here with gratitude the presentation of Lenski's model given by Crossan (*Historical Jesus*, 43–46), where I first came across it. Nuance has been added to Lenski's view of traditional agrarian society by John Kautsky's idea of a commercializing agrarian society in *The Politics of Aristocratic Empires* (Chapel Hill: University of North Carolina Press, 1982). The Lenski-Kautsky model now appears in numerous studies of Galilee. See also Seán Freyne, "Herodian Economics in Galilee: Searching for a Suitable Model," in his *Galilee and Gospel*, 86–113.

23. Lenski, *Power and Privilege*, 266 and 270.

24. Ibid., 281.

25. Ibid., 210, italics his.

26. Richard Horsley, *Galilee: History, Politics, People* (Valley Forge, Pa.: Trinity Press International, 1995), 204; hereafter *Galilee*. I draw here from Horsley, *Galilee*, chap. 9, and his *Archaeology, History, and Society in Galilee*, chap. 3; also K. C. Hanson and Douglas Oakman, *Palestine in the Time of Jesus* (Minneapolis: Fortress, 1998), chap. 4; and Ekkehard Stegemann and Wolfgang Stegemann, *The Jesus Movement: A Social History of Its First Century*, trans. O. C. Dean (Minneapolis: Fortress, 1999), chaps. 1–5.

27. Seán Freyne, *Galilee, Jesus and the Gospels: Literary Approaches and Historical Investigations* (Minneapolis: Fortress, 1988), 172.

28. Meier, *Marginal Jew,* 1:279.

29. Ibid., 281.

30. Ramsay MacMullen, *Roman Social Relations, 50 B.C. to A.D. 384* (New Haven: Yale University Press, 1974), 107–8; cited in Crossan, *Historical Jesus,* 29.

31. Meier, *Marginal Jew,* 1:282.

32. Ibid.

33. Irene Brennan, "Mother of Justice and Peace," *New Blackfriars* 69 (1988): 228–36.

34. Gebara and Bingemer, *Mary, Mother of God, Mother of the Poor,* 113 (see chap. 1, n. 31).

35. Ibid., 120–21.

36. For a chronology of Jesus' life, see Meier, *Marginal Jew,* 1:372–433.

37. Although Herod was originally appointed king by the Romans in 40 B.C.E., it took three years before he could quash popular resistance to his reign, especially in Galilee, where they already knew of his brutality. See Peter Richardson, *Herod, King of the Jews and Friend of the Romans* (Columbia: University of South Carolina Press, 1996).

38. Stegemann and Stegemann, *Jesus Movement,* 112.

39. Josephus, *Antiquities* 17.271–72.

40. Ibid., 2.75

41. Ibid., 17.289.

42. Horsley, *Archaeology, History, and Society,* 32 and 112.

43. Horsley, *Galilee,* 123.

44. Crossan, *Birth of Christianity,* 233.

45. Josephus, *Antiquities* 18.27.

46. Ibid., 18.36.

47. Paraphrase of Horsley, *Archaeology, History, and Society,* 89–90.

48. Horsley, *Galilee,* 219; see also Seán Freyne, "Town and Country Once More: The Case of Roman Galilee," in his *Galilee and Gospel,* 59–72.

49. Sawicki, *Crossing Galilee,* 90.

50. E. P. Sanders, *Judaism: Practice and Belief, 63 BCE–66 CE* (London: SCM Press; Philadelphia: Trinity Press International, 1994), 157–69.

51. Reed, *Archaeology and the Galilean Jesus,* 97.

52. Josephus, *Life* 374–84, cited in Crossan, *Birth of Christianity,* 231.

53. Josephus, *Life* 65–67.

54. Ibid., 384.

55. Horsley, *Galilee,* 221.

56. Philo, *Legatio* 38.302, described and cited in Fredriksen, *Jesus of Nazareth, King of the Jews,* 171.

57. John L. McKenzie, "The Mother of Jesus in the New Testament," in *Mary in the Churches*, ed. Küng and J. Moltmann, 9 (see chap. 2, n. 25).

CHAPTER 8
SECOND TEMPLE JUDAISM: THE RELIGIOUS WORLD

1. Fredriksen, *Jesus of Nazareth, King of the Jews*, 62 (see chap. 7, n. 6).

2. Sanders, *Judaism: Practice and Belief* (see chap. 7, n. 50), is a treasure-trove of information to which the following pages are indebted. See, however, critique of Sanders's idea of a single, unitary Judaism by Bruce Chilton and Jacob Neusner, *Judaism in the New Testament: Practices and Beliefs* (New York: Routledge & Kegan Paul, 1995), 10–18. Primary sources for individual and temple piety are presented in *Faith and Piety in Early Judaism: Texts and Documents*, ed. George W. E. Nickelsburg and Michael Stone (Philadelphia: Fortress, 1983).

3. Fredriksen, *Jesus of Nazareth, King of the Jews*, 201. A critically enlightening discussion of these purity laws' effect on women's social position is presented by Shaye Cohen, "Menstruants and the Sacred in Judaism and Christianity," in *Women's History and Ancient History*, ed. Sarah Pomeroy (Chapel Hill: University of North Carolina Press, 1991), 273–99; see also Sanders, *Judaism: Practice and Belief*, 71.

4. Amy-Jill Levine, "Second Temple Judaism, Jesus, and Women: Yeast of Eden," *Biblical Interpretation* 2 (1994): 16, critiquing Ben Witherington III, "Women (NT)," in *Anchor Bible Dictionary*, ed. David Noel Freedman (Garden City, N.Y.: Doubleday, 1992), 6:957–61.

5. Paula Fredriksen, "Did Jesus Oppose the Purity Laws?" *Bible Review* 11 (June 1995): 22.

6. Norman Pittenger, *Our Lady: The Mother of Jesus in Christian Faith and Devotion* (London: SCM Press, 1996), 33.

7. Horsley, *Galilee*, 122 (see chap. 7, n. 26).

8. Crossan, *Birth of Christianity*, 575–86 (see chap. 7, n. 8); also Horsley, *Galilee*, 111–27.

9. Reed, *Archaeology and the Galilean Jesus*, 53 (see chap. 7, n. 3).

10. Ibid., 23–61. For a clear explanation of ossuaries, see Crossan, *Birth of Christianity*, 543–44.

11. Horsley, *Archaeology, History, and Society*, 131–53 (see chap. 7, n. 13); see also his *Galilee*, 222–37 ("Synagogues: The Village Assemblies").

12. Josephus, *Antiquities*, 14.235, 260.

13. Horsley, *Galilee*, 236

14. See the fascinating research by Bernadette Brooten, *Women Leaders in the Ancient Synagogue* (Chico, Calif.: Scholars Press, 1982), especially 103–38.

15. Horsley, *Galilee*, 237; also Crossan, *Birth of Christianity*, 159–65; and Sawicki, *Crossing Galilee*, passim (see chap. 7, n. 15).

16. Here I am following closely Fredriksen, *Jesus of Nazareth, King of the Jews*, 54–61.

17. Robert Aron, *The Jewish Jesus* (Maryknoll, N.Y.: Orbis, 1971).

18. Josephus, *Against Apion* 2.175.

19. Fredriksen, *Jesus of Nazareth, King of the Jews*, 61.

20. Sanders, *Judaism: Practice and Belief*, 275.

21. Horsley, *Galilee*, 144–47.

22. Meir Ben-Dov, *In the Shadow of the Temple: The Discovery of Ancient Jerusalem* (New York: Harper & Row, 1985), 77. For the following description I am drawing mainly on Sanders, *Judaism: Practice and Belief*, chaps. 5 and 6; also Fredriksen, *Jesus of Nazareth, King of the Jews*, 42–50; and Sawicki, *Crossing Galilee*, 48–54.

23. Josephus, *Jewish War* 5.199.

24. Ibid., 5.219.

25. Sanders, *Judaism: Practice and Belief*, 79–81.

26. *Aristeas* 92–95, cited by Sanders, *Judaism: Practice and Belief*, 80.

27. Sanders, *Judaism: Practice and Belief*, 81.

28. Ibid.

29. This scenario is a gloss on Sanders's imaginative example (*Judaism: Practice and Belief*, 112–16) with credit also to Fredriksen, *Jesus of Nazareth, King of the Jews*, 42–50.

30. Fredriksen, *Jesus of Nazareth, King of the Jews*, 47.

31. *Mary in the New Testament*, ed. R. E. Brown et al., 284 (see chap. 1, n. 4).

32. Ibid., 173–77.

33. Stegemann and Stegemann, *Jesus Movement*, 215 (see chap. 7, n. 26).

34. See Carolyn Osiek, "Women in House Churches," in *Common Life in the Early Church*, ed. Julian Hills (Harrisburg, Pa.: Trinity Press International, 1998), 300–315, with other examples that include Lydia (Acts 16:14, 40) and Nympha (Col. 4:15).

35. James D. G. Dunn, *The Partings of the Ways: Between Christianity and Judaism and their Significance for the Character of Christianity* (Philadelphia: Trinity Press International, 1991), 152–59. For this complex history, see also Claudia Setzer, *Jewish Responses to Early Christians: History and Polemics, 30–150 C.E.* (Minneapolis: Fortress, 1994); Stephen Wilson, *Related Strangers: Jews and Christians 70–170 C.E.* (Minneapolis: Fortress, 1995); and essays in *Interwoven Destinies*, ed. Eugene Fisher (New York: Paulist, 1993).

36. Fredriksen, *Jesus of Nazareth, King of the Jews*, 12–17.

37. See the explanation in Daniel Harrington, "Retrieving the Jewishness of Jesus: Recent Developments," in *The Historical Jesus Through Catholic and Jewish*

Eyes, ed. Leonard Greenspoon, Dennis Hamm, and Bryan LeBeau (Harrisburg, Pa.: Trinity Press International, 2000), 67–84.

38. See the excellent discussion in Mary Boys, *Has God Only One Blessing? Judaism as a Source of Christian Self-Understanding* (New York: Paulist, 2000).

39. Dunn, *Partings of the Ways,* 230.

40. Alan Segal, *Rebecca's Children: Judaism and Christianity in the Roman World* (Cambridge, Mass.: Harvard University Press, 1987).

CHAPTER 9
WOMEN: THE SOCIAL-CULTURAL WORLD

1. Rosemary Radford Ruether's early analysis in, *New Woman, New Earth,* 64 (see chap. 1, n. 14); see her *Faith and Fratricide: The Theological Roots of Anti-Semitism* (New York: Seabury, 1979).

2. Amy-Jill Levine, "Second Temple Judaism, Jesus, and Women," *Biblical Interpretation* 2 (1994): 11.

3. Judith Plaskow, "Christian Feminism and Anti-Judaism," *Cross Currents* 28 (1978): 306; reprinted as "Blaming the Jews for the Birth of Patriarchy," *Lilith* 7 (1980/5741): 11–13. Her analysis is further developed in "Anti-Judaism in Feminist Christian Interpretation," in *Searching the Scriptures,* volume 1, *A Feminist Introduction,* ed. Elisabeth Schüssler Fiorenza (New York: Crossroad, 1993), 117–29.

4. Susannah Heschel, "Anti-Judaism in Christian Feminist Theology," *Tikkun* 5, no. 3 (May, June 1990): 25–28, 95–97, at 97; see her edited work, *On Being a Jewish Feminist: A Reader* (New York: Schocken, 1983).

5. Elisabeth Schüssler Fiorenza, *But She Said: Feminist Practices of Biblical Interpretation* (Boston: Beacon, 1992); and her *Jesus and the Politics of Interpretation* (New York: Continuum, 2000), 115–44; see also Deborah McCauley and Annette Daum, "Jewish-Christian Feminist Dialogue: A Wholistic Vision," *Union Seminary Quarterly Review* 38 (1983): 147–90; and Katherina von Kellenbach, *Anti-Judaism in Feminist Religious Writings* (Atlanta, Ga.: Scholars Press, 1990).

6. Plaskow, "Christian Feminism and Anti-Judaism," 308. Many feminist scholars credit the early work by Leonard Swidler, *Women in Judaism: The Status of Women in Formative Judaism* (Metuchen, N.J.: Scarecrow Press, 1976) with focusing on the question of women, although they take issue with his use of sources.

7. Tal Ilan, *Jewish Women in Greco-Roman Palestine: An Inquiry into Image and Status* (Tübingen: Mohr-Siebeck, 1995); and eadem, *Mine and Yours Are Hers: Retrieving Women's History from Rabbinic Literature* (Leiden: Brill, 1997); her work attempts a critical use of rabbinic sources to glimpse women's actual lives.

Judith Romney Wegner also makes connections between later law and earlier Jewish practice (*Chattel or Person? The Status of Women in the Mishnah* [New York: Oxford University Press, 1988]). Contrary to simply reading off first-century conditions from the Talmud, these studies use careful methodology to sift and judge at every point.

8. Barbara Geller Nathanson, "Toward a Multicultural Ecumenical History of Women in the First Century/ies C.E.," in *Searching the Scriptures*, ed. Schüssler Fiorenza, 1:272–89, with excellent notes.

9. Randall Chesnutt, "Revelatory Experiences Attributed to Biblical Women," in *"Women Like This": New Perspectives on Jewish Women in the Greco-Roman World*, ed. Amy-Jill Levine (Atlanta, Ga.: Scholars Press, 1991), 107–25; a different take is offered by Ross Shepard Kraemer, *When Aseneth Met Joseph: A Late Antique Tale of the Biblical Patriarch and His Egyptian Wife, Revisited* (New York: Oxford University Press, 1998).

10. Ross Shepard Kraemer, "Jewish Women and Christian Origins: Some Caveats," in *Women and Christian Origins*, ed. Ross Shepard Kraemer and Mary Rose D'Angelo (New York: Oxford University Press, 1999), 44; see also Kraemer "Jewish Women and Women's Judaism(s) at the Beginning of Christianity," in the same volume, pp. 50–79.

11. Brooten, *Women Leaders in the Ancient Synagogue* (see chap. 8, n. 14).

12. Ross Shepard Kraemer, *Maenads, Martyrs, Matrons, Monastics: A Sourcebook on Women's Religions in the Greco-Roman World* (Philadelphia: Fortress, 1988); see also her analysis in *Her Share of the Blessings: Women's Religions among Pagans, Jews, and Christians in the Greco-Roman World* (New York: Oxford University Press, 1992).

13. Bernadette Brooten, "Jewish Women's History in the Roman Period: A Task for Christian Theology," *Harvard Theological Review* 79 (1986): 22–30—an insightful programmatic essay; and her "Early Christian Women and Their Cultural Context: Issues of Method in Historical Reconstruction," in *Feminist Perspectives on Biblical Scholarship*, ed. Yarbro Collins, 65–92 (see chap. 3, n. 6).

14. Barbara Geller Nathanson, "Reflections on the Silent Woman of Ancient Judaism and her Pagan Roman Counterpart," in *The Listening Heart: Essays in Wisdom and the Psalms in Honor of Roland Murphy*, ed. Kenneth Hoglund (Sheffield: JSOT Press, 1987), 273; also *"Women Like This": New Perspectives on Jewish Women in the Greco-Roman World*, ed. Levine; and Cheryl Ann Brown, *No Longer Be Silent: First Century Jewish Portraits of Biblical Women* (Louisville, Ky.: Westminster John Knox, 1992).

15. Schüssler Fiorenza, *Jesus and the Politics of Interpretation*, 137.

16. Carol Meyers, "Everyday Life: Women in the Period of the Hebrew Bible," in *Women's Bible Commentary*, ed. Carol Newsom and Sharon Ringe (Louisville, Ky.: Westminster John Knox, 1998), 256.

17. Schalom Ben-Chorin, "A Jewish View of the Mother of Jesus," in *Mary in the Churches*, ed. Küng and J. Moltmann, 12 (see chap. 2, n. 25).

18. Jane Schaberg, *The Illegitimacy of Jesus: A Feminist Theological Interpretation of the Infancy Narratives* (New York: Crossroad, 1990), 42–45; and Brown, *Birth of the Messiah*, 123–24 (see chap. 5, n. 32). For background, see Bruce Malina, *The New Testament World: Insights from Cultural Anthropology* (Atlanta: John Knox, 1991), 94–121 ("Kinship and Marriage"); for a critical assessment of Malina's approach, see Mary Ann Tolbert, "Social, Sociological, and Anthropological Methods," in *Searching the Scriptures*, ed. Schüssler Fiorenza, 1:255–72; and Joel Green, "The Social Status of Mary in Luke 1:5–2:52: A Plea for Methodological Integration," *Biblica* 73 (1992): 457–72.

19. Brown, *Birth of the Messiah*, 304.

20. Ibid., 305. Brown makes the important distinction that "unanimity of the Fathers has value in interpreting God's revelation, but the Fathers of the Church had no more knowledge about Mary's historical intentions than we have and no other way of gaining that knowledge than we have" (p. 304 n. 24).

21. Meyers, "Everyday Life," 253.

22. Miriam Peskowitz, "Family/ies in Antiquity: Evidence from Tannaitic Literature and Roman Galilean Architecture," in *The Jewish Family in Antiquity*, ed. Shaye Cohen (Atlanta: Scholars Press, 1993), 33, citing D. Fiensy, *The Social History of Palestine in the Herodian Period* (Lewiston: Edwin Mellen Press, 1991), 145.

23. Joseph A. Fitzmyer, "Saint Joseph in the New Testament," *Josephinum Journal of Theology* 7, nos. 1–2 (2000): 18–30.

24. Brown, *Birth of the Messiah*, 503.

25. Meier, *Marginal Jew*, 1:318 (see chap. 7, n. 5); see his "The Brothers and Sisters of Jesus in Ecumenical Perspective," *Catholic Biblical Quarterly* 54 (1992): 1–28, where he suggests using the Vatican II teaching on the "hierarchy of truths" to remove this disputed question from the path to unity, given its marginal importance in scripture and the obscurity of data available for resolving it.

26. *Mary in the New Testament*, ed. R. E. Brown et al., 87 (see chap 1, n. 4).

27. Ibid., 66 n. 124.

28. Ben-Chorin, "Jewish View of the Mother of Jesus," 13.

29. Ranke-Heinemann, *Eunuchs for the Kingdom of Heaven*, 341 (see chap. 2, n. 31).

30. The sign is that of a dove that flies out of his staff (his staff "blooms"), leading to traditional artistic portraits of Joseph with a lily (see chap. 7, n. 1).

31. Meier, *Marginal Jew*, 1:326; for a full, lucid discussion, see pp. 316–32.

32. McKenzie, "The Mother of Jesus in the New Testament," in *Mary in the Churches*, ed. Küng and J. Moltmann, 6.

33. Meier, *Marginal Jew*, 1:331. It should be noted for Catholic readers that this book bears the *imprimatur*. Meier points to the groundbreaking study by Rudolf

Pesch, *Das Markusevangelium* (Freiburg: Herder, 1976), which created controversy in Germany over its claim that these were biological brothers and sisters, yet was not censured.

34. John McHugh discusses all three ancient positions at length (*The Mother of Jesus in the New Testament* [Garden City, N.Y.: Doubleday, 1975], 200–254).

35. Leo Gafney, "Jesus at Home," *America* 175, no. 3 (August 3–10, 1996): 17.

36. Josephus, *Jewish Antiquities* 20.199–203; see discussion in Meier, *Marginal Jew*, 1:57–59. There may be another extrabiblical witness to this brother in an Aramaic inscription discovered in 2002. Found on an ancient bone box, called an ossuary, it reads, "James, son of Joseph, brother of Jesus"; see André Lemaire, "Burial Box of James, the Brother of Jesus," *Biblical Archaeology Review* 28, no. 6 (November–December 2002): 24.

37. Meyers, "Everyday Life," 251–59. See also Amy Wordelman, "Everyday Life: Women of the New Testament Period," in *Women's Bible Commentary*, ed Newsom and Ringe, 482–88, which provides background from the wider Roman empire.

38. Meyers, "Everyday Life," 254.

39. Ibid.

40. Jacob Neusner, *Judaism in the Beginning of Christianity* (Philadelphia: Fortress, 1984), 59.

41. Luise Schottroff, *Lydia's Impatient Sisters: A Feminist Social History of Early Christianity*, trans. Barbara Rumscheidt and Martin Rumscheidt (Louisville, Ky.: Westminster John Knox, 1995), 85. Levine argues to the contrary that in the symbolic universe of Judaism and the early church, yeast represents moral corruption ("Second Temple Judaism," 24–25 [see chap. 8, n. 4]).

42. Meyers, "Everyday Life," 255.

43. Ibid.

44. Ibid., 256. See also O. Larry Yarbrough, "Parents and Children in the Jewish Family of Antiquity," in *Jewish Family in Antiquity*, ed. Cohen, 39–59.

45. Meyers, "Everyday Life," 256.

46. Ibid., 257. Kathleen Corley also argues the thesis that lower-class women long enjoyed more freedom in the public realm (*Private Women, Public Meals: Social Conflict in the Synoptic Tradition* [Peabody, Mass.: Hendrickson, 1993]).

47. Klaus Schreiner, *Maria: Jungfrau, Mutter, Herrscherin* (Munich: Hanser Verlag, 1994), 116, in a chapter entitled "Maria, die Intellektuelle."

48. Horsley, *Archaeology, History and Society in Galilee*, 156 (see chap. 7, n. 13).

49. Meier, *Marginal Jew*, 1:255–56.

50. Crossan, *Birth of Christianity*, 234 (see chap. 7, n. 8).

51. Reed, *Archaeology and the Galilean Jesus*, 131 (see chap. 7, n. 3).

52. Horsley, *Galilee*, 246 (see chap. 7, n. 26).

53. Robert Hughes, "When Beauty was Virtue," *Time* 158 (December 24, 2001): 60–62.

54. Norris, *Meditations on Mary*, 16–17 (see chap. 2, n. 53).

CHAPTER 10
THE DANGEROUS MEMORY OF MARY:
A MOSAIC

1. There are additional brief allusions to Mary in other Gospel scenes as well as implied references to her in passages in Paul's letters where the subject is Jesus' birth according to the flesh. For a full listing, see the Table of Contents in *Mary in the New Testament*, ed. R. E. Brown et al., ix–xi (see chap. 1, n. 4).

2. The most developed treatment available in English is Raymond E. Brown, *The Birth of the Messiah* (see chap. 5, n. 32), especially 25–41 ("Scholarship and the Infancy Narratives").

3. Vatican II's presentation of Mary follows this pattern; see the Dogmatic Constitution on the Church (*Lumen Gentium*), chapter 8.

4. Some translations say "besides women and children," others, "to say nothing of women and children"; see Megan McKenna, *Not Counting Women and Children* (Maryknoll, N.Y.: Orbis, 1998).

5. Elisabeth Schüssler Fiorenza, *Wisdom Ways: Introducing Feminist Biblical Interpretation* (Maryknoll, N.Y.: Orbis, 2001). In what follows I draw on this lucid introduction to feminist methods and their interpretive power. For earlier working of these methods, consult the bibliographic essay by Janice Capel Anderson, "Mapping Feminist Biblical Criticism: The American Scene, 1983–90," *Critical Review of Books in Religion* 4 (1991): 21–44.

6. Elisabeth Schüssler Fiorenza, "Transforming the Legacy of *The Woman's Bible*," in *Searching the Scriptures*, ed. Schüssler Fiorenza, 1:11 (see chap. 9, n. 3).

7. For the significance of this scene for the question of women's ministry; see Raymond E. Brown, "Roles of Women in the Fourth Gospel," in his *The Community of the Beloved Disciple* (New York: Paulist, 1979), 183–98; and Sandra Schneiders, "Women in the Fourth Gospel and the Role of Women in the Contemporary Church," *Biblical Theology Bulletin* 12 (1982): 35–45.

8. Barbara Reid, *Choosing the Better Part? Women in the Gospel of Luke* (Collegeville, Minn.: Liturgical Press/Michael Glazier, 1996), 160; see also the groundbreaking interpretation of Elisabeth Schüssler Fiorenza, "A Feminist Critical Interpretation for Liberation: Martha and Mary: Lk 10:38–42," *Religion and Intellectual Life* 3 (1986): 21–36, reprised in *But She Said*, 57–76 (see chap. 9, n. 5).

9. Reid, *Choosing the Better Part?* 54.

10. Mary Rose D'Angelo, "Women in Luke-Acts: A Redactional View," *Journal of Biblical Literature* 109 (1990): 461; her "Re-presentations of Women in the Gospel of Matthew and Luke-Acts," in *Women and Christian Origins*, ed. Kraemer and D'Angelo, 171–95 (see chap. 9, n. 10); and Turid Karlsen Seim, "The Gospel of Luke," in *Searching the Scriptures*, volume 2, *A Feminist Commentary*, ed. Elisabeth Schüssler Fiorenza (New York: Crossroad, 1993), 728–62.

11. Jane Schaberg, "Luke," in *Women's Bible Commentary*, ed. Newsom and Ringe, 380 (see chap. 9, n. 16).

12. D'Angelo, "Women in Luke-Acts: A Redactional View," 461.

13. The relevant biblical passage will be noted at the beginning of each scene. Readers are encouraged to read the passage in full. Unless otherwise noted, direct quotations used in each tessera can be found within the passage cited at the beginning.

14. Mary Ann Tolbert, "Mark," in *Women's Bible Commentary*, ed. Newsom and Ringe, 358–59.

15. Joan Mitchell, *Beyond Fear and Silence: A Feminist-Literary Reading of Mark* (New York: Continuum, 2001), 63.

16. Ben-Chorin, "A Jewish View of the Mother of Jesus," in *Mary in the Churches*, ed. Küng and J. Moltmann, 14 (see chap. 2, n. 25).

17. Donald Senior, "Gospel Portrait of Mary: Images and Symbols from the Synoptic Tradition," in *Mary, Woman of Nazareth*, ed. Doris Donnelly (New York: Paulist, 1989), 93.

18. Joanna Dewey, "The Gospel of Mark," in *Searching the Scriptures*, ed. Schüssler Fiorenza, 2:478.

19. Hisako Kinukawa, *Women and Jesus in Mark: A Japanese Feminist Perspective* (Maryknoll, N.Y.: Orbis, 1994).

20. *Mary in the New Testament*, ed. R. E. Brown et al., 284.

21. Ben-Chorin, "A Jewish View of the Mother of Jesus," 15–16; emphasis in the original.

22. Dewey, "Gospel of Mark," 482.

23. Nel Noddings, *Women and Evil* (Berkeley: University of California Press, 1989).

24. Sara Ruddick, "Maternal Thinking," *Feminist Studies* 6 (1980): 342–67; eadem, *Maternal Thinking* (see chap. 3, n. 15).

25. Daphne Merkin, "A Mother's Influence," *New Yorker* 75, no. 21 (August 2, 1999): 28.

26. *Mary in the New Testament*, ed. R. E. Brown et al., 284.

27. Elaine Wainwright, "The Gospel of Matthew," in *Searching the Scriptures*, ed. Schüssler Fiorenza, 2:641–44; and Amy-Jill Levine, "Matthew," in *Women's Bible Commentary*, ed. Newsom and Ringe, 340–41.

28. Elaine Wainwright, *Shall We Look for Another? A Feminist Rereading of the Matthean Jesus* (Maryknoll, N.Y.: Orbis, 1998), 56.

29. Trible, *God and the Rhetoric of Sexuality*, 195 (see chap. 3, n. 9).

30. While this law dealt with the marriage of a widow to a brother of her deceased husband, it was also interpreted more widely to include the obligation of other male family members.

31. Schaberg, *Illegitimacy of Jesus*, 24 (see chap. 9, n. 18).

32. Ibid., 26.

33. Ibid., 32.

34. Brown, *Birth of the Messiah*, 73.

35. *Mary in the New Testament*, ed. R. E. Brown et al., 82.

36. Wainwright, "Gospel of Matthew," 642, 643. Amy-Jill Levine argues in a different vein: what is important is not extramarital sexual activity but Matthew's recognition that these women are examples of higher righteousness that challenges and teaches the men in powerful positions ("Matthew"; see n. 27 above). See also Katharine Doob Sakenfeld, "Tamar, Rahab, Ruth, and the Wife of Uriah: The Company Mary Keeps in Matthew's Gospel," in *Blessed One: Protestant Perspectives on Mary*, ed. Gaventa and Rigby, 21–31 (see chap. 1, n. 39).

37. Senior, "Gospel Portrait of Mary," 102.

38. Schaberg, *Illegitimacy of Jesus*, 74; see pp. 32–33 for precise logical connections between the four foremothers and Mary.

39. Senior, "Gospel Portrait of Mary," 103.

40. Ibid., 107.

41. Wainwright, "Gospel of Matthew," 643.

42. Brown, *Birth of the Messiah*, 534–42 (Appendix V, "The Charge of Illegitimacy"); and *Mary in the New Testament*, ed. R. E. Brown et al., 256, 261–62.

43. Schaberg, *Illegitimacy of Jesus*, 1, 18, 74, 67, 199.

44. Ibid., 193. Not all criticism of Schaberg has been temperate or intelligent, charitable or wise. See her account of abusive reactions to her scholarship, "A Feminist Experience of Historical-Jesus Scholarship," in *Whose Historical Jesus?* ed. William Arnal and Michel Desjardins (Waterloo, Ont.: Wilfrid Laurier University Press, 1997), 146–60. Based on the axiom that the personal is political, she offers astute analysis of how the fierce reaction to her feminist scholarship carries a reactionary agenda.

45. Levine, "Matthew," 340.

46. Barbara Reid, review of *The Illegitimacy of Jesus, Catholic Biblical Quarterly* 52 (1990): 364–65.

47. Schottroff, *Lydia's Impatient Sisters*, 201 (see chap. 9, n. 41).

48. Reid, *Choosing the Better Part?* 84.

49. The problem is detailed in *Women Resisting Violence: Spirituality for Life*, ed. Mary John Mananzan et al. (Maryknoll, N.Y.: Orbis, 1996); see especially Elisabeth Schüssler Fiorenza, "Ties that Bind: Domestic Violence Against Women," ibid., 39–55; *Violence against Women*, ed. Elisabeth Schüssler Fiorenza and Shawn Copeland (Maryknoll, N.Y.: Orbis, 1994); and *Violence against Women and Children: A Christian Sourcebook*, ed. Carol Adams and Marie Fortune (New York: Continuum, 1995).

50. Dom Sebastian Moore, "The Bedded Axle-Tree," in *Jesus Crucified and Risen: Essays in Spirituality in Honor of Dom Sebastian Moore*, ed. William Loewe and Vernon Gregson (Collegeville, Minn.: Liturgical Press, 1998), 220.

51. Ibid., 223.

52. For a survey of the discussion in Europe and North America, see Joseph A. Fitzmyer, "The Virginal Conception of Jesus in the New Testament," in his *To Advance the Gospel: New Testament Studies* (New York: Crossroad, 1981), 41–78, with extensive bibliography; and Brown, *Birth of the Messiah*, 517–33 (Appendix IV, "Virginal Conception"), with bibliography.

53. Raymond Brown, *The Virginal Conception and Bodily Resurrection of Jesus* (New York: Paulist, 1973), 66.

54. Brown, *Birth of the Messiah*, 527.

55. *Mary in the New Testament,* ed. R. E. Brown et al., 96.

56. Van Austin Harvey presents an excellent discussion of this issue of intellectual integrity with regard to the quest for the historical Jesus (*The Historian and the Believer* [New York: Macmillan, 1966]).

57. Vatican II, Dogmatic Constitution on Divine Revelation (*Dei Verbum*) §11.

58. Elaine Wainwright disagrees with the majority scholarly opinion that Matthew attributes divine sonship to Jesus in this text (*Shall We Look for Another?* 59).

59. Brown, *Birth of the Messiah*, 124; also Fitzmyer, "Virginal Conception of Jesus in the New Testament," 54.

60. Jürgen Moltmann, *The Way of Jesus Christ: Christology in Messianic Dimensions*, trans. Margaret Kohl (Minneapolis: Fortress, 1990), 83; see pp. 82–87 ("Christ's Birth in the Spirit from a Theological Perspective").

61. Gerhard Delling, "*parthenos,*" in *Theological Dictionary of the New Testament,* ed. Gerhard Kittel and Gerhard Friedrich (Grand Rapids: Eerdmans, 1977), 5:835.

62. Frans Jozef von Beeck, "Born of the Virgin Mary: Toward a *Sprachregelung* on a Delicate Point of Doctrine," *Pacifica: Australian Theological Studies* 14 (June 2001): 128.

63. Ibid., 139.

64. Ibid., 142.

65. Brown, *Birth of the Messiah*, 531.

66. Schaberg, *Illegitimacy of Jesus*, 2.

67. Joseph Ratzinger, *Introduction to Christianity* (New York: Seabury, 1968), 207–8.

68. Levine, "Matthew," 341.

69. Janice Capel Anderson, "Mary's Difference: Gender and Patriarchy in the Birth Narratives," *Journal of Religion* 67 (1987): 183–202.

70. Wainwright, "Gospel of Matthew," 2:643.

71. Schaberg, *Illegitimacy of Jesus*, 199.

72. Wainwright, "Gospel of Matthew," in *Searching the Scriptures*, 2:676; see also her *Towards a Feminist Critical Reading of the Gospel according to Matthew* (Berlin: de Gruyter, 1991).

73. Ibid., 10, 198.

74. Sojourner Truth at the Woman's Rights Convention, Akron, Ohio, May 28, 1851; in *Sojourner Truth as Orator*, 103–4 (see chap. 3, n. 47).

75. Brown, *Birth of the Messiah*, 167.

76. Wainwright, *Shall We Look for Another?* 61–62.

77. Brown, *Birth of the Messiah*, 168; see this section for fascinating historical examples of envoys from the East coming to Palestine or to Rome with gifts.

78. Richard Horsley, *The Liberation of Christmas: The Infancy Narratives in Social Context* (New York: Crossroad, 1986), 53–58.

79. Wainwright, *Shall We Look for Another?* 63.

80. See Michael Crosby, *House of Disciples: Church, Economics, and Justice in Matthew* (Maryknoll, N.Y.: Orbis, 1988) for analysis of the house as a key metaphor in this Gospel.

81. Wainwright, *Shall We Look for Another?* 63.

82. Ibid.

83. Brown, *Birth of the Messiah*, 232.

84. See graphic reflections in Peter Daino, *Mary, Mother of Sorrows, Mother of Defiance* (Maryknoll, N.Y.: Orbis, 1993); and Megan McKenna, *Mary, Shadow of Grace* (Maryknoll, N.Y.: Orbis, 1995), 62–77.

85. Letter from U.N. High Commission for Refugees, May 2002.

86. Catholic Relief Services, *The Wooden Bell* 13 (October 2002): 1, 4.

87. Balasuriya, *Mary and Human Liberation*, 126–27 (see chap. 2, n. 24).

88. See *New Testament Apocrypha*, ed. Hennecke and Schneemelcher, 1:410 (see chap. 7, n. 1).

89. Ibid., 413. Though railed against by Jerome and condemned by popes, this literature was immensely popular up through the Middle Ages.

90. Josephus, *War* 33.6 §600; *Jewish Antiquities* 17.6.5 §§174–78; cited in Brown, *Birth of the Messiah*, 226.

91. Comment by Wainwright, *Shall We Look for Another?* 58, glossing Schüssler Fiorenza, *Jesus, Miriam's Child, Sophia's Prophet* (see chap. 2, n. 67).

92. Wainwright, *Shall We Look for Another?* 66.

93. Ibid., 65.

94. Wainwright, "Gospel of Matthew," 2:644.

95. See Trible, *God and the Rhetoric of Sexuality*, 31–59, for the exegesis of compassion as womb-love; Wainwright draws on this work to interpret both fulfillment citations in this pericope in an original feminist way as bearing female images of God.

96. McKenna, *Mary, Shadow of Grace*, 76.

97. Daino, *Mary, Mother of Sorrows, Mother of Defiance*, 14–15.

98. Joseph A. Fitzmyer, S.J., *The Gospel According to Luke I–IX*, Anchor Bible 28 (Garden City, N.Y.: Doubleday, 1981), 927–28; Brown, *Birth of the Messiah*, 316–19.

99. See chart in *Mary in the New Testament*, ed. R. E. Brown et al., 112.

100. J. P. Audet shows how closely the annunciation to Mary follows the call of Gideon ("L'Annonce à Marie," *Revue Biblique* 63 [1956]: 346–74).

101. See the development of this argument by Schaberg, *Illegitimacy of Jesus,* 101–30; Klemens Stock, "Die Berufung Marias (Lk 1:26–38)," *Biblica* 61 (1980): 457–91; Ignace de la Potterie, *Mary in the Mystery of the Covenant,* trans. Bertrand Buby (New York: Alba House, 1992), 7–10; M. Miguens, *Mary, The Servant of the Lord: An Ecumenical Proposal* (Boston: St. Paul, 1979); and B. Hubbard, "Commissioning Stories in Luke-Acts," *Semeia* 8 (1977): 103–26. While noting the marvelous birth motif, all also interpret the annunciation scene as a prophetic calling comparable to that of some prophets of the Hebrew Bible.

102. Richard Sklba, "Mary and the 'Anawim,'" in *Mary, Woman of Nazareth,* ed. Donnelly, 124.

103. John Calvin, *Commentary on a Harmony of the Evangelists Matthew, Mark, and Luke,* volume 1, trans. William Pringle (reprint, Grand Rapids: Baker Book House, 1989), 42.

104. Schaberg, *Illegitimacy of Jesus,* 115; see also pp. 112–17.

105. Carsten Colpe, "*ho huios tou anthrōpou,*" in *Theological Dictionary of the New Testament,* ed. Kittel and Friedrich, 7:400; see also *Exegetical Dictionary of the New Testament,* ed. Horst Balz and Gerhard Schneider (Grand Rapids: Eerdmans, 1991), 2:34–35.

106. *Mary in the New Testament,* ed. R. E. Brown et al., 121; Brown, *Birth of the Messiah,* 309–16.

107. Fitzmyer, *Gospel According to Luke I–IX,* 335.

108. Schaberg, *Illegitimacy of Jesus,* 111.

109. This theme is developed by Mary Callaway, *Sing, O Barren One: A Study in Comparative Midrash* (Atlanta: Scholars Press, 1986), 91–114.

110. Schaberg, *Illegitimacy of Jesus,* 131.

111. Schottroff, *Lydia's Impatient Sisters,* 194ff.

112. Luke Timothy Johnson, *The Gospel of Luke* (Collegeville, Minn.: Liturgical Press, 1991), 38.

113. Diana Hayes, *And Still We Rise: An Introduction to Black Liberation Theology* (New York: Paulist, 1996), 173.

114. Ana María Bidegain, "Women and the Theology of Liberation," in *Through Her Eyes: Women's Theology from Latin America,* ed. Elsa Tamez (Maryknoll, N.Y.: Orbis, 1989) 34.

115. Chung Hyun Kyung, *Struggle to Be the Sun Again,* 78–79 (see chap. 1, n. 21).

116. Norris, *Meditations on Mary,* 32 (see chap. 2, n. 53).

117. Schaberg, *Illegitimacy of Jesus,* 134, quoting Soares Prabhu.

118. Saiving, "The Human Situation: A Feminine View," 108–9 (see chap. 3, n. 16).

119. Catharina Halkes, *Mary: Yesterday, Today, and Tomorrow,* 68 (see chap. 4, n. 20).

120. Rosemary Radford Ruether, "She's a Sign of God's Liberating Power," *The Other Side* 104 (1980): 18; see also Marie-Louise Gubler, "Luke's Portrait of Mary," *Theology Digest* 36 (1989): 19–21.

121. Gebara and Bingemer, *Mary, Mother of God, Mother of the Poor*, 67 (see chap. 1, n. 31). See Anne Thurston, "Mary and the Intelligence of the Heart," *Doctrine and Life* 51 (2001): 337–45.

122. The phrase comes from Jürgen Moltmann's essay "Joy in the Revolution of God," in his *The Gospel of Liberation* (Waco, Tex.: Word Books, 1973), 113.

123. Schaberg, "Luke," 284.

124. Ambrose, *De institutione virginis* 14.87; in Hugo Rahner, *Our Lady and the Church*, trans. Sebastian Bullough (New York: Pantheon Books, 1961), 9; see also Alois Grillmeier, "Maria Prophetin," in his *Mit ihm und in ihm: Christologische Forschungen und Perspektiven* (Freiburg: Herder, 1975), 198–216.

125. Irenaeus, *Adv. Haer.* 3.10.2–3; cited in Hugo Rahner, *Our Lady and the Church*, 7–8.

126. Schottroff, *Lydia's Impatient Sisters*, 191.

127. Renita Weems, *Just a Sister Away: A Womanist Vision of Women's Relationships in the Bible* (San Diego, Calif.: Lura Media, 1988), 113–25.

128. Tina Pippin, "The Politics of Meeting: Women and Power in the New Testament, in *That They Might Live: Power, Empowerment, and Leadership in the Church*, ed. Michael Downey (New York: Crossroad, 1991), 13–24.

129. Schottroff, *Lydia's Impatient Sisters*, 193.

130. Susan Ross, "He Has Pulled Down the Mighty from Their Thrones and Has Exalted the Lowly," in *That They Might Live*, ed. Downey, 145–59.

131. Reid, *Women in the Gospel of Luke*, 55.

132. Schottroff, *Lydia's Impatient Sisters*, 200.

133. Callaway, *Sing, O Barren One*, 100–114.

134. The ideas in this section come from Reid, *Choosing the Better Part?* 55–85.

135. This phrase was coined by Mary Catherine Hilkert, *Naming Grace: Preaching and the Sacramental Imagination* (New York: Continuum, 1997).

136. *Mary in the New Testament*, ed. R. E. Brown et al., 136.

137. We follow those scholars who attribute the whole victory hymn in Exodus to Miriam and the women, though it was later attributed to Moses; see Reid, *Women in the Gospel of Luke*, 76; Brown, *Birth of the Messiah*, 466 n. 63. See also Walter Vogels, "Le Magnificat, Marie et Israël," *Eglise et Theologie* 6 (1975): 279–96; and Aschkenasy, *Eve's Journey*, 13 (see chap 2, n. 18), where it is noted that ancient representations and figurines show women holding tambourines.

138. Dorothee Soelle, *The Silent Cry: Mysticism and Resistance*, trans. Barbara Rumscheidt and Martin Rumscheidt (Minneapolis: Fortress, 2001), as well as Schillebeeckx, *Christ*, 790–839 (chap. 3, n. 10).

139. Samuel Terrien, *The Magnificat: Musicians as Biblical Interpreters* (New York: Paulist, 1995), 11.

140. Martin Luther, *The Magnificat* (Minneapolis: Augsburg, 1967), 20.

141. Ibid., 23. See Donal Flanagan, "Luther on the Magnificat," *Ephemerides Mariologicae* 24 (1974): 161–78; and Kathleen Hurty, "Mary, Luther, and the Quest for Ecumenical Images," 61–74 (see chap. 1, n. 40).

142. Singapore Conference, "Summary Statement on Feminist Mariology," in *Feminist Theology from the Third World*, ed. King, 272–73 (see chap. 1, n. 37).

143. Luise Schottroff suggests that the Beatitudes provide the immediate theological context for the Magnificat in Luke ("Das Magnificat und die älteste Tradition über Jesus von Nazareth," *Evangelische Theologie* 38 [1978]: 298–313).

144. Schaberg, "Luke," 373.

145. Sermon preached by Bonhoeffer on the Third Sunday of Advent in 1933; in Dietrich Bonhoeffer, *The Mystery of Holy Night*, ed. Manfred Weber (New York: Crossroad, 1996), 6 (translated by Peter Heinegg from Bonhoeffer, *Werke*, volume 9).

146. Brown, *Birth of the Messiah*, 350–55; see also Sklba, "Mary and the 'Anawim,'" 123–32.

147. Horsley, *Liberation of Christmas*, 63–67 and 110–14.

148. Ibid., 110. Horsley draws attention to the chart of parallels in Brown, *Birth of the Messiah*, 358–60.

149. R. J. Raja, "Mary and the Marginalized," *Vidyajyoti* 51 (1987): 223.

150. Norris, *Meditations on Mary*, 14.

151. Gustavo Gutiérrez, *The God of Life*, trans. Matthew O'Connell (Maryknoll, N.Y.: Orbis, 1991), 185; see the whole essay on the Magnificat, pp. 164–86.

152. John Haught, *God after Darwin: A Theology of Evolution* (Boulder, Colo.: Westview Press, 2000), 98. Note the following from the *New York Times Magazine*: "The average household in America now pulls in about $42,000 a year. The average household headed by someone with a college degree makes $71,400 a year. A professional degree pushes average household income to more than $100,000. If you are, say, a member of one of these college-grad households with a family income of around $75,000, you probably make more than 95% of people on this planet. You are richer than 99.9 percent of the human beings who have ever lived. You are stinking rich" (David Brooks, "Why the U.S. Will Always Be Rich," *The New York Times Magazine* [June 9, 2002]: 88). Meanwhile, the gap between rich and poor grows increasingly large even in the United States (Paul Krugman, "The End of Middle-Class America," *The New York Times Magazine* [October 20, 2002]: 62–67, 76–78, 141–42).

153. Edward Schillebeeckx, *God Among Us: The Gospel Proclaimed* (New York: Crossroad, 1983), 20–26.

154. Terrien, *The Magnificat*, 52.

155. Anderson, "Mary's Difference: Gender and Patriarchy in the Birth Narratives," 197; and Rosemary Radford Ruether, "She's a Sign of God's Liberating Power," 17–21.

156. Daino, *Mary, Mother of Sorrows, Mother of Defiance*, 90.

157. Schaberg, "Luke," 373.

158. Boff, *Maternal Face of God*, 33 (see chap. 2, n. 64).

159. Gebara and Bingemer, *Mary, Mother of God, Mother of the Poor*, 168.

160. Ibid., 165.

161. Gubler, "Luke's Portrait of Mary," 23.

162. Ibid.

163. Ross, "He Has Pulled Down the Mighty from Their Thrones . . . ," 145.

164. Ruether, *Mary, The Feminine Face of the Church*, 33–34 (see chap. 5, n. 9).

165. Norris, *Meditations on Mary*, 16.

166. Schaberg, *Illegitimacy of Jesus*, 130; see 92–101.

167. Puebla §1135n, cited in Gutiérrez, *God of Life*, 165.

168. Boff, *Maternal Face of God*, 192.

169. Gebara and Bingemer, *Mary, Mother of God, Mother of the Poor*, 159–71.

170. Ibid., 72; and Julia Esquivel, "Liberation, Theology, and Women," in *New Eyes for Reading: Biblical and Theological Reflections by Women from the Third World*, ed. John Pobee and Barbel von Wartenberg-Potter (Bloomington, Ind.: Meyer Stone Books, 1987), 21–24; and *Feminist Theology from the Third World*, ed. King, 204–8, 271–74.

171. Luther, *Commentary on the Magnificat*, 19.

172. This registration took place when Herod the Great's son Archelaus was deposed; Judea was to be turned into a Roman province, so property needed to be newly assessed; Quirinius, governor of Syria, was in charge of the event; the people of Judea again revolted; see Brown, *Birth of the Messiah*, 547–56 (Appendix VII).

173. Johnson, *Gospel of Luke*, 52.

174. Balasuriya, *Mary and Human Liberation*, 123.

175. Charles Homer Giblin, "Reflections on the Sign of the Manger," *Catholic Biblical Quarterly* 29 (1967): 87–101.

176. Amy Wordelman, "Everyday Life: Women of the New Testament Period," in *Women's Bible Commentary*, ed. Newsom and Ringe, 486.

177. *New Testament Apocrypha*, ed. Hennecke and Schneemelcher, 383–85 (see chap. 7, n. 1).

178. Malone, *Women & Christianity*, 1:158 (see chap. 2, n. 30).

179. Gutiérrez, *God of Life*, 175.

180. Brown, *Birth of the Messiah*, 153 n. 344; Fitzmyer, *Gospel According to Luke I–IX*, 421.

181. *Mary in the New Testament*, ed. R. E. Brown et al., 150–51.

182. J. Cheryl Exum, "Mother in Israel: A Familiar Story Reconsidered," in *Feminist Interpretation of the Bible*, ed. Letty Russell (Philadelphia: Westminster, 1985), 73–85.

183. Brown, *Birth of the Messiah*, 447–50.

184. Judith Plaskow, "Bringing a Daughter into the Covenant," in *Womanspirit Rising*, ed. Christ and Plaskow, 179–86 (see chap. 4, n. 34); also Reid, *Women in the Gospel of Luke*, 87.

185. Luke mentions fulfillment of the Mosaic Law or Torah in five verses: vv. 22, 23, 24, 27, and 39; references are to Lev. 12:2-8 and Exod. 13:2, 12.

186. Brown, *Birth of the Messiah*, 462; see pp. 462–66 for what follows.

187. Reid, *Women in the Gospel of Luke*, 88.

188. Norris, *Meditations on Mary*, 16.

189. Katoppo, *Compassionate and Free*, 23 (see chap. 2, n. 46).

190. Brown, "The Meaning of Modern New Testament Studies for an Ecumenical Understanding of Mary," 100 n. 99 (see chap. 5, n. 2).

191. See Richard Dillon, "Wisdom Tradition and Sacramental Retrospect in the Cana Account (Jn 2:1–11)," *Catholic Biblical Quarterly* 24 (1962): 268–96.

192. Raymond Brown presents an extensive discussion of the genre, sources, and multiple meanings of this passage (*The Gospel According to John I–XII*, Anchor Bible 29 [Garden City, N.Y.: Doubleday, 1966] 97–112). See also Raymond Collins, "Mary in the Fourth Gospel: A Decade of Johannine Studies," *Louvain Studies* 3 (1970): 99–142; and Judith Lieu, "The Mother of the Son in the Fourth Gospel," *Journal of Biblical Literature* 117 (1998): 61–77.

193. Gebara and Bingemer, *Mary, Mother of God, Mother of the Poor*, 80; this liberation analysis is marred by a latent anti-Judaism that equates the Law of Moses with the wine that has run out.

194. Juan Alfaro, "The Mariology of the Fourth Gospel: Mary and the Struggles for Liberation," *Biblical Theology Bulletin* 10 (1980): 14.

195. Raja, "Mary and the Marginalized," 227; see also Balasuriya, *Mary and Human Liberation*, 184.

196. Mary Rose D'Angelo, "(Re)presentations of Women in the Gospels: John and Mark," in *Women and Christian Origins*, ed. Kraemer and D'Angelo, 136.

197. See the groundbreaking study by Jane Schaberg, *The Resurrection of Mary Magdalene: Legends, Apocrypha, and the Christian Testament* (New York: Continuum, 2002); and Katherine Ludwig Jansen, "Maria Magdalena: *Apostolorum Apostola*," in *Women Preachers and Prophets through Two Millennia of Christianity*, ed. Beverly Mayne Kienzle and Pamela J. Walker (Berkeley: University of California Press, 1998), 57–96.

198. Sandra Schneiders, *Written That You May Believe: Encountering Jesus in the Fourth Gospel* (New York: Crossroad, 1999), 113.

199. Schüssler Fiorenza, *In Memory of Her*, 326 (see chap. 2, n. 13).

200. Adele Reinhartz, "The Gospel of John," *Searching the Scriptures*, ed. Schüssler Fiorenza, 2:568.

201. Schüssler Fiorenza, *In Memory of Her*, 327.

202. Raymond Brown, *The Gospel According to John XIII–XXI*, Anchor Bible 29A (Garden City, N.Y.: Doubleday, 1970), 904; see comparative chart of these

women in idem, *The Death of the Messiah: From Gethsemane to the Grave: A Commentary on the Passion Narratives in the Four Gospels*, 2 volumes, Anchor Bible Reference Library (New York: Doubleday, 1993), 2:1016.

203. Pheme Perkins, "Mary in Johannine Traditions," in *Mary, Woman of Nazareth*, ed. Donnelly, 114; see Gail O'Day, "John," in *Women's Bible Commentary*, ed. Newsom and Ringe, 381–93.

204. Raymond Brown, *The Community of the Beloved Disciple* (New York: Paulist, 1979), 198; see pp. 183–98 (Appendix II, "Roles of Women in the Fourth Gospel").

205. Brown, *Gospel According to John XIII–XXI*, 926; Schüssler Fiorenza, *In Memory of Her*, 331–36.

206. *Mary in the New Testament*, ed. R. E. Brown et al., 210.

207. David Flusser, "Mary and Israel," in Jaroslav Pelikan, David Flusser, and Justin Lang, *Mary: Images of the Mother of Jesus in Jewish and Christian Perspective* (Philadelphia: Fortress, 1986).

208. Chung Hyun Kyung, *Struggle to Be the Sun Again*, 79; and *We Dare to Dream*, ed. Fabella and Park, 149 (see chap. 1, n. 36).

209. Consuelo del Prado, "I Sense God Another Way," in *Through Her Eyes*, 143.

210. Balasuriya, *Mary and Human Liberation*, 143–44.

211. Brown, *Birth of the Messiah*, 431 n. 76.

212. E. P. Sanders, *The Historical Figure of Jesus* (New York: Penguin Books, 1993), 124.

213. Johnson, *Gospel of Luke*, 388; Johnson continues, "There is a definite air of male superiority in this response."

214. Tal Ilan, "In the Footsteps of Jesus: Jewish Women in a Jewish Movement," in *Transformative Encounters: Jesus and Women Re-viewed*, ed. Ingrid Kitzberger (Leiden: Brill, 2000), 116.

215. Elizabeth Cady Stanton, *The Woman's Bible*, part 2, 143, cited in Mary Jo Weaver, *New Catholic Women*, 208 (see chap. 1, n. 28).

216. Gail O'Day, "Acts," in *Women's Bible Commentary*, ed. Newsom and Ringe, 401.

217. The literature is vast; for a sampling, see Elisabeth Schüssler Fiorenza's classic *In Memory of Her*, 160–284; O'Day, "Acts," 394–402; Clarice Martin, "Acts of the Apostles," in *Searching the Scriptures*, ed. Schüssler Fiorenza, 2:763–99; Mary Rose D'Angelo, "Re-presentations of Women in the Gospel of Matthew and Luke-Acts," in *Women and Christian Origins*, ed. Kraemer and D'Angelo, 171–95.

218. For the following citations, see "The Gospel according to Mary," in *New Testament Apocrypha*, ed. Hennecke and Schneemelcher, 1:340–44; and Karen King, "The Gospel of Mary Magdalene," in *Searching the Scriptures*, ed. Schüssler Fiorenza, 2:601–34.

219. René Laurentin, "Mary: Model of the Charismatic," in *Mary, the Spirit and the Church*, ed. Vincent Branick (New York: Paulist, 1980), 30–32.

220. Anne Johnson, "Pentecost," in her *Miryam of Nazareth: Women of Strength & Wisdom* (Notre Dame, Ind.: Ave Maria Press, 1984), 117–20.

CHAPTER 11
MARY, FRIEND OF GOD AND PROPHET

1. For extensive discussion of these principles, see Elizabeth Johnson, *Friends of God and Prophets: A Feminist Theological Reading of the Communion of Saints* (New York: Continuum, 1998). The point of this condensed presentation is not only to fill in background for those who have not read that book, but to lift up theological principles that shape this chapter's marian theology.

2. Elisabeth Schüssler Fiorenza analyzes how this text expresses the self-definition of the early church, with sociological ramifications: "Justified by All Her Children: Struggle, Memory, Vision," in *The Power of Naming*, ed. Schüssler Fiorenza, 339–57 (see chap. 1, n. 42).

3. William James, *The Varieties of Religious Experience* (New York: Longmans, Green, 1923), 358.

4. David Matzko, "Postmodernism, Saints and Scoundrels," *Modern Theology* 9 (1993): 36 n. 36.

5. Stephen Wilson, "Introduction," in *Saints and Their Cults: Studies in Religious Sociology, Folklore, and History*, ed. Stephen Wilson (London and New York: Cambridge University Press, 1983), 23; and Johnson, *Friends of God and Prophets*, 86–93.

6. Jeremy Boissevain, in *Patrons and Clients in Mediterranean Societies*, ed. Ernest Gellner and John Waterbury (London: Duckworth, 1977), 94.

7. "The Martyrdom of Polycarp," in *The Acts of the Christian Martyrs*, ed. Herbert Musurillo (Oxford: Oxford University Press, 1962), 16–17.

8. Augustine, Sermon 273.2, in *Sermons*, 8:17 (see chap. 6, n. 3).

9. Augustine, Sermon 306c.1, in *Sermons*, 9:37.

10. Ibid., 9:36–37.

11. Ibid.

12. Augustine, Sermon 306.10, in *Sermons*, 9:24.

13. Johann Baptist Metz, *Faith in History and Society*, trans. David Smith (New York: Seabury, 1980), especially "The dangerous memory of the freedom of Jesus Christ" (pp. 88–99) and "Categories: Memory, Narrative, Solidarity" (pp. 184–237). See also Walter Brennan, *The Sacred Memory of Mary* (New York: Paulist, 1988), which argues for the importance of the church's liturgical memory of Mary, but with fewer political ramifications.

14. For the tradition that ensued from the silencing of Mary Magdalene's

voice, see Mary Catherine Hilkert, "Women Preaching the Gospel," in her *Naming Grace*, 144–65 (see chap. 10, n. 135).

15. *In Our Own Voices: Four Centuries of American Women's Religious Writing*, ed. Rosemary Radford Ruether and Rosemary Skinner Keller (San Francisco: HarperCollins, 1995), 179–81.

16. David Power, *The Eucharistic Mystery: Revitalizing the Tradition* (New York: Crossroad, 1992), 312–51.

17. Paul VI, Apostolic Letter *Marialis Cultis* §§42–55 (see chap. 6, n. 34).

18. Published by Pax Christi USA, 348 East Tenth Street, Erie, PA 16503.

19. Miriam Therese Winter, *WomanWord: A Feminist Lectionary and Psalter ~ Women of the New Testament* (New York: Crossroad, 1990); eadem, *The Gospel according to Mary: A New Testament for Women* (New York: Crossroad, 1993).

20. Ann Johnson, *Miryam of Nazareth, Woman of Strength and Wisdom; Miryam of Jerusalem, Teacher of the Disciples; Miryam of Judah, Witness in Truth and Tradition* (Notre Dame, Ind.: Ave Maria Press, 1984, 1987, 1991).

21. Harry Nasuti, "Historical Narrative and Identity in the Psalms," *Horizons in Biblical Theology* 23 (2001): 132–53, at 148.

22. *The People's Companion to the Breviary: The Liturgy of the Hours with Inclusive Language* (Indianapolis: Carmelites of Indianapolis, 1997), printed on the inside back cover.

Index of Subjects and Names

371

Index of Ancient Sources

Christian Apocrypha

"*Friends of God and Prophets* is one of those rare must-read books which not only illustrates that a lively and living articulation of traditional doctrinal symbols is possible for the contemporary world, but which so engages readers that they will likely find their own reflections spinning off in myriad directions, living plants which grow from the seeds which this book plants. . . . It is this combination of lucidity and theological depth which argues that this book is deserving of a very wide audience indeed."　　　　—*Anglican Theological Review*

"Some of [Johnson's] critique is aimed at, and perhaps most pertinent to, Roman Catholic religious practices, but her central themes are relevant for the whole church. She articulates Christian faith in a way that also reaches out to those outside the church. I find this book and *She Who Is* particularly helpful for women of faith who are struggling with the church."
　　　　—*Sewanee Theological Review*

"As always, Johnson's scholarship is impeccable and her writing accessible. This book is a joy to read, its gift is a sense of inheritance and connection with millions of very real people in our faith history, its message is of continuing solidarity for the future."　　　　—*Sisters Today*

"Throughout this book Johnson's poetic style engages readers with wit and grace as she interlocks an unlikely set of themes. She is unbending in her feminist critique of injustice, the structures of church and society that bring untold suffering to human persons, and to the natural life that surrounds all. She is astute in selection of biblical passages that provide the backbone to a work that releases the energy and dynamism of the communion of saints. Her effort to let 'the symbol sing again' is a vibrant success."
　　　　—*Journal of the American Academy of Religion*

Lightning Source UK Ltd.
Milton Keynes UK
UKOW07f1546041214

242635UK00001B/80/P